ECONOMIC CONSEQUENCES OF THE SIZE OF NATIONS

*Proceedings of a Conference
held by the International Economic Association*

EDITED BY

E. A. G. ROBINSON

LONDON
MACMILLAN & CO LTD
NEW YORK · ST MARTIN'S PRESS
1963

MACMILLIAN AND COMPANY LIMITED
St Martin's Street London WC 2
also Bombay Calcutta Madras Melbourne

THE MACMILLIAN COMPANY OF CANADA LIMITED
Toronto

ST MARTIN'S PRESS INC
New York

PRINTED IN GREAT BRITAIN

CONTENTS

PART I

THE PROBLEM

PART II

CASE STUDIES OF EFFICIENT LARGE AND SMALL NATIONS

PART III

SIZE AND EFFICIENCY

v

Contents

Contents

PART VII

REPORT ON THE PROCEEDINGS

ACKNOWLEDGEMENTS

THE International Economic Association wishes to thank all those who did much to ensure the success of the Lisbon Conference. Special gratitude is due to the Portuguese Government, to Professor Amzalak and the Sociedade Portuguesa de Ciencias Economicas, and to the management and staff of the Hotel Tivoli.

LIST OF PARTICIPANTS

Professor M. B. Amzalak
University of Lisbon, Portugal

Professor L. Baudin
University of Paris, France

M. L. Duquesne de la Vinelle
University of Louvain,
Belgium

Professor Corwin D. Edwards
University of Chicago, U.S.A.

Professor H. S. Ellis
University of California,
Berkeley, U.S.A.

Professor S. Fabricant
New York University, U.S.A.

Professor E. Gudin
Rio de Janeiro, Brazil

Professor D. Hague
University of Sheffield,
England

Professor W. Hoffmann
University of Münster,
Germany

Professor J. Jewkes
Merton College, Oxford

Professor W. A. Jöhr
Handelshochschule, St. Gallen,
Switzerland

Professor G. Leduc
University of Paris, France

Professor E. Lindahl
University of Uppsala, Sweden

Professor G. Marcy
University of Aix-en-Provence,
France

Dr. V. A. Marsan
Rome, Italy

Professor D. Patinkin
The Hebrew University,
Jerusalem, Israel

Professor G. Pereira
University of Lisbon, Portugal

Professor L. T. Pinto
University of Lisbon, Portugal

Professor W. Prest
University of Melbourne,
Australia

Professor E. A. G. Robinson
Sidney Sussex College,
Cambridge, England

Dr. K. W. Rothschild
Österreichisches Institut
für Wirtschaftsforschung,
Vienna

Professor T. Scitovsky
Stanford University, U.S.A.

Professor de Seabra
University of Oporto, Portugal

Professor G. Stigler
Columbia University, New
York, U.S.A.

Professor I. Svennilson
Socialvetenskapliga Institutet,
Stockholm

Professor L. Tarshis
Stanford University, U.S.A.

Professor Teixeira Ribeira
University of Coimbra,
Portugal

Professor R. Triffin
Yale University, U.S.A.

M. P. Uri
European Coal and Steel
Community, Luxemburg

Professor C. N. Vakil
UNESCO Research Centre,
Calcutta, India

Professor P. J. Verdoorn
Centraalplanbureau, The
Hague, Netherlands

Professor J. Weiller
University of Paris, France

FORMULATION OF THE ISSUES
FOR THE CONFERENCE

PROGRAMME COMMITTEE

THE Programme Committee attempted to formulate, for the benefit of the writers of the various papers to be delivered to the Conference and printed in this volume, the major issues which seemed to require discussion. This formulation is here reprinted, both because reference is made to it in some of the papers and because it serves to focus sharply for the reader the problems that seemed to the Committee to require discussion.

The economist regards differences of the size of nations primarily from the point of view of the opportunities which any given size offers or fails to offer for securing the greatest possible economies and regularity of production, in so far as these depend on scale of production.

He tends to identify the area of the nation with the area within which (a) goods, (b) factors of production, *i.e.* labour and skills, capital, materials, can move freely.

The problems which seem most to need future investigation include the following :

(1) How far does scale of production within the individual plant (the unit of technical production) depend upon and vary with the size of the market as a whole ?

(2) How far are the economies of scale exhaustible ? Would firms ordinarily have higher productivity if they were larger ? What are the principal obstacles and limitations to the growth of the firm ? Is there some limit in theory and practice, in most cases, beyond which further economies of scale are unimportant ?

(3) How is the character of the market influenced by the multiplicity of firms in the market ? How far is the character and competitive state of the market dependent on its size and growth ? How does the size of the market affect the behaviour and planning of the individual business ?

(4) How far does freedom of movement of goods, resulting from free trade, customs unions, etc., permit · the enlargement of markets without the necessity for political unity ?

(5) How far (in contradiction to 4) is the size of the market affected by

the community of tastes and habits which goes with political unity and national homogeneity ?

(6) At what size, in practice, are the chief economies of scale reached ? Does a national market of 150 million persons provide substantial economies not available with one of 50 million or of 10 million ?

(7) How far (amplifying 6) is the productive efficiency of the U.S.A. the consequence of the size of the U.S. market ? How do we explain the relatively high level of productivity and income per head of, *e.g.*, Canada, Australia, Sweden, Switzerland, all of which are comparatively small nations ?

(8) How far is a market which is largely an export market more risky ? How far does the existence of such risks diminish willingness to develop new activities and new methods ? How far is the existence of a large home market important to the efficiency of firms in the export market ?

(9) How far do national barriers, in fact, prevent the movement of goods and of labour, techniques, materials, and capital ? How far can customs unions, the relations of metropolitan and dependent territories, inter-commonwealth relations, etc., provide opportunities for enlarging markets and permitting specialization on products in which different countries have comparative advantages ?

(10) How far is a large nation more stable than a small one

(*a*) in consequence of a smaller dependence on international trade in general ;

(*b*) in consequence of a smaller dependence on its ability to sell a small range of exported goods ;

(*c*) in consequence of wider opportunities for adjusting its economy to changes in both markets and technologies ?

(11) How far does a large nation have superior economic power and a stronger bargaining position ?

(12) How far does the existence of a single currency, and/or a single credit policy facilitate trade where differences of currency, etc., would make it more difficult ?

(13) How far does a small nation have an advantage in its capacity to adjust more quickly its policies to changing conditions ?

(14) How far does a large or small nation have an advantage in that a given expenditure per head on administration or defence is more productive ?

(15) Is research and development work likely to achieve greater results in a large nation ?

INTRODUCTION

By E. A. G. ROBINSON

It would, I think, be impertinent to describe the purpose of the 1957 Conference of the International Economic Association as 'An Inquiry into the Nature and Causes of the Wealth of Nations'. Yet in a broad sense we were engaged in returning to the great issues with which Adam Smith was concerned. It is paradoxical that in the hundred and eighty years since his book was first published the relation of the size of nations to their economic prosperity and to their level of income per head has received comparatively little academic discussion. Both in the writing of papers and in their subsequent discussion many of us had a feeling of incredulity when we failed to discover a volume of antecedent literature such as the subject seemed to have deserved.

The economic consequences of the size of nations afford none the less a subject that well deserves more attention. The practical arguments for the establishment of common markets and free-trade areas are based on the premise that there are economies of scale which are not exhausted within the limits of the size of nations as we know them today, but which could be achieved within the limits of the sizes of nations, or of trading areas, which it might be practicable to create. We did, in fact, try to ask ourselves what were the economic advantages of a nation with a population, let us say, of 150 million, as compared with those of a nation of, say, 50 million, or of, say, 15 million. To answer such a question involves, necessarily, some attempt to judge at what size of market the principal economies of scale are likely to be exhausted. It is a criticism of most of the academic work in this field that in the past it has been qualitative rather than quantitative and has not lent itself to generalized statistical analysis. Much of the actual political discussion, on the other hand, of the merits of integration would seem to any professional economist to have been based upon arguments and evidence that were at best superficial and at worst the purest nonsense. One cannot hope to convince anyone with a rudimentary understanding of the rules of logic of the validity of the argument : 'The United States is rich ; the United States has a large free-trade area ; have a large free-trade area and you will be rich'. One could with equal validity and cogency be persuaded to achieve riches by adopting any other characteristic of the United States, from its constitution to its consumption of newsprint.

We set ourselves, therefore, to analyse more academically the essentials of the problem. We began by asking why the concept of a nation is relevant and important to economic analysis. The answer, provided by Professor Svennilson, is clear. The boundary of the nation represents a point of discontinuity ; it represents a change in the degree of mobility of almost all the factors of production, of labour more especially, but in hardly less degree also of capital and credit, since currency and banking systems are co-terminous with nations ; it represents above all a discontinuity in the mobility of goods. To some extent these discontinuities are the result of real differences which follow national boundaries : differences of language, of education and skill, of a sense of community of outlook and interest. Such real differences are not capable of being wholly removed by the integration of the separate nations of today into larger units. But in great part the discontinuities are artificial. They derive from the existence of tariffs or other trade restrictions, of limits to the convertibility of currencies and the transfer of credits, of limits to the movement of workers or of other persons imposed either by governments or by trade unions.

These discontinuities have not been uniform in degree, either as between all nations or at different periods of time. Some political units which may juridically be entitled to be called 'nations' are so effectively integrated into larger economies that the degree of real discontinuity is negligible : Monaco, for example, or Andorra, or the Vatican City. Indeed, the concept of the nation would be largely irrelevant from the point of view of economic analysis if everywhere all that is practicable were done to minimize discontinuities and to promote mobility. It was, perhaps, because the classical economists tended to assume such freedom of movement that they tended not to emphasize the concept of the nation.

In our own generation the nation has acquired a new and increasing importance, because it is the unit of government action and of economic authority. Within the confines of its national boundaries, a modern government uses its budgetary system as an instrument of economic policy ; within those boundaries, with the aid of the central bank, it maintains full employment, promotes economic development, and keeps its balance of payments under control. Within those national boundaries, individuals have rights to the benefits of the welfare state, both in terms of social services and of the more general benefits of economic policy and environment. Thus the discontinuities are tending to become more pronounced.

Introduction

The nation is acquiring increasing significance as an economic factor.

If an academic conference is to discuss the importance of some concept it is inevitable that it should demand that the concept shall be properly defined. Our French colleagues, steeped in the tradition of Descartes, were particularly insistent that one could not discuss the size of nations without first defining what one meant by size. It seems clear, however, that one has to be prepared to discuss not one single concept of size, but any or all of various concepts. For some purposes it is relevant and significant to discuss the relation of the number of persons comprising the population to the average productivity per head of that population. For some purposes — ability to provide a market for an optimum plant in some industry, for example — one is concerned, not with numbers but with expenditure, and it is relevant to discuss the size of the total home market of the country (the product of numbers and of average income). For some purposes, again, it is relevant to have in mind the size not only of a nation with its home market, but also with its normal export markets. It need not be stressed that if nations are ranked by population, the ranking is by no means the same as if they are ranked by national income ; and if they are ranked by the size of a closely integrated market — as, for example, France and the Outre-mer, or the United Kingdom and the Sterling Area — the ranking will again be substantially different. It is, however, difficult — as was pointed out in the discussion — wholly to avoid some circularity of argument : since the size of the population influences the size of the market and thus productivity, the size of the market already embodies some of the economic consequences of the size of a nation. What is more important in practice is that a nation that is rich, for reasons of rich natural resources and high individual productivity, can afford to be smaller in terms of population than a less richly endowed country without suffering from the penalties of markets inadequate to sustain efficient production.

With this background to our problems we went on to look at the actual advantages and handicaps of some of the bigger and smaller countries. As an example of a rich large country we took the United States. As examples of the recalcitrant exceptions to any rule that large countries and high income per head are uniquely associated, we took Switzerland and Belgium, with glances also at the experience of Sweden. The outcome of our discussions of these examples was a belief that it was easy to exaggerate the importance of scale among the many factors that influence productivity. Switzerland succeeds in adding to many natural disadvantages of raw material supplies and of limitations of agricultural land what most people would regard as additional handicaps in the form of cartelized industries and a protected agriculture. Yet with a very high level of individual efficiency and hard work, an exceptionally high ratio of exports to home sales in her own specialized industries, and a high capital per head thanks to the attraction of refugee capital, she manages to achieve a level of income per head equal to or greater than that of most comparable nations of substantially larger size. Putting it slightly differently, Switzerland has managed to secure the necessary economies of scale in her chief manufacturing industries by a very heavy reliance on export markets.

It was less easy to understand how Belgium succeeded in achieving so high a level of income per head. Her raw material resources, though better than those of Switzerland, are not exceptional. She benefits considerably, it is true, by her integration with the Congo Belge and its rich resources of a character now greatly in demand. But the principal explanation must again be the unfashionable one of individual efficiency and hard work, allied to economic policies which have allowed her to benefit as far as possible from foreign trade. Relatively few of her industrial undertakings are of very great size. She does not equal Switzerland in her dependence on export markets to permit the advantages of scale. Our discussion of M. Duquesne de la Vinelle's paper left us, I think, inclined to the view that lack of economies of scale had not gravely handicapped the Belgian economy.

I have deliberately taken those two papers out of their order and before Professor Fabricant's discussion of the American economy, because from their discussion emerged a number of factors very relevant to the great question of the explanation of high American productivity. The discussion of his paper left his broad conclusions standing. Economies of scale form a part of the explanation of the remarkable efficiency of the American economy, but only a part. One must look for many of the advantages to the very high level of individual efficiency and the high general *tempo* of work that it permits, to the high standards of general technical education, to the high capital per head, and, above all, to the exceptional natural resources of the United States. But while recognizing these immensely important factors in the American situation, both Professor Fabricant and his American colleagues were convinced that the scale of the American economy was in part also responsible for the high productivity. The scale of the market did not merely permit more easily the achievement of the minimum size required for maximum technical efficiency — to judge from Professor Bain's *Barriers to*

Introduction

New Competition the size of market required for that is very substantially less in most industries than that afforded by the American market. It meant also that the market as a whole, and in all its regions, was very much more competitive and that firms and plants both could and did specialize more narrowly and concentrate their efforts on a more limited range of products. At the same time the addition of an efficient unit of production to the market required less growth of the market to justify it, risks were to that extent reduced, and confidence in a necessary minimum of expansion more readily created. Thus the advantages of scale were far more ramifying than might at first glance be supposed.

Forewarned by these earlier discussions, we were ready to proceed to rather more fundamental analysis of the factors that determine the extent and exhaustibility of the economies of scale, with the assistance of two papers by Professor John Jewkes and Professor Corwin Edwards. What emerged from those papers and our discussion of them would seem to be this : outside of a few exceptional industries most technical economies are exhausted by firms of quite moderate size. Even relatively small and poor countries can have a number of firms of the minimum size to give full, or almost full, technical efficiency. We found ourselves reluctant to speak of optimum size, if that is taken to imply a size not only such that anything smaller has not achieved the full possible economies of scale but also that any further expansion would lead to diseconomies. We tended to speak rather of minimum efficient size with the implication that beyond that size there was a plateau of constant cost.

There was little evidence, as Professor Jewkes' paper made clear, that, as measured by numbers of employees, units of production are getting significantly larger. But with increasing productivity the real value of the output of the average unit was probably increasing. There are, however, various significant differences between the patterns of industrial activity and structure of larger and smaller countries. In the first place, there are certain industries or groups of industries which are ordinarily found in larger countries and not found in smaller countries. Larger countries normally possess an automobile industry, an aircraft industry, locomotive building, heavy machinery building, both mechanical and electrical. Smaller countries rarely possess any of these industries. The dividing line seems ordinarily to come between 10 and 15 million of population, though it is not difficult to find exceptions — Australia, for example.

Secondly, there tend, as has emerged above in relation to the United States, to be differences in the degree of diversification of industries. In small markets firms tend to be less specialized and more diversified. Many products are produced within each plant and the firm tends to be more concerned with the problems of shifting production from one product to another as circumstances dictate than with making an outstanding success of any single one product. Not a little of the success of the American economy would seem to derive from the concentration of all the efforts of a concern on mastering the problems of design and production of a quite narrow range of products. This difference in the degree of diversification seemed to hold good even at a substantial size of national market. The differences between the United States, on the one hand, and France or the United Kingdom on the other hand, seemed as significant as those between the latter and some of the nations of 10-15 million, though here again the differences were important.

Thirdly, there appeared to be differences in the character of competition. In small markets it was easier to develop monopoly. With the smaller number of firms of minimum efficient size that the market could keep employed, competition was more often of the character that exists when competitors are few, and oligopoly prevails, than of that which exists when competitors are many and anonymous and their reactions are likely to be aggressive rather than co-operative.

Fourthly, in almost all the larger economies the general specialization of firms extended to the specialization of service industries, with additional opportunities for producers to narrow, so far as they might wish, the range of processes for which they made themselves responsible and to extend, with advantage to themselves, their dependence on the services of these specialist firms to the greatest possible extent. There were marked differences in this respect again not only between the very small nations and those of around 50 million, but also between the latter and the United States, as an example of the very big.

It would not be easy, or indeed fair to the variety of opinions held by participants, to try to establish any quantitative conclusions from this part of our discussions. It is not going too far, perhaps, to say that it seemed to be our general impression that most of the major industrial economies of scale could be achieved by a relatively high-income nation of 50 million; that nations of 10-15 million were probably too small to get all the technical economies available; that the industrial economies of scale beyond a size of 50 million were mainly those that derive from a change in the character of competition and of specialization — a change which may, if one relies on the contrasts between American and other experience, be explained partly by scale, but may also be attributed to differences of national outlook and to differences in the legal handling of the problems of monopoly, as well as to differences consequent on income and expenditure per head, and due, in part at least, to a richer endowment of natural resources.

We next addressed ourselves to the problems of adaptability. Did large nations enjoy an advantage because the secular declines of certain activities could be offset by the growth of others and by the more ready movement of resources to the points of growth ? Did smaller nations enjoy an advantage because they were more homogeneous, more closely integrated, more flexible in both political and economic organization ? This proved a singularly difficult issue to define and test. In practice, as the very interesting analysis of Professor Leduc brought out, some small nations have grown at least as rapidly as some large ones. That was, perhaps, to be expected. A small nation is often to be compared with a region within a large one ; and regions within the large nations — California, for example, within the past decade or two — have grown immensely faster than the large nation as a whole. And, as Professor Weiller showed, no clear answer was to be expected from a mere statistical comparison of large and small which did not take account of external trade, with its attendant advantages and its attendant risks. Seen in terms of the problems of Italy and India, with the aid of M. Marsan and of Professor Vakil, development was in various respects easier if a large and fairly assured market was there to be served. From the point of view of Italy, membership of a European Common Market opened up many new opportunities. In Italian conditions, and within the existing home market of Italy, a minimum unit of reasonable technological efficiency required something approaching the whole of the home market, so that not only was investment risky, but also industry tended to be too nearly monopolistic.

This group of problems led inevitably to the wider problem of the extent to which external trade could and did provide an effective escape from the penalties of smallness. It was clear that for a variety of countries it had, in fact, done so. Great Britain in the nineteenth century and Switzerland in the twentieth were only two of the more obvious examples of nations which had enjoyed the economies of scale in their manufacturing industries. to an extent quite impossible within the limits of the home market. And it remained true, as a broad generalization, that the smaller was a national economy, the higher the ratio of imports to gross national product. The smaller nations, in particular, had a higher rate of exchange of manufactures against manufactures.

But though external trade provided an escape, it was generally agreed, as brought out by the papers contributed by Professor Scitovsky and Professor Marcy, that it was a somewhat precarious escape. The uncertainties of political interventions and tariff changes were such as to make investment in the export trade appreciably more risky. Production for a market in a different currency area involved the risks not only of the convertibility of currencies, but also of differing rates of inflation and of consequent difficulties in maintaining competitive prices. Tastes, which were relatively homogeneous in a home market, might differ widely in the export markets, both regarded collectively and as between different export markets ; thus to an increasing extent goods had to be specially tailored for export markets and the full economies of mass production and standardization were harder to obtain. Some were led on by this to argue the need for a large home market as a springboard for the export market, and to give the confidence to plan expansions of productive capacity. The earlier success of Britain and the more recent success of Switzerland in developing great export trades with relatively small home markets once again called any too dogmatic extension of this argument greatly in question.

If foreign trade, with the uncertainties that exist today, provided an escape that is only partly satisfactory, how can a more satisfactory and less uncertain solution be organized ? Clearly there are two possibilities. The first solution, and fundamentally the more desirable solution, is that provided by the concepts enshrined in the GATT — the attempt to create progressively a relatively free trade world, permitting the more general exchange of products equally between all nations, and setting no restrictions on the directions in which trade should flow. The second solution, and to any academic economist a *pis aller*, is the creation of customs unions or other regional systems for the encouragement of mutual trade on a less than world-wide scale.

If a freely trading world system were achievable, few would doubt its superiority, purely as a trading system. But some would argue that, the freer is the trade, the more closely must any group of freely trading nations keep in step ; that a limited group of freely trading nations can more reasonably hope to co-ordinate sufficiently their monetary, fiscal, and other economic policies. A decision to prefer the creation of a customs union to more strenuous attempts to create a world system is an empirical and political decision as to what is practically achievable, rather than an economic decision as to what is inherently the more desirable. It is a decision that may well be different for different nations within any potential grouping. The issue which such a group of nations must consider is the likelihood that the trade-creating effects of the customs union will predominate over the trade-diverting aspects. It was impossible for those who came from nations which were inclined to fear the trade-diverting aspects of possible customs unions not to be impressed by the convictions of their French, German, Italian, and Benelux colleagues that a common market in Europe would be greatly trade creating.

It was not for us, as a group of academic economists, to reach political conclusions, and we made no attempt to do so. We regarded our functions as limited to the clarification of the issues with which we were concerned. The papers here printed and the discussions of them are best left to speak for themselves. If I may be allowed to emphasize one of the impressions left on my own mind, it is that large size is not a panacea. It may well contribute to economic improvement, but it is unlikely to alter the orders of magnitude of the real incomes that nations have in the past provided for themselves from their efforts applied to their natural resources. The better and more scientific use of those resources is what ultimately matters, and size of market is only one ingredient in that more effective use.

The advantages which may potentially accrue from increase of size of market may quite easily be lost if a group of collaborating economies fail to co-ordinate their policies effectively, operate at less than full capacity, restrict their investment, and thus individually and collectively grow less rapidly. If a group of countries are to gain, they must be prepared from the first to recognize and accept significant losses of individual sovereignty over their economic affairs. That is the price of the gain.

We were anxious, as economists, to confine ourselves to the economic issues. But we could not conceal from ourselves that some of the strongest arguments for economic integration are political, and concerned with defence, rather than economic. In order to have this in mind one paper attempted some analysis of the economies of scale as applied to administration and defence. As its author, I think I may emphasize its limitations. Statistical comparison of the costs of public services of any kind runs into the problems of the standards of the services provided. Two valuable studies, one by Miss Alison Martin and Professor Arthur Lewis and the other by Milton Gilbert and Irving Kravis, throw some light on the actual expenditures of different countries. It is very difficult to draw from them any safe or worthwhile inferences regarding the possible economies of scale. In the large field of social services, density of population is probably more important than absolute population. In the field of defence, it was clear that the United States was making a larger real expenditure per head of population than the other countries considered, and spending at comparable prices a larger part of gross national product on defence. But equally clearly this expenditure almost certainly gave a higher level of effective defence and included aid to others, so that no inference regarding economies of scale was conceivably possible. Purely analytical argument suggests, however, that economies of scale may reasonably be expected. While our argument was inevitably inconclusive, without it we should have been omitting what is obviously a major consideration.

But this discussion served, I think, to reinforce one general impression. The economic arguments for the further integration of nations, so as to create wider markets, are not overwhelmingly conclusive. If considerable progress were believed possible in the direction of a freer world system, so that the trade-creating aspects of any more limited and regional integration were less important relatively to its trade-diverting aspects, the arguments for integration would become increasingly the political and defence arguments. It is sometimes difficult for an economist, aware of the limitations of the economic arguments, not to feel that, if the political arguments are strong as he believes them to be, the protagonists of integration should more frankly rest themselves on them.

But it would be wrong not to stress in conclusion one significant point. It may be open to argument whether the economies of scale to be achieved by integrating a number of nations, already of the order of 50 million in population, are great. There are probably significant economies of integrating nations of the size of 10 to 15 million. But in neither case is there any danger of loss of efficiency by doing so, if the larger nations that emerge conduct their affairs with equal efficiency. There are no possibilities of diseconomies of scale arising from the excessive size of the market. There are no penalties for being bigger than the minimum size, if such there be, that will exhaust the economies of scale, provided that a centralized economic policy is not collectively more protectionist against the outside world or slower at making the adjustments of economic policy that will keep the parts of the large integrated unit continuously operating at a high level of production. Quite apart, moreover, from permitting economies of scale, a wide area of relatively free trade may give gains by permitting greater regional specialization on products for which the resources of a region have special comparative advantages.

PART I

THE PROBLEM

Chapter 1

THE CONCEPT OF THE NATION AND ITS RELEVANCE TO ECONOMIC ANALYSIS

BY

I. SVENNILSON
University of Stockholm

I. THE GENERAL PROBLEM

THE nation is a geographical unit cut out as a strip from the world map. What is the reason for treating it as a unit in economic analysis ? What kind of discontinuities are there that distinguish the national unit from other units, smaller or larger than the individual nation ? Why and to what extent are these discontinuities relevant to economic analysis ?

The answer depends, of course, on the kind of problems we want to analyse. There seem to be three types of problems that the present conference has in mind, all related to the advantages and disadvantages of the size of nations : (*a*) for international trade ; (*b*) for the efficiency of national activity ; (*c*) for national economic growth.

It is, indeed, quite unnecessary to discuss whether the nation as a unit has any relevance in the analysis of such problems. Of course it has. The purpose of this paper is only to draw attention to the great variety of sorts of nations with which we are confronted, and to discuss the dependence of the position of a nation on the character of the individual regional units and on the international *milieu* in which it lives.

The basic fact is evidently one of *political authority* ; a nation can be defined as an area in which a *central government* exercises political authority. This again means that a nation can be regarded as a *unit of action* in economic analysis. But the power of the national government to act and its will to act may vary within very wide limits. We must analyse the distribution of power in relation to the economic area comprised by a nation before we can draw conclusions about the 'economic consequences of the size of nations'. This is true as well of its 'internal' as its 'external' activities. In this respect a nation is a strictly relative concept.

I

However, a nation means a lot more than a system of political authority. Political authority cannot even be assessed, if it is not related to a series of *cultural* and *institutional* facts.

Among the cultural facts may be mentioned language, religion, level of education, and among the institutional facts the organization of private and local units of action. In a market economy, the structure of various markets, for labour, credit, commodities, and so on, are important aspects of this organization. Further, we must take into account the traditions and institutions for consultation and negotiation between central government and private individuals, enterprises and organizations.

All these characteristics — political, cultural, and institutional — determine to what degree we can speak of the 'integration' of a national economy, which makes the nation a relevant unit from an economic point of view.

In some cases, a nation may be so loosely integrated that a discussion in national terms becomes quite irrelevant. At the other extreme, the integration may be so tight and so sharply limited by national frontiers that the nation functions like a well-integrated private firm.

The relevance of the nation in economic analysis is, however, also dependent on the *international milieu* in which it is placed, that is to say, on the structure and policy of the nations with which it has its main economic contacts, actual and potential. First, this *milieu* will decide what parameters of action are at the disposal of national units of action in their international transactions. Secondly, the use of these parameters of action will depend on the actual policy and institutions of these other nations. Of special relevance is the effect of these policies and institutions on the mobility of resources in the widest sense — labour, capital, and technical knowledge. A liberal policy on the 'foreign' side towards international mobility may tend to wipe out the discontinuity of markets at frontiers, and make the nation *de facto* less relevant as a unit in economic analysis. The position of a nation in the international community may then approach that of a region in relation to a national economic system.

The international relation which seems to be most fundamental is the fact that international credits are not unlimited, while at the same time for most nations foreign currency reserves are of limited size. In foreign trade each nation has to pay its way. It is therefore faced with an international liquidity problem, corresponding to that of a private firm in a national market. The need to balance its international payments imposes certain restrictions on national policy and creates interrelations between various parts of a national economy ; restrictions and interrelations which do not exist, or at least not in the same degree, for a region within a country. This is perhaps the most important discontinuity in economic relations that coincides with national frontiers.

These various aspects of the nation as a unit in economic analysis will be discussed in more detail in the following paragraphs.

II. DEGREES OF NATIONAL INTEGRATION

(a) Political Aspects

The authority of central government may vary between nothing and infinity. The maximum is found in the totalitarian state without local or private autonomy in relation to central government. Such a 'nationalized' economy functions as a large private enterprise. The government monopolizes all resources within its national territory. Internal and external activities may be co-ordinated in a plan. In this plan, the various regions and industries are more or less efficiently integrated to serve the ends of central government, it may be consumption, progress, or military potential. If we want to make a clear case of the economies of size, we should compare such totalitarian nations, their bargaining power in the world market, their efficiency in production, and their ability to promote development.

The types of economies which, I imagine, we mainly want to discuss are, however, much more complicated as regards their system of authority, and consequently their way of functioning, internally and externally. They represent various degrees of decentralization, either regionally, to the extent that they form a federation of states or that they maintain some other type of partial local autonomy, or structurally, to the extent that they accept a certain degree of autonomy of private units of action (individuals, firms, or organizations).

The case of a federal nation illustrates the relativity of the concept of a nation. The discontinuity of economic relations may, in fact, be as marked, or even more clearly marked, at the borders of each state as at the borders of the federation.

The autonomy of private institutions may also reduce the importance of national frontiers. As an extreme case which illustrates this point, we may take a subsidiary of a foreign firm that has established itself in a less developed country to exploit one of its natural resources, say, oil or iron ore, mainly for export. Depending on the laws of the country in question, the firm may maintain a considerable autonomy both in its internal and in its external transactions. It may be independent of internal finance and other scarce national resources, and may conduct its international business independently. The relation of its activities to the rest of the national economy may be just as loose as those of any local firm producing for a national market in relation to other regional activities.

This is an extreme case ; most private firms are, of course, more closely integrated in the national market system, depending on it for resources and sales outlets, more dependent on the nation's position in the system of international trade and payments, more tightly 'controlled' by national policy. But the existence of partly autonomous private units of action introduces an element of relativity in the concept of the nation which cannot be overlooked.

(b) The Framework of National Institutions — the 'Welfare State'

This is, of course, not the place to analyse all the interrelations of a political, psychological, and socio-economic nature that exist within a nation. That would demand a much more profound analysis in terms of political science. My task can only be to indicate broadly some facts and tendencies that make the nation a relevant unit from an economic point of view.

One long-term trend in modern history has been the development of national institutions. This development has its background in the growth of *political nationalism* that has been regarded as a typical feature of history from the nineteenth century onwards.

Political nationalism is, of course, closely interrelated with psychological attitudes, best described as *chauvinism*. Its content is a certain discriminatory attitude towards what is national and what is foreign. It may concern people, literature, mountains, architecture, or what you will. There may, of course, be regional counterparts to this chauvinism, but against the background of political nationalism, international conflicts, and lack of international contacts, chauvinism tends to concentrate around national 'values'. In most countries it has found a new basis in the manifestations of the modern welfare state.

Many books would have to be written to describe the highly organized modern welfare state. It exists in as many varieties as there are countries ; its organization may vary from the totalitarian to the liberal type. Any detailed description must, therefore, of necessity require a volume. When I try to indicate a few general characteristics, I can only illustrate my remarks by referring to the varieties that are found in north-western Europe. I leave it to the reader to decide what can be extrapolated to other countries.

The basic fact of the welfare state seems to be the ambition of the national government in relation to economic activities within the nation. This ambition may be expressed in such terms as equality, full employment, and development. To promote these ends, the government applies economic policy — fiscal, monetary, and so on — which regulates the conditions under which private individuals, firms, and organizations may conduct their business. Production and trade are mainly left to private initiative, but central and local governments appear to a varying extent as organizers of public services and, exceptionally, of basic industries. The activities of private firms are only in part directly controlled by government, but the social pressure on private firms and organizations, ultimately in the shape of the risk of extended government control or even nationalization, is such that they tend to fall in line with the policy of the government. The government carries out its policy with the aid of a highly differentiated public administration, manned by civil servants who represent the government view. Typical fields of activity for this administration are education, research, health, social welfare, labour conditions, credit market (central bank), transport (roads, railways, water, and air transport), telecommunications, various industries (agriculture, fishing, forestry). In such fields the administration may establish standards of operation, regulate prices, distribute subsidies, or operate nationalized services.

Another important feature of this type of welfare state is the growing strength of non-governmental national organizations. One of their main functions is to represent the interests of various industries, not only in relation to the policy of the government but also in relation to each other. What distinguishes this highly organized state from the corporate state is that government powers are not transferred to organizations. Instead there is a system of consultation and bargaining between organizations, and between central government and organizations.

A constant issue is the distribution of the national income, which is typically being recorded more and more perfectly in national accounts. These may be said to symbolize the economic integration of the welfare state. It is symptomatic that, as a rule, they do not exist for regions, nor for groups of nations. National income is regarded as a common national asset, which is redistributed by fiscal, monetary, and other policies. In principle, all groups and regions are regarded as having the same rights to 'welfare' and, as a result of the parliamentary equation, equalizing income transfers are made to old people, children, sick people, unemployed, local communities with a weak income base, and sometimes to weak industries. Progressive tax systems reduce the differences in personal income. Price support programmes and import tariffs, taxes on corporations form other parts of this system of income redistribution. Regional equality of standards tends to be maintained by government contributions to schools and social services, by running nationalized transport in less developed regions at a loss, and by an all-inclusive national electricity grid system.

The tendency towards national uniformity of standards and income is also reinforced by nation-wide organizations in the labour market. The stronger the top organizations of labour and employers are, the more will regional or other differences in wages tend to disappear. This tendency will also be strengthened by a nation-wide labour exchange system, which increases the mobility of labour.

In this way, clear discontinuities in income and standards appear at national frontiers, while corresponding regional differences tend to be eliminated. As a result of these tendencies towards uniformity, it is becoming relevant to speak of the 'national' wage level, the 'national' standard of living, and the 'national' income distribution, all of which are concepts relevant to economic analysis.

The discontinuity of incomes at national frontiers has its repercussions on attitudes towards immigration of labour from countries with lower standards. Mass immigration is restricted, and permission for a foreigner to work tends in practice to depend on acceptance of the rules of national collective agreements.

The uniformity of standards makes the home market a fairly uniform unit with a standardized consumer choice. To 'keep up with the Joneses' becomes a reality as equalization is approached. A large majority of the population may, for example, simultaneously decide to use a new expensive consumer durable, such as a television set. The standardization of consumer choice is increased by organized education of the consumer and by nation-wide advertising; a nation-wide daily and weekly press being one of the mediums through which the uniformity of the home market is commercially exploited. This does not necessarily mean that foreign-produced goods are less favoured in the national market. But the national press can be used to appeal to and strengthen traditional taste or confidence in the quality of national brands. This confidence has a solid background in the good-will creating general information about 'our' steel industry, 'our' electrical industry, and so on — their history, their technical performances, their success in the export market. (How often does the public learn such things about foreign industries ? The big American firms like Ford and General Motors seem to be exceptions to this rule.) Organized control of consumer products, safety regulations, and the like may further strengthen a preference for home-made products.

In a progressive welfare state the government is concerned with national progress. Increases in national output and standards of living are eagerly watched. There are plans for improving housing and public services. Future increases are mortgaged in sweeping pension schemes which play an important rôle in the competition between political parties. The rates of saving and capital accumulation are, as main factors in economic growth, one important concern of government policy. Since the war, plans for investment (at prevailing rates of interest) have, in most countries within this group, tended to exceed the capacity to invest without inflation. The result has been various policies directed to curb investment.

Against this background, investment abroad has, from the government point of view, been regarded as undesirable, even if the yield of such investment is comparably high. If investment were regarded as solely the concern of a private investor, it would be only the yield of the capital that counted. The government of a welfare state, however, is concerned not only with the capital yield but with the total increase of income for capital and labour together that follows from investment, and this increase can be completely harvested only if investment is made at home. A welfare government is, typically, uninterested in standards of living abroad.

The result of this policy has been the development of exclusive domestic capital markets and, as a consequence, different rates of capital accumulation in various nations. Even if private commercial banks maintain traditions of international contact, they have been drawn into the organization of the credit and capital markets on national lines. It would lead too far to analyse what this means for the integration of business and production. It is, however, evident that debts and claims open the door for business contacts and various types of co-operation in production. An active hierarchy of bank leaders may have a strong influence on the development of industry and the combination of business interests, and in most welfare states the national home market is their exclusive playground.

One of the important factors in the establishment of integrated national economies is the tendency towards the concentration of the bank system into larger units. In most countries there seems to have been a development from smaller provincial banks to large banks operating on a national scale. The reasons for this development may be complicated. But if (for the sake of discussion) we assume that the main reasons are economies of scale and capacity to handle volumes of credit facilities corresponding to the capital needs of modern industries, and if we further assume (which may not be true) that these volumes are the same in large and small countries, we would expect to find a smaller number of large commercial banks in small than in large countries. In any case, the number of large private banks in the small states of northern Europe is restricted to a few. This may mean a concentration of power, and in any case will mean possibilities of easy personal contacts in all matters that concern economic activity. These contacts, of course, include the central bank and may lead to a policy in which commercial banks act as an extended arm of central government.

The effect of national economic policy on private production is mainly decided by its effect on wages, prices, and other factors in the market. Within this framework, private industry may be autonomous, for example as regards investment, production exports and imports. There are many varieties in the relation of individual firms to the 'national industry' in the same field and to the corresponding industries in other countries. There are great differences, for example, between the small firm in a home market industry and the big exporting firm with subsidiaries in other countries. Industrial organizations of the 'trade association' type may carry out joint work on problems of technical development, standardization, etc. They may, however, also do work on problems of national policy for a branch of industry, sometimes under pressure from government or trade unions. Cartels that regulate prices or production are, as a rule, organized on a nation-wide basis, at the same time as they may represent the national industries in international cartels. Both as regards national and international relations, the conditions under which private firms operate vary to such an extent from one branch of industry to another that they can be described only by special case studies.

National long-term plans, which are established even in some countries which are mainly based on private enterprise in industry, are among the most important instruments for the co-ordination of activities in national industries. These national plans cannot, in fact, be more than forecasts based on plans of private and public enterprises and on targets for the economic policy of the national government. They can be regarded as a kind of explicit consolidation of the mutual adjustment of plans, private and public, that takes place continuously in an integrated welfare economy of the type just described. Various industries can, in the light of such a plan, adjust their input-output relations to other industries (for example, steel-works and shipyards) and government services (electric power, transport) may find a more realistic basis for their development programmes.

III. DEGREES OF INTERNATIONAL INTEGRATION

From the point of view of national planning, public and private, developments abroad represent uncertainties outside the control or influence of national units of action. Leaving aside the risk of war, there are other uncertainties, such as changes in exchange rates, tariffs, quotas, rights to transfer of profits, and so on, which make foreign markets less reliable as a place for permanent activities. Markets abroad which have been built up at a considerable cost may be lost overnight as a result of sudden changes in the policy of other nations. This risk factor is no doubt one of the strongest factors working towards exclusive national integration. The reduction of this risk or its complete elimination is one of the most important aspects of international co-operation.

To eliminate all types of discontinuities in economic relations between highly organized welfare states would, of course, be a very complex problem. One can distinguish various more or less far-reaching steps in this direction :

(i) arrangements for negotiation on a *do ut des* basis ;
(ii) abandonment of certain political powers to an international organization which acts in the interest of several nations ;
(iii) establishment of an international understanding which may ultimately result in an effective economic federation or union.

Various types of international activities which have been created in the post-war years may illustrate developments in these directions. The following examples may be classified in one or other of these groups : tariff negotiations, free trade areas, customs unions, international monetary and financial institutions, agreements about free exchange of labour (joint labour market), international grid systems, integrated tariffs and car pools for inland transport, the Coal and Steel Community, Euratom.

It would lead too far to discuss in detail how far such international contacts and associations go in eliminating the discontinuities at national borders. The preceding summary description of the institutions of the highly organized welfare state gives an indication of how many national ties need to be complemented by corresponding international ties in order to approach international integration. The welfare idea is so deeply rooted that its manifestations within the national framework can be superseded only by corresponding institutions of an international welfare community. How this can be made is an important subject for investigation.

The relation of national economic structures to international markets may be illustrated by two cases : credit and technical knowledge.

(i) *The Market for Credit*

There is hardly, any field in which discontinuities at national frontiers are so sharp as in the market for credit. The inside picture of the welfare state in this respect has been discussed in a preceding paragraph. But the actual degree of international disintegration naturally depends on the structure of international markets for credit.

In the discussion of these problems we may distinguish the short- and long-term relations. Since the war, most progress has been made in creating systems of international short-term credit (IMF and EPU). To the extent that national accounts are balanced over a number of years, such systems do not conflict with narrow national welfare interests. On the contrary, they provide the oil in the machinery of international trade which prevents short-term changes in trade-flow from creating cumulative tendencies towards trade restrictions. In this way, a viable system of international short-term credit reduces the uncertainties that nations meet in their transactions abroad. Experience since the last world war has also shown that such credit arrangements facilitate an expansion of mutual trade. In these ways, they favour an integration beyond national frontiers.

Less progress has been made in solving the problem of long-term imbalances in foreign payments of individual nations. Such imbalances are always bound to occur, not only for reasons of inflationary mismanagement of internal monetary policy. Structural changes in world demand take place which shift the position of various export products and consequently of the total exports of countries specializing in various directions.

The problem of long-term imbalance is also closely related to that of economic expansion. Internal economic growth will (with given trade restrictions) lead to growing imports. On the other hand, a corresponding expansion of traditional exports may be limited by domestic national resources or by trends in world demand. A conversion of exports into new lines may demand

heavy investment (which would create internal inflationary imbalance) and, in any case, a development of internal resources of
skill and technical knowledge that take a long time to acquire. The
position of weak international liquidity may then (in the absence
of possibilities of long-term credit) last for a long period or even
become more or less permanent as a result of a vicious circle of
weak external liquidity, low internal investment, and slow change
in the economic structure.

It may be said that the positive correlation between dominating
exports and internal economic development in general may be
overcome by a rational monetary and currency policy. A deflation
of the internal cost level (in relation to the cost level of competing
countries) or a depreciation of the currency may make new export
industries competitive in the world market. In this way, various
nations may attain a balance according to the rules of comparative
advantage. Countries with a high comparative advantage on the
basis of some special natural resources will tend to specialize in
that direction, while other countries without such resources or with
resources in a less favourable world market position will develop
manufactures which are locally less bound to natural resources (the
process is further complicated by such factors as the relative supply
of capital, labour, and specialized technical talent).

Such possibilities do not, however, eliminate the fact that it may
take a long time to carry through a conversion of the national
economic structure. In the intermediate period a depreciation may
have little effect on the international liquidity position, while a
deflationary internal policy slows down economic development in
general. A depreciation may, as a result of unfavourable trade
elasticities, even affect the balance of payments in an adverse way,
and may tend to raise the internal cost level. Governments may,
therefore, prefer to extend their economic policy to a state-directed
development policy under the cover of import restrictions. This
shift towards a centrally planned economy means a movement
towards a closer national integration.

These relations between external liquidity position and internal
national development seem to be relevant for our discussion in two
different ways. First, an ample supply of international long-term
credit would tend to loosen the ties between various national industries, and would make the discontinuities at national frontiers less
marked. Second, it is likely that small countries will be more
exposed to the hazards of favourable and unfavourable changes in
their liquidity position.

'Small' and 'large' nations can be distinguished only in an

arbitrary way. Irrespective of how we define 'size' it is, however, likely that most small countries have a more specialized export industry than large countries. This follows from the distribution of natural resources over the world surface, from regional differences in climate and traditions, and from advantages in specialization and large-scale production. It is easy to find examples where agricultural or forest products, fish, ore, oil, or shipping dominate the exports of small countries. Large countries are less likely to have all their export eggs in one or a few baskets. There is, therefore, an *a priori* likelihood that small countries will more often find themselves for periods in a favourable or unfavourable situation as regards the trends and potentialities of their dominating exports.

Some small countries may have the good luck of an easy development situation as a result of favourable market trends for their dominating export products. Others may be in the opposite position. As a consequence, a particular industry in two countries (for which conditions in all other respects are similar) will develop quite differently, depending on the position of the dominating export industries with which it is combined within the same narrow frontiers. The risk of falling for periods into the category of countries with adverse trends for their dominating exports seems to me to be the greatest disadvantage of most small nations.

(ii) *The Mobility of Technical Knowledge*

Technical knowledge is, on the whole, the most mobile factor in international relations. Boundaries in this field are more dependent on levels of education and scientific training than on nationality.

It is true that the system of education and research is tending to get more closely integrated in a welfare state, irrespective of its political system. Technical education is, as a rule, co-ordinated on a nation-wide basis, and geared to the structure of national industries. Basic research is mainly financed by government, and government-sponsored boards often distribute funds according to a strategy of national development. Results of this research are made available to the whole national industry without discrimination. Technical development work, on the other hand, is carried out mainly in individual industrial firms, which accumulate the know-how in their special field. There may, however, exist a national system for exchange of experience, which is centred around universities, professional organizations, trade associations, or industry-wide research institutes. Sharing of technical knowledge is, besides, often the result of business or financial contacts that may be especially close within national frontiers.

These national systems in the field of research and technical know-how are, however, only partly exclusive. In the Western world there are (with the important exception of defence secrets) no iron curtains in the field of technology. This is true at least of basic research. Scientists have maintained a spirt of international open door, which is only exceptionally closed to protect national interests. As regards applied technology and know-how, there are, of course, more restrictions in international exchange. But on the whole the difference in mobility within and across national borders does not appear to be sharp.

International contacts through professional and industrial organizations or directly between firms are, generally speaking, less frequent. But foreign technicians, patents, and know-how can often be bought from other countries. Firms may even prefer to grant patent licences or a sharing of know-how to a firm in another country, provided that it does not compete in their markets at home and abroad. Many examples of agreements to this effect can be found in the literature on international restrictive business practices, but the great majority of such agreements have not been registered. But in any case knowledge about industrial methods tends to leak out from one country to another through independent consultants, through firms who deliver machinery, through the press and technical textbooks.

The difference between national and international mobility of technical knowledge may be a matter of no more than a time-lag. In a field where progress in technical knowledge is rapid such a time-lag may represent a great disadvantage. To the extent that small countries are specialized in research, technical development work, and production, this time-lag (which works both ways) should not, however, represent a handicap in international competition.

Chapter 2

ECONOMIC GROWTH OF SMALL NATIONS [1]

BY

S. KUZNETS
Johns Hopkins University

I. WHAT CONSTITUTES A SMALL NATION?

BY a small nation I mean an independent sovereign state, with a population of ten million or less. Setting the dividing line at ten million is a rough decision, made with an eye to the distribution of nations by size as it exists today and has existed over the last fifty to seventy-five years. Were I to draw the line for 1800, it would have been at a much lower number — considering that the largest state within the European family of nations at that time had a population below forty million. And were I to draw it a hundred years hence, the dividing line would be far higher — assuming no devastating demographic catastrophe.

Just as the dividing line is relative to the distribution of nations by size at a given historical epoch, so it is relative to differences in the economic and social potentials that we wish to emphasize. For some industries, even a fifty million nation is too small to provide a sound economic base ; for others, a community of five million may, under reasonable assumptions, supply an adequate long-term market. Conversely, as we move the dividing line up and down, the weight of the various arguments submitted in the paper changes. Whatever will be said of the limits upon diversity of resources, range of possible industries, dependence upon foreign trade, and other problems of economic efficiency, applies with greater force to nations whose population is below five million than to those whose population is close to the dividing line of ten million, and with progressively reduced weight as we move up in the scale of size.

Of about eighty independent states, recognized in 1952, as many

[1] This paper was prepared for a symposium on 'The Challenge of Development' on the occasion of the inauguration of the new building of the Eliezer Kaplan School at the Hebrew University, Jerusalem, and is published with the consent of the Kaplan School authorities.

as forty-seven, or more than half, can be characterized as small —
if we use the criterion just proposed.[1] True, they constitute but a
limited fraction of the total population of independent states : these
forty-seven nations account for only 171 out of some 2258 million,
or less than 8 per cent. At the other extreme, the four very large
states — China, India, the U.S.S.R., and the United States —
account for 1198 million, or over half.[2] But this contrast in size
makes it all the more important to consider some distinctive problems of economic growth of small nations. They can be viewed
as so many experiments in economic growth ; and while the diversity
among them is great, some general features associated with their
small size can perhaps be found.

A note of advance caution must be sounded about the generalizations to be suggested below. For lack of adequate comparative
statistics and other data, of time to assemble those available, and of
space to present them, it is impossible to offer fully documented
analysis ; and the statements are necessarily tentative hypotheses.
In other words, they indicate the results we would expect to find,
and are not positive generalizations fully buttressed by comprehensive evidence. The data provided are illustrative rather than
conclusive. But in combination with some general supporting
analysis, they suffice to indicate that the challenge of economic
growth has particular overtones for small nations, and that in the
current active concern with problems of economic growth more
attention should be paid to the effect of size than has heretofore
been the case.

II. THE CHARACTERISTICS OF A SMALL NATION

The first general observation is that the economic structure of
small nations is typically less diversified than that of larger units.
This means that some of the full variety of industries observed in
the larger nations is either lacking or only barely represented in
many small nations. Conversely, it means that the economic structure — the proportional distribution of output and of productive

---

[1] See United Nations data as grouped in W. S. and E. S. Woytinsky, *World
Commerce and Governments* (Twentieth Century Fund, 1955), Tables 194 and 196,
pp. 564-66. Nine minor splinter units like Vatican City, Andorra, Monaco, etc.,
are excluded.
[2] *Ibid.* The population figure used for China in this source is 464 million.
According to the recent census, the population of mainland China is close to 570
million ; and if this figure is accepted, the share of the four large states becomes
even larger.

factors — of the small nations is more concentrated in a few industrial sectors.[1]

Diversification of economic structure, in the sense indicated, is a function of the level of economic development reflected in such commonly accepted indexes as, for example, real national product *per capita*. When the level of economic development and *per capita* product is low, a large share of the country's economy is devoted to agriculture, and diversity within non-agricultural pursuits is narrowly limited. It is only when *per capita* economic performance is sufficiently high that non-agricultural activities can attain importance, and a wide range of economic activities can emerge in response to the variety of human wants.

It follows that the difference between small and large nations in range of diversity of the typical economic structure would be clear only in comparisons of nations at about the same level of development. But with this qualification, the general statement should hold. Even if we compared two nations, both underdeveloped, but one small and the other large, we would expect the range of economic activities to be wider in the latter than in the former — particularly if our observations penetrate below the broad economic sectors and distinguish divisions within agriculture, mining, and so on. But the contrast in diversification would be particularly conspicuous for two economically advanced nations : the high levels of technological and economic performance would permit, *except for differences in size*, a wide range of economic activities and products — from necessities to luxuries, from commodities to services, from consumer goods to producer goods.

There are three reasons for expecting the greater concentration of economic structure of small nations, particularly in comparisons for states that are fairly well-advanced on the scale of economic growth. The first lies in the size of the area and its limiting effect on the supply of natural, irreproducible resources. Most of the nations that are small in population are also small in area. Of the 47 small nations mentioned above, 19 had areas of less than 20 thousand square miles each, and another 15 areas of between 20 and 50 thousand square miles each. Only 2 (Australia and Libya) had areas of over 500 thousand square miles ; and in these the proportions of desert land are large.[2] The large states had, on the whole, much larger areas, although the correlation between area

---

[1] I am using 'industry' and 'industrial sector' in the widest sense to denote any distinctive branch of a country's productive system — agriculture, mining, manufacturing, any other commodity-producing branch, or any of the numerous service activities.

[2] See Woytinsky, *op. cit.*, Table 196.

and population is not perfect, and exceptions come easily to mind.

The availability of a variety of mineral and other natural resources, useful at a given level of technology, is largely a function of area. Generally, a large area will have much greater variety than a small area — of minerals, of climate, of topography, of mixture of land and water, and so on. This does not mean that small nations possess *no* natural resources : all it means is that any one of them is likely to have a lesser variety. Denmark has great natural endowments for certain types of agriculture and for activities connected with water, but it has no sources of mechanical energy — neither coal nor oil nor hydropower. Some small Arab states have great oil resources, but very little else. As a further illustration of this obvious point, we draw attention to the fact that several of the smaller nations are completely land-locked : Switzerland is a conspicuous example among the economically developed, and Paraguay, Nepal, and Mongolia among the under-developed. Of the thirty-three larger countries only one, Czechoslovakia, is cut off from the sea.

The second reason lies in the conflict between the minimum or optimum scale of plant for some industries, and the limited domestic market of small nations. Because of the minimum, let alone the optimum, scale of plant required for some industries, for example, aircraft, automobiles and trucks, large machine tools, heavy electrical equipment, heavy railroad equipment — their inclusion in the domestic productive system of a small nation would be extremely uneconomical unless it could count on a substantial foreign market. And heavy reliance on foreign markets is not a sound base for many industries. Despite intense nationalism and strong security feelings that are perhaps warranted, there are compelling economic factors that make it impossible for a small nation to have even a single basic plant for a number of industries that are feasible for a larger country at the same level of economic development. This implies particularly to industries of advanced technology which require large-scale production, since costs would otherwise be prohibitively high because of the mechanical energy and the complex fabrication techniques needed to turn out acceptable final products. The fact of the matter is that none of the forty-seven small countries mentioned above has an aircraft industry ; none has an integrated automobile production industry (as distinct from assembly or parts plants) ; and few, even among the advanced, produce heavy railroad stock — to mention but a few illustrations.

The third reason is, in a sense, the complement of the first two. While a small nation may lack many natural resources, its supply of a few may give it a marked comparative advantage over larger countries whose supply may be as large or larger absolutely, but much lower on a per head or per unit of need basis. Likewise, while a small nation cannot afford to adopt large-scale industries, it may have advantages with respect to some fabrication processes. The existence of such foci of comparative advantage may mean concentration upon them — to a much greater extent than required in larger nations : with population small, labour and other economic resources can be more fully absorbed in a few economic activities. If a small nation has even a relatively small supply of some resource of world-wide use, such as oil — a much smaller supply than say the United States or the U.S.S.R. — it may well concentrate on this valuable resource to the point where little labour force and few other resources are left for other domestic production, excepting, of course, essential goods that cannot be imported. And what is true of oil is true also of coal and iron, natural advantages for shipping (which looms so large in Norway), or the peculiar advantages of a skilled labour force and an experienced entrepreneurial class (as in Switzerland with its watch and other high-skill manufactures). Since every nation is by definition the repository of a distinctive historical heritage, as well as the occupant of a distinctive portion of the earth's surface, pre-conditions for some specific advantages always exist ; and concentration on the latter in the small nations may, *ipso facto*, mean lack of resources for many other *domestically* located activities.

III. FOREIGN TRADE IN THE ECONOMY OF A SMALL NATION

Given the tendency of small nations to concentrate economic production on a limited range of activities, the second general proposition follows. Foreign trade is of greater weight in the economic activity of small nations than in that of larger units. This is particularly true of nations that have developed and attained fairly high levels of *per capita* output and consumption. For at these levels, the variety of goods demanded by ultimate consumers is far wider than that of domestic output of final goods. But it is likely to be true even of under-developed countries, for they tend to have some comparative advantages, some resources that permit exports to world markets — whether jute, bananas, oil, coffee, or copra. The weight of these exports (and correspondingly generated imports), in relation to total activity, is likely to be greater in small than in equally under-developed but larger countries.

Two illustrations of this broad generalization can be briefly presented. The first, for the year 1938–39, relates imports and exports to national income plus imports for each of fifty-three countries.[1] The rank correlation between size of country, as measured by its population, and the ratio of exports to total product plus imports is -0.44; that between population size and the import ratio is -0.56. Both coefficients are statistically significant at a demanding level of confidence, and suggest that, by and large, the smaller the country, the larger the ratio of exports or imports to total output. It is interesting that a similar correlation coefficient between *per capita* income and the import ratio is only 0.15, and that between *per capita* income and the export ratio is 0.02 — neither statistically significant ; and the indication is that, at least for this sample, there is no significant association between foreign trade ratios and the level of *per capita* income.

Another statistical demonstration, this time for 1949, can be derived from Table 25 in the Woytinsky volume already quoted,

TABLE I (A)

SIZE OF NATION AND FOREIGN TRADE

Thirty States with Higher *Per Capita* Incomes, 1949
Arranged in Decreasing Order of Population Size

Group	Average population (millions)	Average income *per cap.* (U.S. $)	Average foreign trade *per cap.* (U.S. $)	(4) as % of (3)
(1)	(2)	(3)	(4)	(5)
1. First five	69·0	653	142	21·8
2. Second five	15·0	399	176	44·1
3. Third five	10·2	429	252	58·8
4. Fourth five	6·2	360	234	65·0
5. Fifth five	3·9	579	306	52·9
6. Sixth five	1·3	447	374	83·6

where *per capita* income and *per capita* foreign trade (sum of imports and exports), all in United States dollars, are given for sixty independent states. From Table 197 we have the population total for each state. By arranging the thirty states with the higher *per capita*

---

[1] The denominator in the ratio measures total available product within the country. A more appropriate measure would be the sum of gross national product and imports, but the results of the correlation would be the same. The underlying data are presented in an unpublished statistical appendix to my paper, 'Toward a Theory of Economic Growth', *National Policy for Economic Welfare at Home and Abroad*, edited by Robert Lekachman (Doubleday and Co., 1955).

incomes by decreasing size of population, and averaging (without weighting) the *per capita* incomes and the *per capita* foreign trade levels for successive groups of five countries, we secure the results given in Table I (A).

With one exception, the ratio of foreign trade to national income rises as the average size of population declines — and the result would be the same if foreign trade were related to national income or to gross national product plus imports. In contrast, there is no clear association between the ratio of foreign trade to income and *per capita* income. For three of the six groups, in which the range of *per capita* income is fairly narrow — from $399 to $447 — the ratio of foreign trade to income ranges from 44 to 84 per cent (lines 2, 3, and 6).

The same calculation for the thirty nations with lower *per capita* income, most of them under-developed, yields the following results :

TABLE I (B)

SIZE OF NATION AND FOREIGN TRADE

Thirty States with Lower *Per Capita* Incomes, 1949
Arranged in Decreasing Order of Population Size

Group	Average population (millions)	Average income *per cap.* (U.S. $)	Average foreign trade *per cap.* (U.S. $)	(4) as % of (3)
(1)	(2)	(3)	(4)	(5)
1. First five	214·2	52	19·6	37·7
2. Second five	29·1	100	44·0	43·8
3. Third five	16·4	59	27·2	46·1
4. Fourth five	5·5	84	56·6	67·4
5. Fifth five	2·7	68	41·4	61·1
6. Sixth five	1·2	101	65·0	64·2

Here we find the same relationship — a rise in the ratio of foreign trade to national income as population size declines. But the association is not as regular and the range not as pronounced as among the more developed countries. This finding suggests, as might have been expected, that foreign trade by the less developed countries is subject to the more accidental influences of availability of world-wide marketable resources. Some of the larger nations may, because of that circumstance, be as heavily engaged in foreign trade as (or more than) the small units in the array.

Three additional comments may illuminate further the implications of the greater relative share of foreign trade in the economic activity of small nations.

(1) As already indicated, this greater share is largely the consequence, and complement, of the greater concentration of the economic structure of small nations on a narrower range of activities. Yet one aspect of this connection was not stressed explicitly. To the extent that the balance of advantages plays a part in the choice of sectors, the smaller area of the small nations permits more effective competition and substitution by imports and more effective development of exports than in nations with larger areas. Transportation costs constitute an important factor in the calculation of advantages for many commodities. In a nation with a large area, whose population is not concentrated on the boundaries (as is likely to be the case), the transportation cost advantage for domestic producers *vis-à-vis* would-be importers would be far greater than in a country with a small area, particularly one that is a close neighbour of a much larger country. Furthermore, concentration on exports would be relatively more limited in a large country, particularly if its transportation network is not well developed — as is the case with many under-developed countries ; and the smaller nations can specialize in some world-traded export to a greater relative extent without running into prohibitive costs of long-distance transportation from the interior. This specification of transport cost elements as an item in the balance of advantages that would lead to greater engagement in world trade by small area nations is but part of an argument already advanced — but it merits explicit mention in connection with the statistical findings on the foreign trade ratios.

(2) Exports may flow to many or to a few countries, imports may come from many or from a few countries. Accompanying the heavier reliance of small countries on foreign trade is a greater tendency on their part to rely on imports from and exports to but a few countries — with such concentration particularly noticeable in exports.

An interesting analysis of this aspect of the foreign trade network was made over a decade ago by Albert O. Hirschman.[1] His index of concentration is the square root of the sums of the squares of the percentage share of n countries in the exports or imports of a given country. Complete concentration, in the sense that the exports or imports involve ties with just *one* country, yields an index of 100 ; complete dispersion, if exports go to 100 countries (or imports

---

[1] See his *National Power and the Structure of Foreign Trade* (University of California Press, 1945), particularly Chapter VI, pp. 98-116.

come from 100 countries) and if these share equally, yields an index of 10. I took Mr. Hirschman's indexes for 1938 (the last year shown in his tables) for three areas — western Europe (including central and southern), the British Empire, and Latin America. Within each of these areas I calculated simple arithmetic means of the indexes, separately for the larger and the smaller countries distinguished by size of population. The results were as follows :

TABLE II
CONCENTRATION OF FOREIGN TRADE

Area and subgroup	Countries included	Average index of concentration	
		Exports	Imports
(1)	(2)	(3)	(4)
Europe			
Larger countries	U.K., Netherlands, Czechoslovakia, Belgium, Portugal	27·7	27·2
Smaller countries	Sweden, Norway, Denmark, Finland, Switzerland	41·0	36·4
British Empire			
Larger countries	India, Nigeria, Egypt, Union of South Africa	55·0	45·8
Smaller countries	Ceylon, British Malaya, Australia, New Zealand, Eire	65·1	45·1
Latin America			
Larger countries	Brazil, Argentina, Mexico, Colombia, Peru	49·5	45·7
Smaller countries	Chile,* Cuba, Bolivia, Ecuador, Uruguay	53·6	44·5

* The index for exports from Chile (not given by Hirschman) I assumed was slightly higher than the index for imports (42·0 compared with 40·6).

While necessarily crude, the measures point unmistakably to the tendency of small countries to concentrate their foreign trade, particularly exports, in one or a few countries — usually large. In extreme cases, this tendency results in the satellite position of some small countries to their larger neighbours — *e.g.* Eire in relation to the U.K., many Latin American countries and possibly Canada in relation to the United States, and, recently, some countries in Eastern Europe in relation to the U.S.S.R. Even when no geographical or political compulsions are involved, it may be easier for a small country to concentrate its exports in one or two major purchaser countries than to diversify the geographic destination of its exports too much ; and correspondingly it may be easier to import goods from one or two major sources.

(3) The concentration in few countries of destination of exports and few countries of origin of imports of small nations, in contrast to the dispersion of the foreign trade of the larger countries, is partly a matter of size : of two totals being distributed, the larger will, because of its very size, be more easily directed into more channels.

This difference in size is of bearing upon another type of international flow, fairly closely connected with commodity trade — capital investment. It has not been unusual for some small countries in the past to derive, over long periods, a substantial proportion of their total capital investment from abroad, *e.g.* Sweden from the 1860s to World War I and Canada from 1870 to World War I. In Sweden from 1860 to 1890 more than half of domestic net capital formation came from abroad ; and the proportion was not much below that for Canada from 1901 to 1920.[1] A similar case could probably be established for Australia. A large country could derive a large proportion of its capital formation from abroad only if its domestic savings were rather small. But conditions that would restrict the flow of domestic savings would most likely also discourage foreign capital investment — unless it was politically guaranteed or protected by empire-colony relations, or involved political commitments as was so common in foreign loans in the nineteenth century. Under such conditions, the borrower country would naturally shrink from too onerous a burden of foreign capital investment. On the other hand, in a large country, conditions that are relatively favourable for domestic savings and domestically financed capital formation, and that result in a large flow of domestic savings, could not induce a flow of foreign funds *large* enough to equal a high fraction of domestic capital formation (as was the case in the post-Civil War United States). Only in small countries can conditions favourable to both domestic growth and foreign capital investment produce, because of the small size of the borrower *vis-à-vis* the would-be lenders, a long-run situation in which a large proportion of domestically located capital formation is financed from abroad.

[1] See my ' International Differences in Capital Formation and Financing', *Capital Formation and Economic Growth*, edited by Moses Abramovitz, Universities-National Bureau Committee for Economic Research (Princeton University Press 1956), particularly Table II-4, p. 71.

IV. EFFECTS OF SIZE WHERE FOREIGN TRADE
IS IMPOSSIBLE

While foreign trade permits concentration of a small country's activity in the economically advantageous sectors, not all goods needed for domestic use can be imported ; nor can a country's economic growth be securely built upon exports to a few countries of destination. It follows that, for various reasons to be noted, the international division of labour stops far short of the economic optimum — in larger as well as in small countries. The question here is whether the factors that limit the international division of labour and compel countries to be more autarkic than warranted by economic calculation have greater adverse bearing upon small than upon larger countries — and thus inhibit economic growth in the former more than in the latter.

Without attempting to deal with them fully, we distinguish the technological from the social factors. The technological factors are prominent in those economic activities in which the producer must be in close proximity, spatially or culturally, to the ultimate consumers, for otherwise transportation and transfer costs would be extremely heavy proportionately to final cost. Many types of economic goods fall into this category and cannot therefore be imported. The simplest case is bulky commodities with high transportation costs. Another illustration is construction and installation activities within a country which can be rendered on a continuous and satisfactory basis only by domestically located labour. But the condition is most typical of service activities — those provided by retail trade, personal service establishments, the educational system, the curative and other professions, and, above all, by government. By a stretch of the imagination, and given modern transportation facilities, one can visualize an arrangement by which a fleet of airplanes would bring in daily hordes of foreign experts in these services, trained to perform them in accordance with the country's needs and customs ; thus permitting the residents to concentrate on what may be to them economically more advantageous activities. Yet, even if in this imaginary arrangement we could ignore the social factors that would make it unacceptable to the importing country, the costs — not only of transportation, but also of training the imported performers in the language and *mores* of the country — would still be prohibitively large. This whole range of activities, unlike those embodied in standardized commodities of wide international use that can be easily handled in foreign trade, are so closely geared to the distinctive social pattern of the user country that the sheer technological difficulty of importing compels their performance by that country's long-term residents.

The question which arises is whether this necessarily domestic performance in such fields means greater per unit cost in the small than in the larger countries. In other words, is the optimum scale of performance of these activities so large that the smaller scale firms commensurate with the needs of the small countries mean uneconomically high unit costs? Offhand, the answer for most products in this category would be in the negative — particularly domestically bound services. Because of their close connection with the needs of individual consumers, these activities tend to be small-scale the world over. After all, there are no giant plants for providing professional, educational, or business services even in the larger countries; and construction activity is, on the average, a small-scale industry even in a country like the United States.

Yet the answer must be qualified in two respects. First, for professional and educational activities, whose quality is dependent upon participation in the intellectual life of a wide community, too close a tie to the distinctive language and the limited professional group of a small country is a serious drawback. All other conditions being equal, a country with a larger population can, at a lesser cost, develop the variety of specialities in the intellectual hierarchy, and provide the tools for adequate participation in the world community of advanced knowledge. A smaller country can accomplish these ends only through more widespread multilinguality, and a proportionately (to its total resources) more costly and conscious effort to offset the effects of the small size of its professional community.

Second, even in other service activities (and in construction), in larger countries enough large-scale production may be possible to make, again *ceteris paribus*, for greater efficiency, *i.e.* lower unit costs. In the larger countries there is room for giant construction companies which can use more advanced technology in the construction of many large-scale plants, office buildings, or apartment houses. There is room for well-organized chain systems of retail stores, repaid service establishments, and the like. And there is room for economy of scale even in local transportation, financial establishments, business services, and so forth. It is, consequently, quite possible that, like professional activities, many other domestically bound activities would be relatively more costly in a small than in a larger country ; although not even the order of magnitudes involved can be suggested.[1]

The social factors that limit reliance by countries on international trade are essentially political. Given the structuring of the world in independent, sovereign states, the existence of aggressive tendencies, and of perhaps less importance, the vagaries of economic policy of various countries — no one country can safely allow its future to depend on exports to a few markets, or on imports that may be cut off in times of emergency. So long as international anarchy prevails, and so long as political independence is desired, there will be justification for keeping within a country's boundaries activities whose products are indispensable and whose supply might be cut off ; for devoting a substantial proportion of resources to economically unproductive uses, for example, military training and armaments ; and for limiting the economically profitable use of resources if it makes the country too dependent in the long run.

Whether the extra costs of these uneconomical uses of resources for the sake of security are proportionately greater in small than in larger countries is a question that could be dealt with effectively only if we could carefully standardize the objectives, *i.e.* the returns whose relative costliness is to be appraised, and deal properly with such complications as are hidden behind the terms 'alliances', 'blocs', 'leagues', 'counter-blocs', and so on. Purely statistical comparisons of shares of military expenditures in total activity would not lead very far ; and even they cannot be made, given the secrecy and obfuscation that naturally surround these data. Larger countries may be more concerned with aggression than small countries ; larger countries may support some smaller allies, who are thereby relieved of some burdens ; and, above all, direct military outlays may be only a small part of the costs of the uneconomical distortion of a country's productive structure for the sake of external security in an uncertain world.

Yet, if any conjectures in such a murky field can be made, I am inclined to the conclusion that, given defence as the only objective, and given a limitation to reliance upon allies, the burden of the uneconomical use of resources for security purposes would be far larger proportionally for the small countries. The basis for this conclusion is simple : it is not the size of the country but the size of possible opponents that should govern the response. All other

---

[1] The purely economic aspect of the argument may be stated as follows : the transfer costs from one country to another of these economic goods are so heavy on a per unit basis that even large differentials in per unit cost between the two countries would not induce a flow — even with the application of the principle of comparative advantages.

conditions being equal, the relative magnitude of the possible emergency reflected in the size of would-be opponents would naturally be greater for the small than for the larger countries. Indeed, the burdens may be so unequal that alliances may prove to be in the long run the indispensable prerequisite for survival ; and such alliances can be more valuable to the small states than the larger — thus offsetting the original disadvantage of small size. But in this uncertain world, alliances cannot be fully relied upon ; and it is, therefore, reasonable to suggest that, given defence considerations alone, the economic burdens of safeguarding independence are proportionately far heavier in a small than in a large country — again *ceteris paribus*.

V. HOW CAN WE EXPLAIN THE SUCCESS OF SOME SMALL NATIONS ?

It would seem from the discussion so far that small countries are under a greater handicap than large in the task of economic growth. Their small size may not permit them to take full advantage of the potentials of large-scale production and organization ; their defence task *vis-à-vis* the rest of the world may be proportionately greater ; and their reliance on international trade and international division of labour, while greater than for large countries, must still be limited for security reasons, and because many needed goods that are closely interwoven with the country's distinctive culture and indigenous life cannot be imported.

How, then, do some small nations manage to attain high levels of economic growth — for example the Scandinavian countries, Switzerland, let alone Canada, Australia, and others ? And how do some others manage to do so much better than some very large states ? While the answer to this question must be just as sketchy as the propositions advanced in the earlier sections, it should be explicitly formulated — if only as a basis for further thinking.

One possible answer should be heavily discounted. It may be argued that some small nations happen, by a lucky accident, to be endowed with a valuable natural resource — which will be developed by foreign firms (presumably from a larger country) with only benefits accruing to the host country. The suggested inference is then that some small nations reach an economically advanced stage because they happen to possess unusual natural resource endowments.

It need not be denied that in the distribution of natural resources some small nations may be the lucky winners at a given time (and others at other times). But I would still argue that the capacity to take advantage of these hazards of fortune and to make them a basis for sustained economic development is not often given. In the nineteenth century, Brazil was commonly regarded as an Eldorado — and indeed enjoyed several times the position of a supplier of a natural resource in world-wide demand; yet the record of this country's economic growth has not been impressive, and it is not as yet among the economically advanced nations. The existence of a valuable natural resource represents a permissive condition, facilitates — if properly exploited — the transition from the pre-industrial to industrial phases of growth. But unless the nation shows a capacity for modifying its social institutions in time to take advantage of the opportunity, it will have only a transient effect. Advantages in natural resources never last for too long — given continuous changes in technology and its extension to other parts of the world.

To put it differently : *every* small nation has some advantage in natural resources — whether it be location, coastline, minerals, forests, etc. But some show a capacity to build on it, if only as a starting-point, toward a process of sustained economic growth and others do not. The crucial variables are elsewhere, and they must be sought in the nation's social and economic institutions.

Small nations, because of their smaller populations and hence possibly greater homogeneity and closer internal ties, may find it easier to make the social adjustments needed to take advantage of the potentialities of modern technology and economic growth — the terms defined most broadly. This task may prove much harder for the larger countries because the ties that bind their larger populations may be far weaker and thus provide a less secure basis for acceptance, by consent, of social changes which, while in the short run hurting some groups and benefiting others, may be indispensable for adequate growth of the economy as a whole.

This general proposition is comprised of two distinct parts. First, since economic growth is a process of unequal change, of structural shifts within an economy, some established economic interest groups must lose in relative importance and others must gain. Agriculture must recede, relatively, and non-agricultural sectors must advance ; small-scale enterprise may lose out and large-scale enterprises profit ; individual business-men may suffer and impersonal corporations, as well as the wage-earning and salaried classes, benefit. These shifts are usually accomplished partly through differential returns to various groups, where the lagging returns in some sectors set up a pressure for labour and other resources to move into more productive and profitable sectors ; and partly through the action of the state, which even in libertarian countries takes responsibility for secular decisions — on land tenure, on public improvements, on employment conditions, on taxes, on foreign trade, on currency and banking, and so forth. All of this is done in order to resolve conflicts of interest and to contribute positively to the long-term interest of the community at large. Behind these shifts, in response to differential compensation in the relatively free markets, or to legislatively modified conditions of operation, there is bound to be destruction of the traditional patterns of life and existing scales of values — particularly in the older countries where they have been set for a long time — to allow for new patterns, indispensable to economic growth. With the high rate of economic growth in many countries during the last century and a half to two centuries, the structural shifts were also rapid, and the corresponding social adjustments were large — relative to the spans over which they had to be realized. They were in essence revolutions that had to be controlled and channelled if the integral unity of the society was to survive or continuing bottlenecks were to be prevented — either of which eventualities would have promptly put a stop to further economic growth.

The second part of the proposition is that, given the need for rapid and far-reaching social changes to take advantage of potentials of modern economic growth, the small states are likely to have an easier task because of the closer ties among the members of their smaller populations ; because of a possibly greater community of feeling among these smaller populations, due in part to a long background of common historical experience and in part to the lines of communication and connection among them that are closer than in a large country with its diversity of regions and multiplicity of local interests. This is not to deny that many small independent states, particularly some that have emerged recently, are riven by the existence of sizable and hostile minorities or split almost in two by religious, linguistic, and other differences. All that is argued here is that in many small states there exists a strong feeling of community and solidarity, a product of a long-shared historical past, and that in these states social decisions, necessary for the adjustment to the potentials of economic growth, may be far easier to reach than elsewhere. Among the larger nations this task is far more difficult, since the ties among the various sectors of their populations are looser and regional and other cleavages can more readily develop.

The economic and social history of many small countries, now at a high level of economic performance, is replete with past decisions which were crucial for attaining sustained growth and were made by the kind of community-wide agreement that had to be so much more laboriously striven for, or often forcibly imposed, in many larger countries. The example of Denmark, which faced grave problems in the second half of the nineteenth century, when its economic position was undercut by competition of exports from the United States and other large grain exporters, and immediately after its political position was shaken by the loss of Schleswig-Holstein, and the way a solution was found, is a clear case in point. The example of Switzerland, with its long-range policy of neutrality, and decision on the framework of the state, in the relation between the Federal government and the cantons, is another. And the example of Canada and its policy after Confederation is a third.

Two other items of possible evidence of the greater capacity and elasticity of the small states to adjust to what, in the light of our earlier discussion, appear to be greater problems of economic growth (compared with the larger states) may be noted. The first is that the developed small states seem to have succeeded in spreading the fruits of economic growth more widely among their populations than the larger states at comparable levels of income *per capita*. I have no evidence ready to demonstrate this suggestion statistically, but it is my belief that income is distributed more equally among the populations in the Scandinavian countries and Switzerland, than say in the U.K., France, Germany, or even the United States ; and that the same is true of Australia, New Zealand, and perhaps even Canada, compared with the United States. These smaller countries have no proportionately large regions like our South with a *per capita* income distinctly lower than that for the rest of the country. Nor is the differential between *per capita* returns per worker in agriculture and in the non-agricultural sectors as great in many of them as it is in the United States. And their social legislation is surely more advanced than that of the larger countries at comparable *per capita* levels of economic performance.

The second item, of lesser importance, is the greater ease with which the small countries can fit into the interstices of the international trade network than the larger countries — given their greater ease in changing the structure of the domestic economy. Because of their smaller size relative to world markets, and the shorter lines of internal communication, these small countries can adjust more rapidly to changing conditions. There have been many incidents in the history of international trade when the small countries beat their larger competitors to the punch — to use an American colloquialism — by shifting their lines and by selecting the specific adjustment of their limited but skilled resources to take advantage of a changed conjuncture.

VI. SOME CONCLUSIONS

The comments above are but brief exploratory notes on a large problem. While many of them can easily be criticized, and while the whole presentation can be charged with sins of omission and commission, I feel no need to apologize if the remarks attain their main purpose : to suggest the specific aspects of the challenge which economic growth presents to small nations, as distinct from larger ones.

The specific challenge is, to put it briefly, how to use the stronger sense of community, the closer coherence of the population, the greater elasticity of social institutions, to overcome the disadvantage of small size. Limited in its area and variety of natural resources, limited in the number of people within its boundaries, confronted with greater problems of security, the small nation is at a distinct disadvantage. It must compensate essentially by the quality of its people and its social institutions. It must be able to adjust its institutions to the ever-changing technological potentials of peaceful economic growth, more promptly and thoroughly than the large countries can do ordinarily. It can by social consensus rather than by dictatorship, which cannot be relied upon for the long run, reach decisions that hurt some people more than others, for the sake of the longer-range future of the community. It can, by wide agreement, impose great burdens on its population — in learning, in work, in patterns of organization, in savings, in taxation, and so forth ; all of which can be secured in a larger country either by an authoritarian government — with all the disadvantages that this implies — or only after long and costly conflict and delay.

This capacity for 'social invention' can be and is exercised not only in modifying the domestic institutions of a country to take better advantage of the potentials of economic growth, but also in international economic relations. And the greater ease of securing a voluntary consensus in the small countries may make them more effective pioneers in modifying international relations, as it makes them more effective in social invention applied to domestic institutions. The common market movement in Europe indicates quite clearly that when some fairly high levels of economic growth have been passed, the small nation can pioneer new institutional arrangements, now in the sphere of international relations.

The main premise of this paper is that the proper framework of social institutions, capable of continuous and relatively painless adjustment and, in fact, social invention, is an indispensable prerequisite for modern economic growth. Given this premise, the distinctive advantage of small nations lies in this determinant of economic growth — not in technology of production. It is in the evolution of social institutions and organizations that facilitate long-term peaceful type of economic growth (the only type that can be long-term) that both the challenge and the promise of economic growth are particularly great for small nations.

PART II

CASE STUDIES
OF EFFICIENT LARGE AND SMALL NATIONS

Chapter 3

STUDY OF THE SIZE AND EFFICIENCY OF THE AMERICAN ECONOMY

BY

S. FABRICANT
New York University

I. THE PROBLEM

THE problem before us is the link between the size and the efficiency of the United States. The problem might be put narrowly : do the obstacles that political boundaries raise to the movement of goods, men, money, and ideas impose fewer disadvantages on the large economy of the United States than on the smaller economies of other countries ? To this question most of us would nod our heads quickly, and we would support the answer along the following lines. The United States has open to it whatever opportunities for efficiency are provided by wide markets despite the obstacles to international trade. Some, perhaps many, of these opportunities may be open even in countries not nearly as large as the United States ; but there must be some which appear only in the very largest of economies. We may presume, also, that the opportunities opened by wide markets are not neglected in the United States. The vast size of the American economy therefore probably contributes in some degree to the high level of American efficiency.

When more than this is asked about the effect of America's size on its efficiency, the answer cannot be as quick and as confident. Our thinking about the causes of national efficiency in general, and about the rôle of national size in particular, is still largely in the realm of speculation. When we get down to cases, we find ourselves below the level of abstraction at which most theorizing has taken place. I think it is well to recognize this and I shall therefore submit a few questions on points that bother me : What do we mean when we say the American economy is efficient and large ? How might its size contribute to its efficiency ? What do we learn from the bits of statistics that bear on the matter ?

35

II. EFFICIENCY AND ITS MEASUREMENT

That the economy of the United States of America is super-latively efficient, measured by the goods and services it provides its people per head of the population or in return for an hour or year of work, does not need to be argued these days. This is an era in which almost every country seems to be acutely aware of the differ-ence between its level of efficiency so defined and that of the United States, and is striving to narrow the gap or keep it from widening. And, indeed, the gaps are wide, to judge from the available figures. Hardly any other country stands higher today than about six- or seven-tenths of the United States level of real income *per capita* or per time-unit of labour input, and most are below four-tenths.[1]

It is easy, however, to exaggerate the gap between the United States and other countries. In their OEEC study [2] Gilbert and Kravis showed how the use of foreign-exchange rates to convert national products to a common unit can mislead. The *per capita* gross national product of the United Kingdom in 1950 was 37 per cent of the United States level according to money values adjusted by the exchange rates, and 58 per cent according to Gilbert and Kravis's far more reliable quantity index. Yet most comparisons of *per capita* incomes must still be made via exchange rates, as in the United Nations Statistical Paper. The pioneering efforts of Colin Clark [3] need to be extended and improved along the lines followed by OEEC. Even this advance would not carry us as far as we need to go. In calculations of relative income levels, there are still other sources of error, many of which are mentioned in Kuznets's com-parison of China and the United States.[4] On the whole, these too probably make the differences appear wider than they should.

It is not at all likely, of course, that the order of countries with respect to *per capita* income or income per unit of labour time would be seriously affected by improvements in the statistics, so long as we accept something like the usual definition of real income. At any rate, the United States would remain first on the list. Yet the question with which we are dealing is in part at least a quanti-

[1] United Nations, 'National and Per Capita Incomes of Seventy Countries in 1949 Expressed in United States Dollars', *Statistical Papers*, Series E, No. 1, October 1950.

[2] M. Gilbert and I. B. Kravis, *An International Comparison of National Pro-ducts and the Purchasing Power of Currencies*, Organization for European Economic Co-operation, 1954.

[3] C. Clark, *Conditions of Economic Progress*, Macmillan, 1940; 3rd ed., 1957.

[4] S. Kuznets, 'National Income and Industrial Structure', *Proceedings of the International Statistical Conference, 1947*, Vol. V, Calcutta, 1951; reprinted in *Economic Change*, New York, Norton, 1953.

tative one, and it matters whether we are trying to explain a gap of 40 per cent or 60 per cent.

There is a further source of doubt about the width of the gap. Economists, more than most people, are aware of the variety of meanings embraced by the term 'efficiency', as well as of the problem of measuring it. In terms of product *per capita* or per unit of labour time the United States is highly efficient. But how different would the results be if efficiency were measured by the ratio of product to the inputs of the services of all productive agencies or resources? And is not this the more appropriate measure? Labour alone is not the only productive agency; labour time alone does not adequately measure input generally or even the input of labour alone. There is also the stock of tangible and intangible capital that is put to work in American industry.

It is an impressively large stock. According to Goldsmith's recent estimate, the tangible assets of the United States reached a current value at the end of 1955 of more than 1,350,000 million dollars.[1] It seems that a very substantial portion of the tangible capital of the world lies within American borders.

Perhaps of equal importance — no serious calculation has been made of its magnitude and maybe nothing is yet possible — is the investment in the education and training of the American labour force and in the discovery of its talents. Not all of the cumulative expenditures on formal education is investment, for some must be viewed as a form of consumption. Also, the United States goes in for formal education, as contrasted with informal, more than do other countries, and there is therefore some further tendency to overestimate the relative level of United States investment in educational capital. But with all allowance, I would suppose that the value of the existing stock of such capital per head is larger than in other countries.

The investment in scientific, technical, and industrial knowledge — the current term is 'research and development' — is also to be considered. Here, too, not all the expenditures constitute investment, nor is all knowledge the result of a process of investment in the economic sense. But I would judge from clues of rather dubious quality — for example, the research expenditures of government, non-profit institutions, and industry, the size of the population with higher education and particularly with scientific and technical training, the volume of patents — that the economic capital involved is very substantial. Of course, intangible capital

[1] R. W. Goldsmith in *37th Annual Report* of the National Bureau of Economic Research, May 1957.

is not something to which a permanent claim can be staked out. Just as the American economy has at its disposal the 'heritage of all the ages', so does the rest of the world have at its disposal the knowledge accumulated in the United States. Nevertheless, some knowledge is for a time the 'private' possession of the nation that produces it, and the United States is an important producer and therefore possessor of such capital. Moreover, a good deal of the world's knowledge is not at the disposal of considerable sections of the globe, for they lack the other resources required to exploit it, or engage in the kinds of production to which the knowledge is inapplicable.

The common definition of efficiency in terms of the ratio of output to population, labour force, or labour time alone, thus falls short of completeness. One could say, of course, that the other inputs are not thereby ignored; that, in effect, they are counted among the variables that explain efficiency. But however it is done, they must be taken into account and the difficulties of doing so must be met.

Though it is not already here, the time is approaching when the definition of efficiency might be expanded at least to include tangible capital among the inputs in the denominator of the efficiency ratio. Such an alternative measure of efficiency would, I think, reduce the gap between the United States and other countries. I would be surer of this result if the alternative calculation covered the still broader range of inputs. But what gap would remain is one of the questions that I want to put before you. It might not be as big as some people think. I cannot believe that it would vanish.

III. THE DOUGLAS-COBB HYPOTHESIS

Some economists seem to have argued, however, that the vast output of the American economy is entirely, or very largely, the result of the resources at its disposal. The Douglas-Cobb production function [1] may be viewed as the formulation of such an hypothesis, and the statistical work of Douglas and his collaborators [2] as an attempt to test this hypothesis against the experience of the manufacturing industries of the United States and a few other countries.

The authors thought the test favoured their hypothesis. Their

[1] C. W. Cobb and P. H. Douglas, 'A Theory of Production', *American Economic Review*, Supplement, March 1928.

[2] P. H. Douglas, 'Are There Laws of Production?', *American Economic Review*, March 1948.

model fitted neatly enough the indexes of physical output, number of workers, and physical volume of tangible capital for all manufacturing industries in the United States over the period 1899–1922. The implication was that size of nation or market, and much else besides, played no significant rôle in determining output per worker.

In response to criticisms [1] Douglas tried a formula free of the assumption of constant returns to scale, but did not get significantly different results. However, two important developments raised crucial questions about the validity of his results. One consisted of revisions in the basic data : the trend of output was revised upward somewhat,[2] and the trend of capital was revised downward considerably.[3] The other was an extension of the data to cover the period after 1922 [4] — a severe test of the hypothesis. The original Douglas-Cobb formula could no longer be considered a satisfactory interpretation of the known statistics. In particular, the data no longer lent any support to the assumption of constant returns to scale — though, of course, they did not disprove it.[5]

IV. MORE RECENT STATISTICAL WORK

Our present understanding of the basic facts is far better than it was in the 1920s. We now have figures, calculated by Kuznets,[6] and summarized conveniently by Abramovitz,[7] which portray changes in the economy as a whole. From the decade 1869–78 to the decade 1944–53 the real net national product of the United States multiplied 13·3-fold ; population, 3·3 ; man-hours of work, 3·1 ; and capital (tangible assets, net of depreciation, in constant prices), 9·9. Over the period as a whole, then, national product rose more rapidly than population, and more rapidly than either tangible capital or

[1] D. Durand, 'Some Thoughts on Marginal Productivity with Special Reference to Professor Douglas' Analysis', *Journal of Political Economy*, December 1937.

[2] S. Fabricant, *The Output of Manufacturing Industries, 1899–1937*, National Bureau of Economic Research, 1940.

[3] D. Creamer, 'Capital and Output Trends in Manufacturing Industries, 1880–1948', *Occasional Paper 41*, National Bureau of Economic Research, 1954.

[4] Burton Wall, 'A Cobb-Douglas Function for the United States Manufacturing and Mining, 1920–1940' (abstract), *Econometrica*, April 1948.

[5] Douglas tried his hand also at cross-sectional functions for manufacturing in a variety of countries, with results which again seem to leave little room for the scale factor. But the calculations were necessarily in terms of current values and may be viewed as no more than a check on the uniformity of factor prices among industries.

[6] S. Kuznets, *Income and Wealth of the United States, Trends and Structure*, International Association for Research in Income and Wealth, Series II, 1952.

[7] M. Abramovitz, 'Resource and Output Trends in the United States since 1870', *American Economic Review*, May 1956 (reprinted as *Occasional Paper 52*, National Bureau of Economic Research).

labour input. *Per capita*, real net national product increased at an annual rate of 1·9 per cent. Relative to an appropriately weighted combination of man-hours and tangible capital, output grew at an annual average rate of 1·7 per cent. The figures for manufacturing, also greatly improved, lead to essentially similar conclusions.[1]

We may say that the increase of output *per capita* reflects — or may be decomposed into — a slight decline of labour input *per capita*, a substantial rise in tangible capital input *per capita*, and a residual accounting for all other factors. On the assumptions implicit in the calculations, the residual turns out to be the major component — a result quite different from Douglas's. The residual covers the other inputs to which I have referred (such as improvements in the quality of labour input), and efficiency as defined by output per unit of total input (including economies of scale).

V. DIFFICULTIES OF MEASUREMENT OF MARKETS AND INDUSTRIES

The aggregate income or product of the American economy is the best available single measure of its size. Judged by this standard, the United States is clearly first in size among the economies of the world. Expressed even more forcefully, the United States produces and consumes something like a third or two-fifths of the world's output.[2]

No single measure, however, can adequately characterize the various dimensions of size that may be related to efficiency. Size of markets for goods, size of markets for productive factors, area and the character of resources embraced by it, population and its relation to area and resources — all these are involved and about each there are questions.

Consider, for example, size of the markets for goods. It is quite safe to say — with industry defined as it usually is in censuses of manufacturing and the like — that on the average the industries of the United States are substantially larger than those of other countries. But the size of a 'census industry' is no more than a first approximation to the size of the market (or markets) for the goods produced by it. Because the population of the United States is spread over a vast area, with a lower average density than in many

[1] J. Kendrick, 'Productivity Trends : Capital and Labour', *Review of Economics and Statistics*, August 1956 (reprinted as *Occasional Paper 53*, National Bureau of Economic Research); and forthcoming fuller report of the National Bureau.

[2] United Nations 'National and Per Capita Incomes of Seventy Countries in 1949 Expressed in United States Dollars'.

other countries, the size of the census industry will often overstate the size of the market.[1] Compared with a country like Britain, for example, it is hardly likely that transport and distribution in the United States are sufficiently more efficient to offset differences in density in every case. Surely there are more brick industries in the United States than in Britain — though just how many more is a question.

The census-type definition of industry is deficient in another respect. It is based on a classification of establishments that tends to make identical the number of industries in countries like the United States and the United Kingdom, and thus causes American industries to be about as large in relation to British industries, on the average, as the national product of the United States is in relation to British national product. This would not be so if industry were defined to accord with the circumstances of each country. Because of its large variety of climates and resources, the United States is less dependent on foreign trade than other industrialized economies ; it satisfies more of its needs by domestic production than by import ; it therefore has more industries for a given composition of final demand. I would suppose also that because of its high level of income *per capita*, the United States enjoys a more varied consumption, and therefore produces a greater variety of goods and services, and presumably in more industries, than other countries.

Opposed is the impression that American demand is more homogeneous than elsewhere. Because of the absence of social distinctions [2] or for other reasons, tastes tend to be similar. As a result, the population of the United States is, in Marshall's words,[3] 'homogeneous in matters of consumption', and this 'homogeneity of demand creates an unrivalled market for standardized products'. If this were true, the number of industries, products, or markets would tend to be fewer per dollar of national consumption. But whatever the causes of homogeneity of consumption — and the causes may stem not only from tastes but also from the shape of the distribution of income or from economies of scale — we are not sure of its strength. Budget studies, for example, cannot yet help us to build a firm bridge between income distribution and tastes on the one side and consumption homogeneity on the other. Nor are the interesting observations of the Working Parties sent over

---

[1] E. Rothbarth, 'Causes of the Superior Efficiency of U.S.A. Industry as Compared with British Industry', *Economic Journal*, September 1946.

[2] *Ibidem.*

[3] A. Marshall, *Industry and Trade*, Macmillan, 1923.

by the Anglo-American Council on Productivity conclusive.[1] In some significant sense standardization may be more prevalent in the United States than elsewhere (except Russia !). That would be my guess. But we have far to go before we can claim to have systematic and convincing evidence of it.

That the concept of size is vague and the problems of measurement difficult could be further illustrated by reference to other aspects of size. But let us accept as a fact that the United States is large in many different senses of the word, and go on to ask how its large size might affect its efficiency.

VI. THE RELATION OF SIZE TO EFFICIENCY

We begin with Stigler's schematic description of the course of vertical integration and disintegration of firms during the life of an industry : [2]

> Young industries are often strangers to the established economic system. They require new kinds of qualities of materials and hence make their own ; they must overcome technical problems in the use of their products and cannot wait for potential users to overcome them ; they must persuade customers to abandon other commodities and find no specialized merchants to undertake this task. These young industries must design their specialized equipment and often manufacture it, and they must undertake to recruit (historically, often to import) skilled labor. When the industry has obtained a certain size and prospect, many of these tasks are sufficiently important to be turned over to specialists. It becomes profitable for other firms to supply equipment and raw materials, to undertake the marketing of the product and the utilization of by-products, and even to trained skilled labor. And, finally, when the industry begins to decline, these subsidiary, auxiliary, and complementary industries begin also to decline, and eventually the surviving firms must begin to re-appropriate functions which are no longer carried on at a sufficient rate to support independent firms.

This generalized description — with some qualifications mentioned below — seems to fit well the course of events in a variety of industries in the United States and elsewhere. It gives us an explanation of how growth in the size of an industry may, through the increased specialization it makes possible among plants within

[1] Anglo-American Council on Productivity, *Productivity Team Reports*, London, various dates around 1950.

[2] G. Stigler, 'The Division of Labor is Limited by the Extent of the Market', *Journal of Political Economy*, June 1951.

an industry and among industries, lead the way to increased efficiency ; and, of course, it gives us also an explanation of how the size of an industry at a moment in time may be associated with its level of efficiency.

For our purpose — which is not quite Stigler's — the picture is incomplete. As an industry grows, it may also have to go farther afield or scavenge about for materials and other resources. And there may be still other tendencies towards increase in real costs with increase in size, though economists have had some difficulty thinking of examples of these (at any rate, within a static framework) for industries other than those engaged in farming and mining.[1] On the other hand, any technological improvement that is induced by the growth of an industry would strengthen the tendency towards decreasing costs. The net result might be decreasing real costs only to a point, as output rises, and then increase ; or the cost curve might approach a horizontal level, either quickly or slowly ; or it might decline without limit. Presumably the first of the possibilities is the least likely, but general reasoning does not lead to any confident choice among them.[2]

VII. THE INDUSTRY AND THE ECONOMY

Growth in the economy at large also plays a rôle and we need to put individual industries into the context of the economy as a whole.

For one thing, to the extent that economies of scale in individual industries are unlimited, larger countries, having larger industries, will enjoy lower real costs. But this may be less important than the contribution by the size of the whole economy to the efficiency of all its component industries. In a large economy we may expect that the advantages of specialization become available to young industries sooner than in a small economy. An infant industry finds other industries already in the business of manufacturing, if not also designing, specialized equipment. New materials, or at least the tailoring of old materials to new specifications, are

[1] J. Viner, 'Cost Curves and Supply Curves', 1931; reprinted with supplementary notes in *Readings in Price Theory*, Irwin, 1952.

[2] If real costs per unit are measured by money costs deflated by the 'general' price level, its tendency to increase after a point may be strengthened. For increase in an industry's size relative to the economy at large may frequently (not always) bring with it 'external net pecuniary diseconomies of large production' through increasing factor prices (Viner, *op. cit.*). These pecuniary diseconomies cannot arise (or, better put, are ignored) if real costs are defined, as is implicit above, as the physical quantity of input per unit of output. This raises a question about that definition which merits attention.

available from many supplying industries already equipped with machinery, specialized personnel, and wide knowledge and experience. Management, consulting and advertising firms stand ready to aid anyone in developing and launching a new product. In large countries like the United States, therefore, new industries start, so to speak, at a higher level of specialization and presumably also of efficiency. Mature industries, too, benefit from the assistance of other industries to a degree not possible in smaller economies. And old industries can retain some of the advantages of specialization even when they have shrunk to small size.

It is this that Young had in mind when he stated that 'the mechanism of increasing returns is not to be discerned adequately by observing the effects of variations in the size of an individual firm or of a particular industry, for the progressive division and specialization of industries is an essential part of the process by which increasing returns are realized'.[1] Put in other language, the cost curves of industries in a country as large as the United States are generally lower — some slightly, some greatly — than in other countries. Even industries confined to local markets, such as those producing perishable commodities or commodities so heavy that transport costs are high, though they may be no 'larger' in large economies than in small, will tend to be more efficient. For even such industries will benefit from being in large economies if, as is likely, their equipment, supplies, and methods are better because of access to national specialized industries.

On the other hand, the large size of the United States may have also adverse effects on its efficiency. The pressure of a large population consuming huge amounts of material can become heavy even on rich natural resources. Most recently the report of the President's Materials Policy Commission (the Paley Report) focused attention on the limitations of our water supply and on our increasing dependence on foreign sources of raw materials supply. However, the immediate problem seems to be largely that of preparing for the future. Up to now, technological advance has more than offset diminishing returns in most cases ; hardly any industry in the United States for which there are statistics reveals a decline in output per man-hour or per unit of labour and tangible capital combined.[2] Perhaps we might enjoy an even higher income *per capita* if our present population were smaller (though I doubt it), but it is undoubtedly the case that compared with other countries

[1] A. A. Young, 'Increasing Returns and Economic Progress', *Economic Journal*, December 1928.
[2] J. Kendrick, *op. cit.*

our resource position in relation to population or consumption of materials is excellent.

VIII. THE MECHANISM OF INCREASING RETURNS

'The mechanism of increasing returns may not be discerned adequately by observing the effects of variations in the size of an individual firm.'[1] But can we say that the prevalence in the United States of large firms, or large plants or large units of equipment, accounts, even in small part, for the greater efficiency of the country?

There seems to be some doubt even about the prevalence of large economic units in the United States. For a given type of industry, the size of plant in different countries tends to be much alike, according to some evidence.[2] However, these statistics are notoriously sensitive to the coverage of small plants, which frequently varies widely from one United States census to another and presumably also internationally; 'cut-off points' are commonly ignored in making these comparisons; and attention is paid largely to the number of workers per plant, rather than to output per plant. While some similarity cannot be denied, I believe careful comparisons would indicate that the United States has, on the average, not only the largest industries, but also the largest plants — and the largest firms and the largest units of equipment as well.

As for the relation between size of unit and efficiency, the unsatisfactory state of our knowledge was emphasized not long ago by Caleb Smith; and after some discussion of the traps set by accounting data, a 'survivor' test of the most efficient sizes was suggested by Friedman.[3] That test might be applied, in a crude sort of way, to the averages; and if it were, we might conclude, with some qualifications, that economic units are generally large in the United States because large units in the United States are more efficient than small. But it would not follow that the United States is more efficient than other countries because its economic units are larger, on the average, than those of other countries.

Whether large firms devote more resources, proportionately, to research and development than do smaller firms; whether they produce more innovations; whether they are better able to take over and develop new ideas wherever these may originate; whether

[1] A. A. Young, 'Increasing Returns and Economic Progress', *Economic Journal*, December 1928.
[2] J. Jewkes, 'The Size of the Factory', *Economic Journal*, June 1952.
[3] Universities-National Bureau Committee for Economic Research, *Business Concentration and Price Policy*, National Bureau of Economic Research, 1955.

the disproportionately large share of research and development accounted for by large countries is biased towards large-scale production; whether, apart from this bias, technological advances are increasingly of the sort requiring or favouring large-scale production — these are questions which have been discussed widely but not conclusively. If we had clearer answers to them, we might know better than we now do how the scale of American firms, plants, and equipment contributes to the country's efficiency and growth. And we might have a better idea of the disadvantages of small countries in putting the world's stock of technological knowledge to their own uses.

The large economy of the United States may benefit from the fact that large scale of enterprise does not tend to reduce competition — at any rate, to the extent that it would in smaller countries. In more industries of the United States than of smaller countries the firms can be both absolutely large and many in number.[1] But it would be unwise to put this factor making for competition ahead of the anti-trust policy of the United States.

IX. TWO MINOR CONSIDERATIONS

There are a couple of other points which must at least be mentioned.

I have referred to the broad range of resources and climates embraced by the American economy. To some extent, this has had its disadvantages, for it has led to the development of industries that can be kept alive only under the protection of tariff walls or subsidies. On the whole, of course, the possession of a wide range of resources has been beneficial to the country because it has helped avoid the special costs that are incurred in foreign trade. It has also led to the development of a wide range of skills that may make adjustments to shifts in demand and supply easier and faster, and therefore help to maintain efficiency at a level higher than it would otherwise be.

Efficiency is higher also because the American economy provides an unparalleled market for labour and capital free of the obstacles standing at national borders. The United States is not free of all internal obstacles, though there are signs that these are diminishing. Prejudice restricts the movement of labour; our capital market is not yet fully integrated because financial institu-

[1] G. Rosenbluth, *Concentration in Canadian Manufacturing Industries*, National Bureau of Economic Research, 1957.

tions are organized under state charters which in various ways inhibit their freedom of action ; and there are other restrictions on the freedom of domestic markets. But these are surely no greater, and I would guess that generally they are much smaller, than in other countries.

X. INTERNATIONAL COMPARISONS

Though it might 'enrich' our discussion, no list of examples — however long — could provide really convincing evidence of an association between size and efficiency or any quantitative clue to its importance. Can we get any help from the statistics that have been analysed ?

We are all sufficiently familiar with the available information to know that a direct attack, through a simple correlation of national figures on income and income *per capita* such as those I have cited, leads nowhere. It is true that the United States is first in size, measured by total income, and first in efficiency, measured by income *per capita*. But no one would expect the sizes and efficiencies of other countries, measured in the same crude way, to fall into so orderly an array as to trace out a clear line of relationship between the two. And, in fact, no clear picture emerges.[1]

When we turn to the individual industries of the United States and consider their efficiency in relation to their size we must make comparisons with other countries. Comparison of one industry with another within the United States would run up against the difficulty of measuring efficiency : value figures are useless for this purpose. The comparison between countries simplifies our problem also because factors common to all industries of a country are in effect set aside. Unfortunately, however, one of the common factors eliminated is the size of the economy as a whole.

The results obtained from cross-sectional comparisons of the United States and the United Kingdom, which we owe to the ingenuity and labours of Rostas for the pre-war period [2] and of

[1] Mention may be made of an international cross-sectional analysis along Douglas' lines, attempted by a student of his (E. C. Olson, 'Factors Affecting International Differences in Production', *American Economic Review, Papers and Proceedings*, May 1948). Output was taken to be a homogeneous function of labour input, energy consumed, animal stock, and arable area. Fairish fits were obtained, using data for around 1937, but the estimates are very crude and it is, in any case, difficult to interpret the rôle of an item like energy consumption.

[2] L. Rostas, *Comparative Productivity in British and American Industry*, Occasional Paper XIII, National Institute of Economic and Social Research, Cambridge, 1948.

Frankel for the post-war,[1] are not encouraging when information for all available industries is included. (Size is measured by total physical output ; and efficiency, by output per worker.) The correlations are very low. Rostas did not even calculate a correlation coefficient, merely pointing out the lack of relationship, while Frankel obtained a coefficient of only 0·1 for thirty-four industries. As both authors recognized, however, total output is not a good measure of size in the case of localized industries like brewing, brick, and ice cream. With these excluded, correlations of the order of 0·7 are obtained in both the pre- and post-war comparisons ; and the 'elasticity' of relative efficiency with respect to relative size, which is also of interest, is considerably less than unity.

There are also the Gilbert-Kravis comparisons, in which relative prices and relative quantities of final consumption and investment goods are laid out in scatter diagrams. (The comparisons apply not only to the United States and the United Kingdom, but to several other pairs of countries as well.) Distinct correlations are visible in the charts, though no calculations were made of the coefficients. The elasticities seem to be closer to unity than in the case of the Rostas-Frankel type of data.

Although they would pass muster as 'significant' by ordinary statistical standards, none of the correlation coefficients is high.[2] Yet they seem to indicate something, and there is a question, therefore, whether this information can be relied upon, and what interpretation may be made of it.

My impression is that the available data overstate the strength of the relationship between size of industry and efficiency, and the elasticity of efficiency with respect to size. My doubts arise, first, out of the likelihood of spurious correlation. The measures of size and of efficiency are not calculated independently of one another. (The only exception — in part — is the Gilbert-Kravis cross-sectional price-quantity comparisons.) There is a common factor, output, in both measures. This factor is subject to purely statistical error which, I would judge, is fairly considerable. It stems from deficiencies in the basic data and in the aggregates or index numbers summarizing them, and from quality differences. If, owing to such error, the measure of output is too high, so also will be the measure of output per man ; if too small, both will be too small. A source

---

[1] M. Frankel, 'British and American Manufacturing Productivity, A Comparison and Interpretation', *University of Illinois Bulletin*, February 1957.

[2] In fact, Rostas stressed the percentage of variation in relative productivity level that was not 'explained' by size of market. But he had in mind also the largely negative results he had obtained in comparisons of the United Kingdom with Sweden and Holland using the much skimpier data available for these.

of doubt, similar in its effects though perhaps of lesser importance, arises from the tendency of efficiency to fluctuate with level of output : an industry that happens to be enjoying a somewhat better than average level of production in the year for which the comparison is being made, will usually show a somewhat better than average level of efficiency in that year.[1]

Further, as already mentioned, output per man (or per man-hour) is an inadequate measure of efficiency, since it omits inputs other than labour. Information mentioned below suggests that output per unit of labour plus tangible capital or per unit of all inputs (reciprocal of price) would not be as strongly correlated with output as is output per unit of labour alone. Closely related, finally, is the failure of the statistics to take adequate account of specialization among industries. Recall the suggestion that as an industry grows in size, there is a tendency for it to disintegrate vertically. Less labour will be needed directly by the industry per unit of its gross product. Part of this reduction will reflect a real reduction in cost ; the rest, a decline in the ratio of net to gross output (both measured at constant prices), and therefore only a nominal reduction in labour per unit. The usual measures of output per worker will overstate the relative level of efficiency, and the bigger the industry, the larger will the overstatement be.

These considerations lead to no precise conclusion. My hunch is that we should grant the existence of a correlation between the size of an industry and its efficiency, though of a weaker order than most of the figures suggest. There is, then, a question as to how to interpret the results. We have, in fact, something very like the old problem of disentangling demand from supply when calculating elasticities of demand solely from observations on price and quantity, with the further complication that our observations relate to different industries (or products) rather than different outputs and prices of the same industry. Does the U.S.-U.K. comparison of industries trace out the relationship between relative size of industry and relative cost, or does it trace out the relationship between relative price and relative quantity demanded ? The latter possibility does seem less likely than the former. Relative demands for different products may be expected to vary between the United States and Britain because of differences in such underlying factors as population structure, income level, income distribution, 'tastes', and size of 'exclusive' export markets. On the supply side, there is presumably less variation between the two countries. Technological

[1] T. Hultgren, in *37th Annual Report* of the National Bureau of Economic Research, May 1957.

possibilities, for example, may be supposed to be substantially the same in both countries. It is not safe to conclude, however, that variation on the supply side is so small that it does not, in some significant degree, distort the estimate of the elasticity of relative efficiency with respect to relative size. And there are other dangers that would have to be dealt with in a thorough study of the problem.

I have suggested that the elasticity is overstated. If it is not, it indicates rather more influence on the part of size than seems reasonable. Elasticity of relative efficiency (output per worker) with respect to relative size, referring to the U.S.-U.K. comparisons of individual industries, appears to the eye to be of the order of 0·3. So high an elasticity implies that the greater part of the efficiency differential between the United States and the United Kingdom is due to size. If we dare to extend the regression line into a region quite a distance out from the main scatter, it suggests that for industries of the same absolute size U.S. output per man is about 1·3 times that of the United Kingdom. Now, it makes sense, on the basis of the considerations set forth earlier, for a U.S. industry of the same absolute size as the corresponding U.K. industry to have a higher output per worker. But would it be only three-tenths higher, with the rest — the difference between 1·3 and the general average of 2·3 — due entirely to. the greater relative sizes of individual American industries ? There is an interesting problem here which deserves to be tackled properly.[1]

XI. THE EVIDENCE OF THE SERIES

A related and rather more ambiguous type of information is yielded by the analysis of time series. When changes in the national income and income *per capita* of a variety of countries are correlated, comparisons are in effect made of each country at one date with itself at another, thus eliminating some of the differences among countries, and the observations on changes in countries then pooled and examined for a systematic relationship. Kuznets has made such a calculation for such countries as he could assemble — nine-

---

[1] It might be worth mentioning some ways to improve the sort of statistical analysis attempted by Rostas and Frankel. Very briefly, it would be desirable : (1) to include in the analysis the absolute as well as the relative size of the industries; (2) to broaden the period covered, in order to reduce the impact of random and cyclical factors ; (3) to add other countries, especially Canada ; (4) to measure output more exactly, taking account of quality and variety of products and of character and source of materials consumed ; and (5) to develop a more objective basis for excluding 'local' or other 'exceptional' industries from the calculation — or better, for including them in the analysis with appropriate 'correction factors'.

teen at the maximum, for the first half of the twentieth century.[1] (With the exception of the United States, the British Dominions, and Japan the countries are European.) The correlations are all positive and of the order of 0·7 to 0·8.

A correlation equal to about 0·7 is found also between growth in physical output and in output per man or per man-hour in individual industries of the United States over the past half century.[2] Here it is not necessary to confine ourselves to the simple measure of efficiency. When efficiency is measured by output per unit of labour and tangible capital combined, the correlation is smaller, about 0·6, and somewhat less reliable as the number of industries and quality of data are necessarily reduced. It is lower still, about 0·5, when the measure of efficiency is the reciprocal of price — a measure which covers all inputs, including the contribution of material-supplying industries, as in Jones' study.[3] Here, also, changes in relative size were more widely dispersed than changes in relative productivity, and the 'elasticity' of productivity with respect to size was less than one.[4]

These results, too, are infected with a measure of spurious correlation, except for the relationship between change in output and change in price (which are independently estimated). And they are even more difficult to interpret, for no longer can technology and other factors apart from size be kept out of the way, or at least assumed with some validity to be out of the way. In the case of the national aggregates the results are consistent with a rather considerable variety of explanations. Similarly, the data on relative change in individual industries may be interpreted as reflecting the decline in cost per unit as demand and output increase ; but, equally, it could be interpreted as reflecting the increase in demand as costs, and along with them prices, decline.

Given time for adjustment — and we are dealing with long-term processes — substitution possibilities are considerable within a country, and MacDougall[5] has illustrated the effect on relative

[1] S. Kuznets, 'Quantitative Aspects of the Economic Growth of Nations, I. Levels and Variability of Rates of Growth', *Economic Development and Cultural Change*, October 1956.

[2] Similar calculations may be made for the United Kingdom and Canada, for shorter periods, with similar results ; see Colin Clark, *Conditions of Economic Progress*, and A. Maddison, 'Productivity in Canadian Manufacturing, 1935–48', *Canadian Journal of Economic and Political Science*, May 1953.

[3] G. T. Jones, *Increasing Returns*, Cambridge, 1933.

[4] S. Fabricant, *Employment in Manufacturing Industries, 1899–1939*, National Bureau of Economic Research, 1942 ; J. Kendrick, 'Productivity Trends : Capital and Labor', *Review of Economics and Statistics*, 1956.

[5] G. D. A. MacDougall, 'British and American Exports : A Study Suggested by the Theory of Comparative Costs', *Economic Journal*, December 1951 and September 1952.

size of export market of relative costs or price. I am inclined to act as devil's advocate and argue that 'uninduced' technological and organizational advances 'uninduced' by the growth of an industry determine its costs and thus its size. It is a 'spontaneous' innovation that often offers itself as the explanation of the appearance of the young industry to which Stigler referred, and exhaustion of the possibilities of the innovation that contributes to the maturing and eventual decline of that industry. Kuznets [1] and Burns [2] both used this line of reasoning in their explanations of retardation in the rates of growth of individual industries, and I think they were right to do so.

Of course, we are dealing with highly interdependent changes. Necessity is the mother of invention ; but also, as Veblen once remarked, invention is the mother of necessity. The history of the United States reflects both directions of influence and the general case must make room for both. But without more information than is provided by the simple sets of data described above, we will not get far in analysing that complex relationship — and we may not get very far even with more information.

XII. THE AMERICAN ENVIRONMENT

What are obstacles to one people may not be obstacles to another. The receptivity of the American people 'to the most effective and economical goods' caught Marshall's eye. Americans may be willing and able to rise above habit and custom. This businesslike character would affect not only their demand for goods but also their response to income differentials. A good deal of work is proceeding in the United States on community and regional differences in wages and incomes generally,[3] and some on internal migration. Perhaps the results of these and of similar studies for other countries, when they become available, may enable us to judge whether the American people are, in fact, exceptionally mobile, and, indeed, exceptionally enterprising. Americans, I must confess, like to believe that Marshall was right when he referred to the 'germs of high spirit and enterprise' especially latent 'in those who seek new lands'.

[1] S. Kuznets, *Secular Movements in Production and Prices*, Boston, Houghton Mifflin, 1930.
[2] A. F. Burns, *Production Trends in the United States since 1870*, National Bureau of Economic Research, 1934.
[3] Conference on Research in Income and Wealth, *Regional Income*, National Bureau of Economic Research, 1957.

But Marshall also referred to the influence of environment on the spirit of enterprise, and it is better to focus on that.

If American efficiency is to be traced to its sources, we cannot afford to overlook the environment of political and economic institutions that nourishes it. 'A large country has her own advantages', said Marshall. But these must be exploited. 'The extent of the American domestic market, unimpeded by tariff barriers', surely has 'something to do with the matter', said Young. But so has the economic system of the United States, which also may differ in more than one way and in significant degree from the systems of other countries, perhaps even including Britain. The American domestic market is unimpeded by tariff barriers. May it not also be less impeded by other barriers that loom large in domestic markets elsewhere ?

In a world in which so many countries are trying consciously to improve their standards of living, no source of efficiency may be neglected, and the advantages that can be obtained by appropriate measures for lessening the obstacles to international exchange deserve serious attention. Yet the emphasis needs to be broadly on all impediments to trade and enterprise. These may be domestic as well as foreign. About the former, too, something might be done. Larger markets and the advantages they provide will follow in due course, and make further progress easier.

Chapter 4

STUDY OF THE EFFICIENCY OF
A SMALL NATION: SWITZERLAND [1]

BY

W. A.' JÖHR and F. KNESCHAUREK
University of St. Gallen

I. THE ECONOMIC POTENTIAL, PRODUCTIVITY,
AND WELFARE OF SWITZERLAND

THE economic potential of various countries can best be compared in terms of their gross domestic products. This has been done in Table I, and the economic potential of Switzerland, so measured, is seen to be very small. If the gross domestic product of Switzerland is taken to equal 100, that of the United States is 4760, of the United Kingdom 950, of Germany 800, and of Belgium 155. Of the countries listed in the Table, only Austria — with an index of 75 — ranges below Switzerland. A number of different considerations suggest that Switzerland's low economic potential should be reflected in a low level of productivity and welfare. The last two columns of the Table show the contrary.

In the absence of precise knowledge of the working time in certain branches of the economy, more particularly in agriculture, we cannot use gross domestic product per working hour for purposes of international comparisons of productivity, but must instead use gross domestic product per member of the labour force. Here again the United States is at the top of the list and far ahead of all others. But next we find not the group of large European nations, but the small industrial countries of Belgium, Sweden, and Switzerland, with almost identical productivity per member of the labour force. The Netherlands came out in respect of productivity on a level with the group of large European nations headed by Great Britain, while Italy has rather low productivity. Italy's gross domestic product is about four and a half times as great as Switzerland's, but nine times as many people are at work (labour force excluding those unemployed) and the productivity coefficient

TABLE I

ECONOMIC POTENTIAL, PRODUCTIVITY, AND WELFARE IN SELECTED COUNTRIES, 1955

Country	(1) Gross domestic product (Billion Swiss francs at official rates of exchange)	(2) Gross domestic product (Billion Swiss francs adjusted to take account of internal purchasing powers of currencies)	(3) Index (Switzerland =100)	(4) Gross domestic product per head of labour force (000 Sw. francs)	(5) Index (Switzerland =100)	(6) Gross domestic product per head of population (Switzerland =100)
United States	1672	1286	4760	21·0	170	160
United Kingdom	230	255	950	11·2	90	90
France	205	205	760	10·1	83	86
West Germany	172	215	800	10·5	85	82
Italy	95	125	460	6·5	55	50
Netherlands	33	39	145	9·8	80	75
Sweden	38	36	135	12·0	100	97
Belgium	39	41	155	12·4	100	95
Austria	17	20	75	6·2	50	53
Switzerland	27	27	100	12·2	100	100

All indices have been rounded.

(1) Estimates of Gross Domestic Products : *United Nations Monthly Bulletin of Statistics*, Special Tables ; for Belgium : *L'Économie belge et la comptabilité nationale*, Brussels, 1954 ; for Switzerland : *Die Volkswirtschaft*, 1956, No. 10 ; Official exchange rates from *Statistisches Jahrbuch der Schweiz*, 1955.

(2) The adjustment for purchasing power of the currencies concerned has been calculated by converting into Swiss francs the prices paid in different countries for the total of goods and services consumed in Switzerland by an average household (food and clothing, rent, furniture, heating and lighting, other services). A coefficient of 130 for the United States, for example, means that the amount of goods and services consumed by an average Swiss household costs 30 per cent more in Swiss francs converted into dollars in the United States than it does in Swiss francs spent in Switzerland.

(3) Sizes of labour forces from *United Nations Statistical Yearbook*, 1955.

is therefore comparatively low. The same is true of Austria, whose gross domestic product in 1955 was smaller than Switzerland's, while the number of people employed in Austria exceeded those employed in Switzerland by 50 per cent.

Welfare may be measured by real national income per inhabitant. We find again roughly the same order of countries, although with certain differences of absolute level. The differences between the welfare indices and the productivity indices rest largely upon differences in the proportion of labour force to total population. For example, in the United States the labour force is about twenty-eight times as great, but the population thirty-three times as great as in Switzerland, where more women go out to work. Hence the American welfare index is lower than the productivity index. The same is true of Italy, Belgium, the Netherlands, Germany, and Sweden. The opposite conditions prevail in France and Austria. From the point of view of welfare, the position of Switzerland is that the gap between her and the United States is smaller, and that she heads all the countries of Europe.

We are well aware of the numerous sources of error in any international comparison of real domestic product and national income. First of all, the relevant statistics are not altogether comparable, and secondly there is the difficulty of adjusting the figures for comparable purchasing power. But even a margin of error of as much as 10 or 15 per cent either way does not alter the results significantly.

Similarly results are shown by other indices of welfare and productivity, such as the volume of output of separate branches in relation to the workers employed, consumption of power per head of population, the number of motor vehicles, telephones, wireless sets, or household appliances per inhabitant, and the like.

Any comparison of the efficiency of different national economies must take account not only of the flow of goods as such, but, as Alexander Rustow has pointed out, also of the overall conditions of life determined by the economy. Now it is a salient feature of Swiss life that the country has been spared the large industrial and urban agglomerations typical of most industrial countries. The five largest cities together have no more than one million inhabitants; 62 per cent of the population live in townships of less than 10,000 inhabitants. This means that Switzerland suffers far less than do other highly industrialized countries from the disadvantages of agglomeration, such as time-consuming travel to and from work in overcrowded trains and buses, air pollution in large cities and industrial areas, or inaccessibility of the countryside on working

days. If these aspects of welfare were to be included, Switzerland would come still closer to the United States and still further ahead of other European countries.

II. ADVERSE CONDITIONS AFFECTING THE SWISS ECONOMY

It is an unquestionable fact that Switzerland has high levels of productivity and welfare. This fact is all the more astonishing since the country can hardly be said to have been favoured by nature.

The natural basis of the Swiss economy is exceedingly narrow in every respect. The whole country measures barely 41,000 square kilometres. One quarter of this is occupied by lakes and river banks, and, above all, by the glaciers, rock, and stony slopes of the mountains. This is to all intents and purposes totally unproductive soil. Another 11,000 square kilometres, or 27 per cent of the total area, are taken up by mountain pastures with little yield and un-suitable for intensive cultivation.[1] Finally, there are considerable areas of woods and forests, so that barely one quarter of the country's total area is arable land suitable for intensive cultivation. And even this last quarter suffers from steep slopes, poor soil, and a wet and cold climate.

Furthermore, the country is poor in industrial raw material resources worth mining. Apart from hydro-electricity, Switzer-land has practically no raw materials or sources of power. Nearly all her requirements must be imported. In this respect Switzerland has a natural disadvantage even in comparison with other small nations such as Belgium or Sweden.

Switzerland has been called the hub of Europe. It is true that she draws a considerable income from passenger and goods traffic both between North and South and between East and West, but this is more than outweighed by lack of direct access to the sea. Swiss imports, which are the more considerable owing to the country's lack of raw material resources, are thereby burdened with additional freight cost, and export industry is at a competitive dis-advantage with respect to goods for which transport costs are high in relation to price.

Switzerland has, by American standards, no large firms; at best she has a few largish medium-sized firms. The reasons are the country's small size, the pronounced regionalism due to geo-graphical and historical causes, the fragmentation of economic space

---

[1] *Statistisches Jahrbuch der Schweiz*, 1955, p. 142.

due to topographical causes, and finally the lack of any domestic raw materials, the location of which might favour the spatial concentration of industry and production in large plants.

The prevalence of small and very small units can be observed both in agriculture and in industry. Of 238,500 agricultural establishments no fewer than 48,000, or roughly 20 per cent, are smaller than 1 hectare. Nearly 60 per cent of all farms are smaller than 5 hectares. For the sake of comparison it may be mentioned that in Germany the proportion of farms of less than 5 hectares is only 14 per cent. The percentage is still lower in France, in Italy, and, above all, in the United States.[1]

As regards industry, there are at present in the whole of Switzerland no more than 40 plants with more than 1000 workers, and only 9 with more than 3000 workers. Industrial plants with more than 1000 workers account for less than one-half per cent of the total of Swiss industrial plants. By contrast, 82 per cent of all Swiss industrial plants employ less than 50 workers. The largest firm at present employs 12,000 workers, the second largest 9000. And in this connection we may mention the astonishing fact that the tendency towards industrial concentration has increased only quite insignificantly during the last thirty to forty years. The percentage of workers employed in plants with a personnel of more than 1000 is hardly bigger today than it was in 1929. Since, however, the total industrial labour force has greatly increased during this period, the real importance of small and medium-sized plants (up to 500 workers) has actually risen since 1929.[2]

These figures reveal that the Swiss national economy makes very modest use indeed of the possibilities of large-scale, still less of mass, production.

Switzerland is often called the most highly cartelized country in the world. This statement cannot be scientifically proved in the absence of any strict measurement of the degree of monopoly, but the fact remains that cartels play a very significant part in the Swiss economy and that this leads in many (though no doubt not in all) cases to some loss of welfare.

[1] *Statistisches Jahrbuch der Schweiz*, Bern, 1955, p. 143. *Statistisches Jahrbuch für die Bundesrepublik Deutschland*, Wiesbaden, 1956, pp. 130-31.
[2] *Schweizerische Fabrikstatistik*, 1949. *Statistische Quellenwerke der Schweiz*, published by Eidgenössisches Statistisches Amt, Bern, No. 227, pp. 24-26.

III. THE REASONS FOR THE HIGH LEVEL OF PRODUCTIVITY AND WELFARE IN SWITZERLAND

(1) *Freedom from War*

There can be no doubt that the development of productivity and welfare has greatly benefited from the fact that Switzerland has not been involved in any war since the creation of the Federal State in 1848. Wars always reduce the productivity of the warring nation, not least because they always make greater or lesser demands on the country's economic potential. The Second World War provides a striking example of the harmful effects of war on productivity and welfare. In the countries most heavily involved, productivity was much lower in 1945–46 than it had been in 1938, owing to physical destruction, disruption of the transport system, and obsolescence of the remaining plant. The war-damaged countries had to make tremendous efforts immediately after the war merely to regain the ground they had lost on economic development and

CHART I

PRODUCTIVITY IN SWISS AND GERMAN INDUSTRY 1938–55

(Volume of output per worker)

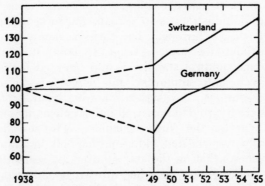

Sources : *Switzerland:* the index of productivity has been calculated on the basis of the social product. The share of industry and crafts (further disaggregation has proved impossible) has been adjusted by the cost-of-living index. The productivity index therefore rests on the following formula :

$$\frac{\text{Index of real net social product of industry and crafts *}}{\text{Index of persons employed in industry and crafts †}}$$

Germany: Statistisches Jahrbuch für die Bundesrepublik Deutschland, 1956, p. 215.

* *Statistisches Jahrbuch der Schweiz*, 1955, pp. 368–9.
† Population censuses of 1930, 1941, and 1950. The figures for the separate years were interpolated with the help of the index of industrial employment.

productivity. This is clearly shown by Chart I, comparing productivity in Switzerland and Western Germany since 1938. While
Swiss productivity had risen considerably above the 1938 level by
1946–47, Western Germany was still well below. Since then
Germany has registered great advances in productivity, but has still
not caught up with the start Switzerland had gained since 1938.
The same is true of France, Italy, Great Britain, Belgium, the
Netherlands, and Austria, among the more important industrial
nations of Europe.

The stability of foreign relations which has flowed from Swiss
neutrality certainly is one of the most important positive factors
which has enabled Switzerland, in spite of her natural handicaps,
to hold her own in the long run among the industrial countries in
the matter of productivity.

(2) *Internal Political Stability*

Internal political stability has been no less important. The
political structure of Switzerland has not changed since 1848. Apart
from a general strike promoted by the socialists, Switzerland has
been spared any major political crisis. Nor has the country ever
known the threat of nationalization, which has paralysed the spirit
of enterprise of industrialists in certain branches of the economy
of other countries of Europe. The Swiss economy has been able
to develop without any obstacles caused by political uncertainty.

This internal political stability is also reflected in the relations
between workers and employers and between trade unions and
employers' federations. Switzerland does not know strikes or lock-
outs, such as are the rule in nearly all industrial countries and which
occasionally paralyse the whole economy. The so-called 'labour
peace' is hardly ever violated and even then only in a minor way.

Table II shows that on the average over the years 1953–55 less
than 30,000 working days were lost in Switzerland through strikes
or lock-outs. This works out at about 18 working days lost annually
per 1000 wage and salary earners ; or, if we take the field more
strictly susceptible to strikes, 24 working days lost annually per
1000 persons employed (other than self-employed) in industry,
crafts, trade, and transport. The corresponding figures for Germany are roughly five times as high as for Switzerland, those for
Sweden, Belgium, and Great Britain more than 7 times as high,
for Canada and Australia about 20 times, and for the United States
about 30 times as high. It is true that the losses through strikes

and lock-outs are everywhere small in relation to the total social product (even in the United States the working hours lost through strikes were no more than 1·5 per 1000 of the hours worked) ; but the economic, political, and social consequences of strong strike movements, such as are the rule in most great industrial countries, should not be underrated.

TABLE II

STRIKES AND LOCK-OUTS IN SELECTED COUNTRIES *

Country	Workers involved	Total wage and salary earners	Working days lost	Working days lost per 1000 persons employed:	
				in the whole economy	in industry, crafts, trade, and transport
U.S.A.	2,000,000	49,300,000	26,000,000	530	770
Australia	400,000	2,490,000	1,000,000	400	450
Canada	60,000	4,085,000	1,400,000	340	500
France	1,500,000	13,392,000	5,500,000	410	760
Great Britain	1,000,000	20,500,000	2,500,000	120	170
Belgium	120,000	2,490,000	400,000	160	210
Germany	90,000	15,630,000	1,500,000	100	140
Japan	1,000,000	13,950,000	3,950,000	280	420
Sweden	20,000	2,400,000	300,000	125	180
Switzerland	1,835	1,600,000	29,000	18	24

* Average 1953–54 ; for Switzerland average 1953–55. Rounded figures.

Sources : *Statistisches Jahrbuch für die Bundesrepublik Deutschland*, 1956 ; *Internationale Uebersichten*, p. 33. *Statistisches Jahrbuch der Schweiz*, 1955, pp. 412-13.

(3) *High Degree of Industrialization*

The studies of Colin Clark, Fourastié, Hoffmann, and other economists confirm the empirical observation that in any national economy it is the industrial sector which registers the greatest advances in productivity.

The picture is basically the same in the United States, Great Britain, France, the Netherlands, Germany, Sweden, and Switzerland :

The long-term rate of increase of productivity in *agriculture* is on the average 1 to 1½ per cent per year. The United States is at the top, France at the bottom, and Switzerland, with 1⅜ per cent, near the top.

The average rate of increase of productivity in *industry* is 1½ to 2½ per cent per year. Again the United States has the highest rate and France the lowest of the countries considered. Switzerland, with 1¾ per cent, comes half-way down the list of countries considered.

The measurement of productivity in the *tertiary sector* (public and private services) is extremely difficult, given the wide differences of conditions which must be expected to be reflected in greatly divergent development. Even in the most favourable cases, however, the rate of increase of productivity does not exceed 1 per cent per year, as has been confirmed over and over again by all serious estimates. The overall rate of increase for the tertiary sector is probably about ½ per cent per year, and this seems quite realistic. It certainly does not appear too low if we remember that in certain branches of the tertiary sector (such as domestic service, public services, the professions) there is by the nature of things hardly any room for an increase in productivity.

It follows that the overall rate of increase of productivity for the whole economy is likely to be the higher the greater is industry's share in the economy. Table III gives some indications on the degree of industrialization of major Western countries.

TABLE III

THE DEGREE OF INDUSTRIALIZATION IN SELECTED COUNTRIES

Country	Year	Total wage and salary earners (thousands)	Wage and salary earners in manufacturing building and power (thousands)	(2) divided by (1) %
		(1)	(2)	(3)
Switzerland	1950	1,600	860	53·6
Belgium	1947	2,490	1,260	51·0
Germany	1950	15,630	7,670	49·0
Great Britain	1951	20,500	9,730	47·5
Sweden	1950	2,385	1,130	47·5
United States	1950	49,300	19,300	40·0
Canada	1951	4,085	1,630	40·0
Netherlands	1947	2,645	1,040	39·0
Italy	1954	12,721	4,875	38·3
France	1946	13,400	4,600	35·0

Rounded figures.

Source: *Statistisches Jahrbuch für die Bundesrepublik Deutschland*, 1956 ; *Internationale Uebersichten*, pp. 28 et seq.

Switzerland heads the list of countries considered. The proportion of the total labour force employed in the manufacturing, building, and power industries is not nearly as high even in the United States as it is in Switzerland. Closest to Switzerland in this respect are Belgium, Western Germany, Great Britain, and Sweden. Clearly the average productivity of the Swiss economy is considerably raised by the dominant part played by industry in the economy as a whole.

(4) *High Relative Level of Exports*

Within the industrial sector as a whole there are generally fairly wide divergences in the development of productivity. Branch-by-branch analysis shows that export industries lead in productivity, whereas branches working mostly for the home market have a

TABLE IV

THE SHARE OF EXPORTS IN SWISS INDUSTRIAL PRODUCTION, 1955

	Exports as a percentage of total output	Exports in million francs
Machines and precision instruments (excluding motor-cars) of which :	*70*	*1,635*
textile machines	90	50
machine tools	80	90
electrical apparatus	75	400
Watches	*95*	*1,077*
Chemicals of which :	*60*	*930*
dyes	95	270
pharmaceutical preparations and perfumes	95	450
Textiles (excluding clothing) of which :	*45*	*750*
cotton	45	250
silk	70	280
embroidery	95	120
wool	15	100
For comparison : *Aggregate net social product*		24,570

Sources : *Handbuch der Schweizerischen Volkswirtschaft*, Schweizerische Gesellschaft für Statistik und Volkswirtschaft, Bern, 1955, Vol. I, pp. 210, 327 *et seq.* ; Vol. II, pp. 170 *et seq.*, 320 *et seq.*, 423, 458, 654 *et seq.*

lower productivity, especially if they are not exposed to the pressure of foreign competition and are protected by tariffs or quantitative restrictions. Now the export intensity of industry is higher in Switzerland than in any other country of the world. Only Belgium comes anywhere near Switzerland in this respect.

Nothing could more strikingly illustrate the export orientation of the Swiss economy than the fact that four important branches of industry (watches, dyes, pharmaceutical preparations and perfumes, and embroideries) export 95 per cent of their output (Table IV).

This high relative level of exports also demonstrates that a nation's small size by no means implies that its market must be small. The statistics of exports by countries confirm this in a striking manner. Total exports in 1955 were 5·6 billion francs, or nearly one quarter of the net social product of Switzerland ; Europe's share was 59·2 per cent, Africa's 5·8 per cent, Asia's 10·3 per cent, North America's 14·4 per cent, Central and South America's 8·1 per cent, and the share of Australia and Oceania 2·2 per cent.

In the field of the watch and chemical industries and in certain branches of the textile industry a considerable part of the exported goods are specialities which are produced in the desired quality in only few other countries, if at all. This enables Swiss products to penetrate comparatively high tariff barriers. It also enables Switzerland to charge rather higher prices for some of her export goods

TABLE V

THE TERMS OF TRADE OF THE SWISS ECONOMY, 1945–56
(1938 = 100)

Year	Export prices	Import prices	Terms of trade
1938	100	100	100
1945	257·3	264·4	97·3
1946	253·2	234·0	108·2
1947	263·5	246·4	107·0
1948	254·4	250·8	101·4
1949	245·9	225·6	108·9
1950	235·7	203·4	115·8
1951	258·5	246·4	104·9
1952	258·9	240·4	107·6
1953	243·0	224·4	108·2
1954	236·0	230·1	102·5
1955	229·0	228·0	100·4
1956	232·0	237·0	97·9

Source : *Statistisches Jahrbuch der Schweiz*, 1955, p. 208 ; 1953, p. 197.

than she could do if her export firms had to compete in world markets with foreign firms under anything like free competition. Switzerland's terms of trade benefit thereby, since her imports contain a much smaller proportion of specialities the prices of which are not keenly competitive.

Indeed, Table V shows that Switzerland's terms of trade have hardly changed during the last twenty years, notwithstanding the much more rapid progress of inflation abroad.

(5) *Subsidiaries in Foreign Countries*

In this connection we may mention another factor which has a favourable influence on Switzerland's productivity and welfare : that is the expansion of Swiss firms beyond the national frontiers, by the creation of foreign subsidiaries or the granting of manufacturing licences to foreign firms. This has a number of advantages.

Countries which, unlike Switzerland herself, do not suffer from lack of domestic raw materials, offer advantages from the point of view of raw material cost. In these circumstances firms whose products have a high raw material content gain from transferring part of their production to foreign sites and thereby reducing unit cost.

These branch establishments abroad, with their more favourable production conditions, also contribute much to the often considerable outlays made by the parent company for technical research and development which are of decisive importance for any long-run improvement in productivity. The parent companies in Switzerland could not possibly finance this on their own. It also happens frequently that the Swiss firms learn new techniques from their foreign subsidiaries and branches or from foreign firms working with Swiss licences.

Finally, quite considerable incomes accrue to Switzerland through the foreign activities of her firms and foreign investment. The amounts involved are about 700 million francs a year and they represent nearly 10 per cent of all income from Swiss foreign economic relations.

Some examples may serve to show the importance of this kind of expansion of manufacturing activities beyond the country's frontiers. One big chemical firm, CIBA S.A., of Basle, at present employs some 20,000 workers and employees. Only 30 per cent of these work in the Swiss plants, rather more than one-third work in the firm's factories in France, Italy, Germany, and Spain, one-fifth in subsidiary companies in North America, and the rest in subsidiary companies elsewhere in the world. Another large company in the food industry, Nestlé Alimentana Company, has plants employing a total personnel of 50,000. But no more than 1500 or 3 per cent of all workers and employees work in Switzerland. Other plants on the European continent employ about 24,000 workers, plants in the Sterling Area about 12,000, and plants in North and South America another 13,000. The engineering company of Brown Boveri, of Baden, runs what is probably the largest industrial works in Switzerland, in which 12,000 workers and staff are employed. But these constitute no more than about one-fifth of the company's total personnel, which at present numbers some 60,000 to 65,000.

(6) *Large Stock of Real Capital*

Productivity largely depends upon capital investment in industry, crafts, and agriculture. Other factors do, of course, have a bearing on the productive efficiency of a national economy, but the technical equipment of the apparatus of production is the prime condition of high productivity.

In this connection we must distinguish :

(*a*) the capital stock which is a factor in the determination of the *level* of productivity at any given moment ;

(*b*) current new investment which influences the *rate of increase* of productivity.

As regards capital stock, Switzerland is one of the richest countries in the world. The Swiss national wealth was estimated at 140 billion francs in 1952, while national income was 20 billion francs. This wealth is the result of uninterrupted capital accumulation for several centuries. As long ago as the eighteenth century Switzerland was the most highly industrialized country of Europe, with more than 200,000 workers employed in the textile industry alone. The proverbial Swiss thrift has also contributed to the country's capital wealth. There is no doubt that all classes of the Swiss population have so far always displayed a very pronounced thriftiness, the most striking — if not the most significant — result of which is the amount of 13 billion francs of *savings deposits* shown in the balance sheets of Swiss banks and distributed over 5 million savings books. If we add savings bonds (which represent another form of the 'small man's' saving) and the savings deposits in life assurance companies, we get a total amount of 27·6 billion francs. For purposes of comparison we may mention that Swiss national income in 1955 amounted to 23·3 billion francs. Furthermore,

66

external and internal political stability provided the conditions of steady economic development and continuously expanding capital formation, conditions which did not obtain in all those many other countries where successive wars repeatedly led to periods of impoverishment.

Marked capital intensity is a feature of Swiss production, especially in industry, transport, and electricity. Average capital per worker in industry is probably 30,000 to 50,000 francs.

(7) High Rate of Investment

The decisive factor for the rate of increase of productivity is an economy's current increase and expansion of real capital. On the average over the years 1951 to 1955, gross domestic investment in Switzerland amounted to about 20 per cent of gross social product, as Table VI shows.

TABLE VI

GROSS INVESTMENT IN SELECTED COUNTRIES

Country	Gross investment as a percentage of gross social product Aver. 1951/55	Gross investment per member of labour force		
		Aggregate gross investment in billion francs, 1955	Labour force millions, 1955	Gross investment per member of labour force in (thousand francs), 1955
	(1)	(2)	(3)	(4)=(2) : (3)
Switzerland	20·0	6·0	2·2	2·70
Western Germany	21·0	40·0	20·7	1·95
Austria	21·5	4·2	3·2	1·30
Netherlands	22·0	7·6	4·0	1·90
Japan	20·4	19·0	36·0	0·55
Sweden	20·0	7·6	3·0	2·55
Italy	19·6	20·0	19·3	1·05
Denmark	17·8	4·7	2·3	2·00
United States	17·2	300·0	61·0	4·90
France	17·0	36·0	20·5	1·75
Belgium	15·0	6·3	3·5	1·80
Great Britain	13·5	37·0	22·9	1·65

Rounded figures:

Sources : (1) and (2) : United Nations, *Monthly Bulletin of Statistics*, special tables of gross social product and capital formation. For Switzerland : *Die Volkswirtschaft*, 1956, No. 10 ; for Belgium : *L'Économie belge et la compatibilité nationale*, Brussels, 1955.

Conversion into Swiss francs on the basis of the official rates of exchange. (3) Compare Table I.

The rate of investment was therefore only just lower than in Western Germany (21 per cent), Jápan (20·4 per cent), and the Netherlands (22 per cent); it was equal to the rate of investment in Sweden (also 20 per cent) and higher than in Italy, France, Belgium, Great Britain, and even the United States (17·2 per cent). If we compare investment per head of the labour force in the different countries, Switzerland is outclassed only by the United States and heads all the other industrial countries of the world.

(8) *High Quality of Labour*

Since the problèm of under-developed countries and of technical assistance to them has moved into the limelight of political and economic discussion throughout the world, the importance of the quality and efficiency of human labour as a determining factor of productivity has been increasingly recognized. The alarmingly low productivity of under-developed countries is regarded as being largely due to the low level of general education, to lack of technical proficiency and experience, and to the absence of any proper standards of labour and professional ethics. As regards Switzerland, the high level of welfare is in large part attributable to the high quality of labour. This in turn is due to the fact that industrialization started very early. The chief positive effect of this long industrialization process is perhaps not so much the level of welfare which has been achieved and maintained through a long period of peace, but the high quality of human labour. It is a matter of common knowledge that each generation hands on to its successor a heritage of professional skill and experience. In an old industrial country this leads to a spiritual preconditioning of people for industrial activities. In under-developed countries tremendous efforts and sacrifices are often involved in teaching people to acquire the habit of technical thinking and feeling for the world of machines. In the industrial regions of Switzerland, on the other hand, even the unskilled worker, for example in the textile industry, soon displays such skill in the handling of machines and such a sure eye for detecting even the smallest faults in the woven materials as can be acquired only by long training and a really professional approach to the work. The achievements of the Swiss watch and machine industry would be unthinkable without the experience of many generations, without a natural skill which may be inherited and without that special 'technical mentality' possessed even by the youngest workers. Furthermore, production in small firms and the almost total absence of mass production methods make particularly high demands on the skill, technical proficiency, and versatility of the workers and thus also contribute to raising the quality of their work.

The Swiss worker also has very strict ethical standards. These are observable even at a very youthful age. Apprentices in vocational training schools often attend many optional courses in addition to the obligatory ones. Entries in professional competitions are usually very numerous. The system of worker's suggestions is very popular and many advances in productivity are due to proposals made by the workers themselves. Many medium-sized and large factories regularly arrange for group visits by the workers' families. These show over and over again how much the worker identifies himself with the firm. One consequence of this is the comparatively small turnover of personnel. Case studies of the basic metals and engineering industries have shown, for instance, that entries and exits per head of personnel are 2-3 times as high in Germany as in Switzerland, 5-7 times as high in Great Britain, and 8-9 times as high in France. The resulting cost reduction and internal stability are obviously greatly to the advantage of the Swiss firm.

Vocational training and its younger branch, vocational guidance, are highly developed in Switzerland. A network of advisory bureaux, which assist youths and their parents in the choice of a profession, now covers the whole country and reaches even into the larger villages. Methods for determining occupational aptitudes have been improved and research intensified. About one-fourth of all the young people who undergo vocational training consult an advisory bureau before choosing their occupations. This system of information and description is excellent in helping young people to choose an occupation for which they are well fitted by aptitude and inclination. At the same time it helps in securing the best employment of the available labour force. Vocational training itself is at a high level, not least thanks to the active participation of the larger firms, which run their own schools and hostels for apprentices and grant scholarships to particularly gifted young people so that they can continue their education at advanced technical or commercial schools.

In these circumstances the relative and absolute numbers of skilled and qualified workers have been rising continuously. During the last fifteen years the annual rates of increase were as follows :

Total labour force	1 per cent
Skilled workers	$1\frac{5}{8}$,,
Clerical staff	$2\frac{5}{6}$,,
Technicians	4 ,,

At present only 12 per cent of the labour force are unskilled workers and their number keeps diminishing not only in relative, but also in absolute, terms. (The average rate of increase per year is 2 per cent.)

(9) *High Level of Research and Entrepreneurial Energy*

It may be that Switzerland has in the most recent decades failed to keep step with the rapid advances of the sciences. Nevertheless scientific research is still at a high level. The mere fact that since the establishment of the Nobel prize ten prizes have been awarded to scientists in the natural sciences and medicine who were resident in Switzerland may be some indication of the achievements of Swiss science. An international reputation is enjoyed by such higher science schools as the Swiss Federal Institute of Technology and the science faculties of some Swiss universities. No less important is the research work going on within the large industrial companies. Export industries, such as the machine industry, the chemical industry, and the textile finishing industry, owe their success largely to the circumstance that their products are continuously improved in the light of the latest research and that the engineers and chemists have been so trained as to be capable of applying the results of research.

Finally we must not overlook the contribution of management. These men are familiar with conditions in a great many countries and are thus able not only to sell their own products, but to adapt them to the special requirements of various areas and civilizations. Although Switzerland is cut off from the sea, the world-wide receptiveness and spirit of her entrepreneurs has, for more than a century, been an essential factor of the Swiss economy.

(10) *Flexibility and Adaptability of the Economy*

Swiss industry has acquired a remarkable degree of flexibility and adaptability to changes in the economic situation. This is due to the closeness of foreign economic relations, whereby Swiss entrepreneurs more than those of any other great industrial country are continuously exposed to the pressure of international competition. It is due also to the small-firm production structure, which means that one-off and small-batch production are the rule rather than mass production. This flexibility and adaptability has a long-term favourable influence on productivity.

Experience has shown that crises and depressions have always caused more or less pronounced reverses of productivity. During the 'thirties, for example, productivity in the United States fell back considerably behind the 1929 levels, owing to the incomplete utilization of capacity and labour (short-time working); it was not until 1938–39 that the levels of ten years previously were reached again. The relative cyclical stability of Switzerland, on the other hand, has been remarkable and one of its main reasons is precisely the flexibility of the Swiss productive equipment. Switzerland's relative cyclical stability is confirmed by the figures in Table VII. If we compare the decline of national income between the top of

TABLE VII

CYCLICAL SENSITIVITY OF SELECTED COUNTRIES DURING THE
DEPRESSION OF THE 1930s

Country	Percentage change of national income between peak of 1929 and bottom of depression
United States	− 51·7
Canada	− 48·4
Germany	− 40·5
Netherlands	− 30·5
Belgium	− 29·0
France	− 28·2
Switzerland	− 21·6
Sweden	− 17·0
United Kingdom	− 15·0

Source : *U.N. National Income Statistics* 1938–1948, New York, 1950.

the boom in 1929 and the bottom of the subsequent depression, we see that Switzerland is among those countries which suffered least from the depression.[1]

IV. FURTHER SPECIAL FEATURES OF THE SWISS ECONOMY [2]

The discussions at the Lisbon Round Table, and in particular Dr. Kuznets' paper 'Economic Growth of Small Nations', suggested

[1] Cf. also Hans Böhi, 'Die Schweiz im welt- und binnenwirtschaftlichen Konjunkturverlauf', *Die Schweiz als Kleinstaat in der Weltwirtschaft*, Schweizerisches Institut für Aussenwirtschafts- und Marktforschung an der Handelshochschule St. Gallen, 1945, p. 83.

[2] [The remainder of the paper here printed represents an addendum to the paper as presented at Lisbon. ED.]

that it might be well to set out some additional factors characteristic of the Swiss economy. These factors have unquestionably contributed to the adaptability of the Swiss economy and thereby to an increase in welfare and productivity. But it is not certain that they have contributed to raise welfare and productivity, as distinct from their effect on cyclical resistance and resilience. For this reason, these factors were not included in Section III above.

(1) *Highly Diversified Production*

Contrary to the assumptions of Dr. Kuznets, which led him to expect that small countries must necessarily specialize on a few branches of production, the Swiss economy is hardly less varied than that of the United States and Germany. This can be seen in Table VIII. It is, in particular, most interesting to observe the close kinship between the Swiss and German patterns of industry and crafts.

(2) *Highly Diversified Exports*

What has been said of the structure of production applies also to the structure of exports. One would expect a small country to have to concentrate on a small number of export products for which it has a comparative advantage ; but Table IX conveys a different picture for Switzerland. First of all, there are many different export industries. Secondly, it is characteristic of Swiss foreign trade that — apart from the watch industry with its relatively uniform products — the major export industries, such as the textile, engineering, and chemical industries, by no means export only one product or group of products, but are successful in the most varied fields.

(3) *Dispersion of Foreign Markets*

Finally, it has been assumed that a small nation's foreign trade must, more than that of a large nation, concentrate on only a few foreign countries, in particular its neighbours. Table X shows that while indeed Germany heads the list of Switzerland's foreign markets with 13·9 per cent of total Swiss exports, the United States follows close behind with 12·2 per cent. The combined share of Switzerland's four neighbours amounts to only 33·6 per cent of total Swiss exports. The table also shows the far-reaching ramifications of the sales channels of Swiss export industry.

TABLE VIII

OCCUPATIONAL STRUCTURE IN SWITZERLAND, THE UNITED
STATES, AND WESTERN GERMANY
1950

Branch	Switzerland		United States		Germany	
	Labour force (thousands)	%	Labour force (thousands)	%	Labour force (thousands)	%
Agriculture	355·4	16·5	6,884	11·7	980·6	6·7
Mining and quarrying	6·2	0·3	966	1·6	835·1	5·7
Building industry	175·2	8·1	3,558	6·0	1,173·5	8·0
Industry and crafts	812·7	37·7	15,662	26·9	6,014·8	41·2
of which :						
Food	87·2	4·0	1,644	2·8	615·3	4·2
Textiles	78·7	3·7	1,295	2·2	668·4	4·6
Clothing	111·4	5·2	1,206	2·1	549·6	3·8
Timber and cork	62·1	2·9	1,219	2·1	523·3	3·6
Paper	19·3	0·9	484	0·8	136·1	0·9
Printing	32·8	1·5	762	1·4	143·9	1·0
Chemicals	35·5	1·6	940	1·6	340·5	2·3
Leather	9·7	0·5	395	0·7	90·6	0·6
Rubber	2·4	0·1	250	0·4	66·6	0·5
Non-metallic minerals	21·7	1·0	524	0·9	157·4	1·1
Basic metals	97·6	4·5	2,294	4·0	927·5	6·4
Heavy and light engineering	168·7	7·8}	3,552	6·1	{1,492·6	10·2
Watches	64·6	3·1}			{ 130·8	0·8
Miscellaneous	2·8	0·1	543	0·9	26·5	0·2
Electricity, gas, water	18·3	0·8	554	0·9	145·7	1·0
Commerce	212·4	9·8	11,225	19·0	1,251·5	8·5
Banking and insurance	40·0	1·9	2,047	3·5	221·5	1·5
Transport	98·0	4·5	3,616	6·1	1,093·1	7·4
Hotels and catering	90·8	4·2	585	1·0	170·3	1·2
Public administration, jurisdiction, defence	85·7	4·0	6,554	11·1	1,330·8	9·1
Private services (lawyers, doctors, education, cultural activities, entertainment, etc.)	167·1	7·8	5,874	9·9	904·5	6·5
Household	111·7	5·2	1,864	3·2	607·6	4·2
Totals	2155·6	100·0	58,835	100·0	14,583	100·0

Sources : For Switzerland : *Statistisches Jahrbuch der Schweiz*, 1956. For
U.S. : Dept. of Commerce, *Survey of Current Business*, National Income Number,
July 1955. For Germany : *Statistisches Jahrbuch für die Bundesrepublik Deutschland*,
1956.

TABLE IX

SWISS EXPORTS BY GROUPS OF PRODUCTS

1956

		Per cent of total exports
Textile industry		13·2
of which':		
cotton yarn and fabrics	4·0	
embroidery	1·9	
artificial silk yarn	1·6	
silk fabrics	1·5	
woollen yarn and fabrics	1·3	
knit fabrics	0·7	
clothing	1·1	
Boots and shoes		0·7
Basic metals		5·6
Machinery		21·5
of which :		
dynamos	1·9	
turbines and pumps	1·2	
oil and gas motors	1·4	
textile and knitting machinery	4·5	
sewing machines	0·8	
printing machinery	0·6	
machine tools	4·4	
air compressors	1·1	
Instruments		7·0
Watch industry		19·9
Chemical industry		16·3
of which :		
pharmaceutical products	7·3	
industrial chemicals	2·8	
dyestuffs	4·5	
Books, periodicals, newspapers . . .		0·7
Food industry		5·9
Other industries		9·2
	Total	100·0

Source : *Jahresbericht 1956 der Schweizerischen Handelsstatistik*, published by the Chief Federal Customs Office, Berne, Part II : *Separate Economic Branches.*

TABLE X

SWISS EXPORTS BY IMPORTING COUNTRIES
1956

Importing country	Per cent of total exports
Twelve largest markets:	
Germany	13·9
United States	12·2
France	8·7
Italy	8·1
United Kingdom	5·2
Belgium-Luxemburg	4·4
Netherlands	4·0
Austria	2·9
Sweden	2·9
China	2·4
India	2·3
Spain	2·0
Others:	
Canada	1·8
Australia	1·4
Brazil	1·3
Denmark	1·3
Argentina	1·2
Venezuela	1·1
Japan	1·1
Mexico	1·0
Czechoslovakia	1·0
Finland	1·0
Egypt	1·0
Norway	0·9
South Africa	0·9
Portugal	0·9
14 other countries in *Europe*	3·6
21 ,, ,, *Africa*	2·5
21 ,, ,, *Asia*	5·4
22 ,, ,, *America*	3·4
4 ,, ,, *Oceania*	0·2
Total	100·0

Notes: (1) The share of the twelve most important foreign markets is 69·0 per cent. (2) Countries outside Europe are printed in italics.

Source : *Jahresbericht 1956 der Schweizerischen Handelsstatistik, op. cit.* Part I : *Countries from which Switzerland buys and to which it sells.*

We may try to measure the regional concentration of exports in terms of the share of a country's exports taken up by their twelve most important foreign markets. This has been done in Table XI,

TABLE XI

REGIONAL CONCENTRATION OF THE EXPORTS

OF SELECTED COUNTRIES

1954

Exporting country	Exports to the twelve most important foreign markets as per cent of total exports
Canada	90·1
Denmark	83·6
Sweden	77·0
Belgium-Luxemburg	73·7
Netherlands	69·0
Switzerland	66·9
Western Germany	64·2
France	59·9
Italy	58·2
United States	53·4
United Kingdom	50·1

Source : *Statistisches Jahrbuch für die Bundesrepublik Deutschland*, 1956, International Comparisons, pp. 80 *et seq.* DM values were converted into Swiss francs at the official rate of exchange.

TABLE XII

EUROPEAN AND EXTRA-EUROPEAN EXPORTS OF SELECTED

EUROPEAN COUNTRIES

1954

Exporting country	Exports to	
	European countries	Extra-European countries
	(Per cent of total exports)	
United Kingdom	33·4	66·6
France	44·3	55·7
Italy	59·0	41·0
Switzerland	59·7	40·3
Western Germany	66·2	33·8
Belgium-Luxemburg	67·7	32·3
Netherlands	68·4	31·6
Sweden	76·9	23·1
Denmark	80·7	19·3

Source : *Statistisches Jahrbuch für die Bundesrepublik Deutschland*, 1956. *Ibid.*

and we see that Switzerland, with 66·9 per cent, has less concentrated exports than other small countries and only slightly more concentrated ones than Western Germany. A further interesting feature is that Switzerland's exports are directed outside Europe roughly in the same degree as those of Italy and rather more so than those of Western Germany (Table XII).

V. CONCLUSION

The preceding analysis has disclosed a number of factors which contribute to Switzerland's high level of productivity and welfare, in spite of small size and other unfavourable circumstances. The authors are content to enumerate these factors without attempting to evaluate their quantitative contribution to the final result. It also remains an open question how productivity and welfare would be affected if the political and economic barriers hampering exchange with other countries were to disappear.

Chapter 5

STUDY OF THE EFFICIENCY OF
A SMALL NATION: BELGIUM[1]

BY

L. DUQUESNE DE LA VINELLE
University of Louvain

I. THE MEANING OF EFFICIENCY

THE first question which arises in discussing the influence of the size of the Belgian economy on its efficiency is that of a standard of measurement for efficiency. This question is less simple than it appears. Consumption might be taken as a yardstick, but it cannot be strictly reduced to production, which is another possible yardstick. Production in its turn might be measured in terms of value or of volume and the two indices do not coincide. It is an open question whether production per member of the labour force is a better standard or production per head of the population. The economic value of leisure ought perhaps to be taken into account so as to neutralize the effects of differences in working time. Finally, income distribution might be considered as one of the elements of economic efficiency.

This catalogue, which is not meant to be exhaustive, shows how necessary it is to adopt some conventional definition in order to avoid a lengthy debate which would not only be intricate but, in this context, beside the point. I propose, as a working hypothesis, to take the development of the volume of production as a yardstick of efficiency. It is true that this means limiting the scope of this paper to one single aspect of economic efficiency, but at least it is an important aspect and one which lends itself readily to fairly accurate international comparison. Such comparison is clearly indispensable.

On the other hand, considerable advantages are to be gained from basing our interpretation on a long-period phenomenon. Any situation is ultimately intelligible only in terms of the series of historical antecedents which led up to it. The present situation of

[1] Translated from the French by Elizabeth Henderson.

78

the Belgian economy can thus be better understood by going back somewhat and taking a long view. Besides, of all the effects which the size of an economy may have on its efficiency, the most important are probably the long-run effects, and it is therefore important to try to identify them. And of all the admissible parameters of economic efficiency, the volume of production lends itself better than any other to an analysis over time.

II. THE INFLUENCE OF A NATION'S SIZE ON THE GENERAL PATTERN OF EXPANSION

Chart I in the Appendix [1] relates to the output of manufacturing industry. Manufacturing industry is much more sensitive to the constraints deriving from the size of the economy than are the extractive industries, whose production is essentially dependent upon the relative abundance of natural resources and their geographical location.

The chart shows the growth of output in the manufacturing industries of Belgium and of the group of countries which are now members of the Organization for European Economic Co-operation. The two curves have the same general shape. The curve for Belgium has, however, some special features which are immediately obvious. While the two curves are closely parallel between 1901 and 1913, the Belgian one rises much more rapidly than the European one between 1921 and 1929. By contrast, the European countries as a whole show considerable progress between 1929 and 1937–38, while Belgium barely reached the 1929/30 level again in 1937–38. Immediately after the Second World War, the Belgian curve starts out from a relatively favourable initial position, but except for 1951, 1954, and 1955 it rises much less rapidly than the European curve.

The determining causes of these divergences would seem to be monetary phenomena and policies, especially the exchange rate.

In this connection it is interesting to observe the movements of the relative level of nominal wages in Belgium. Chart II shows that the strikingly quick expansion of manufacturing production in Belgium during the years immediately following the 1914–1918 war and especially during 1926–29 was clearly linked with a

[1] The chart has been prepared on the basis of statistics presented and published by V. Paretti and G. Bloch, 'Industrial Production in Western Europe and the United States', *Banca Nazionale del Lavoro Quarterly Review*, Rome, December 1956.

depreciation of the international value of Belgian wages, at the exchange rate of that period. By contrast, the very serious difficulties encountered during the subsequent depression, and especially in 1932–34, were associated with a sharp and, given the general economic situation, entirely unwarranted rise in the international value of the Belgian franc. The economy could be rescued only by devaluation, and the principal effect of that was to bring the international value of Belgian wages back to a more or less normal level.

A similar situation can be observed after the last war, during the years 1947 to 1955. Immediately after the war, Belgian wages were, for a number of reasons which cannot be discussed here, well above their historical level. This circumstance seems to have had a sharply restrictive influence on the expansion of output, except in the altogether exceptional conditions of the year 1951. It was not until 1954 that the rate of expansion of manufacturing production in Belgium fell into step with the general European rate of expansion, either because by then the international value of Belgian wages had again come near enough its normal level or because the economy had adjusted itself to a relatively higher wage level.

If this interpretation is correct, it might seem at first sight that the peculiarities in the development of the index of manufacturing output in Belgium had nothing to do with the size of the Belgian economy. Surely all countries, large or small, are liable to experience certain disturbances in their industrial expansion as a result of monetary phenomena or monetary policies. But on second thoughts it will be seen that there are quite considerable differences between the position of a large country and that of a small one.

The political causes of monetary errors are indeed common to both ; but the consequences of these errors are more damaging to small than to large countries. Besides, even the most judicious monetary policy is not always able to avoid all harmful disturbances. For instance, when the international capital markets depending upon the Great Powers are as profoundly disorganized as they were between 1920 and 1930, the maintenance of foreign exchange equilibrium becomes singularly more difficult for small countries. Not more so than for large countries, it may be objected. True enough. But once again, if the difficulty causes errors or failures, their consequences are more damaging to a small country because its foreign relations have such widespread ramifications in its economy. Similar difficulties are created for small countries when the Great Powers pursue completely divergent policies, as they did during the years 1930–40. In the general scramble for safety during the Great Depression some of the Great Powers hung on to the gold standard, others looked for relief in fluctuating exchange rates, yet others took refuge in trying to become self-sufficient. In such circumstances a small country, being more heavily dependent upon foreign trade, is bound to experience serious disturbances, whatever its policy. If it balances its position with respect to one group of countries, it necessarily unbalances it with respect to the others. In a very much milder form, the same thing happened with the economic fluctuations attendant upon the Korean war : while Belgium tried as best she could to maintain her equilibrium *vis-à-vis* the dollar area, she found herself in serious unbalance with the countries of the European Payments Union.

It would seem, therefore, as if a small economy were subject to special difficulties, in so far as its small size amplifies the consequences of the disturbances propagated by the foreign exchange market.

The behaviour of the Belgian economy between 1920 and 1940 shows more than one instance of how the economy of a small country has, in fact, been buffeted between the divergent impulses it has received from abroad, ever since ill-advised economic policies together with adversity have upset the former orderly pattern of the wage relations. Careful examination shows also that economic policy has never — or hardly ever — been able to take a middle road between these divergences. Between 1924 and 1932 Belgian wages kept in line with French ones ; from 1935 to 1938 they followed British wages ; and from 1949 to 1955 American ones. Thus every major turn in economic policy led Belgian wages to align themselves with the wages of the Great Power in whose wake the Belgian economy was following.

It is therefore not enough to grant that however astute a small country's economic policy may be, it will never enable that country to escape the disturbances imposed upon it by the lack of co-ordination in the policies of the Great Powers. In addition, these disturbances are certainly aggravated by the fact that any alignment with one or the other group tends to become so complete that the economy of the small country swings either all one way or all the other. For example, it becomes imperative in such cases for a small country to transfer its sales from one group of markets to another according to circumstances, or to redistribute sales among groups of products. Thereby it becomes more difficult to stabilize the flow of business, long-term industrial risks increase, and with them also the obstacles to a balanced growth of production.

The intensity of the compelling influences [1] undergone by the Belgian economy as the result of these successive alignments is reflected in the index of manufacturing production. In both the periods 1924–32 and 1935–38, this index closely followed that of the country whose wage index was the model of Belgian wages. Since 1948 the parallelism is less striking, but it should be noted that the dislocation of wages during that period is a matter more of relative levels than of relative movements.

The question may, of course, be asked whether it was inevitable that economic policy should have led to such close alignments and was unable to find a middle way. This is a complex problem which cannot be fully analysed in this paper. Nevertheless, we are probably right in thinking at first sight that the choices open to economic policy do not allow of infinite graduations ; an economic policy seems to be an indivisible whole made up of interdependent elements ruled by the central idea. There are thus bound to be certain discontinuities between one policy and another. In these circumstances the permanent search for a middle way would no doubt be harder than a succession of alignments.

III. THE INFLUENCE OF A NATION'S SIZE ON THE PATTERN OF INDUSTRIAL EXPANSION

Analysis of manufacturing production by branches of industry also leads to interesting results. It shows that, as compared with the European average, the rate of expansion of the textile industry in Belgium was above average while the rate of expansion of the chemical and basic metals industries was about average ; in engineering and the food industry the Belgian rates of expansion were below the European average.

This is strange, seeing that the general European rate of expansion was greatest in the engineering industries and weakest in textiles. The Belgian economy seems to have gone against the general European current, showing most vitality where Europe as a whole showed least and vice versa.

These peculiarities of industrial development in Belgium may be explained by means of various hypotheses which are largely complementary.

We may first note that the Belgian textile industry is mainly located in Flanders and that the chemical industry's main expansion

[1] I refer to the phenomenon that Professor Perroux has appropriately termed a 'domination effect'.

was centred in the north-east of the country. Now these are precisely the regions with the largest population growth during the period considered. The engineering industries, on the other hand, are mainly located in the south of the country where there was a marked decline in population growth. It seems reasonable to suppose that this demographic factor was not wholly irrelevant to the pattern of Belgian industrial development between 1900 and 1955. Indeed in the long period industrial development may follow rather than command the distribution of professional skills. Or, more precisely, the occupational traditions proper to the various regions tend to endure because the new generations spontaneously adopt a pattern corresponding to the past and present needs of industry which they extrapolate into the future. This leads to a certain inertia in the supply of skills to which industry must in turn partially adapt itself. This hypothesis does not, of course, give us a full explanation. For example, it is of no help in interpreting the relative lag of the food industry.

IV. TARIFF POLICY

Belgium's comparatively liberal tariff policy may furnish a first and important complementary explanation. It should be noted here that tariff policy itself must be viewed in relation to the country's geographical situation and the smallness of its domestic market. Belgium has an excellent sea-port and good communications with the most highly industrialized regions of Western Europe, but she lacks raw materials other than coal, and her exports have been hampered by protectionism elsewhere ; [1] in these circumstances she took recourse to a policy of low tariffs.

However surprising at first sight, this was a logical step to take. The highly industrialized economy of Belgium can be balanced only by exporting manufactured goods. When a country's industry has to export a high proportion of its products, the advantages of tariff protection are greatly reduced, since it helps only domestic sales ; at the same time the disadvantages of protection are greater when a large proportion of raw materials needs to be imported, which is also the case in Belgium. It is therefore entirely reasonable that Belgium should have striven to encourage her export

[1] The geographical distribution of Belgium's exports of ammonium sulphate provides a typical example of the difficulties which protectionism may create for a small country's industry. As the table shows, the principal markets for this product are Spain and Portugal, India and the Far East. The quantities sold in western and northern Europe are negligible.

industries by imposing only low customs duties or none on imported raw materials and semi-manufactures, rather than to protect her 'domestic' industries by high tariffs.

This tariff policy must have afforded specific support to those industries which were the main sources of the flow of exports from the beginning of the period considered. In fact, Belgium's traditional export industries since before the First World War — the textile, chemical, and basic metals industries — have maintained their place as such and their relative expansion was greatest. On the other hand, the food and engineering industries, which were initially less specialized on exports, fell behind the average European rate of expansion. It can thus be inferred that Belgium's tariff policy, which was determined both by her geographical position and by the smallness of her domestic market, had some influence on the pattern of industrial development.

This inference is reinforced by the consideration that the advantages derived from low or zero tariffs on imported raw materials or semi-manufactures must be all the greater when these constitute a large component in the cost of the goods exported after manufacture. In other words, a policy designed to lower the prices of imported factors of production is of more especial benefit to short production processes. Now metal manufactures, and more particularly light engineering, unquestionably have the longest periods of production, whereas the textile industries have far the shortest, because the different production stages can readily be dissociated from each other.

V. TRANSPORT POLICY

This leads us to consider also the influence of transport policy. Belgium's economic policy has been very consistent in reinforcing its attempts to cheapen imported factors of production by a policy of low transport costs. Tariff policy and transport policy have cumulative effects, since imported raw materials are often heavy and bulky. At the same time, cheap transport also favours less intensive production processes, because they are more sensitive to the freight rates of rail and river transport both inward and outward. The policy of cheap transport has specific effects distinct from those of a low tariff policy only to the extent that low freight rates specifically favour the industries whose products are heavy. But this difference does not prevent the two policies from being complementary and forming a consistent whole. In any case, their combined effect provides a fairly good explanation of the relative success of Belgian industry in the field of textiles, basic metals, and chemicals, and of its relative lag in engineering.

Tariff policy and transport policy were certainly motivated by the same reasons. What indeed could be more reasonable, at any rate at first sight, than that a country with a favourable geographical position but of small size should try to intensify its relations with foreign countries by cheap transport, particularly when there are no major obstacles of a topographical nature ? This policy also fitted in with the idea of stimulating the exploitation of coal, which is the only natural resource which the country possesses. There is no doubt that this was rational, at least until comparatively recently.

VI. GOVERNMENT EXPENDITURE AND THE ENGINEERING INDUSTRIES

Another important observation needs to be made with respect to the manufacture of metals. Of all the industries considered in this paper, engineering most closely depends upon public, and more particularly military, orders. For certain branches, such as aircraft or rolling stock, the government is far and away the principal consumer on the domestic market. At the same time, these are industries where very large economies of scale can be realized. But precisely by virtue of its size, a small country cannot provide a sufficiently large and stable domestic market to enable this kind of industry to reach its optimal economic dimensions. This is a point which must not be overlooked in any attempt to explain the comparatively slow expansion of the Belgian engineering industry, which in the past had a flourishing production of rolling stock and whose motor-car and aircraft production got off to a brilliant, though short-lived, start.

The disadvantage arising from the smallness of public consumption remains very real, even though the example of other small countries suggests that the obstacle is not an insuperable one, since it may be circumvented by appropriate specialization in the products destined for private consumption. The mere fact that the choice of lines of production is limited is a handicap, not to mention the resulting absence of the advantages deriving from technical complementarities and in particular of certain types of external economy. Thus a firm making farm tractors would gain if there were, within the same country, another firm making jeeps. In more general terms this means that any solution of the problem of national specialization must take into account the external economies of which firms are deprived if specialization is pushed to the point of causing a structural impoverishment of the branches of industry in which the nation intends to specialize. This principle, for example, justifies the size of the Belgian nitrogen industry, even though it involves having to export a large proportion of the output in difficult conditions and to distant markets. But the production of ammonia enables the coke and iron and steel industries to realize external economies by using certain by-products of the cokeries. Obviously these external economies would be greater in Belgium if the small size of the domestic market did not make it necessary to export so much to distant markets.

VII. CONCLUSIONS

The preceding analysis unquestionably permits the conclusion that the effects of the small size of the nation on the efficiency of its industry are numerous and complex.

With respect to the most general aspect of the question, the Belgian example shows very clearly that it may sometimes be difficult for a small country to co-ordinate its monetary, budgetary, and social policies with those of the Great Powers. When the latter pursue divergent policies there is no perfect solution to the problem, even in theory, because there is no way of avoiding disturbances which are harmful to the proper functioning of the economy. It is indeed doubtful whether it is at all possible in practice to follow a middle-of-the-road policy which in principle might minimize the disturbances. Belgium was, in fact, during the inter-war period, tossed this way or that by one influence or another. Certainly there was room for improvement in the wisdom of her policies, but we must remember the circumstances. The parallelism between the French and the Belgian economies prior to 1933 was conditioned by moral and psychological attitudes as much as by economic facts. Brussels was looking to Paris. Before the salutary decision was taken to look to London instead, the Belgian economy had undergone the disastrous effect of deflation and had suffered all the more since, before 1929, it had yielded even more than France to the temptations of an inflationary policy.

As regards the pattern of industrial production, we can say that the country's small size has been an important contributory factor in the choice of an economic policy of low tariffs and cheap transport. The other contributory factors were the country's geographical position and the fact that it possesses only one important natural resource, coal, which had to be exploited on a large scale if the economy was to prosper. The combination of these policies in the context of a small domestic market and of the given initial industrial structure at the beginning of the century go a long way towards explaining why Belgium paradoxically displayed greater relative efficiency in the textile and heavy industries than in the engineering and food industries. In the case of the engineering industry an additional explanation lies in the smallness of public consumption.

The immediate result of this explanation is to show how the size of Belgium has directly or indirectly conditioned the efficiency of certain branches of manufacturing industry. But some conclusions may also be drawn for industry as a whole.

MM. Paretti and Bloch have demonstrated in their study mentioned above that an analysis of the industrial development of the principal European countries and the United States shows a correlation between the relative degree of development in the engineering industries and the speed of general expansion. In other words, the countries where the engineering industries grew fastest in relation to total industrial production also had the highest general rate of expansion. Equally, the countries where the engineering industries are relatively largest have achieved the highest levels of production per head.

These results of MM. Paretti and Bloch can no doubt be explained by the fact that the price- and income-elasticities of demand for engineering products were higher, during the period considered, than for any other category of goods. It may also be that technical innovations reduced costs in the engineering industries more than elsewhere. In any case, other studies [1] show most impressively that the share of engineering and electrical products in world trade has grown continuously to the point of completely altering, in the space of fifty years, the structure of the main industrial countries' foreign trade.

All this suggests that if Belgium had been able to specialize more on engineering products and less on basic metals and textiles, she might have experienced a more rapid general expansion. Must we rush to the conclusion, then, that her industrial orientation was ill-advised? For my part, I should not be inclined to say so.

First of all even the most careful analysis of one individual case cannot yield absolutely certain results. All that can be claimed for

[1] *Cf.*, for example, H. Tyszynksi, 'World Trade in Manufactured Commodities', *The Manchester School of Economic and Social Studies*, September 1951, and Ingvar Svennilson, *Growth and Stagnation in the European Economy*, Economic Commission for Europe, Geneva, 1955.

the relations of cause and effect between economic policy and industrial development which have been discussed in this paper is that they are plausible. No more can be claimed, given the historical nature of this study.

On the other hand, it is quite certain that Belgium's industrial orientation was determined by the country's geographical situation and size. I have shown that from this point of view Belgian policy has been consistent. Thus if the pattern of Belgian industry is not as perfect as it might be, the size of the nation is largely responsible. This applies, of course, to the past and not to the future.

The history of the Belgian economy suggests yet another conclusion which I would not wish to pass over in silence. Again I start out from the fact that in the long period the most efficient of the Belgian industries were those which were more typically export industries. I have explained this in terms of economic policy, but I do not think that this explanation reflects the full significance of what has happened. Economic policy is not omnipotent and it would be illusory to think that it could have incisive and permanent effects on the development of any branch of industry in the absence of the spontaneous working of economic forces.

It should be stressed once more that I am not here concerned with formal proof : the interpretation of the facts rests on a judgement which must remain partly subjective. The facts have happened once only and under the impact of a combination of influences ; it is not possible to disentangle the separate influences. Having said this, I cannot help feeling that if the Belgian export industries [1] have been more successful than the others, it must be because, having once gained a foothold on the world market, these industries there encountered conditions which were by and large more propitious to progress than the conditions on the more limited domestic market.

Geographical position, natural resources, and economic policy may provide a sufficient explanation of why certain industries did and others did not specialize in export trade. But this does not fully explain why it was the export industries rather than the others which equalled or surpassed the average rate of expansion in Europe. This seems paradoxical, considering the modern protectionist practices both of Great Powers and under-developed countries. At any rate, if the development had been the other way around, probably few economists would have been surprised.

The apparent contradiction cannot be entirely resolved without

---

[1] Their expansion should be understood in general terms. It would obviously be possible to find localized failures within an export industry as a whole.

assuming that by and large — and in spite of protectionism — an export industry in a small country finds more favourable conditions for expansion than do other industries. The most important of these favourable conditions is the scale of the productive equipment as regards both the whole industry and separate firms, because of external economies. This is probably the reason why the Belgian textile industry can realize economies of scale thanks to its foreign markets. Another favourable condition which may be quite important is of an intellectual nature. Constant contact with foreign markets widens the outlook of entrepreneurs and managing staff, keeps them on the alert and stimulates their inventiveness.

The situation of industry in small countries may perhaps best be expressed in terms of a black-and-white alternative (with all the arbitrary simplification this entails) : either an industry surmounts the obstacles surrounding export markets and finds better than average chances of expansion, or it does not surmount these obstacles and then its chances of expansion remain below average. It would be interesting to see whether the industrial development of other small countries confirms this hypothesis.

NOTES CONCERNING THE SOURCES OF THE STATISTICS

1. Production indices : V. Paretti and G. Bloch, 'Industrial Production in Western Europe and the United States 1901 to 1955', in *Banca Nazionale del Lavoro Quarterly Review*, Rome, December 1956.
2. Wage indices :
   Belgium : 1901–13 : M. Peeters, 'L'Évolution des salaires en Belgique de 1831–1913', in *Bulletin de l'Institut de Recherches Économiques et Sociales*, Louvain, 1939.
   1924–38 : Documentation of the Institut de Recherches Économiques et Sociales and *Bulletin d'Information et de Documentation de la Banque Nationale de Belgique*.
   1948–55 : Statistics published by 'Industrie', Brussels.
   United States : Historical Statistics series no. D 111-116 and 121-133 and 263.
   Germany, France, and United Kingdom :
   1901–35 : R. Kucynsky, 'Labour Conditions in Western Europe'.
   1936–38 : I.L.O. Geneva.
   1949–55 : Statistics published by 'Industrie', Brussels.

For all countries considered, weekly wages have been taken for the period 1901–38 and hourly wages for 1949–55.

For all European countries, wages exclude the employers' contributions to Social Security until 1938 and include them after 1949.

APPENDIX

INDEX OF THE VOLUME OF PRODUCTION OF MANUFACTURING INDUSTRY
(1938 = 100)

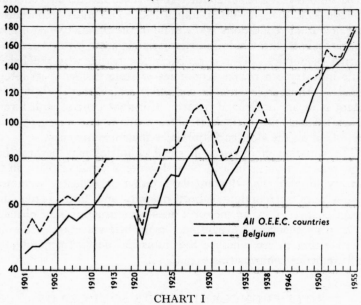

All O.E.E.C. countries

Belgium

CHART I

COMPARISONS OF TRENDS OF WAGES *
(1913 = 100)

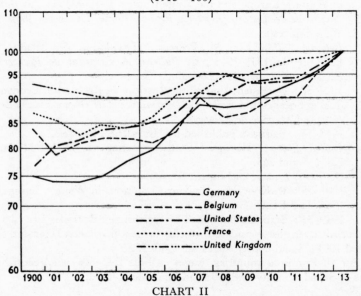

Germany

Belgium

United States

France

United Kingdom

CHART II

* Converted into Belgian francs at the current exchange rate.

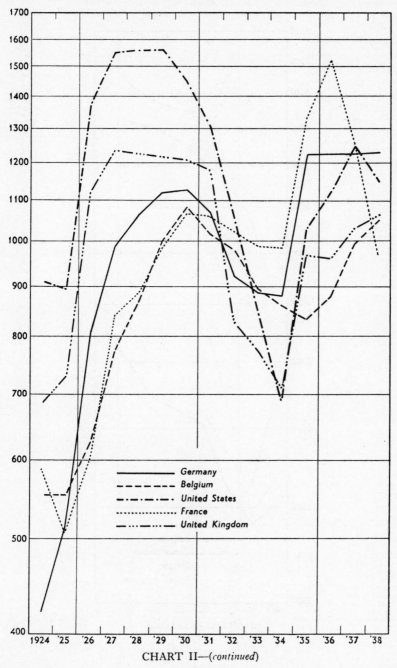

CHART II—(*continued*)

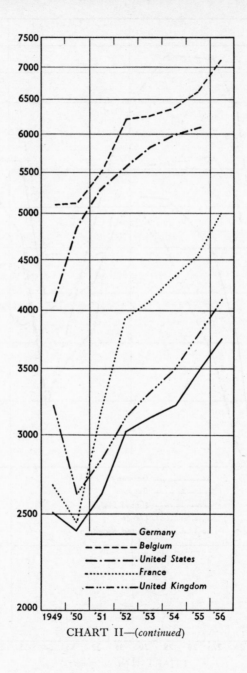

CHART II—(*continued*)

Chapter 6

ARE THE ECONOMIES OF SCALE UNLIMITED?

J. JEWKES
Oxford University

I. THE PROBLEM

THE short answer to this question is, of course, no. If it were otherwise, the structure of industry would be different from what it is. If size, automatically and without qualification, were an advantage — as weight in a boxer — there would be many fewer cases in history where large industrial units, particularly those which have come into existence full grown or have attained their size swiftly, find that the very magnitude of their operations, far from being an unmixed blessing, is the source of their sharpest and most persistent anxieties.[1] The best analyses of the administrative process itself have shown that, with increasing size, the complexities of the task of maintaining proper interrelations between the parts inevitably and progressively increase.[2] And all subjective experience suggests that as the human brain is subjected to the strain of absorbing more and more information and integrating it for the purpose of making decisions, there is a point at which its synthesizing power will begin to fail.

I assume, however, that what is expected of me is not a short answer but a moderately long one. There are certainly limits. But where do they lie? Have the limits shifted their position and are they likely to shift further in the future? As I understand my task in the symposium, it constitutes an invitation to try to answer two questions (and let me hurry on to say that I can provide answers

[1] Interesting cases are to be found in the history of the United States Steel Corporation, the Lancashire Cotton Corporation, and most of the British nationalized industries. In the British coal-mining industry, for example, it was often urged, before nationalization, that the size of the new organization was one argument in favour of nationalization ; now it is common to hear it said that unless the coal-mining industry can 'solve the problems of size' the full advantages of nationalization will not be obtainable.

[2] See especially M. Polanyi, *The Logic of Liberty*, Chapter 8, 'The Span of Central Direction'.

95

to neither of them) : are there some countries where the domestic market for various products, important in the industrial scheme of things, is smaller than the optimum scale of output ? and in such cases, even assuming a free trading world, are the producers (or would-be producers) of those articles in those countries at a dis-advantage in selling abroad, or for that matter in selling at home ?

I suppose that I must be concerned more with the first question than with the second. For the second leads into all sorts of high-ways and byways — is it easier to conduct export trade than domestic trade ? must an industry have a substantial domestic market, as a 'spring-board' as it is usually put, if it is to have a flourishing export trade ? — which would lead me far astray. But with either question a balanced answer is highly elusive for two main reasons. In trying to determine the results of size we can, of course, rely to some degree upon analysis but, in the main, we have to depend upon experience, and, unfortunately, experience presents us with results in which the effects of size are mixed up inextricably with the consequences of other forces. I do not suppose, for example, that anyone really thinks that the inability of British producers of watches or of United States producers of ships to sell in a com-petitive world market has much to do with the size of the factories or the firms in which these articles are made. Or that the dominance in world markets of Swiss manufacturers of watches, or Irish manufacturers of linen, or British manufacturers of woollen goods, can be explained by a study of size. Nor do I suppose anyone would bother to look in that direction for an explanation of some of the great spectacular bursts of success in exports, such as that of the Japanese in textiles between the wars or that of the Germans in the past few years. Second, in both the questions raised above, we get hopelessly bogged down in the definition of a product. If we regard the motor-car as the product, some countries do not have a car industry and there must be some good reason for this. But if we think of the knobs on the cigarette-lighters of the cars as the product, there seems to be no obvious reason, certainly no reason connected with size, why these should not be made any-where, and, for all I know, they may well be made in those countries which do not make motor-cars.

It is, however, sometimes possible to throw light upon un-answerable questions by asking and answering other related questions where it seems feasible to get a little nearer to certainty. Other papers have dealt with the relation, for different countries, between the volume of manufactured goods produced and the volume ex-ported. I should like to know, although perhaps this is too much to hope for, what were the sizes of the factories and the firms in which were made the industrial goods entering into world trade and whether the firms making the industrial goods entering into exports were usually firms specializing in exports or possessing substantial home markets also. All this, however, is hardly my task. I propose to confine myself to much more venerable matters on which already generations of economists have exhausted themselves. What evidence is there about the limits to be derived from larger industrial units ? And I propose to examine this subject under the two heads established by age-long tradition : economies in the factory and economies in the firm.

II. TRENDS IN SIZE

Considerably more than one-half of the manufacturing output of the Western world is produced in factories employing less than 500 workers. In the various important industrial countries the average-sized factory produces somewhere between 0·0003 per cent and 0·001 per cent of the total manufacturing output. Put in that way it might well seem to an inhabitant of another planet, examining these figures for the first time and knowing nothing about our controversies, that there were ample opportunities in a freely trading world for small factories and small countries. But that deduction may be, and indeed is, challenged by some authorities on two grounds :

(1) That whatever may be the present position, powerful forces, discernible in the past and certain to continue in operation in the future, will change all this and make the considerably larger factory a much more normal thing and/or

(2) That to look at overall average figures is misleading ; for there are certain industries where large-scale factory operation is the rule and these cases have some special importance either in the sense that these are the industries destined to expand most rapidly or in the sense that the general economic expansion of the country is crucially dependent upon their presence, without them nothing else avails. That is to say, no industrial country can be really viable unless it has an iron and steel industry, a chemical industry, a motor-car industry, an electrical engineering industry, and perhaps an aircraft industry.

I suggest that we should consider here both the facts and, what I suspect is almost as important, the standpoint from which attempts are made to interpret the facts. As for the facts, I am bound to confess that I feel completely mystified by the way in which different people can look at the same set of figures and apparently read them differently.[1] I will not go into details about these conflicting readings, they are all published material.[2] But for the writing of this paper I have gone over the statistical material once again and I present my conclusions in summary form.

Looking first at the period up to 1939, I can find no industrial country where the actual number of factories was declining. Nor can I find any country where the figures of the average size of factory measured in terms of wage earners suggest any significant trend either upwards or downwards. When one considers the long stretch of statistics available, this appears to me to be a remarkable and significant fact. I cannot think its significance is shaken by any conceivable refinements that can be made in the simple figures. It may be that the wage earner is not the ideal unit in terms of which to measure the size of a factory, but it is the best we have and it is one which is highly relevant to some of our discussions. One may strive to make allowances, some cutting in one direction some in the other, for changes in hours of work over the period, changes in the proportions of salaried workers and wage earners, changes in the prevalence of shift systems, spurious variations in size as between years of prosperity and years of depression — but none of these seem to me to undermine the meaning of the fact that in the United States in 1914 the average factory held 37·3 workers and in 1939 held 42·8 workers, and that in most other countries the figures reveal the same kind of stability.

What has happened since 1939 ? The war destroyed many things, and among them the comparability of these figures of average size. But starting again with the comparable figures since the

---

[1] I cannot refrain from inviting the reader to compare the following statements :
'Over the whole period from 1899 (to 1937) the average size of establishment, as measured by the annual average number of wage earners per establishment, displayed considerable stability with evidence of some upward trend. There were increases from 1914 to 1919 and from 1935 to 1937 which were traceable, in part, to a more complete utilization of plants' (Temporary National Economic Committee, Monograph No. 27, *The Structure of Industry*).
'Taking manufacturing as a whole between 1904 and 1939 American plants doubled their average (arithmetic mean) number of wage earners ; but they more than quadrupled their average horse-power' (P. Sargant Florence, *The Logic of British and American Industry*, p. 30).
'What I am anxious to point out is that . . . the average size of factory is in fact *slowly creeping up* almost everywhere.' (My italics.) (P. Sargant Florence, 'The Size of the Factory', *Economic Journal*, September 1954.)

[2] See J. Jewkes, 'The Size of the Factory', *Economic Journal*, June 1952 ; P. Sargant Florence, 'The Size of the Factory', *Economic Journal*, September 1954 ; G. R. Allen, 'The Size of the Factory in Sweden', *Economic Journal*, December 1953.

end of the war there seems to be no evidence of any tendency for sizes to increase in the United States, Canada, or Australia.[1] Indeed a recent wide survey of this matter in ten countries, by the International Labour Office, recorded the conclusion that 'the average size of industrial establishment on the whole has not changed greatly since 1931, though there is a fairly widespread tendency towards an increase in the proportion of labour employed in the largest size-group establishments'.[2] And in all these countries the number of establishments appears to be increasing.

In the case of Germany we have figures for only 1953 and 1954 and there was an increase in the size of the factory between these two years. But it is in Great Britain that we find the most important, and intriguing, exception. Between 1950 and 1955 the average number of employees per establishment increased from 126 to 140 and the number of establishments fell slightly. The increase in size was found in chemicals, engineering, vehicles and food, drink and tobacco. The size fell in textiles, clothing, leather and leather goods. This may mean that significant changes are occurring in Great Britain. Whether it signifies that Britain is now destined to become the real home of large-scale industrial operations or whether it indicates that, due to a general lack of enterprise, small firms are no longer establishing themselves at the old rate in that country, is a matter on which we will have to wait and see.

How far is it true that, even if the average has not been changing much, the shape of the distribution curve has changed so that the largest-sized factories account for an increasing proportion of total employment ? Information on this subject before the Second World War is practically confined to the United States. I can find no evidence that the proportionate importance of establishments with more than 1000 wage earners in that country between 1914 and 1937 was on the increase. Since the war, on the other hand, in the United States the proportion of all employees found in factories with 2500 or more employees has increased from 17·7 per cent in 1947 to 20·0 per cent in 1952. The same is true of Great Britain, where the proportion of total employees found in factories with more than 2000 employees increased from 18·4 per cent in 1950 to 20·6 per cent in 1955. Although the period since the end of the war for which we have statistics is a short one, I think this increasing importance of the largest-sized factories may well be significant.

From all this evidence I would myself be content to draw these

[1] The figures are given in the Appendix.
[2] *International Labour Review*, June 1956, 'The Size of Industrial Establishments'.

deductions, which in the circumstances I consider highly restrained. If there are pervasive and powerful forces making for increased size of factories, then they cannot have been operating long, because so far they have produced no remarkable results. If, on the other hand, there are forces acting in this direction which are deep-seated and have long been in operation, they cannot be very powerful, because they have not produced conspicuous effects.

The interpretation of all such figures depends enormously upon one's prepossessions. If one starts out with a feeling that there must be *something* in the idea of the economies of scale, if one sees in increasing size the working out of an inner logic in industry, then one naturally has a highly perceptive eye for any movements which appear to confirm this. And this is a happy and secure position from which to discuss these matters. For if the figures move in the expected direction well and good. If they do not, this can be explained as a failure on the part of the business man to seize swiftly and adequately the possibilities of economy open to him, and to grasp the inner logic of industrial dynamics as the economist sees it. But since the sky is always a different colour if one is standing on one's head it may be worth while employing that posture occasionally. If one begins with the fact that after a century and a half of rapid industrial expansion, of extraordinary technical progress, and of generalized belief in the virtues of size, it still remains true that the average factory in the United States or Great Britain employs only two- or three-score people, then the mind intuitively begins to search for the diseconomies of scale, and what seems to be really worthy of our curiosity and our labours is some explanation of why the increase in average size has not been more evident.

III. THE GROWTH OF SPECIALIST FIRMS

When we turn to those industries where the factories are largest and are growing most rapidly, I have one point to make which is certainly not new but of which, in my opinion, sufficient notice is not taken. It is that these big factories are normally nourished with supplies and parts from many other much smaller factories either within or without 'the industry'. I have tried to pick out the picture [1] for 'motor vehicles and parts' in the United States ; it is roughly as follows :

[1] Based on *Report of the Federal Trade Commission on the Concentration of Productive Facilities*, 1947, and *Report of the Federal Trade Commission on the Divergence between Plant and Company Concentration*, 1947.

TABLE I

MOTOR VEHICLES AND PARTS IN THE UNITED STATES
1947

	All companies	Automobile assembling companies	Other companies
Number of Companies	779	8	771
Number of Plants	963	130	833
Value added by Manufacture ($m.)	3577	2150	1427
Value added per Plant ($m.)	3·71	16·5	1·61
Value added per Company ($m.)	4·59	268·7	1·85

That is to say, in this industry about two-fifths of the added value arises out of companies with an average added value of $m. 1·85 and an added value per plant of $m. 1·61.

I have not been able to obtain the same statistics for Great Britain, but one motor-car firm, usually regarded as highly integrated, has provided me with detailed figures. They show that of the total factory cost of a car, between 33 per cent and 45 per cent (varying with the type of car) consists of the cost of bought-out finished materials ready for immediate assembly. These parts were supplied by some 500 firms, covering a very wide range of size, but very much smaller on the average than the car firm itself.

Even in the classic examples of big firms with big factories which, over a long period, have actively pursued a policy of integration, the degree of dependence upon outsiders always seems to be surprisingly high. Thus the United States Steel Corporation buys goods and services from 54,000 outside suppliers. The Ford Company of America in 1949 was reported to be purchasing 20,000 items costing around $m. 700 from 7000 vendors.

So the question I ask myself is this. Even if the giant assembling and manufacturing plants are likely to be found in a few big countries, why should not the bits and pieces, massive in their totality, be made in other smaller industrial countries? Whatever the answer is, it cannot be because these bits and pieces can only be made economically in very large factories.

At this point I would like to make a general comment, which relates equally to factories and firms but which is perhaps best referred to whilst we have in mind this case of the American motor-car industry. I wonder whether those who are interested in the structure of industry have not pondered far too long over, and emphasized far too much, the importance of the idea of the optimum size of factory or firm and far too little the idea of an optimum *distribution* by size of factory and firm in an industry. When one considers within any one part of the manufacturing system which can usefully be defined as 'an industry', the different products, technical processes, and market conditions ; the contrast between those bits of the industry where probably conservatism and caution pay best and those bits where imagination and daring produce the results ; the virtues that may reside in having some firms which are temporarily satisfied with their lot and others which are dissatisfied, either because they are small and want to be bigger or because they are smaller than they used to be and are anxious about their decline ; the diverse kinds of ability to be found among different entrepreneurs — when one considers all these things, does it not lead to the presumption that a range, and one particular range more than any other, of sizes among the units will make for optimum efficiency ? Or, to put this same idea in another way, industrial units of varying size exist together in a mutually independent fashion and that it is the study of communities and not of individuals which might best reward our attentions. Or to put the idea in a more concrete form by advancing a very reckless hypothesis, might it not be that, in the long run, the industrial strength of the United States resides just as much in the extraordinary multiplicity of small factories and firms as it does in the small number of large factories and firms ?

Nothing could be further from my mind than an attempt to resurrect, in the study of industrial structure, the biological analogies formerly so popular. But I cannot refrain from pointing out that in the earlier biological parallels employed by economists, what was weak was not so much the economics as the biology. Plant men, in fact, are much more interested in plant ecology, in plant communities than in anything else. I do not know what kind of forest Marshall had in mind in his famous 'trees of the forest' illustration. But it was certainly not like any forest I have ever seen where the interesting thing usually is that plants of different sizes, shapes, forms of growth, methods of sustenance exist in a balanced symbiosis of competition and co-operation, with the large often as dependent for their existence on the small as the small on the large.

IV. ECONOMY AND SCALE IN THE FIRM

I now turn to the second half of my remit : economy and scale in the firm. Here the facts are less plentiful because, for all practical purposes, they apply only to the United States (the degree to which American economists and statisticians have outstripped their colleagues in other countries in their knowledge of the detail of industrial structure is a matter for envy and admiration although, quite recently, there has been a welcome return of interest in this subject in Great Britain). But even in the United States, of course, we know less about changes in the average size of firm, and the size distribution, than of factories. Nevertheless it is intriguing that in the United States the number of manufacturing firms roughly doubled between 1919–24 and 1952,[1] the number of employees in manufacturing roughly doubled, and industrial production increased by 150 per cent. Which suggests that the size of firm remained roughly constant in terms of employees and increased by 50 per cent in terms of output.

Discussions regarding the economies of scale in the firm have in recent years taken two rather sudden twists, the very occurrence of which seem to be of consequence. First, there has been a considerable toning down recently of the earlier, alarmist accounts of the degree of 'industrial concentration' and the speed at which it is increasing ; second, there has been a switch of emphasis from the economies of large-scale operation associated with manufacturing and selling to the economies connected with research and the development of inventions.

I suppose the first of these moves was set going by the celebrated article of Professor Adelman in 1951 in which he concluded that since 1900 'the odds are better than even that there has actually been some decline in industrial concentration. It is a good bet that there has at least been no actual increase ; and the odds do seem high against any substantial increase.'[2] In my opinion the criticisms which have been advanced of his work hardly seem to have shaken his tentative conclusions. And, as far as I know, no disagreement at all has been expressed with his proposition that 'since 1931 there has at least been no further concentration'. The effect of this, and other work by Stigler,[3] Nutter,[4] and Kaplan,[5] has been to give us a slant on the whole subject of industrial concentration

---

[1] M. A. Adelman, 'The Current Wave of Mergers Analysed'. Paper given to American Management Association, Conference on Mergers and Acquisitions, October 31st, 1956.

[2] M. A. Adelman, 'The Measurement of Industrial Concentration', *The Review of Economics and Statistics*, November 1951. See also the symposium on this paper in the *Review of Economics and Statistics*, May 1952.

[3] G. J. Stigler, *Five Lectures on Economic Problems*.

[4] G. W. Nutter, *The Extent of Enterprise Monopoly in the United States, 1899–1939*.

[5] A. D. H. Kaplan, *Big Enterprise in a Competitive System*.

in the United States very different from that which most of us were disposed to accept when Berle and Means published their first spectacular statistics and even more spectacular reflections upon their social and economic meaning.

Indeed, when we look back now at the earlier generalizations about industrial concentration, it is interesting to note how conflicting they were as to *when* this industrial concentration occurred and how persistent it was.[1]

Economists, and in this they are perhaps no better and no worse than other scientists, do not find it difficult to discard one theory, purporting to explain one set of what are supposed to be reliable observations on economic phenomena, and to take up a rival theory if these observations prove to be faulty. While it was thought that industrial concentration was on the increase, it was commonly argued that mergers largely explained this; when it was found that industrial concentration was not increasing, it was discovered, at least for the United States, that the merger movement, after the great boom in amalgamations at the beginning of the century, was not so decisive a factor as had been imagined.[2]

I do not suppose anyone would doubt the occurrence of the second change of emphasis which I mentioned : the modern disposition to stress much less the advantages which the big firm has over the smaller in the actual making and selling of things and to write up the advantages of size (and even of a degree of monopoly, though that is another story) in conducting research, producing innovations and getting them into proper form for the market. I need hardly point out that there is not a sharp dividing line between the two things : inventors may reduce costs of manufacturing existing products as well as bring into existence new products. Nevertheless, I think there is an important distinction here — it is reflected in the relative infrequency with which large firms now boast of reductions in price and the relative frequency with which they do so about their expenditure on research, their path-breaking

[1] Thus Galbraith's 'the present pattern of concentration was apparently achieved prior to World War I' (*Survey of Contemporary Economics*, p. 122) may be compared with Samuelson's 'the tremendous concentration of economic power in these giant corporations . . . did not grow overnight. Up till the New Deal of 1933, their percentage importance steadily mounted. Throughout the 1930s and up to World War II they grew some but just about held their own, relatively speaking' (*Economics*, 1948, p. 125).

[2] J. Lintner and J. K. Butters, 'Effect of Mergers on Industrial Concentration', *Review of Economics and Statistics*, February 1950; J. W. Markham, 'Survey of the Evidence and Findings on Mergers', Paper presented to the Conference on Business Concentration and Price Policy, Princeton, June 1952 ; M. A. Adelman, 'The Current Wave of Mergers Analysed', Paper read before American Management Association Conference on Mergers and Acquisitions, October 1956 ; J. F. Weston, *The Role of Mergers*.

innovations and technical progress, or about the fact that '*x* per cent of their present day products did not exist *y* years ago'. It is well exemplified by comparing the prospectuses of new amalgamations in the first thirty years of this century, wherein much of the talk was invariably about manufacturing economies, with such prospectuses today, where the stress is usually laid upon the possibilities opened up for research on an extended scale.

I do not profess to understand the reasons for this change. It may be that economies of manufacturing and selling are not really so important as has up to now been supposed. It may be that they are still as important but that they have been transcended by other types of economies. Or it may be that, in a world which now so passionately believes that science is 'wonderful', firms dare not, in the interests of their share values and their power to raise capital, ignore the appeal made to the investing public by accounts of serried masses of Ph.D.s, accommodated in palatial laboratories and working with incredibly expensive equipment, moving forward under a common direction into the scientific unknown.

Much has been written on the question of whether larger firms show lower costs and prices than smaller firms and so much of it is conflicting or inconclusive that scholars, and particularly American scholars, may well plead for an end to such studies. But perhaps you will bear with me if I mention some impressions which I draw from recent events and studies in Great Britain where, up to now, the literature on these comparisons has been relatively scanty. I do not think, for example, that our experience with nationalization lends support to the idea that increased size inevitably brings in its wake lower costs and prices. I doubt whether really big amalgamations in the last few years, particularly that of Nuffield and Austin into the British Motor Corporation, accounting for about one-half of the motor vehicle output of the country, have provided evidence of such economies. These, however, are opinions, although perhaps by now fairly widely held opinions. On top of them we have had, since the war, in Britain two major sets of investigations into industrial organization, each of which has thrown up a considerable amount of evidence, qualitative and statistical, of the relative efficiency of firms of different size, evidence which has been, I think, oddly ignored.

Between 1946 and 1948 a number of official committees, so-called Working Parties, published reports upon a number of British industries. In some of these studies attention was devoted to the relation between size and efficiency and, whilst the findings are in all cases tentative, the verdict was not usually in favour of the largest firms as the following quotations show. The Wool Report says :

'The evidence is hardly sufficient to warrant any conclusions in favour of the superior efficiency of firms in the larger size groups.'

The Lace Report :

'In the lace furnishing section the most economical unit is in the small or small-medium firm . . . the very small and very large firms seem to show definite weakness.'

The Furniture Report :

'The gap between the best and the worst firms is very nearly as large in the large and medium size groups as it is in the smaller ones . . . the complete absence of any indication of any direct relationship between size and such measures of efficiency as have been available to us is somewhat surprising.'

The Boots and Shoes Report :

'It is impossible to draw any conclusions as to the relations between size and efficiency from this sample enquiry. . . . The enquiry seems to show rather that there are great differences between the performance of individual firms in each size group.'

What is perhaps most interesting in some of these comments is the surprise expressed by the investigators that they did not find what they expected to find.

Again, since 1948, the British Monopolies Commission has made studies of a fairly wide range of British industries. In ten of its reports the Commission has provided evidence of the relative costs and profits of different-sized firms. In only one of these cases, that relating to electronic valves and cathode-ray tubes, was it found that the largest producer showed the lowest costs. In the other cases there seems to have been no evidence that size and efficiency moved together. Thus in the Tyres Report : [1]

'It is not always the same manufacturer who shows the lowest profits or the higher costs and vice versa. Nor is it invariably the smaller manufacturers whose costs are higher and profits lower than the larger manufacturers.'

In the Report on Rubber Footwear : [2]

'Dunlop's (the largest producer) costs were considerably above those of the lowest producer in four of the five lines costed.'

[1] The Monopolies and Restrictive Practices Commission *Report on the Supply and Export of Pneumatic Tyres*, Paragraph 434.
[2] The Monopolies and Restrictive Practices Commission *Report on the Supply of Certain Rubber Footwear*, Paragraph 219.

In the Report on Metal Windows and Doors : [1]

'About three-quarters of the costs submitted by Crittall (the largest producer) and well over half those submitted by another of the three largest members were below the weighted average, while about one-quarter of the costs of each of these two companies were the lowest costs submitted. In the case of the third of the three largest companies, however, over half of the company's costings were the highest submitted and only 1% were below the weighted average.'

In the Report on Calico Printing,[2] where common prices were being charged, the evidence suggests that the profits on net turnover or on capital of the C.P.A. (the largest producer) had not been higher than those of the smaller firms. In the Report on Semi-Manufactures of Copper,[3] the Commission reached the following conclusion :

'There is no apparent correlation between the rate of profit achieved and the size of the concern, or the range of products made, or membership or non-membership of the associations, although the larger units with a wide range of production tend to achieve rates of profit at or below the average level and some concerns with a very limited range of products achieved rates of profit well above the average.'

In the Report on Electric Lamps [4] the Commission came to the conclusion that the two largest firms showed costs which were in the middle of the range for the whole industry. In the Report on Insulated Electric Wires and Cables [5] the conclusion was :

'In the samples submitted the costs of the largest cable maker, the B.I.C.C., are not among the five lowest for any one of the six types of mains cable or the seven types of rubber cable ; their costs are among the three lowest for a number of types of covered conductor, but in only one of these cases did more than four members submit costs.'

In the Report on Matches [6] the Commission showed that the largest.

[1] The Monopolies and Restrictive Practices Commission *Report on the Supply of Standard Metal Windows and Doors*, Paragraph 137.

[2] Monopolies and Restrictive Practices Commission *Report on the Process of Calico Printing*, Paragraphs 147-49.

[3] Monopolies and Restrictive Practices Commission *Report on the Supply and Export of Certain Semi-Manufactures of Copper and Copper-Based Alloys*, Paragraph 245.

[4] Monopolies and Restrictive Practices Commission *Report on the Supply of Electric Lamps*, Paragraph 215, and Table 9, Appendix 15.

[5] Monopolies and Restrictive Practices Commission *Report on the Supply of Insulated Electric Wires and Cables*, Paragraph 249.

[6] Monopolies and Restrictive Practices Commission *Report on the Supply and Export of Matches and Match-Making Machinery*, Paragraphs 166-69.

firm, responsible for more than one-half of the industry's output, was not the lowest cost producer.

V. RESEARCH AS AN ECONOMY OF SCALE

How true is it that of recent years a new kind of economy of scale has pushed itself to the forefront; that the minimum scale on which industrial research can be effectively pursued is very large but that, so conducted, it brings such high yields that the smaller firms are inevitably left behind ? At first blush, this is a rather odd idea; for the essence of an innovation is that the path to it is not known beforehand and, in the absence of a guiding direction, it seems difficult to conceive of a large team of research workers being organized to any purpose. I would have expected economists, above all men, to be slightly mystified by the idea, for they cannot really believe that the important progress in economic science in the past half century has been the result of the work of large co-ordinated teams endowed with massive resources and elaborate equipments. Science and technology, as it is related to industry, may, however, be different.

How far is it true that technical progress has become largely dependent upon the work of big industrial research laboratories which belong, and indeed could only be afforded by, large industrial firms ? With two colleagues (admittedly a team but a tiny one) I have spent a good deal of time recently attempting to draw together a few facts on this subject. The results will, I hope, shortly be published.[1] Perhaps I may be permitted to summarize the general impressions which have been formed in our minds by this work.

First, one word about definitions, which are the curse of this subject, and to which I should be devoting much more space than this paper will allow me. It is imperative to draw a distinction between innovation and the development of inventions. Of course, it cannot be drawn sharply. But some ideas clearly are more novel, some changes are more radical than others. At one end of the spectrum is invention, at the other end is development.

So far as *invention* is concerned it was found that in sixty case histories of what might be regarded as important twentieth-century inventions, the new ideas had arisen in a most bewildering assortment of circumstances and from very different sources. The individual inventor is certainly not dead. Smallish firms have had

[1] *The Sources of Invention*, by John Jewkes, David Sawers, and Richard Stillerman. Macmillan, 1958.

their successes. Very large firms have remarkable achievements to
their credit. Some idea of the range of these diverse sets of circumstances can be indicated by the brief mention of a few cases. At
one extreme is, for example, nylon : discovered in the du Pont
laboratories by W. H. Carothers, a Harvard scientist, and developed
and marketed by that firm — perhaps the greatest research scoop
of all time and a spectacular illustration of success in large-scale
research. This case has captured the public imagination and has
perhaps over-dominated our thinking on all these matters. At the
other extreme is the jet engine, a case of simultaneous invention by
Frank Whittle, whilst an Air Force cadet in England, and Von
Ohain, an engineering undergraduate in Germany. In this case
invention, and indeed the early stages of development, occurred
before the aero-engineering firms gave any encouragement or
showed any interest. The jet engine is just as clearly a case of
individual invention as was the invention of the steam engine or the
steam turbine. So far as the conditions under which their work
was carried out, the scale of resources which they employed, the
temperament and motives of the inventors themselves were concerned, Whittle might have been an eighteenth- or nineteenth-
century inventor and James Watt a twentieth-century inventor.

Or take two cases roughly in the middle of the range. The
discovery in 1929 of a method of rendering cotton and viscose
fabrics highly resistant to creasing was the outstanding, perhaps
the only, major non-mechanical advance conceived of and fully exploited within the textile industry proper in this century. The story
is a remarkable one in many ways. The new process, whilst not
wholly split off from earlier knowledge, had no extensive scientific
background. It has continued to hold the field almost unchallenged
since its discovery. The case is a rare one in that the scientists and
technologists were told the object at which they should aim and,
after seven or eight years of fruitless search, they finally scored a
resounding success. But for our present purpose the interesting
points are these. The discovery was made in the research laboratory of Tootal, Broadhurst, Lee, which is a medium-sized firm in
the Lancashire cotton industry. No one of the large chemical
firms seems to have been pressing towards the same answers. And
the original discovery, as indeed the carrying on of development,
were the result of the work of a relatively small team of research
people. This I would consider an outstanding illustration of
achievement by a moderately sized firm. Another fascinating
case of the same kind is that of the evolution and development of
hot strip rolling in the steel industry. This is perhaps the most

important twentieth-century innovation in this industry. The credit for it goes to John B. Tytus, who had had no technical education but had taken up a post in the American Rolling Mill Company in 1904. Between 1904 and 1920 he continued to work on his ideas with some encouragement from his firm. In 1923 the first continuous mill was completed and the methods patented. In some ways this is a case of individual invention, but Tytus had the backing of a steel company, which was not among the large steel operators of the United States, all of whom subsequently had to take out licences under the Armco patents.

Of course, the sample of cases we have been able to examine is small, I hope other workers will try to make it larger. Of course, we may have got the stories wrong, for there is no subject under the sun in which myth, rumour, exaggeration, and national prestige play a more distorting part than in the attribution of the credit of particular inventions (and Russia is not the only country which thinks it invented everything, every country thinks that). But I feel we have collected sufficient information to satisfy ourselves generally on two points. The one is that if, in the last fifty years or even the last thirty years, we had had the advantage only of the inventions issuing from large research laboratories in large firms, the world would be much poorer than it actually is. The other is that there is a much closer similarity as to the conditions under which invention arose between the nineteenth century and the twentieth century than is commonly supposed; the world is not such a new place as all that; what the large-scale industrial laboratory has to give us in future will probably be a supplement to, rather than a complete substitute for, innovations arising in other ways and at other points.

The *development* of inventions may be another matter; that was not, in fact, the immediate object of our study. It may be that, to an increasing degree, successful development to the point at which a product is placed on the market calls for larger and larger expenditures which, in effect, will mean that smaller firms, however they may exist in the future, are not going to make a living by putting on the market products embodying radically new ideas. I confess that it needs a good deal of courage in these days to be a sceptic when one is invited to admire, and recognize, the necessity of : wind tunnels costing millions of pounds for testing designs for supersonic aircraft; machines for getting pressures of 100,000 atmospheres or for getting within 0·1 per cent of zero temperature; or cyclotrons costing £9 million. But, recalling that even if nylon cost $20 million to develop, the development of a practical jet engine was taken quite a long way by Whittle for £20,000, let me face the hazards of being a doubter.

One interesting question is why development costs seem to be growing all the time. Is there some general law, arising out of the nature of modern science, the character of modern technology, or the pattern of modern markets, indicating that a new idea of a given inventive content will increasingly cost more to develop? If so, this would in one sense be surprising. For it might be supposed that scientific and technical advance would make for economy in the effort of development; that costly empirical testing could be replaced by quicker and cheaper scientific calculation; that cul-de-sacs could be perceived before they had been pursued too far; that scientific market research would render less hazardous the commercial introduction of a new product. Why should technical progress make everything cheaper except the process of development? Why should scientists and technologists find ways by which we can economize in everything except themselves?

A point to notice here is that the conditions under which much industrial research has been carried on in recent years have probably been conducive to prodigality, even to waste. In the United States and Great Britain, for example, between one-third and one-half of the research expenditures of manufacturing firms are met by the government. These subsidies are, of course, connected with defence. This explains why such a high proportion of the total cost of research and development is found in such industries as aircraft, electrical equipment, scientific instruments, and telecommunications. In the United States 84 per cent of the research expenditures of manufacturing firms in aircraft is met by the Federal Government; in electrical equipment, 54 per cent; in scientific instruments, 45 per cent; in telecommunications and broadcasting, 52 per cent. In a period of feverish rearmament, with these heavy state subsidies, it is hardly to be expected that great importance would be attached to economy in research and development. We must further remember that, so long as the money is there, the sky is really the limit in research and development. If men become interested in knowing what happens to chemical compounds when subjected to high pressures, it is always possible at some cost to devise a machine which will produce pressures greater than have ever been produced before. But whether such costs are justifiable is frequently a gamble, involving judgements of a highly difficult and hazardous kind.

But doubtless there are good reasons, both technical and commercial, why development costs of a magnitude unparalleled in the nineteenth century are now fairly common. The greater the stock of technical knowledge, the wider the range of effort which may be brought to bear on any development task. There are now more different possible routes for reaching a pre-determined target, more ways of spending money which offer some chance of success. In the twentieth century we have cases of widespread empirical research, such as the search for new strains of penicillin, which can be extremely costly and to which there is no close parallel in the nineteenth century. Again, on the technical side, the increased cost of modern development may be attributable to the greater caution of manufacturers in not taking their products out of the factory or moving beyond a pilot plant stage until they are convinced that full-scale manufacture is wholly feasible. The absence of such discretion in the nineteenth century sometimes led to serious mistakes and consequent loss of time and money.

On the market side, too, it is easy to see why development costs tend to rise. Products in these days are more carefully tested in the laboratory before being released to the consumer in order to avoid a loss of reputation through the appearance of unsuspected defects. More dangerous products and processes are now made use of — atomic energy, vaccines, toxic insecticides, and so on ; in these cases special security precautions must be worked out in the public interest before anything is put on to the market.

But in the few important cases of the development of an invention I have been able to look at in any detail, I find one point intriguing. The cost of development is often great because the company is in a hurry ; if the development were carried out more slowly it would be much cheaper. And the company is in a hurry because it is afraid of competition. Where the invention is available for licensing or is in the public domain, one company fears that some other will complete the development first. Even where a company has the master patents it cannot be sure that some other parallel but not infringing work is going on elsewhere which may deprive it of its commercial priority and the fruits of its work.

Development costs may, therefore, be increasing because of the increased intensity of competition arising from rapid technical progress on a very wide front. And the larger companies obviously have a healthy respect for such competitive powers in the hands of smaller firms. They have good reasons for that : success in development has not always gone to the large battalions. The first regular system of high definition television broadcasting in the world was set up in Great Britain in 1935 as the result of the work of a small team, under the direction of I. Schonberg, in Electrical and Musical Industries Ltd., a much smaller company than many others then engaged in the development of television. The improvements in insulin since 1923 have not, for the most part, been the work of large industrial research laboratories. And the same may be said to be true in the history of the development of the cotton picker, air-conditioning equipment, automatic transmissions, power steering, magnetic recording, and synthetic detergents.

I hasten to say, however, that I am not reaching any conclusions here ; the important point I have to make is that we badly need to know more about development and about how and where it has occurred. It is really not sufficient to talk in terms of a few cases, spectacular though these may be.

VI. FOREIGN TRADE AS AN ESCAPE FROM SMALLNESS

I fear I have strayed far from the immediate point with which this conference is concerned. But I imagine that nearly everything I have said is mildly in favour of the view that the mere size of a country is not of itself a very important determining influence of its industrial achievements. If the crazier man-made blocks to trade were absent, no country, provided of course the other conditions were favourable, need suffer greatly from the fact that it has only a small domestic market, whatever branch of industry to which the native genius of its people might call it.

Some blocks to trade, not government created, there will presumably always be. I suppose that there are a lot of intangible reasons, if I may come back to a point I raised earlier, why the poppet valves on the Cadillac (if the Cadillac in these days has anything so old-fashioned as a poppet valve), even if not made by General Motors itself, are more likely to be made by an American manufacturer than a manufacturer in Sweden, Switzerland, France, or Great Britain. The proximity of supplier and customer must be a help in technical affairs where things may go wrong and have to be put right quickly ; between one country and another there are a thousand and one minor differences in engineering techniques, methods of producing drawings, standard specifications of dimensions, and so on, all of which will give something of a pull to the poppet valve manufacturer in Detroit.

But even here I would be somewhat optimistic. One of the sharper shocks I received in the last war was the recognition that it was extremely difficult, and for a time indeed it seemed virtually impossible, for an American manufacturer to produce a British designed aero-engine, the Merlin, which would fit into a British-built aeroplane body. Even with the best will in the world, the task of making exactly the same product on both sides of the Atlantic seemed to be frustrated by an incredible tangle of minor but compounding complexities. In the event, this problem was solved — but only by recourse to an almost unparalleled degree of co-operation on every level between Rolls Royce and Packards.

Yet that type of close international collaboration has in the post-war world apparently become much more common. Rolls Royce itself has provided one example by building engines for fitting into airframes' of many foreign designs and it has close links, for other types of work, with a number of American companies. This illustration is not unique among British companies. I have no doubt that firms, such as Sulzer Bros. or Brown Boveri in Switzerland, and equally famous engineering firms in other smaller countries, are doing much the same thing. And one might therefore hope and expect that the creation of a more perfect international market in this way would run down into the smaller bits and pieces that are finally drawn together in complex assemblies of motor-cars, aeroplanes, electronic equipment, and so on ; and that, even if it proved to be true that the main assembling points would remain few and located mainly in the larger countries, that need be no serious deterrent to the exploitation of the authentic industrial abilities of smaller countries.

STATISTICAL APPENDIX

THE SIZE OF FACTORIES

UNITED STATES *

	Average number of employees	Volume of production per establishment (1947 = 100)
1947	59·3	100
1950	59·7	109
1951	59·5	110
1952	60·1	112

* Establishments with 1 or more employees.

CANADA *

	Average number of employees	Volume of production per establishment (1939=100)
1939	53·4	100
1944	78·1	173
1950	59·8	129
1951	61·2	132
1952	59·8	128
1953	61·2	136

* Establishments with 5 or more employees (wage earners and salary earners).

AUSTRALIA *

	Average number of employees	Volume of production per factory (1945–6=100)
1945–46	37·8	100
1949–50	35·2	100
1951–52	35·1	98

* Factories with 5 or more employees (wage earners and salary earners).

GERMANY *

	Average number of employees	Volume of production per establishment (1953=100)
1953	108·2	100
1954	114·2	112

* Establishments with over 10 employees.

GREAT BRITAIN *

AVERAGE NUMBER OF EMPLOYEES BY INDUSTRY GROUPS

	1950	1952	1955
Treatment of Non-Metalliferous Mining Products other than Coal	114	114	116
Chemical and Allied Trades	164	170	195
Metal Manufacture	272	272	287
Engineering	189	198	209
Vehicles	150	156	182
Precision Instruments	91	93	102
Textiles	145	130	139
Leather and Leather Goods	63	55	60
Clothing	85	79	82
Food, Drink, and Tobacco	92	96	116
Paper and Printing	101	100	111
Wood, Cork, etc.	81	80	92
Total Manufacturing	126	127	140

* Establishments with 11 employees and more.

Chapter 7

SIZE OF MARKETS, SCALE OF FIRMS, AND THE CHARACTER OF COMPETITION

BY

C. D. EDWARDS
University of Chicago

I. THE DIFFICULTIES OF MEASUREMENT

ECONOMIC theorists attempt to make the term 'market' one of precision, pertaining to a single commodity and to a community of buyers and sellers who are so intimately associated with one another that a single price emerges from their bargaining. Even small countries are large enough to contain, for most commodities, more than one market thus defined. Presumably we are not concerned here with the variety of market magnitudes to be found within a single country and the influence of this variety upon industrial organization. Our interest is in differences from country to country in the size of business enterprises and the vigour of competition. Accordingly, I shall discuss the effect upon these, not of the size of the market, but of the size of the national economy.

Unfortunately, the concept of a national economy is fuzzy and is incapable of exact measurement. The size of a nation's economy is not even approximately expressed in the area or population of the national state. It is roughly reflected by the size of the gross national product. But in considering the relation between the organization of industry and the size of the economy, we must beware of circular reasoning if we measure the economy by such an income standard ; for the gross national product is probably affected by industrial organization, and it is difficult to separate the sequences that run from size to organization from those that run from organization to size.

The boundaries appropriate to the concept of an economy are sometimes not those of the national state. Within states having a large area, economic life may be regionalized to such an extent that, for many purposes, the country contains more than one economy. The economy of Brazil is thus segmented, and in the United States the Pacific seaboard is partially separated from the Centre and East by mountains, deserts, and arid plains. Moreover, international trade may be important enough to extend an economy beyond the national borders. The precise economic significance of the national frontier is highly variable. It differs from country to country with the importance of trade barriers, obstacles to international investment and payment, and obstacles to the movement of population. For any one country it differs from time to time. For one country at one time there is a complex pattern, with different degrees of segregation applied to different commodities and with commodities treated differently from population movements and perhaps from investments. Thus the conception of the national economy is necessarily loose, and generalizations as to its significance must be equally loose.

These ambiguities are peculiarly troublesome in approaching problems of size ; for there is probably a difference in degree of segregation between the economies of large states and those of small states. It is usually impossible for a small state to be self-sufficient. Liberal import policies are usually necessary, and substantial exports are often essential. Countries that are large in the sense that they have a large gross domestic product based upon a relatively large population and large area have the opportunity to be more self-sufficient and sometimes grasp it. Moreover, a state that is large in area but not compact may be peculiarly susceptible to regionalization. So far as there are such differences, as well as differences in gross product, between big and little countries, the apparent difference in the size of their economies is likely to be deceptive.

The concept of the business enterprise is even more tricky than that of the economy. The techniques of business organization have outrun the conceptual apparatus of economics. We still talk as though a business enterprise consists of a single legal entity controlling a single plant that produces a single commodity, and, therefore, finding its opportunities in a single market. In fact, however, one plant may produce several commodities and serve several markets. One legal entity may control several plants, thus increasing the practicability of diversification and the likelihood of a gap between the unit of control and the unit of technical efficiency. One business undertaking may express itself in a considerable number of corporate entities bound together with varying degrees of tightness by ownership, common management, and communities of interest created by contractual arrangements. The linkage among these corporate entities is sometimes so complex as to arouse dispute as to where the boundaries of the undertaking are located. For example, in the United States the Supreme Court recently held, in effect, that

Du Pont controlled General Motors after a lower court had denied the existence of such control.

Since these elaborations of the scope of business enterprise are closely related to the size of the concern, they are peculiarly important for topics having to do with size. The Federal Trade Commission recently provided pertinent information about the diversification of the thousand largest manufacturing enterprises in the United States. Only 78 of these thousand concerns confined their production to one class of products and only 134 limited themselves to a single producing establishment.[1] The most diversified concern shipped products that fell into 129 product classes. The most diversified establishment produced more than 20 product classes. The company with the largest number of points of production had 358 manufacturing establishments. There was a substantial difference in diversification between the larger and smaller companies. Among the largest 50 companies, 33 made shipments in more than 20 product classes. In the next group of 50, only 16 did so, and in the remaining 900, only 32. Among the largest 50 companies, 26 operated in more than 15 industries. Among the next 50, only 16 did so, and among the remaining 900, only 28. Though the diversification of most of the thousand was appreciable, it increased with the size of the concern. The bigness of the largest enterprises was derived partly from their spread across products and industries, rather than their dominance of single-industry markets.[2]

Similarly, the complexity of the structure of control and the discrepancy between the size of the legal entity and the size of the undertaking tend to be greatest in the largest companies. To acquaint junior executives with the maze of holding companies and interlocking official and contractual relationships that constitute its structure, one large American corporate combine has offered a formal course on company organization that meets three times a week for an academic year. Corporate structures including scores of subsidiaries at one or more levels of subordination are common among the largest companies. Some of the subsidiary relationships rest upon majority stock ownership ; others upon minority interests that give effective control. Sometimes two or more parent companies participate in the ownership of certain subsidiaries. For

[1] The Commission's study followed the standard industrial classification, in which sub-classes are indicated by numbers with more digits. In this discussion, the term 'industry' is used to mean 4-digit classes and 'product class' to mean 5-digit classes. Within a single product class there are often several products.

[2] Federal Trade Commission, *Industrial Concentration and Product Diversification in the Thousand Largest Manufacturing Companies*, U.S. Government Printing Office, 1957.

example, much of the oil production of the Middle East is controlled by a company the stock of which is owned by five corporate stock-holders, of whom four have equal holdings amounting to 23·75 per cent each. Two of these corporate stock-holders are, in turn, subsidiaries of two great oil companies and a third is the corporate device by which two other great oil companies share its holdings equally. In such situations, the boundaries of the business enterprise are, to say the least, indistinct, but they clearly are not set by the limits of a single product, a single market, or a single legal entity.

The third concept, the character of competition, is not quantitative. It has to do with the quality of institutional arrangements and modes of behaviour. There is no need to retrace the history of the controversy over workable competition in order to make the point that the standards by which the vigour of competition is to be determined are matters of enduring dispute and that often the application of these controversial standards to particular bodies of fact does not produce agreed conclusions.

What, then, is the relation of the size of that complexly indefinite thing, the national economy, to that complexly indefinite thing, the business enterprise, and to that controversial thing, the character of competition ?

II. THE RELATION OF THE SIZE OF THE ENTERPRISE TO THE SIZE OF THE ECONOMY

Even in the simplest case only a part of the answer is simple. If we exclude our greatest difficulties by hypothesis, as economists often permit themselves to do, we may assume a model in which the economies of large countries are not regionalized and the economies of all countries are neatly segregated at their national boundaries. Within each of the nation-wide markets of each economy are enterprises confining themselves to single products and organized as easily identifiable entities. In such a model, the size of the national economy would limit the size of the commodity markets and the size of these, in turn, would limit the size and number of business enterprises. In larger markets there would be room for more enterprises of a given size. In smaller markets, large enterprises would be possible only with highly concentrated production that would probably change the character of competition. Since there would be more larger markets in the larger economy, concentration, with its effects upon competition, would be more common in the smaller economy.

However, even in the smaller countries, concentration would appear only in a segment of the economy. The sizes of markets and of business enterprises would differ from one industry to another, and thus many industries would be capable of supporting numerous enterprises. Concentration would be found in those industries the country was barely large enough to support.

But even in this model, the significance of the result is not clear. We cannot safely assume that for any one industry or product there is a particular size of enterprise that best expresses the economies of scale and that, therefore, the opportunities for bigness provided by the market have a fixed relationship to technological performance. The fact that in many industries concerns of widely different sizes continue to exist side by side suggests that, if there are penalties in being bigger or smaller than a narrowly defined optimum, they are not very great. Scattered and inconclusive cost studies seem to suggest, but not prove, that costs of production may remain unchanged over a considerable range of output and that it is common for the lowest costs to appear at neither the top nor the bottom when enterprises are arranged in order of size.[1] We must distrust both the view that there is an identifiable optimum size and that it is to be found in the biggest enterprises.

Moreover, we should not presume that even the one-product, one-market enterprises of our model attain sizes that express merely the economies of scale. If bigness increases bargaining power or gives any of the profits of monopoly, it is worth pursuing whether or not it increases efficiency. It is reasonable to expect that, even if the size that is most efficient can be sharply defined, concerns will often try to grow bigger and will sometimes succeed. Thus, it is not safe to assume that when the size of the market limits the size of an enterprise it is limiting productive efficiency, nor that in a market where there is not room for enough big enterprises to preserve competition the choice is between monopoly and inefficiency.

Moreover, while it may be true that in small countries the market limits the size of an enterprise more often than in large countries, it is not clearly true that each increment of growth in the national economy tends to increase the average size of enterprises. In large industries there appear to be conflicting tendencies.

---

[1] Though external economies are relevant to the economies of scale in a discussion of the bigness of an industry or of a national economy, they are not pertinent here. An increase in the size of an industry would affect its external economies, whether or not there was a change in the size of enterprises in the industry.

Increasing mechanization, self-service, vertical integration, increase in the number of establishments under a single ownership — all these become possible and sometimes take place, with a consequent increase in the size of the biggest concerns. By sub-division of processes, more narrow specialization of establishments and separate ownership of the specialized activities also become possible. These developments create opportunities for enterprises smaller than would previously have been practicable. Indeed, the trends toward increase and decrease in size are likely to be commingled. The large producer may buy an increasing number of components for his product from small producers. The large manufacturer may sell chiefly to small distributors and the large distributor may buy chiefly from small manufacturers. In part, such opposite tendencies express the diverse technological opportunities created by the growth of an industry. In part, they express the strategy of power, for the big concern is more clearly powerful in transactions with small concerns than in transactions with other big ones. Thus, bigness and smallness may both be promoted by the growth of an economy or a market.

If, disregarding these complexities, we assume that in the larger markets of larger economies the level of industrial concentration tends to be higher, the character of competition is doubtless affected by this fact. But we cannot safely assume that the effect is necessarily to reduce competition. The degree of concentration is important as one of the significant conditions pertinent to a diagnosis of the patterns of behaviour of an industry. Thus, if concentration is very low, we need not look for monopoly or oligopoly, and we may expect that if there is collusion it will be overtly manifested. We may also assume that the tactics of competition are those appropriate to a market in which one's competitors are anonymous. If most of the industry is controlled by a few concerns, we may assume that the tactics of competition consist in rivalry with identified competitors, and we may inquire whether the circumstances and policies of these competitors are so similar that each concern can rely upon the oligopolistic forbearance of the others. We may also look for signs that forbearance has evolved into collusion. If concentration is still higher, we may look for monopolistic policies in the largest enterprise. Except at the highest levels of concentration, it is not certain that competition must be impaired, even though its nature may have been changed. The significance of a change in concentration is substantial if the change is great enough to substitute competition with identified rivals for anonymous competition or to remove the possibility of one kind of impairment of competition and substitute another. But significant changes do not appear continuously in small increments from the lowest concentration to the highest. Instead, there are likely to be sensitive stretches, within which the importance of change is great, and insensitive stretches within which it is slight, particularly in the lower part of the concentration scale. Moreover, a given level of concentration, as measured by any of the accepted techniques of measurement, may actually reflect different patterns of relative size among the largest enterprises and different patterns of relative size and number among the rest of those in the industry, and these differences may have important influences upon the competitive result. Both for these reasons and because concentration is only one of several influences bearing upon the vigour of competition, we cannot assume that in all cases more concentration means less competition. The symptom justifies an inquiry, but does not justify a diagnosis without inquiry.

III. NATIONAL AND INTERNATIONAL CONCERNS

If we discard the assumptions of this simplified model, much of the foregoing analysis must be abandoned. Enterprises may be big because they are diversified. They, and the markets they serve, may extend across national boundaries. Bigness may be achieved, not only through the growth of a legal entity, but through merger and other forms of affiliation. With these facts recognized, the market is not necessarily confined within the national boundary and the large enterprise is typically not confined within a single industry nor necessarily confined within a single country.

This pattern is much closer to reality than the previous one. That there is a substantial amount of international trade and investment and even a limited amount of international population movement is the starting-point for a discussion of the economic relations between countries. That great business enterprises are typically international may not be equally well recognized, but it is true. At the outbreak of the Second World War, N. V. Philips had subsidiaries in the United Kingdom and four of its dominions, eleven European countries, nine Latin American countries, and two Middle Eastern countries. One or more of the three largest oil companies had producing, refining, or distributing subsidiaries, several or joint, in every significant country that would admit them. The pattern of international operation varied with the political climate. Where national states imposed no handicap upon foreign corporations, productive or distributive establishments were often set up in various countries under a single corporate name. Where foreign concerns were excluded or handicapped, similar establishments were set up through corporate subsidiaries domestically organized but controlled abroad. Where a colour of domestic ownership was desirable, minority stock interests were sold to nationals of the countries that issued the corporate charters. Where even this arrangement was forbidden, the international enterprise often found it possible to do business by cloaking its control under the mask of trusteeships, intermediate dummy holding companies, or long-term contracts that established an effective pooling of interests among concerns that were nominally separate. Even under the stimulus of the Second World War, belligerent governments did not wholly succeed in breaking the ties between the portions of great corporate combines that lay on opposite sides of the battle lines.

Where the size of single markets does not set limits for corporate size, a corporation may grow big by embracing a wider segment of industry horizontally and vertically. Even if it encounters obstacles in buying and selling beyond the national boundaries, it may, like the Hudson's Bay Company or Union Minière, become large in a relatively small economy. Indeed, if the economy is small enough to produce conditions of monopoly or of non-competitive oligopoly in the markets in which a relatively large concern buys and sells, these conditions may intensify the incentives for that concern to grow by vertical integrations. At most, the size of the country can have only a minor effect upon the size of the business enterprises in the country.

However, the size of the country probably does have a significant effect upon the structure of large enterprises. If the national economy is small, a domestic concern can become big only by diversification. If the economy reaches beyond the national boundaries, a concern may also grow big by following it there. In large countries, the large enterprises may be — but need not be and usually are not — domestic concerns that limit themselves wholly to a single large industry. In small countries they cannot be of this kind. They must be local branches of large international combines or be diversified or both.

The size of the country may affect the quality of competition by affecting the number and structure rather than the size of business enterprises. In industries that do not contain large diversified enterprises, cartelization is likely to be more difficult in larger countries because the enterprises to be cartelized are more numerous there. In industries occupied by large diversified concerns a similar effect probably will be produced in a different way. When large diversified concerns approach one another as competitors, their substantial resources and varied experience enable each concern to enter new lines of activity more readily than could one newly established or highly specialized. The exposure of each large diversified enterprise to the potential competition of the others is a check upon oligopolistic and monopolistic policies in the exploitation of markets in which production is highly concentrated. When such large diversified enterprises are in collusion, they usually try to allocate fields of business activity so as to minimize their competition with one another. Their incentives to compete or to agree are derived from the strategy of the total position of each in the various markets it occupies or could readily enter, and cannot be deduced by examining their productive potential in a single market. In general, however, if there are many diversified concerns, the incentive to compete is substantial and the opportunity to work out satisfactory terms of agreement is slight; whereas if there are few diversified concerns competition is less attractive and agreement is easier. In a small country, unless concerns are international, there is room for fewer larger diversified enterprises than in a large one. Hence, unless foreign trade is as easy as domestic trade, the competitive aspects of diversification are likely to be less important in small countries and the allocative aspects more important.

Similarly, in a small country, a specialized enterprise, if large, is likely to be large because it is international; and its domestic segment is likely to be a small part of its total size. The significant rivals of an international concern, whether or not it is diversified, are usually other large international companies. The policies of such companies toward one another are determined, not by their interests in a single country, considered separately, but by their position *vis-à-vis* one another in all of the various countries in which they are or might be in contact. Like the diversified companies in a single country, these international companies evolve strategies appropriate to their respective total positions, with such subordination of advantage in particular markets as may be necessary. An international company may compete vigorously in one country if it is doing so everywhere, or if it regards that country as a testing ground in which to show its strength before negotiating with its rivals. It is unlikely to be lured into competition in one country if a competitive policy there is inconsistent with its interest in a broad international agreement. Like diversified companies in single countries, international enterprises often have incentives to allocate markets in order to avoid competition ; and since national markets can be readily segregated, the segments that are allocated are likely to be the national markets of particular countries. When a part of the world is thus territorially allocated, competition in the remaining territory is often avoided by organizing joint subsidiaries to exploit unallocated areas or by agreeing upon sales quotas in countries jointly occupied. So far as the attractiveness and feasibility of such international cartelization depend upon the size and number of business enterprises, the relevant question is the degree of concentration in the industry throughout the world ; not in the portion of the industry that lies in a particular country.

Nevertheless, the impact of an international cartel is likely to be greater upon a small country than upon a large one. In countries so small that there is room for few concerns in the relevant industry, the impact is at its maximum. Countries in which there is no significant domestic production will be allocated as export markets, with recognition of the historical interests and current bargaining strength of the members of the cartel. Countries in which there is only one producing enterprise are likely to be allocated to that enterprise ; and thereafter entry from outside is not to be expected and the appearance of new domestic competition is less probable than before. Countries with very few enterprises producing in the relevant industry may be reduced to single-enterprise countries by the fusion of the local establishments of the members of the cartel ; or they may experience the gentle and decorous competition that takes place among concerns that have accepted quota restrictions upon sales. Where the domestic portion of the relevant industry is larger and the participating concerns are more numerous, the cartel will be less effective. Participation in the international cartel is likely to be possible only if the members of the industry are first brought together in a domestic cartel. But the members of the domestic industry cannot always agree, and where they do so the agreement is sometimes unstable. Indeed, some enterprises are likely to be wholly domestic, and diversities of interest between concerns that are wholly domestic and concerns that are international may be great enough to constitute major obstacles to domestic agreement. Moreover, if domestic governmental policy opposes cartelization, the domestic enterprises can be kept out of both domestic and international agreements. Hence, small countries are more vulnerable than large ones to monopolistic developments at home that are part of international programmes of cartelization.

IV. EFFECTS UPON COMPETITION

But though these aspects of the size of a country probably are significant, I suspect that their effect upon competition is overshadowed by other less direct influences. To discuss these adequately would require more time and space than is available here. I shall confine myself, therefore, to the statement of a point of view and of some of the principal propositions upon which it rests, illustrating the relevance of these propositions rather than arguing their validity. I do this with deference, since, in part, I shall trespass upon subjects assigned to other participants in this conference. I hope I may be forgiven for any appearance of dogmatism introduced into the discussion by my brevity.

One of the most important ways in which the size of a country may affect the character of its competition seems to be through the effect of size upon cultural variety and upon the rate of institutional and technological change. Countries with a homogeneous culture probably tend to be less competitive than countries that are culturally more diversified. Both collusion and monopoly flourish best in coherent groups. Group solidarity promotes collusion. Similarity among members of the group limits the variety of competitive ventures that must be suppressed. But where the customs, ways of thought, and loyalties of different segments of the business community are diverse, agreement among these segments is likely to be difficult and the members of each segment are likely to offer a different kind of competitive threat to the rest.

Similarly, countries where change is slow probably tend to be less competitive than those where change is rapid. Where technology and markets change only slightly or slowly, powerful enterprises can flourish without showing great foresight or great flexibility. Where markets are shifting and technology is changing, experiment is attractive and the enterprise that is willing to compete can explore the new possibilities before a would-be monopoly can reconcile itself to disturbance of the *status quo*. In a changing economy, new products and new producers appear. Thus the demand encountered by established concerns in selling established commodities is made more elastic and less susceptible to market exploitation.

The homogeneous and unchanging economy tends to be overgrown by a tangle of vested interests and restrictive practices, some rooted in formal arrangements and some in hardened customs. In a heterogeneous and changing economy, as in woodland that is often cleared, there is room for new growth and opportunity for new kinds of vegetation.

This general relationship is significantly modified by the patent laws. Most industrial countries grant monopolies for a limited period of time as a reward for invention. In some segments of industry, business enterprises have found it desirable to extend their own patent estates and avoid being controlled by the patents of others through a process of organized research that undoubtedly makes technology more dynamic. Yet they have assembled patents and exchanged patent rights in ways that sometimes convert the monopoly of particular inventions into monopoly of particular industries. Through a succession of patents, they have prevented the time limits of the patents from terminating these broader monopolies. Even in such cases, however, there is impressive evidence to support the view that monopolistic incentives tend to retard the introduction of new processes while fomenting the discovery of them. Moreover, the technological competition that underlies the patent monopolies has usually produced a pattern of moderated and unstable monopoly, in various respects less objectionable than monopolies in industries not exposed to rapid change.

If competition is stimulated by cultural variety and change, it should follow that countries exposed to the interaction of cultures tend to be more competitive than those that are culturally homogeneous and that countries with rapidly changing economies tend to be more competitive than those whose economies are stable. One should expect the maritime states to be generally more competitive than those inland, at least prior to the age of air transportation. One should not be surprised that competitive policy and the theory of competition came to first flower in England, the foremost sea trader.

Diversity and change are somewhat more likely to be associated with big countries than with small ones. Small countries tend to be culturally unified. Large countries are less apt to be so. Though modern systems of communication and transportation have tended to break down cultural diversity in large populations, the influences of varying climate, resources, industries, regional traditions, and the like have not disappeared in the large states. Indeed, as the United States has come to take its economic unity more for granted, there appears to have been a revival of self-conscious regionalism. The lack of homogeneity has clearly contributed to the development and to the effectiveness of the American anti-trust policy. Our first anti-trust law was passed largely because of the resistance of the farmers and small business-men of the West to restrictive controls by power groups on the Eastern seaboard. To this day, there is often a sectional cleavage in congressional votes upon important matters of anti-trust policy.

Moreover, the breadth and diversity of our economy has facilitated private efforts to escape from restrictive controls. One recurrent problem is the gradual consolidation of institutional arrangements and technological methods in an industrial centre, followed by collective resistance to new entrants and new ways of doing things. A common escape is for the newcomers to establish themselves in a locality in which the industry has not previously flourished, to try their new methods there, and, by competition, to bring about reluctant changes or the withering away of the industry in the old industrial centre. In a large country, the shifts in industrial location through which competition is thus recurrently renewed are both feasible and tolerable. In a small country, the reach of the vested interests might extend to the national boundaries and the government may curb new competition from other countries as inconsistent with the national interest.

Technological and institutional change are more probable in large countries not only because of the possibility of escape from restriction by vested interests, but also because there are more resources to invest in change. The large country has more funds for research, a field for experiment wide enough to try a greater number of new proposals, and more trained people who may develop new ideas. The statistical probability of a flash of genius is presumably no greater per thousand of population in a big country than in a small one, but there are not only more people to have flashes ; there are also the technicians to carry out a systematic programme of research large enough to explore all the variant possibilities implicit in a particular bright idea. Forms of business organization and market organization, as well as technology in the narrow sense, are likely to be more dynamic for these reasons. Moreover, in the technological field the fact that the limits of any single patent run with the national boundaries means that the best market for a patent is likely to lie in a large country and that the expenses of development are most likely to be quickly recovered in a large economy. The flow of technological ideas across national boundaries is likely to be more conspicuous from the small countries to the large than in the reverse direction.

Thus the dynamic forces of variety and change that foster competition tend to be stronger in big countries than in small ones.

To suggest that these influences exist is not, of course, to weigh their absolute or relative importance. Other influences — cultural, economic, and technical — can also be related to the size of firms and to the vigour of competition.[1]

Moreover, the dynamic quality of a culture cannot be adequately summarized in its variety and susceptibility to change. The willingness of cultural groups to receive new ideas is itself subject to change and to control through educational processes. A homogeneous society may look curiously and experimentally at the world. A multi-variant culture may enrich itself through cross-fertilization of ideas or may exhaust itself in the struggles of its various elements for supremacy. Political policy may encourage or repress change and may tolerate or curb restrictive practices. The boundaries of national states, the trade barriers at national boundaries, the policies of large enterprises, the changes in population, the changes in technology — these are not invariant natural phenomena but complex manifestations of human institutions, in which both purpose and understanding play a significant part. It is probably true that the economies of large states tend to be more competitive than those of small states. But it is probably equally true, and more important, that the economies of states which foster competition tend to be more competitive than those of states which do not regard competition as a major aim of public policy.

[1] In the United States, for example, the influence of the frontier and of the democratic political tradition were obviously significant. A large part of the population had come to North America to escape institutions, political and economic, that were thought to be unsatisfactory. Frontier conditions encouraged self-reliance, emphasis upon opportunity and feelings of personal equality that had a sustained influence in breaking down restrictions of various kinds. The fetters of custom, status, and vested interest were weak enough to be broken.

The influence of the democratic tradition is equally clear. The United States was founded upon revolt against autocratic absentee government, and the policies of that government in supporting vested economic interests were central among the grievances that produced revolution. It was a short step from belief in the diffusion of political power to belief in the diffusion of economic power.

PART IV

SIZE OF NATION AND DYNAMIC ADJUSTMENT

Chapter 8

THE PROBLEMS OF DEVELOPING COUNTRIES

BY

C. N. VAKIL and P. R. BRAHMANANDA

University of Bombay

I. CONCEPTS OF A NATION AND ITS SIZE

THE relationship between geographical area, population size, and
the level of economic efficiency and the rate of development is one
of the leading topics of current economic discussion. The issue
has gained considerable political and practical importance because
of the various efforts being made among both the developed and
the under-developed countries to work out new patterns of market
alignment. This paper concentrates attention upon the analysis of
the way in which the factor of size in respect of both population and
area can affect the nature and rate of development. Section I
differentiates between the economic and political concepts of
'nationhood'. Section II examines the nature of the supposed
links in the relationship between size and the level of economic
efficiency. Section III works out the concept of optimum size of a
nation, taking into account the crucial economic factors. Section IV
examines the various possible types of effects which differences in
size along with other factors can exert upon the dynamic processes.
Section V examines the special problems of under-developed
countries vis-à-vis size. It briefly deals with the possibilities and
implications of market expansion programmes. Section VI draws
attention to the economic consequences of the pursuit of a policy of
aggressive 'nationhood'.

Among political scientists there is considerable discussion about
what exactly constitutes a nation. Various factors, like geographical
contiguity, ethnic and racial homogeneity, common heritage in
regard to cultural and other values, allegiance to a common political
head, prevalence of common aspirations and ambitions, are included
in the concept of nation. The clarification of the above concept
from an economic point of view has not, however, received due
attention. For example, mere geographical, racial, climatic, cultural,

or political factors alone are not important here. The economist's concept of nation would include some assumptions concerning the absence of tariff barriers within the geographical limits of a nation, prevalence of a high degree of mobility between different groups and sectors in the economy, the existence of a certain similarity in regard to the strength and intensity of reactions to various forms of economic stimuli, and such other factors. In other words, the term 'nation', when looked at from an economic point of view, assumes the existence of a fair measure of *economic homogeneity*. This would imply that the different sections of the people have somewhat similar outlook in their want and preference patterns in regard to commodities and jobs ; that a fair degree of uniformity would prevail in regard to the response of individuals and different groups regarding changes in prices, wages, interest rates, profit rates, tax changes, etc. ; and that there would be some similarity in regard to the choice structure between effort and income ; and so on.

The term 'Size' is somewhat ambiguous and may refer to either area or population. Large-sized countries may be sparsely populated, while small-sized countries may have high density. From the economist's point of view, geographical size, other conditions given, has significance because of the possibility that a large-sized country may possess a larger quantity of natural resources or a greater diversity in their supply and conjunctural advantages in climate. Thus, the larger the size, the larger the resource base, and other conditions given, the greater the *capacity* to have a larger-sized population. On the other hand, if we emphasize the population aspect in size, we find that some countries with a small geographical size have a very large population though with low *per capita* incomes and poor productivity levels. A large-sized country may, however, have a relatively smaller population but with high *per capita* standards and productivity levels. Thus, contradictory trends in living standards and productivity levels will be found if we try to correlate them positively with the geographical area and size of population.

The economist, however, emphasizes the significance of geographical and population size upon the size of the market. But the concept of 'market' has both demand and supply aspects. A country large in size and in population may, none the less, have low incomes, just as another country small in size but also large in population may yet have low incomes. Thus, the level of *per capita* income is, or perhaps can be, more important than the size of population or the geographical area. From the point of view of potentialities, large population or even large size may be of limited significance. In fact, largeness in area may even become a handicap in this respect. There is, however, the possibility that a large geographical size would, other conditions given, connote a richer supply base, and if the supply base is also rich from a potential point of view so that there is a large gap between the actual levels of utilization of resources and their potential supply, a large population might connote the possibility of higher incomes and hence of a larger-sized market. Other conditions given, if resources are abundant in relation to population, productivity levels can potentially rise, and the economy has considerable scope of expansion, the process having increasing returns.

Thus geographical size is by itself not very significant, even if we assume that there is a fairly similar degree of economic homogeneity between the countries of equal size. Further information about the relative endowment of different countries in regard to natural resources both in quantity and quality is needed. We want to know whether there are substantial climatic differences ; whether the size and growth of population are fairly similar ; whether the pattern of institutions, sets of laws, socio-religious customs, are similar, and so on. These different factors are closely interrelated and it would be difficult to single out any particular factor as *the* determining influence. Hence, so many diverse factors affect the economic well-being of different countries that it is extremely difficult to isolate the factor of size to ascertain its impact upon the dynamic course and prospects of an economy.

Thus, we find in actual practice that two countries with equal size in the world today may have very great differences in regard to the current levels of standard of living and the potentialities for such standards in future. We also find that some of the countries with a smaller size have been able to have very high standards of living. They have attained high levels of improvement in methods of production technique and have large capital stock as compared to countries much bigger in size. Nor even among the developed countries does it follow that the capital stock is proportionate to geographical size or population, or that the actual standards of living tend to remain the same or grow with size. In fact, we cannot draw any definitive conclusion that a small country is invariably worse off in relation to a large country or that a small country is invariably better off than a large country or that the size of a country is a matter of indifference. It is just not possible to derive the level of development from the size alone.

II. SIZE AND EFFICIENCY

At the outset it may appear that a large country, other conditions equal, would have greater advantages as against a small country. For example, firstly, whatever the size of a country, some minimum expenditure has to be incurred in regard to the maintenance of administration. Administrative overheads do not increase proportionately with size. It is true that a small country is put to some handicap in this respect because of the indivisibility in this item of expenditure. Secondly, whatever the size of the country, certain minimum expenditure has to be incurred in regard to defence. It is very difficult in modern days to distinguish between military expenditure needed in some absolute sense for defence and that which is necessary to maintain the relative military position of the country. Defence expenditure is not necessarily proportionate to size. A small country is again at a disadvantage here. Thirdly, there are a number of items of expenditure on transportation, communications, and other public utility services which are generally a function of size. Here again, a small country is to a certain extent at a disadvantage. Fourthly, a country's bargaining position *vis-à-vis* other countries is not determined purely by economic forces. Relative size may play an important part in this case ; in other words, there may be special advantages in the case of a large country. The most important advantages arise, however, from the spread of the cost of the establishment and maintenance of various economic institutions. They arise from the common currency, credit and exchange arrangements resulting from an integrated monetary and banking system. The large costs of the establishment and operation of scientific laboratories and the technical training institutes can also be spread out. Another factor is the possibility of the development of specialization. It may also be possible to diversify the economic structure.

The purely economic argument in respect of size runs as follows :

(*a*) The larger the size of the firms, the lower the unit cost of production. This is because of economies of scale, which arise on account of indivisibilities.

(*b*) The larger the aggregate market, the larger would be the size of the firms. Here the assumption is that an increase in the size of the market would imply an expansion in the size of the firms. This in its turn would lead to the gains arising on account of the economies of scale.

(*c*) The larger the size of a country, the larger would be the aggregate market. The assumption here is that the larger the size, the larger would be the resource base, and the larger the population, the larger would be the magnitude of demand.

The argument about the superiority of a large-sized nation is based upon the above three critical links. If the argument is to stand, there must first be economies of scale, which cannot be exploited if the average size of the firm is small, given the aggregate market ; secondly, an increase in the size of the market must lead automatically to an increase in the size of the firms ; thirdly, an increase in the size of a country must lead to an increase in the size of the market. If the reasoning is to be valid, it is necessary that it should be wholly impossible to reap the economies simply through reorganization, with given size in regard to the market. In other words, a number of economies are derived entirely from the aggregate size of the firms.

It is difficult to acquiesce in the view that all the above links would necessarily hold. For example, it is not clear whether the size of the firms is positively correlated with the size of the nations. In a broad sense, it is true that there *are* economies of scale to the *economy* in the sense that an expansion in size gets over various types of indivisibilities. The argument in respect of positive correlation of efficiency with size must assume that it is not possible to overcome the indivisibilities through any method other than an expansion of the size. Perhaps the most difficult link to be satisfied is that between the size of the market and the size of the country. It is clear that a mere increase in size may or may not connote an actual expansion of the market. In the case of several underdeveloped countries facing acute population pressure it almost certainly does not. As pointed out earlier, the economist's argument assumes not only that an increase in size would permit an increase in the capacity to produce but also that such conditions exist that the increase in income is realized in practice.

III. THE OPTIMUM SIZE OF A NATION

Assuming, however, that the above links do operate, it appears that, for a large country, there are increasing returns arising on account of indivisibilities (as also certain windfall advantages). From this it may be reasonable to infer that, as in the case of individual firms, there is an optimum size for a country from an economic point of view. Such 'optimum' has normally to be subjected to various qualifying considerations.

A preliminary clarification of such an 'optimum size' needs to be given. Assuming that the average density of population remains the same, if a slight *increase* in area and in population leads to a long-period *increase* in the average net product per worker, then the current size of the country may be said to be less than optimum. If a slight *increase* in area and population with constant density leads to a *decrease* in the per worker productivity in the long period, then the size of the country is *more* than optimum. Here, of course, we exclude the impact of changes in technology and in methods of production due to reasons other than variation in size. Further, the use of the term 'slight increase' in area and population implies that the average resource potentiality of the increment of land is the same as that of the existing land, and that, qualitatively, the increment of population is similar to that of the existing population. We are also assuming away the complications arising on account of the possibility of new barriers in transport and communications, etc. Thus, the concept of optimum size is subject to the same limitations as the concept of optimum population. The change in productivity is, however, to be reckoned *after* taking into account the adjustments arising as a result of the change in size. A certain time-lag is inevitable here.

If a country, however, *has* to invest in various indivisible administrative, economic, and political overheads, and if larger size would permit the cost of these fixed overheads to be distributed over a larger base, there is obviously a possibility of increasing returns. The country's size is less than optimum. On the other hand, if there are diseconomies in organization and there is a possibility of violent exposure to crisis if the size is increased, then a reduction in size would be beneficial. It is very difficult to cite cases in which the size of a country is more than optimum, for very often there would be a possibility of improvement in productivity if the size of population could be slightly decreased, or, population remaining the same, if the geographical size could be increased. If, therefore, the *per capita* product can rise with a slight increase in size, population being the same, then obviously the country is of less than optimum geographical size. If, with a given population, a slight decrease in size could lead to a rise in average product per worker, then the size is more than optimum. This would be the case in which the administrative and other overheads could be slightly reduced in the long period if the size could be reduced somewhat. With a given geographical area, a slight increase in population might lead to a rise in per worker productivity. Here, the country is less than of an optimum size with respect to population, as there are vast potentialities in land and other forms of natural resources. Another case would be that in which, with a given size, a decrease in population would lead to a rise in per worker productivity. This case is similar to that in which, with a given population, a slight increase in area would lead to a rise in product per worker. In these cases the country's size with respect to either population or area is less than optimum.

The concept of optimum is useful only in abstract discussion. In the real world, however, it is difficult to attach practical and quantitative significance because any given country's pattern of activities and of specialization tends to be historically orientated towards the needs and requirements of the trading world as a whole.

IV. SIZE AND GROWTH

It is necessary, therefore, to examine the relationship between size and the reaction tempo and patterns in different countries in the light of various dynamic changes under different sets of assumptions. Let us assume that different countries differ in respect of size ; the size of population is proportionate to geographical size ; the supply of agricultural land in terms of quantity and quality is also proportionate to size ; the supply of other forms of natural resources like minerals, water, hydro-electric potentialities, etc., is also proportionate to size ; the composition of population in regard to age structure, sex ratio, etc., is similar in different countries and is not affected by variations in geographical size ; the conjunctural advantages arising out of climatic and other reasons are also similar in the different countries. In such a situation, would the relative difference of sizes matter in respect of rates of capital formation, patterns of techniques, adjustment capacity of countries in respect of emergencies, both economic and non-economic, etc. ? Would the potentialities of growth in these different countries *also* be affected by the size factor ?

The answers to the above queries would yet be not unambiguous. In spite of the rigid framework of assumptions, the critical factor would be whether the size factor would by itself lead to particular forms of production functions as well as levels of costs and returns. The classical analysis as popularized in Smith's *Wealth of Nations* emphasizes the possibility of increasing returns with enlarged population sizes. As other factors would relatively be proportionate to population, a larger population would, on this analysis, give more room for specialization of talents. The quality of labour would improve ; productivity levels would rise ; there would thus be scope for considerable division of labour. In such a case, country A, whose size is double that of country B, would manifest any or a sum of the following characteristics :

(i) The capital stock in country A would be more than double the capital stock in country B. The *per capita* wealth would, therefore, be higher in country A than in country B.

(ii) The level of real wages in country A would be higher than in country B.

(iii) The rate of capital formation and/or the rate of rise in real wages would be greater in country A than in country B. From the familiar Keynesian hypothesis about the relationship between consumption and income, one may say that the large-sized country would be subject to business fluctuations of a larger amplitude. As the relationship between consumption and wealth from a long-period point of view is not clear, it is difficult to say anything more precise about the course of business cycles in the two types of countries.

Another important factor in this connection is that some diseconomies might emerge beyond a stage when population size increases. From an aggregate point of view, the problem of co-ordination would be important in this connection though, if the other factors are available and are proportionate to size, it is not clear as to when and how increasing returns would end. The other advantages arising out of a large-sized *per capita* wealth and income would be available in the case of large-sized countries. The latter's capacity for bearing through a programme of forced savings arising out of needs of war and military preparations would be greater. Further, the large-sized country would be in a better position to carry through rapidly programmes of new changes in technology. Thus, there might be a certain extent of cumulation in the rate of growth of levels of living and/or of wealth in the case of the large-sized country.

The above conclusions would be true provided the rigid framework of the assumptions is satisfied. In the real world it is never so, and there are wide differences between different-sized countries in respect of the population size and structure and composition, availability of land and other forms of natural resources, geographical and climatic advantages, etc. In fact, it is only in the context of a proportionate availability of other factors and conjunctural advantages that size might happen to be the important factor.

It is necessary, therefore, to relax the framework of assumptions and to move some steps nearer reality. Let us first take up the case of availability of agricultural land. It is not true that the size of country A, which is double that of country B, would also be equipped with double the quantity of agricultural land. The term 'land' has to be interpreted here in such a way that qualitative factors are subsumed. In other words, population and other factors being given, a country double the size of another may or may not have proportionate advantages in the supply of agricultural land from the qualitative and/or from the quantitative point of view. Let us first assume that country A is relatively deficient in respect of land. Obviously, the further question emerges as to whether the volume and rate of growth of production of food and of agricultural raw materials for industrial purposes would be adequate, taking into account population needs. It may be that at any point of time, the shortage of land in relation to the size and growth of population may not have an immediate impact upon economic well-being. The land limit might enter at a later stage, so that if population growth is given, a large-sized country deficient in land in the above sense might at a later stage come into serious difficulties on account of diminishing returns or of a continuing crisis in regard to production of food and agricultural raw materials. This may be reflected in the emergence of long-period pressures upon the country's balance of payments. Any under-developed country which is forced to depend upon imports from other countries in regard to supplies of food and agricultural raw materials would tend to face an economic situation of anxiety, particularly in foreign trade. The scope of adjustments is not great, and the country's policy will have to be conducted within certain rigid contours.

Assuming that it is possible to overcome the obstacles arising on account of diminishing returns and the increasing pressure of population on land, through changes in technology, it follows that the rate of growth of living standards would in any case be still lower than would have been the case if the land supply was relatively larger.

Thus, if the supply of land is not proportionate to size, and population variation *is* proportionate, a large-sized country would tend ultimately to get into difficulties. It might be necessary in such a country to set in motion forces which would reduce the rate of growth of population. Such a country, further, will have to be dependent upon the emergence of land-saving innovations and upon foreign trade to a greater extent than a small-sized country.

Let us now take up the case wherein the size of population is proportionate to geographical size, but in one case the supply of land is relatively abundant. Here, obviously, a country with a larger amount of land will have better economic prospects.

It might be that, in fact, the size of population is too meagre in relation to land supply so that potential development would be conditional upon an increase in the rate of growth of population or immigration. There may be increasing returns in such a process. Here, of course, a country with more abundant land is potentially worse off in a sense that it cannot utilize to the maximum extent the available resource opportunities.

The next factor is the availability of resources other than land. The mining and mineral resources are, to some extent, independent of size. Country A which is double country B will not necessarily have double the quantum of mining and mineral resources. If population and other factors are proportionate to size, obviously the rate of development of a large-sized country would be affected adversely. The same factors as in the case of land would be valid here too. A large-sized country with a large population will have to think in terms of synthetic substitutes if it has to overcome the shortages.

On the other hand, it may happen that a large-sized country may also have abundant resources not merely of land but also of other types, but is not in a position to utilize its advantages fully because supply of population is not sufficient. In such a case, there might be increasing returns with a rise in population growth or through immigration.

The next factor to be taken into account is the distribution of geographical and climatic advantages. A large-sized country would not ordinarily have adversities in weather. It may happen that a large-sized country would be in a better position to recover from adversities due to climatic reasons like draughts, floods, and unequal distribution of rainfall over the year, etc. This would be so because in a large-sized country, except on rare occasions, there would not be a short-fall in rains in all areas. So also with regard to other climatic adversities there is always a possibility of counterbalancing forces. Thus, such a country would not be so much worse off during periods of climatic adversities.

Similar comments may be made in respect of the distribution of rivers, mountains, etc. Mere size is not the only important factor in all cases. It may be that a small country may be most favourably equipped in regard to climatic and weather conditions and a large country may so lie within a particular geographical range that it has absolutely no advantages arising on account of this.

The above remarks also apply in regard to conjunctural advantages like proximity to the sea, availability of hydro-electric resources, etc.

It may be that the population of two countries may be proportionate to size, but because of geographical reasons within the country, the different parts of the large-sized country are not easily accessible to each other. There are natural barriers in the way of mobility of men and materials. If these barriers are of a strong character and their impact has been felt over long centuries, there might be wide differences in the characteristics of labour. This would imply that a large-sized country would just consist of a number of economically heterogeneous parts. In such cases, the advantages of size may all be nearly lost. To overcome the disadvantages, large expenditure on transport and communications and preliminary educational overheads may be necessary. From this, the next step is to consider cases where differences due to religion, language, casts, customs, and such other sociological factors might be preventing the attainment of a higher degree of economic homogeneity.

Another interesting case would be that of two nations which are equal in size but one is different from the other in that geographical contiguity is absent in one. Here, obviously, the potentialities of increased returns would be limited and there might be various indivisibilities which tend to detract resources from productive investments.

From the above discussion, it appears that more detailed data about the various aspects of an economy are needed before one can generalize about the relationship between size and economic well-being. It may be, and it is so in practice, that a small-sized nation *may* be at the spearhead of industrial advance, may even be in a position to sustain a larger-sized population under higher-living standards than a large-sized country can. The disadvantages due to a possibility of deficiency in the size of the market may be more than overcome by rising incomes, though the rate and the period of termination of high rates of growth would depend upon factors like availability of land, the quality of technological advance, the advantages of foreign trade, etc. From an economic point of view many of the disadvantages arising out of deficiency of size may be overcome by the creation of conditions favouring free movement of factors of production and commodities. The absence of tariff barriers as well as relative freedom in regard to movement of capital and labour would be of very great help in this connection. To the extent, however, that the feeling of nationhood is strong, there would be difficulties in the way of migration of labour. All adjustments, therefore, will have to be concentrated upon flow of capital. The relative economic cost from the current to the temporal points of view of movement of labour as against those of capital would determine the net balance of advantage in this respect.

It may be thus generally argued that if there is freedom in regard to international movements of factors and goods and there is no restriction whatsoever upon the movement of population, the disadvantages due to a relatively small size may be overcome. Though this might have been true during the nineteenth century, it does not have much validity today in the current political context. The deficiencies in regard to political size cannot be completely overcome through alternative countervailing arrangements or through the break up of the barriers against free movement. In the first place, any given nation, whatsoever its size, would tend to be worried about the possible re-emergence of tariff barriers. It might be that supplies of strategic raw materials might be suddenly cut off or become suddenly scarce. There may be a fear that other nations might develop new techniques, new products, and factors. It may not be found advisable to give up the special advantages that are at present accruing to any particular nation because of certain arrangements with countries outside the 'free' area. To the extent that a policy of greater freedom is adopted in the international sphere, some nations may be afraid that they may be subjected to the serious impact of the repercussions arising on account of crises in related countries. There is also a possibility that as a result of a greater extent of freedom of trade and an enlargement of the size of the market, some countries may benefit more than others. Most of these fears and uncertainties are inherent in any process of expansion of the market which is independent of political size. The gains arising on account of a deficiency in the latter cannot therefore be completely overcome. The difficulty in any countervailing arrangement is that the relative gains and losses cannot be potentially appropriated by any one particular country. The distribution of gains and losses *within* a particular country would, however, not be subject to the same qualifications.

V. THE SPECIAL PROBLEM OF UNDER-DEVELOPED COUNTRIES

The special problems of under-developed countries *vis-à-vis* size may briefly be examined. The under-developed countries may be divided into three broad categories. In the first, there are those countries which are relatively large-sized in area but which have a very high density in population. These countries are less than optimum in respect of geographical size but more than optimum in respect of population. There are a number of indivisible items of expenditure which have to be incurred if the conventional requirements of political nationhood are to be satisfied. The impact of such size-orientated expenditure would be keenly felt primarily because the level of income is low, and the annual meagre ratio of savings to income hardly permits any increase in *per capita* living standards. The problem in such economies is one of the maximization of the rate of savings. This would imply a considerable reduction in avoidable unproductive investments or consumption. A substantial increase in productive capacity might, however, require a large increase in expenditure on transport and communications. The required volume of savings may not be forthcoming within the particular country. If geographical size is given, obviously the way out would be through a reduction in population growth rates. The problem will be difficult if the existing size itself is too large so that for a fairly long period to come, reductions in population growth rates would not be of much help. Given the supply of land (determined by size), there would be possibilities of increases in agricultural production and productivity, but, once again, the population factor would tend to depress the chances of any considerable increase in living standards. The population factor in market expansion takes the form of an increasing pressure upon diminishing return activities like agriculture. Hence, actually, as *per capita* and per worker productivity would tend to be depressed below that level which would have been attained if population, size, and growth rates had been less, mere large size in respect of population connotes no scope for increasing returns. The country's resource potentialities may be vast in absolute terms but in *per capita* terms they may be fairly meagre, and the potential limits up to which standards can be raised would also be low. Such a country might seek expansion outlets in other countries. It may import land-orientated products and export manufactured goods. But, then, the scope is not much inasmuch as at low incomes and low productivity levels the level of specialization would be low. Owing to the low rate of accumulation, the country's capacity to produce on competitive terms those goods which are largely demanded in other countries would be meagre. Foreign trade, therefore, does not offer much of a way out. The position becomes chronic if, because of population pressure, the country is forced to import land-orientated products without, however, sufficient capacity to produce the required quantities of other goods in exchange.

In category two can be included those under-developed countries which have a large geographical size but have a relatively low volume of population. There is scope for increasing returns if population size could increase. At present, the country's size of population is less than optimum. In such a country the current levels of income and productivity may be low ; the vast potential resources might, however, remain unutilized or under-utilized because of the insufficiency of population. The size of the market is too meagre to permit large-scale specialization and the needed industrial diversification. There are no intrinsic supply difficulties, particularly in respect of land-orientated products, but the question is one of the need of accumulation of a large quantity of capital before accelerated rates of income growth can be obtained. Immigration and accelerated population growth rates would have beneficial repercussions upon the economy.

In the third category may be placed those under-developed countries whose geographical size as well as population are not much out of proportion with each other, but whose absolute size is small so that very large overheads are to be incurred upon the maintenance of the convention of nationhood. A number of such countries together might constitute a potential base for large-scale expansion and each might gain in the process of integration.

Let us examine briefly the implications of market expansion schemes with reference to under-developed countries :

(*a*) Two or more under-developed countries, all of them having acute population pressure and hence relatively deficient in land, and with meagre industrial and technological base, get into an integrated 'market expansion' programme. In this case, it does not appear that there would be substantial gains from the integration. The different countries are relatively deficient more or less in the same factors. A country which is slightly more developed than the others might, however, derive considerable advantages in such expansion schemes, but this aggravates cumulatively the inequalities between the different countries. No wonder that, from the economic point of view, under-developed countries geographically contiguous to each other do not much relish the idea of integrated market programmes. Another complicating factor is that in the world, as it is today, a number of under-developed countries have close relationship with some developed country or other, and it is difficult to fashion out a new pattern of relationship amongst the under-developed countries in such a way that economic integration becomes feasible.

(*b*) An under-developed country whose size in respect of area is less than optimum, or whose size in respect of population is more than optimum, gets integrated with another under-developed country whose size in respect of area is more than optimum, or whose size in respect of population is less than optimum. This particular type of integration has considerable potentialities. The relative shortage in factor endowment in the different countries can be compensated by some common arrangements. Success would, however, depend upon the degree of permissible freedom in respect of population movements. As both the countries are under-developed and their capacity to save is meagre, the integration will succeed most when it is possible to obtain supplies of fixed capital, technical skill, etc., from some of the developed countries. In the absence of the latter, there would be considerable opposition by the trade unions in the population-sparse country against any large-scale inflow of population from another low-income country. Population movements can, however, be considerably facilitated if there is a guarantee of inflow of complementary capital from some of the developed countries.

(*c*) One or more under-developed countries get into integrated market arrangements with a developed country. The general picture here would be that of several developed countries having a ring of under-developed satellites around them. In earlier days, owing to historical and other reasons, such arrangements were frowned upon as the reflection of imperialism or of exploitation. Such arrangements, however, continue to exist despite the attainment of freedom in several under-developed countries in recent years. It follows that there must be strong *economic* reasons making for the continuance of such an arrangement. In fact, amongst the under-developed countries there is a race, as it were, to get into some sort of workable arrangement for the inflow of capital and technical skill with some of the leading developed countries. In the absence of arrangements of the pattern (*b*), it is natural to suppose that one or more countries, short of capital but abundant in labour, would tend to get into working arrangements with one or many developed countries, which have, actual or potential, capital to export. The developed countries particularly are richly endowed with those factors in which the under-developed countries are deficient. Any acceleration in the rate of development in the latter leads to an increased extent of dependence upon the former, though an ultimate objective of such plans might be to *reduce* the extent of such dependence. There is, however, a feeling amongst the under-developed countries that the process of such exchange would be more beneficial if the relative share of benefits accruing to the under-developed countries could be increased.

(*d*) Finally, we may take up the case of one or more small-sized under-developed countries in which the relative proportion between land and population is fairly satisfactory, and which get into integrated arrangements amongst themselves with a view to reducing the impact of indivisibilities in the process. This type of arrangements would be beneficial from the point of view of the different countries. The success would, however, depend upon the distribution of gains from such arrangements and the attitudes of different countries towards one another in respect of the above.

Another complicating factor in all market expansion is that it might have different qualitative connotations. For example, if two of more equally developed countries are integrated in an economic sense, the resulting impact would be different from that in a case wherein the developed country or a group of such countries get integrated with another or a group of under-developed countries. In the latter case, particularly, there are large advantages in the case of commodities capable of mass production. Further, as several under-developed countries tend to export raw materials and minerals in exchange for finished consumers' or capital goods, the developed countries particularly may stand to gain in the process, because the supply of raw materials and minerals would be assured. If a group of developed countries integrate, there may be advantages in terms of cost of production, which lead to a fall in prices ; but such gains may be mostly accruing to the inhabitants in the developed countries in the form of higher wages. The relatively less-developed countries may not stand to gain so much though the demand for some other raw materials and land-orientated products would be augmented.

There are also some reasons why the under-developed countries have a reason to be sceptical of the benefits to themselves of such a process. For example, in the first place, this would tend to upset the schemes discussed in (c). If the different planets come together with a view to obtaining countervailing advantages from another highly developed large-sized planet, there would tend to be a considerable dislocation in the relationship *between* the planets and satellites. Firstly, the extent of dependence upon raw materials and processed products might tend to be reduced, if synthetic substitutes emerge or the search for them is accelerated. Secondly, part of the capital which is at present flowing to the under-developed countries might find an internal outlet and may not be available for export to the under-developed countries. In the third place, the market for some of the finished products of the under-developed countries amongst themselves or in the rest of the world might suffer. Integration arrangements among the developed countries might lead to a shrinkage in the market for the products of some of the under-developed countries rather than for an expansion of the market in the highly developed countries. The repercussions of such programmes, however, require much deeper study.

VI. ECONOMIC NATIONALISM

Finally, a few words may be added about the case of a nation which is too small from the point of view of the capacity to obtain economies of scale and of mass production but which seeks to *assert*, however, its nationhood. Such a nation would like to equip itself with most of the economic and political institutions which are characteristic of a large or developed nation. For example, it is necessary to maintain a reasonably large defence force. The expenditure on this account would naturally be a first draft upon the nation's resources. A reasonably large expenditure will also have to be incurred in maintaining a foreign service with provision for embassies, consulates, etc. The foreign exchange resources would be partly strained on this account. There is also expenditure on account of the costs of membership of various international bodies. In all these cases there might be countervailing advantages. A nation might like to have its own currency and foreign exchange arrangements. Advantages due to a link with some established foreign currency might have to be given up. Expenditure will have to be incurred in establishing and maintaining a Central Bank as well as a network of commercial banks dealing in internal as well as external transactions. An independent currency would imply the need for substantial gold reserves. Here, again, the advantages on account of the link with a foreign currency may have to be abandoned. If such a nation pursues also a policy of economic nationalism, tariffs may be necessary with consequent current disadvantages, though these may *prove* beneficial from a long-period point of view. New industries may have to be fostered and developed, though the internal market is not sufficient to warrant the large initial indivisible expenditure. The feeling of nationhood may assert itself in the form of the regulation of inflow of foreign capital or of discriminatory attitude against the growth of foreign businesses at home. In some cases the need for self-sufficiency might reflect itself in the considerably large capital expenditure upon various capital goods industries (particularly in steel). Here, again, the market may or may not be sufficient to warrant the above expenditure. There may also be restrictions upon migration. Even though the country might afford to have a larger population with consequent advantages, these may have to be given up because of the pursuit of a policy of nationalization. Immigration may be forbidden or may be selective. The feeling of nationhood might assert itself also in the giving up of certain existing cultural institutions and in the development of new ones.

Thus the desire to assert political nationhood has its economic counterparts. As a result, there might be considerable transitional costs which may or may not be counterbalanced by current or long-period gains. The idea of national self-sufficiency in various economic spheres under certain conditions would definitely lead to considerable mal-allocation of resources. Excess capacity in certain fields might be a consequence of this. It may be that a particular nation may not be so well-equipped in technical skill; may not be in possession of the required quantity and quality of entrepreneurial and managerial capacity; its administrative cadre may take some time before the nationals can be completely trained. Discrimination against employment of foreigners in indigenous business and government might lead to certain disadvantages. The regulation of the inflow of foreign capital might create a disincentive against the flow of capital. Because of its independent currency arrangements, it may be difficult for this particular country to float loans in world markets under as favourable conditions as would be desirable. While there is no doubt that to some extent these costs are inevitable in the emerging process of a nationhood, in some cases nationalism might go too far with consequent disadvantages. Not in all cases is it true that the growth of nationhood would lead automatically to the distrust of foreigners and to the emergence of independent arrangements everywhere. The exact course of events would depend upon past experience of nationals in their relationship with foreigners, and upon the current or expected political atmosphere in the international world.

Chapter 9

THE EXPERIENCE OF ITALY [1]

BY

V. A. MARSAN

Rome

I. THE PROBLEMS OF ITALY [2]

THE size of the market is a problem of which Italians are becoming vividly aware. In spite of the high rates of increase of production and exports after the war, the need to overcome the limitations of the domestic market is being sharply emphasized by the constant advance of modern production techniques and by the fact that other countries are favoured, when competing with Italy, by the large size of their domestic markets. Such limitations are now regarded as a serious obstacle to a full development of the national economy, and this widespread belief is expressed, in particular, by Italy's readiness to join in the various endeavours towards international economic integration which have recently led to the establishment of the European Economic Community. It is worth pointing out that the decision to become a member of the EEC has met in the country with almost universal approval on grounds of economic as well as political expediency. Such approval is all the more significant in a nation where protectionist policies are traditional and which has but recently emerged from a period of economic autarky and is confronted with grave problems of unemployment and under-development.

Italy, with a population of 48 million, has at present a *per capita* income which is 40 to 60 per cent below that of other European countries with similar populations, such as France, Germany, and Great Britain. It is therefore easy to understand why, in the Italian case, we can speak of a limited market. But this market is further restricted by the prevalence of an oligopolistic structure which a high tariff protection has helped to create in many sectors and, above all, by the existence of a very wide gap between the average income levels of the Southern regions — which account for almost

[1] Translated from the Italian by N. Livenziani.
[2] I am indebted to Professor Pasquale Saraceno for many helpful suggestions.

38 per cent of the Italian population — and the rest of the country. In terms of *per capita* income the disparity is of the order of 2 to 1, and clearly puts an additional constraint on the country's industry, which has concentrated, and continued to develop, mainly in the North, where the pattern and level of consumption are very different from those prevailing in the South. Low and inelastic demand in this area expresses the typical conditions of under-development so frequently met with in the economic literature of today. While the further growth of the North is now undoubtedly hampered by the economic backwardness of the South, the development policy currently under way in the latter is highly conditioned by the existence of a Northern industry which often helps, but in certain cases may also hinder, the progress of the South. This means that in addition to the usual problems characteristic of a small national market, we find in the Italian case the special problems inherent in a situation of structural disequilibrium originating from the fact that a large section of the domestic market did not take part in the process of industrialization, which started when the country became politically unified almost a hundred years ago.

In the concluding section of this paper I propose briefly to examine the objectives and instruments of Italy's current development policy in the context of the particular conditions under which the national economy has developed so far. First I shall try to show what in my opinion are the main effects of the present size of the Italian domestic market, which such policy is basically designed to overcome.

II. DOMESTIC MARKET AND EXPORT MARKET

The growing importance of the size of the market in a modern economy is linked chiefly to the corresponding increase of the minimum scale of the plant which, if fully and stably exploited, can ensure minimum unit costs. The technical, organizational, and market factors which favour this increase of scale [1] do not operate with the same intensity in the various sectors, but the trend has generally been towards a larger scale and will probably become more marked in the near future owing to recent technological developments.

The greater the economies of scale in a given sector, the greater are the disadvantages for the firm which, owing to an insufficient

---

[1] In this context scale is measured by productive capacity since this is best suited for reference to the size of the market.

outlet, is obliged either to operate with equipment of inefficient scale or, conversely, to utilize efficient large-scale plant below capacity. Clearly, the importance of the domestic market in determining the size of the firm's outlet is in inverse proportion to the possibility it has of relying on a stable export market. In principle, export sales can supplement domestic sales to the extent of ensuring the profitability of an efficient scale of production in sectors where it would otherwise be impossible.

In practice, of course, the difficulties which the exporting firm is up against are well known. The fluctuations of foreign demand, and even the possibility of a complete closing up of certain export markets, involve great risks. To these must be added the cost, sometimes very high, of entering into markets where exporters of other countries are already firmly established ; moreover, foreign competitors have the frequent advantage over the exporters of a small country like Italy not only of large home markets but also of preferential treatment on many export markets. As a rule, the exporting firm's commercial organization must therefore be relatively larger than that of the firm which confines itself to the domestic market, and this while access to foreign markets is far more hazardous. This means, as a rule, that exports can supplement the home market only for a comparatively small proportion of the firm's total output in the sectors where the scale of efficient production is in excess of the domestic outlet.

If we examine the composition of Italian exports, we can see that the products mainly represented are, characteristically, those for which a sufficiently protected home market ensures the economic operation of technically efficient plants. For instance, textiles in 1955 accounted for 15 per cent of Italian exports against a corresponding percentage of 5 for Western Germany and of 11 for the United Kingdom. It is worth noting that Italy's percentage share of the aggregate textile exports of seven European industrial countries [1] has risen from 5·1 per cent in 1913 to 9·5 per cent in 1928 and to 11·8 per cent in 1955 (see Table I).

This growing proportion, at a time when the foreign sales of European textiles are undergoing a general crisis (in 1955 the value of the seven countries' textile exports was lower than in 1928, as shown by the table), indicates that Italy has some difficulty in changing the pattern of her exports in favour of other industrial products, as the major countries of Europe are doing. It is significant that Italy's share of the total exports of the seven countries in the three years considered in Table I should still be distinctly

[1] U.K., Germany, France, Italy, Belgium-Luxemburg, Switzerland, Sweden.

larger for textiles than for any other commodity group with the exception of foodstuffs, while in the case of other countries in the group which are also traditionally textile-makers, the weight of textiles in the group's total exports is today below that of engineering products (as in the case of the United Kingdom) or of both engineering and chemical products (Western Germany). The comparative smallness of the optimal textile unit (together with its modest technical complexity) means that the flow of exports is easily checked by the rise of a textile industry in the importing countries, and also that in a phase of declining exports, such as the present one, the industry can continue to operate profitably without changing very much the prevailing scale of the plant.

The problem of scale in relation to the size of both the domestic and the export market is of special importance in the field of capital goods and, where Italy is concerned, also in that of durable consumer goods, the demand for which is linked to a high standard of living. The problem, of course, varies a good deal in degree from one sector to another.

In the chemical industry, for example, the economies of large scale make their weight felt only partially in the production and marketing phases. In the principal branches of chemical production the capacity of the technical unit ensuring competitive costs does not, as a rule, exceed the possibilities of absorption of the Italian market. In spite of a late start, Italy's chemical industry has successfully developed a fairly wide range of products (especially fertilizers and artificial fibres, and now also pharmaceuticals and plastic materials). But in contrast with the countries which are the main chemical producers, the ratio of exports to national output is rather low (in the average less than 10 per cent). Taking the total exports of the seven industrial countries previously considered, the percentage share of Italian chemical exports, though undoubtedly on the increase, is still at a level (5·6 per cent in 1955) which is less than half that of textile exports. Italy's handicap in this sector lies mainly in the field of research, since in the modern chemical industry this is typically the phase in which the economies of large scale are important and where, as a consequence, the major countries have a decisive advantage. But I shall revert to this subject later.

In the vast sector of the metal industries, on the contrary, the existence of large-scale economies has had a more direct bearing on the possibility of expanding in Italy a number of lines of production ; in such cases the smallness of the domestic market has often made it impossible either to export successfully or indeed to meet domestic demand otherwise than by importing. Wide margins of idle capacity are a recurring phenomenon in many lines of engineering production (*e.g.* shipbuilding, railway rolling-stock, heavy electric machinery), and frequently exports of these products can be undertaken only at unremunerative prices.

Under the circumstances it is hardly surprising that Italy should be a large importer of engineering products — both capital and consumer goods. As to exports, the more stable and profitable are constituted to a large extent by a few mass-produced goods which have a sufficient domestic outlet (given the existing tariff protection) and have reached high technical standards (for instance, utility cars,[1] motor-scooters, sewing machines, and office machinery). It should be added that, in the case of most of those products, materials account for a comparatively small part of the total cost. Where such products are concerned the proportion of export to domestic sales is not pushed by the firms beyond a certain point, their policy being to limit the risks of ups and downs in foreign demand over which they have no control. Engineering exports include also a number of special machines and high-quality products (such as passenger ships) for which production of long runs, let alone mass-production, is out of the question. As in the preceding case, the technical quality of many of these products is such as to give them a leading position in the world market, so that their competitiveness is largely independent of the scale of production. In this particular field the ratio of exports to total output can be very high (as much as 80 per cent for certain types of steel-making equipment, for instance).

These achievements cannot, however, blind us to the fact that in many other branches of engineering the possibility of exporting is heavily curtailed by the size of Italy's domestic market, which is a handicap when competition has to be faced from foreign manufacturers who are firmly established in their own much larger national markets and hence in the world market. On the whole, Italian engineering exports are today only slightly above imports ; and their percentage share of the country's total exports, although a growing one, is still far below the levels which are characteristic of the major industrial countries (in 1955 this ratio was 20 per cent against Germany's and Britain's 37 to 40 per cent). It is also significant that, in spite of the progress made, in 1955 Italy's contribution to the total engineering exports of the seven countries listed

[1] In 1956 motor-cars in the under-1-litre class represented 59 per cent of Italian motor-car production against an average of 33 per cent for the major European producers (U.K., W. Germany, France, Italy, and Sweden). The corresponding percentages for exports in 1955 were 28 per cent for Italy alone against 19 per cent for the total of the five countries.

in Table I was less than 5 per cent, a level below that of textiles and chemicals.

A point worth making is that the development of the Italian engineering industry has been traditionally hampered by the problem of steel supplies. In Italy steel has been, until recently, produced at a high cost in plants of uneconomic scale or else imported at high prices, especially in periods of expanding world demand, as post-war experience shows. The development of Italian steel-making in its turn has been hampered more by the smallness of the domestic outlet than by the insufficiency of raw materials supplies. The high cost of steel does help to explain the difficulties and problems of a number of engineering branches where its incidence on the production cost is particularly high (shipbuilding, railway rolling-stock, heavy industrial equipment). Unfortunately these are frequently the very branches where Italy is otherwise favoured by the fact that they are unsuitable for highly mechanized production in long runs and where the efficient scale therefore tends to be small.

Owing to the concurrence of circumstances and factors, which I propose to deal with later, the Italian steel industry started after the war and has since considerably carried forward a remarkable process of modernization and rationalization, which high world demand in recent years has done much to help. The disparity between Italian costs and those of the main European steel-makers having been reduced, a major obstacle to the development of Italian engineering is now in part removed. But it cannot be denied that the competitiveness of Italian steel, as now produced by up-to-date mills, depends to a decisive extent on whether current economic expansion will continue at a rate sufficient to call for intensive utilization of capacity, not only in Italy but also in the rest of Europe, thus preventing the younger Italian steel industry from being overpowered by competitors who are better prepared to overcome a critical phase. The amazing progress made by Italian steel producers after the war should not blind us to the fact that the balance recently attained is still a precarious one.

The limited reliance that can be placed on exports is even more evident in the case of foodstuffs, which are nevertheless the main item on the Italian list. In spite of Italy's outstanding natural advantages as regards some agricultural products and of the comparative absence of a problem of scale, the difficulties of increasing exports in this field are well known to be particularly serious. An expansion of fruit and vegetable crops, entailing adequate investment in irrigation and in processing and marketing facilities, has no doubt been held up so far by the strongly protectionist policies of European countries which are potential consumers of Italian products. An additional factor has been discrimination (as in the case of England and France) in favour of products from dependent overseas territories. It is significant that the ratio of exports to output, even of the most typical Italian crops, has been in the past forty years almost stationary and sometimes has actually declined, as shown by the data in Table II. The fact is that Italy has encountered obstacles to expansion in a specialized field of export production where she has many natural advantages and which affects a large part of her working population — in particular, the Southern regions where the problem of excess labour is most acute and where it is hardest to create new jobs in other activities.

We may conclude from what has been said so far that the Italian case is good proof of the outstanding rôle of a large national market in the development of an efficient and well-balanced industrial and agricultural system.

III. THE PROBLEM OF RESEARCH

The conclusions arrived at as regards the economies of scale in the production phase apply even more forcibly to that of research and experimentation, which play so important a rôle in modern industry.

It was pointed out earlier, in dealing with exports, that the scale of production and the size of the home market are of secondary importance in the case of products of superior technical quality — that is, of products which constitute important innovations and which, if adequately marketed, can sell easily both at home and abroad. Leadership in the technical field, however, can be achieved only if the facilities available for research and development in all their various phases are highly efficient. This is pre-eminently true of chemical and engineering industries, and, in fact, in all the major industrial countries these two sectors account for more than half of the total expenditure and personnel devoted to research. In these industries, moreover, there is a minimum scale for effective research facilities, involving a large, fixed cost than can usually be shouldered by the small firms — that is to say, by most of the firms in a country like Italy. Moreover, in the major countries the government contributes very substantially to the organization and financing of applied as well as of fundamental research. This, as is well known, takes place both in industry (particularly in the aircraft and nuclear fields which are of military interest) and, more generally, in agriculture where, indeed, applied research at farm level is practically non-existent. A few data will suffice to give an idea of the position of inferiority, in this field, of a poor country like Italy.

As regards fundamental research, where Italy has nevertheless a tradition of long standing, the main centres constituted by the universities suffer from a chronic lack of resources. At present the Italian scientific faculties can rely, in total, on public funds and other income of the order of $8 million a year, to be distributed among the more than one thousand institutes attached to them. The utter inadequacy of such an endowment sufficiently explains why Italian researchers are constantly emigrating to richer countries where they can find laboratories equipped for organized and systematic work. The best-known case has been in the field of nuclear research. Under these circumstances, even the solution of sending young scholarship students to scientific institutes abroad often means, in the end, that research personnel is definitely lost to other nations.

From the point of view of teaching, the Italian university faculties are no better off. For 100,000 undergraduates, they have at present slightly over 1000 professors, 2700 lecturers, and 2500 assistants. The latter especially seem very few (one to every 40 undergraduates) compared with the requirements of modern technical and scientific training.

The lack of technicians and researchers is perhaps even more serious from the quantitative than the qualitative standpoint. A recent study [1] of the increased requirements of technical personnel in relation to the advent of automation points out that the number of technicians and researchers in all sectors of production (including agriculture) which Italy will need by 1975 is of the order of one and a half million. This means that the universities and specialized institutes should turn out a number of new graduates and trained personnel which is about six times the current yearly rate.

Hence in Italy the organization and financing of research becomes to a much greater extent than elsewhere the responsibility of the individual industrial firms. The nature and scope of research requirements vary, of course, from one sector to another. As indicated earlier, they are especially large in the chemical industry and in certain branches of engineering, and in these cases only the big firms are in a position to finance such long-term investment without external help. No doubt there are instances of big Italian firms

---

[1] Gino Martinoli, 'L' automazione e la necessità di una adeguata preparazione culturale in Italia', in *Proceedings of the Conference on Problems of Automation*, Milan, April 8th–13th, 1956.

which have undertaken research and development of inventions with a high degree of success both in the chemical field (for example, fertilizers, plastic materials) and in engineering (calculating machines). In fact, whenever new products or processes could be developed, these firms not only expanded their export sales considerably but were able also to start the construction of new plant abroad. (In the branch of nitrogenous fertilizers, for example, the Montecatini Company has built, in little more than thirty years, about 150 plants in various countries with an aggregate capacity which accounts for about 13 per cent of the world total.)

However, the fact must be faced that these are exceptional cases and that, particularly in engineering, the majority of the so-called research laboratories actually do not go beyond mere testing and inspection of current products and processes. The wide practice of resorting to foreign manufacturing licences (apart from the fact that it does not eliminate the need for a further research effort on the part of the licensee firm to adjust the imported techniques to local conditions and keep them up-to-date) is a compromise solution which places the firm in a definitely subordinate position, particularly in the export markets. The organization of research in favour of the small firms (for instance, on a co-operative basis) suffers from well-known limitations, and in Italy is almost non-existent. The conclusion that forces itself upon us is that, in a field of such fundamental importance for economic progress, Italy suffers from a serious handicap which is largely a consequence of the modest economic size of the country.

IV. CONCENTRATION AND SPECIALIZATION

It has earlier been stressed that the choice of the scale of production on the part of the firm is usually conditioned, in the first place, by the size of the domestic market. Other things being equal, this size is in direct proportion to the degree in which the individual firm has been able to concentrate in its hands the production of the sector in which it operates. A high degree of specialization within the sector has similar effects. And the incentive to attain a high level of concentration and/or specialization is more or less strong in relation to the importance of scale economies in the various sectors and to the degree of competition with which the firm is confronted. In the textile industry, for instance, numerous firms can operate at an optimum scale even if the home market is not a large one, whereas in the steel industry and in a number of chemical and engineering branches the opposite is true.[1]

There are numerous sectors where, owing to the limited size of the home market, an economic scale of production entails a position very close to monopoly. If one considers the percentage share of national output accounted for by one or very few firms (often grouped together) it appears that concentration of industry is now very high in Italy in far more sectors than is the case in larger-sized economies. The basic reason, even if not the only one and not in every case, is that in many sectors the capacity of efficient plant is very close to, and sometimes larger than, the domestic outlet. Over and above the incentive of higher returns as the scale of production increases, the advantage mentioned earlier of enlarging the scale of research activities may also play a decisive part. It is certainly not by chance that in Italy productivity tends to be highest and technical progress most satisfactory in the very sectors where concentration is greatest.[2]

The major drawback of such widespread conditions of monopoly or oligopoly is perhaps constituted by the price policy which, thanks also to the existing tariff protection, is applied in many of the country's industrial sectors and whereby the increases of productivity achieved by the firm are largely turned into higher profits and wages and not into price reductions. In a situation like Italy's, where there is serious unemployment and where many sectors and regions lag very much behind in technical progress and capital accumulation, such distribution of the fruits of productivity increases tends to widen the gaps between income levels and between rates of growth. The disadvantage is greatest for Italian agriculture (and hence for the under-developed Southern regions which are mainly agricultural) where productivity cannot be raised to rates comparable to industry's because of the pressure of over-population, and where compensatory price adjustments are precluded by the structure of the market. If we bear in mind that 41 per cent of Italy's active population is engaged in agriculture and that 38 per

---

[1] The scale alternatives open to a firm are often limited not only for strictly technical but also for economic reasons. For example, the profitability of a smaller scale of production (which, as a rule, means a smaller degree of mechanization) may depend on whether it is possible to maintain wages during the life of the plant at a level which is actually below the established minimum in a given national market. This is the case in Italy, where the new industries in the South are obliged to pay wages which are only slightly below the legal minima in the industrial regions of the North (and this in spite of the fact that the workers engaged locally would otherwise be unemployed or at any rate unproductive). This circumstance helps to explain the advanced technical level (and therefore the tendency to large-scale operation) of most of the new industries set up in the South in recent years.

[2] Among the sectors for which data are available, the highest increases in productivity between 1950 and 1955 were registered by those where concentration is also very high, such as chemicals, steel, and motor-car manufacturing.

cent of the country's total population live in the South, it is easy to see how such a problem should be of fundamental importance for Italy's economic development, and all the more so because the possibility of finding outlets for many industrial products depends, sometimes to a decisive extent, on the progress of agriculture and on the well-being of the rural population.[1]

There are many cases, however, where production in a restricted national market such as Italy's is carried out by a large number of inefficient firms of sub-optimal size or working much below capacity, which survive behind the shelter of tariff protection in a market whence competition has been, more or less tacitly, banished. The situation is one of patent inability to achieve adequate technical progress, and the external diseconomies of these inefficient firms and sectors have a cumulative effect in holding up the growth of the system as a whole.

A remedy might be found in greater specialization of the firms in the sectors in question, which would result in lower costs. But the obstacle here lies precisely in the oligopolistic situation in which an industry can operate with a price structure which ensures a more or less satisfactory profit to each firm in spite of inefficient methods of production. In these circumstances it is extremely improbable that a process of rationalization would be spontaneously undertaken by agreement between the firms. In Italy the outstanding instance after the war has been in the steel industry, where such a process was rendered possible by the exceptional rise in steel demand and by the enlightened policy conducted by the State-owned group which controls a vast proportion of the country's capacity (80 per cent for pig iron and 50 per cent for steel). In the engineering industry, on the other hand, the problem of rationalization still looms large in the case of several branches (industrial machinery, tractors, railway rolling-stock, shipbuilding) ; and given the importance of this sector for the growth of investment and exports, the persistence of this situation must be regarded as a serious handicap to the Italian industrial system.

A comparison between engineering in Italy and in other countries shows that the position of Italy is still far from satisfactory. Table III

---

[1] Italian trade unions have recently pressed very strongly for a reduction of working hours in industries where productivity increases have been largest and most rapid (steel, motor-vehicles, chemicals). In this connection the Advisory Committee for the Government Ten-Year Development Plan has submitted an official report in which it is stressed that in relation to the objectives of Italian development policy, 'productivity increases . . . should be utilised to a maximum degree in favour of the whole national economy through a systematic adjustment of the price structure to productivity's trends'. For a theoretical and more general analysis of this problem, see P. Sylos Labini, *Oligopolio e progresso tecnico*, Milan, 1957.

indicates that Italy's percentage share of European manufacturing output is noticeably lower in the case of engineering, while it is above average in the case of chemicals and textiles — that is to say, in two sectors where, respectively, a considerable degree of concentration has been achieved in Italy and where the economies of large scale are negligible.

V. OBJECTIVES AND INSTRUMENTS FOR ITALY'S ECONOMIC DEVELOPMENT

The conclusion we must arrive at is that the comparative smallness of the Italian market is of itself a serious obstacle to the development, on an adequate scale, of the process of industrialization, which is now a precondition of the country's general development. This is true not only of a backward region like the South, where private investment may be altogether unprofitable in many lines of activity in which the minimum scale of operation is a large one, but also of the industrialized regions where, in the present phase of rapid technological progress, the constraint of an insufficient domestic outlet is felt more and more keenly.

The main remedy resorted to in the past by Italy, like all late-comers on the industrial scene, was tariff protection. But the inadequacies of such a policy, originally justified by this late start, became, with time, more and more apparent. On the one side, it encouraged the formation of the monopolistic and oligopolistic structures of which mention was made earlier, with the accompanying adverse effects on the country's general economic growth; on the other side, it proved utterly incapable of ensuring the expansion of some of the sectors which are of strategic importance for balanced industrialization and which are particularly affected by the smallness of domestic outlets, such as steel and heavy engineering.

In these circumstances the need for public action became imperative; and the government, in certain cases, went so far as to take over and directly operate industrial firms, particularly in basic sectors where the minimum capacity of modern equipment is sometimes in considerable excess of domestic demand and where capital requirements are, in Italy, beyond the possibilities of private entrepreneurs. A case in point is that of blast-furnace-based steel-making: this was developed entirely by public enterprise, while private enterprise concentrated on steel-making based on scrap, requiring smaller-scale equipment which also can be run more flexibly. Now that Italian steel consumption has risen to 6 million tons a year against little over 2 million before the war and is steadily growing, the government's policy has proved a long-sighted one, since any further expansion of cold-charge plant is barred by the scarcity of scrap. But that the need should have arisen for a country like Italy to entrust to an unusual degree its industrial development to public enterprise, which often and for long periods has proved unable to yield normal returns, must be regarded as a symptom of weakness on the part of an industrial system which nevertheless comprises highly dynamic sectors and firms. And the danger is that these elements of weakness will increase now that the intensified rate of scientific and technological progress may bring about revolutionary changes in the industry of countries which are major competitors.

Hence the economic grounds for Italy's recent policy in favour of economic integration with other European countries. The prospect of increased competition and at the same time of stable widened outlets, which the European Economic Community offers to Italy, should urge Italian producers to adopt the most up-to-date techniques and an efficient scale and specialization of production, both in industry and in agriculture.

The many problems — briefly indicated in Section 2 — which an expansion of agricultural and industrial exports will involve should be more easily solved in the sphere of the new Community with the gradual establishment of a preferential area for the output of member countries — an area which potentially multiplies the 'home' market for Italian producers by four. This preferential area, created by means of a common external tariff, can offset the effects of stiffer internal competition and, in the case of Italy, also of competition with non-member countries, since the common tariff will tend to be fixed below Italy's present average level. Moreover, the new expanded market should make it possible to sever the often unavoidable link between large scale and control of the market, mentioned in Section 4.[1] As to research, apart from the opportunity of common undertakings as in the field of nuclear energy, where Euratom will offer obvious advantages to a country like Italy, a wider market basis should be an incentive for its development within the firms operating in the more rapidly progressing sectors.

There is, of course, the danger that the initial imbalance between Italy's economy and those of other members may crystallize and eventually aggravate the problems of under-development which Italy still has to solve. It should be emphasized, on the other hand,

[1] It should be mentioned that one of the tasks devolving on the common institutions is to prevent the formation of monopolies and cartels.

that the Treaty envisages much more than a mere customs union, since it includes an institutional set-up and a whole series of procedures and safeguards designed to ensure an orderly and balanced development of income and employment in all the member countries. In particular, the objectives of the Ten-Year Development scheme adopted by the Italian government at the close of 1954 have been formally acknowledged, in an annex to the Treaty, as 'objectives of common interest'.

The approval of the Ten-Year scheme makes it now possible to define in a concrete way the nature and order of magnitude of the problems which Italy is facing. The basic objectives may be summarized as follows : 4 million new jobs are to be provided outside agriculture ; the growth of the Southern regions is to be intensified, in particular through an increase in industrial income of about 175 per cent in ten years against an increase of 61 per cent in the rest of the country ; the balance of payments gap is to be closed at a high level of foreign trade, involving an export increase of the order of 60 per cent, considerably larger than that of imports which is put at 43 per cent.

According to the estimates given in the scheme, these objectives can only be attained on the basis of a 5 per cent average yearly rate of growth of national income during a period of ten years. The fact that the government is now committed to a programme of long-term economic policy designed to ensure the achievement of these objectives, and of the required rate of income growth, adds a new dimension to the Italian market. This overall rate of growth constitutes an important point of reference for private investors, who can assess the profitability, as regards size and location, of new enterprise in the various sectors of production in relation to the prospects opened out by government development policies. This expected rate of growth will be the more effective in reducing the handicap of a small home market in so far as it will presumably be higher than the rates simultaneously achieved by the countries competing with Italy in the world market.

What a high overall rate of growth can mean in actual practice is best illustrated by the development of steel after the war, as previously described. It should be emphasized that the expansion of this sector has undoubtedly been helped by the creation in 1952 of the European Coal and Steel Community, which was a powerful incentive for Italian producers to undertake modernization of their plant, and which, at the same time, made possible an effective regulation of the critical market for steel scrap. Moreover, Italy was granted a transitional five-year period of decreasing tariff protection.

Obviously, Italy is confident that her membership of the European Economic Community will lead, with time, to similar overall results, and will equally favour a high rate of economic growth and help to eliminate the present wide disparities between levels of income of member-countries.

It may be stated in conclusion that an efficient long-term development policy at home, and her gradual integration in a common market implemented according to the same principles and with the same safeguards as the Coal and Steel Community, can open to Italy entirely new prospects in the next few years. Indeed, without the expectation of a balanced expansion it would be impossible to intensify the industrialization of Southern Italy, a process which can be viable only if carried out at modern technical levels and if extended over a range of sectors with sufficient momentum to support the region's increase of employment and income without extraordinary outside help. The development of industry in the South cannot, on the other hand, be conceived as disjoined from the simultaneous growth of the industrialized Northern regions. A formulation of this point which has since often been quoted is that 'a problem which appears as one of regional industrialisation is in reality a national problem of development of the Italian industry'.[1]

It is possible that certain industries cannot be expanded or even started in the South because excess capacity already exists elsewhere in the country (as in the case of the textile industry). Apart from this, given the present scale of efficient operation in many industrial sectors, and given the size of the Italian market, it is likely that in several cases the creation of even one optimal unit may be enough to meet additional demand for some years. Hence the paramount importance of locating such new units in the South as soon as the situation warrants it ; indeed, to set them up in other regions would mean considerably to delay any growth in the South of the industries in question.

We may conclude that the prospects opened by the common European market strengthen and widen, at least potentially, the basis which alone makes possible in Italy and in its Southern regions the development of efficient industrial units. Specialization in agriculture, which is an important precondition for an increase of income and exports, should be equally favoured by the creation of the EEC.

The government's development policy has a decisive rôle to play in promoting both the location of new industry in the South

[1] Pasquale Saraceno, 'Necessità e prospettive dello sviluppo industriale nelle regioni meridionali', in Proceedings of the 2nd Conference at Naples, promoted by the Cassa per il Mezzogiorno, November 1953.

and the structural transformation of agriculture. As regards the former, we already have concrete instances of promising industrial developments in the South promoted by large private concerns from the North (especially in the chemical and engineering industries) and by public enterprise (such as a new integrated steel unit and a nuclear power plant, for which plans have been laid recently).

The difficulties of Italy's current economic policy cannot, of course, be ignored. This policy does, however, seem to hold out the promise that the obstacles to the solution of the economic and social problems of a country which is still poor, and in that sense small, will ultimately be overcome.

STATISTICAL APPENDIX

Table I

Italy's Share of Total Exports of Seven European Countries *
1913, 1928, 1955

Commodity groups	Years	Total exports of 7 countries *		Italy's share of 7 countries' total
		$ million	Index 1913=100	%
Total exports	1913	7,924·4	100	6·1
	1928	10,870·2	137	7·0
	1955	26,727·4	337	7·0
of which :				
Food, drink, and tobacco	1913	933·2	100	15·7
	1928	1,056·7	113	16·6
	1955	2,041·6	219	20·2
Textiles	1913	1,984·7	100	5·1
	1928	2,772·0	140	9·5
	1955	2,673·2	135	11·8
Chemicals	1913	398·9	100	2·5
	1928	604·9	152	3·2
	1955	1,080·5	522	5·6
Machinery and transport equipment	1913	778·2	100	1·9
	1928	1,353·0	174	3·1
	1955	7 690·1	988	4·8

* United Kingdom, Germany, France, Italy, Belgium-Luxemburg, Sweden, Switzerland.

Sources : 1913 and 1928 : Svennilson, *Growth and Stagnation in the European Economy*, Geneva, 1954 ; 1955 : OEEC Trade Statistics.

TABLE II

RATIO OF EXPORTS TO GROSS VALUE OF ITALIAN PRODUCTION
OF CERTAIN AGRICULTURAL COMMODITIES

Products	1911–14	1950–53
	%	%
Vegetables	7·4	9·3
Fruits	22·2	28·4
Wine	2·9	2·2
Olive oil	20·6	0·5

Source : G. G. Dell' Angelo, *L' esportazione agricola italiana*
(to be published by SVIMEZ).

TABLE III

SHARE OF FIVE COUNTRIES IN TOTAL EUROPEAN PRODUCTION
IN CERTAIN MANUFACTURING SECTORS IN 1955
(Volume of European production in each sector in 1955=100)

	Total manu-facturing	Textiles	Mechanical products	Chemicals
United Kingdom	30·0	22·0	33·8	25·9
Germany	23·3	19·5	24·9	23·8
France	14·4	15·9	15·4	14·0
Italy	8·6	12·2	5·0	17·5
Sweden	4·1	2·0	4·7	1·4

Source: V. Paretti and G. Bloch, 'Industrial Production in W. Europe and
the United States, 1901 to 1955', *Banca Nazionale del Lavoro Quarterly Review*,
December 1956.

Chapter 10

SIZE AND VIABILITY: THE LESSON OF AUSTRIA

K. W. ROTHSCHILD

Österreichisches Institut für Wirtschaftsforschung, Vienna

I. ADJUSTMENT TO THE LOSS OF AN EMPIRE

THERE is hardly any country in the world where the problem of size and its economic significance has met with such widespread interest as in Austria between the two wars. This was not due to a particular smallness of the country. With its (at present) 7 million inhabitants it is far from standing at the end of the queue when the nations are lined up by size.[1] Nor can it be said that Austria is particularly poorly endowed by nature. With timber and iron ore, with sufficient water for extensive hydro-electric projects, and with a variety of other resources and of human skills, Austria does not compare badly even with a well-to-do country like Switzerland, and certainly comes off far better than many other small countries where the question of 'economic viability' has never been raised.

No, the reasons for the drawn-out discussion on the economic viability of post-First-World-War Austria were of a different nature. They had their roots in special historical and political circumstances, though that was not generally recognized at the time.

The end of the First World War certainly found Austria in a very precarious condition. Not only had a war been lost and had left a rather badly managed economy more or less in ruins; on top of this came the dissolution of the Habsburg monarchy. The former central province of an empire of 50 million suddenly shrunk to an independent country of some 6½ million inhabitants faced by quickly growing tariff walls around its former markets. To this new situation the Austrian economy was not at all well adjusted. Many industries had developed over wide regions of the old empire and found themselves suddenly torn into separate parts. In the

[1] In the usual alphabetic order *Österreich*, thanks to the vagaries of the English and French transformation of foreign names, stands even near the top of the queue.

textile industry, for instance, spinning had been mainly concentrated in Austria, while weaving had its main base in Czechoslovakia. Now the co-operation between these two branches was hampered by tariffs and administrative difficulties. Similar conditions prevailed in other industries. Far-reaching changes became necessary in public administration and in the field of banking and finance. Austria, once the centre of the imperial and capitalist domination over the outer provinces of the Habsburg empire, had to cut down the over-sized apparatus which had served these needs. Numerous civil servants, bank clerks, and other salaried employees lost their jobs. The chances for young people to enter occupations of this kind became very slim indeed.

Most of these structural difficulties were projected into the size discussion. The question of size overshadowed all other problems.[1] The shock of being reduced from a big to a small country resulted in a very acute size pessimism, particularly among the articulate middle classes who, after having lost some of their well-protected job opportunities, tended to take an equally poor view of the nation's chances as they took of their own. Such size pessimism in a mother country which has lost some of its territories is not a peculiarly Austrian phenomenon.[2] Distinct signs of it could be seen after World War II in the Netherlands and even in big countries like Britain and France. In Austria the symptoms of this illness were, however, particularly severe, mainly for three reasons.

---

[1] A typical example for the confused way in which everything was made a problem of size was the widely quoted hydrocephalic analogy of the 'water-head Vienna'. Vienna, so it was said, was 'far too big' for the new Austria, with its more than 28 per cent of the country's inhabitants. Now, 28 per cent of a country's population in the capital (today the percentage is still 25 per cent) is certainly an uncommonly high proportion, the share in comparable countries usually being 10 per cent or less (see Table I in the Appendix). The *economic* problem was, however, not the *size* of Vienna but the fact that its economic structure had been largely geared to the administrative and financial requirements of the Eastern hinterland and to the special demands of the Court. With their disappearance the basis for the city's existence was shaken. Nowadays, with the economic structure of Vienna having adapted itself to the changed circumstances, nobody talks any more of the 'water-head Vienna', though the percentage of people living in the capital is almost as big as in 1918. The historical fact of the dissolution of the Habsburg Reich has left Austria with a large proportion of its city population concentrated in one town — the capital. If one adds the — economically more significant — number of people living in cities over 100,000 inhabitants, and calculated their share in the total population, then Austria ceases to be a special case. This share (about a third of the population) is smaller in Austria than in Great Britain and not much bigger than in Western Germany (see Table I). It would become even more average if we included medium-sized towns whose number is particularly small in Austria.

[2] The size pessimism was completely absent in the newly created states, Czechoslovakia, Hungary, etc., though they were faced with similar structural problems. The spirit of national liberation provided the stimulus for an active and optimistic readjustment policy. Also, the middle classes had more to gain than to lose from the change.

(1) The dismemberment came after a lost war, when the economy was hardly functioning and when spirits were rather low.

(2) The areas dissociated from Austria were much more vital to her economy than the overseas territories lost by the Netherlands, Britain, and France in recent years.

(3) A very decisive part in keeping up the disbelief in the viability of the first Austrian republic was played by German propaganda. The German 'Anschluss'-apostles gave massive support to every single doubt in Austria's capacity to solve her problems within her own 'narrow' frontiers. It was typical for this influence that it did not only stress the smallness of Austria but also discarded all solutions other than an 'Anschluss'.

Under these conditions it is perhaps not so strange that size pessimism reached rather high proportions in Austria. A flood of literature on the problem of size and viability was published with the pessimists by far in the ascendancy, though important voices were raised against them.[1] And a German writer could say, with some exaggeration but not completely without foundation: 'Austria's population is convinced that the country is not viable'.[2] In fact, the rather strange and historically not very frequent situation arose in which the protagonists of a country proclaimed its insufficient economic basis, while outsiders — particularly those who were immune to Germany's propaganda influence or were opposed to German expansion — went almost into lyrics when describing the country's potentialities. Thus, while Austria's leading economic publicist declared that the 'Anschluss' of Austria to Germany was an economic necessity,[3] Layton and Rist in their famous 1925 Report to the League of Nations on the economic conditions in Austria affirmed their belief in the country's viability, and in the same year the Czech economist Antonin Basch wrote: 'Austria is *not*, as is often erroneously said, an *economically poor* State, but one with very considerable economic assets ensuring it a sound economic existence and prosperity'.[4]

With feeling inside the country tuned so low the task of recuperation and readjustment, difficult under any circumstances, could not but prove almost unattainable. Investment activity was sluggish, with short-run speculations very much to the fore; business and government alike hesitated for a long time to look at the new

---

[1] Notable among them was Friedrich Hertz. See, for instance, his *Ist Österreich wirklich lebensfähig?* (Vienna, 1921).

[2] S. Schilder, *Der Streit um die Lebensfähigkeit Österreichs* (Stuttgart, 1926).

[3] Gustav Stolper in numerous articles and pamphlets. See, for instance, his *Deutsch-Österreich als Sozial- und Wirtschafts-Problem* (Munich, 1921), p. 144.

[4] A. Basch and J. Dvoracek, *Austria and its Economic Existence* (Prague, 1925), p. 9. Italics in the original.

situation realistically and no proper direction was given to aid the necessary long-run adjustments. Thus Austria's economic development after the First World War suffered from severe stagnationist elements. True, the recovery of production in the 'twenties was quite noticeable — in fact, in the first half of that decade it was faster than the increase in production in Germany, who suffered from a stabilization crisis, and in the second half it surpassed Britain's growth rate, which was hampered by deflation (see Table II), but it was quite insufficient in view of the low level to which production had fallen at the end of the war. Unemployment remained a heavy social and economic burden on the country even in 1929, when the world boom had reduced this problem to an acceptable level in most other countries ; comparable rates of unemployment could only be found in deflationist Britain and in Germany where a heavy modernization movement had upset the labour market (see Table III). A particularly intractable problem was the country's balance of trade deficit, which all through the 'twenties remained at an uncomfortably high level. In 1929, for instance, only two-thirds of the imports were paid for by exports. Even countries in whose balance of payments invisible items played a far greater positive rôle than in Austria — Great Britain, Italy, Norway — had a better relation between imports and exports (see Table IV). The stickiness of the problems reaffirmed the conviction in some circles that the country's size was insufficient, though a comparison with other small countries would have shown that Austria's experiences were not to be generalized.

The adjustment of the economy to the new environment which had proceeded slowly — too slowly — in the 'twenties, made, by force of circumstances, more rapid progress during the 'thirties. By 1937, the last year of Austria's pre-war independence, the country had somehow managed to find its feet. The balance of trade problem no longer loomed as a constant threat over the economy ; 84 per cent of the imports were now covered by exports and the remaining gap was bridged by the receipts from an extended tourist traffic and through other invisible items. The dependence on foreign credits had been removed and the foreign indebtedness could be reduced.

But this development towards economic independence took place under the shadow of the crisis. Therefore it was a sort of retrogressive development. Deflation reigned all through the period. The foreign trade problem was not solved by an expansion in exports but by a sharp reduction in imports. Their volume (measured in prices of 1937) declined by 41 per cent between 1929 and 1937. This decline could only be brought about by a sharp turn towards greater self-sufficiency. The main beneficiaries of this protectionist movement were agriculture and the basic industries, the latter also prospering from the war-induced demand for iron and steel products in Germany, Italy, and Japan. The proportion of people working in agriculture and the basic industries increased during the recovery period 1931–37. If we agree with Colin Clark that economic progress is best exemplified by the movement of labour from primary to secondary and tertiary industries,[1] this solution of the Austrian problem could hardly be called a progressive one. The labour-intensive manufacturing and service industries, suffering from deflationist and low-wage policies, were hardly touched by the recovery. Unemployment, therefore, continued to be a major headache. The number of unemployed, which had reached its highest level in 1933 with an average of more than 400,000 people registered at the labour exchanges, could only be reduced to 320,000 in 1937 ; in 1929 — not a very satisfactory year either, as we saw — it had stood at 192,000.

To the size addicts in Austria the question gradually ceased to be whether the country could live within its narrow frontiers. The stress was now laid on the question : could it live *well* ?

II. AFTER THE SECOND WORLD WAR

After World War II, in 1945, Austria found herself in a situation not unlike that of 1918. Again the economy was ruined and disorganized, again the country was carved out of a bigger economic unit of which it had been a part, again it inherited an economic structure that had not been designed for the needs and opportunities of the 7 million nation. The big iron and steel works in Linz, the over-sized aluminium works in Ranshofen, the viscose factory in Lenzing — to name the most important enterprises erected during the German occupation — were partly unfinished torsos planned for a greater European market under German hegemony. Their location was guided more by security considerations than by a strictly economic calculus. Considering that the development of mass production techniques had not stood still in the past thirty years, economic size should have played, if anything, a much larger part in 1945 than in 1918. In fact, however, apart from a short revival of the 'viability' debate in 1945 and 1946, the subject of size has

[1] See Colin Clark, *The Conditions of Economic Progress* (3rd edition, London, 1957), particularly Ch. IX.

— in noticeable contrast to the inter-war years — disappeared from practically all discussions on Austria's future.

The reason for this change is to be found in the fact that, in spite of all the similarities with 1918, the psychological and objective conditions for Austria's economic revival and adjustment were more favourable in 1945 than thirty years earlier.[1] Three points in particular should be mentioned.

(1) In contrast to 1918 the population now had the recollection of an economically independent Austria. Even if that recollection was none too cheerful, an independent existence within the republic's frontiers at least no longer seemed the absurdity which it had appeared to many people in 1918.

(2) The structural incongruities that existed in 1945 affected mainly the heavy industries. The consumption goods and service industries, which had been the main headache after 1918, suffered recently from retarded growth rather than from over-development. The big post-war reconstruction boom and the subsequent armaments drive in large parts of the world enabled Austria's expanded heavy industry to find an outlet in exports which would have been undreamt off in pre-war days.[2] The same circumstances which eased the change-over from a war to a peace economy in the United States and elsewhere helped Austria (so far) to avoid the pains of adjustment which had weighed so heavily on her economy in the 'twenties. With the considerable profits earned in the post-war years the new industries could be assimilated into the Austrian economy, the destruction repaired, and incomplete and lop-sided projects rounded off.

(3) The actual experience of incorporation in the German Reich during the 1938–45 period has cured many people of the once so widespread and emotionally fortified belief in the 'Anschluss' as a solution for all problems.[3]

[1] It is, of course, not difficult to make such a statement after the event. In fact, the present writer expressed the same opinion ten years ago. See K. W. Rothschild, *Austria's Economic Development between the Two Wars* (London, 1947), Ch. VII. For a different view see, for instance, Hans Bayer, *Die Zukunft der österreichischen Volkswirtschaft* (Innsbruck, 1947) : 'If one compares the situation in 1918 and 1945 one cannot but come to the conclusion that today the starting position for the Austrian economy is less favourable and certainly not better than thirty years ago' (p. 13). In the same pamphlet, however, Professor Bayer expressed the opinion that Austria could enter a more prosperous era if the economic mistakes of the past were avoided.

[2] Iron and steel exports, for instance, which in 1937 represented less than 10 per cent of total exports, accounted in 1956 for 16 per cent out of an export volume more than double the size of that of 1937.

[3] This is not to say that the 'Anschluss' idea is completely dead. Thirty years of continuous ideological propaganda are not shaken off as easily as all that. Though little is said openly on that matter, an 'Anschluss' as the 'natural' solution to Austria's economic future still lingers on in the minds of some Austrians and quite a number of Germans.

With these more favourable conditions surrounding its second birth the Austrian republic could march along a remarkably different economic route compared with that of thirty years ago. Investment activity is much stronger and more long-term orientated than in the days of the first republic. Then there is, of course, the world boom to help matters, and also a greater awareness of the deflationist errors of by-gone days. All this has resulted in the disappearance of a 'special' Austrian situation. In fact, what is perhaps most surprising is the similarity of 'small' Austria's post-war development with that of 'big' Western Germany.[1] In both countries the rate of increase in industrial production and in the volume of exports lies considerably above the Western European average (see Tables V and VI). The difference was particularly wide up till about 1950. At that time it was due to the very low starting point in Austria and Western Germany which permitted rather high rates of growth ;[2] but it has also persisted in the boom period that started in 1954. The performance in the employment field also shows some striking similarities between Western Germany and Austria. Both countries have a significantly higher percentage of unemployment than Britain, Switzerland, and the countries of Northern Europe (due to some structural factors and an unduly high seasonal unemployment in wintertime), and both countries experienced a post-stabilization unemployment problem in the years 1948–50 (see Table VII). Other similarities could also be quoted.[3]

Since the post-1945 adjustment of Austria to the changed environment took place in an expanding world economy, the progress was

[1] The comparison with Western Germany seems more appropriate than with other big countries in Western Europe because there are important parallels. Like Western Germany, Austria had to start from scratch ; both countries had an export-orientated rather than a (directly) armaments-orientated economy ; the Ministers in charge of economic affairs (Erhard in Germany and Kamitz in Austria) are motivated by similar ideas on economic policy. There are, of course, also numerous differences : nationalized industries play an important part in Austria but not in Germany ; the socialists are in the (coalition) government in Austria but in opposition in Germany ; and so on and so forth. But these differences do not weigh heavily enough to rob the comparison of its significance.

[2] For the same reason the Western German growth rates of that period were considerably higher than the Austrian ones. Compared with 1938 the indices of industrial production for Austria, Western Germany, and OEEC-Europe stood in 1948 at 92, 52, and 101 respectively; the indices of export volume at 54, 19, and 79.

About the reasons for high rates of growth in badly damaged industrial economies, see A. Sauvy, 'Développement économique et répartition professionnelle de la population', *Revue d'Économie Politique* (May-June 1956), pp. 372 ff.

[3] The parallels shown above are all in the 'real' sphere. In the monetary field the recent history of the two countries has less in common. On the whole, inflationary trends have been more marked in Austria than in Germany and the Austrian Schilling has not reached the same degree of 'hardness' as the D-Mark. Also, Austria has not experienced such a persistent balance of trade surplus as has Germany. But — apart from the first post-war years — the chronic balance of payments worries which so plagued Austria in the 'twenties have been overcome.

174

not only smoother than in the inter-war period, but it was also quite clearly in the 'right' direction. The share of the population working in agriculture (and their absolute number) has declined sharply, while industry has rapidly gained in importance (see Table VIII). In 1910 agriculture and forestry were clearly leading among the three big economic branches (agriculture, industry, services); in 1934 they were just about equal with industry; yet in the post-war years industrial employment has clearly taken the lead and is continuous by increasing its share. From an agrarian-industrial country Austria has changed into a predominantly industrial country with an important agricultural sector. In fact, Austria's employment structure, as exemplified by the three main divisions, is rapidly approaching the type of structure which Western Germany exhibited before the war. (Since then Western Germany has proceeded further with the shift of employment from primary to tertiary occupations. See Table VIII).[1]

The favourable Austrian development since World War II — the 'Austrian miracle' — should not blind us to certain weaknesses and dangers. We saw that the recovery process has been greatly helped by an exceptional world boom which reduced the need for adjustments to a minimum. A decline in international boom conditions would quite probably put a severe strain on the Austrian economy. The slight stagnation in Western economic growth in the years 1952 and 1953 provided a very serious warning. In these years Austria's industrial expansion suddenly dropped behind the Western European average and her unemployment percentage jumped from less than 6 to 9 per cent.[2] The economic effects might have been even more marked had not exports obtained a strong stimulus by the devaluation of the Schilling early in 1953.

An actual *decline* in world economic activity could have much more serious consequences. Austria's export trade and the entire economy have become dependent, to an uncomfortably high degree,

---

[1] There is one speciality in Austria's structural development: the share of services has actually declined between 1910 and 1951. Part of this phenomenon is explained by the fact that domestic servants (plentifully supplied by the poorer provinces in the days of the Habsburg empire) were employed to an abnormally high extent — for a European country — in imperial Austria and that this exceptional feature has gradually disappeared. If we leave out domestic service, we get for the remaining service-employment the usual rising trend, though the rise is comparatively slow. This is to be explained by the previously mentioned over-grown administrative and financial apparatus Austria had inherited from the monarchy, which had to be cut down to the needs of the smaller country. This acted as a counter-weight to the 'normal' tendency towards increasing tertiary employment. Now that this contrary influence has worked itself out, the usual trend will probably become more clearly observable.

[2] Western Germany maintained her above-the-average performance also in these two years.

on the building, armaments, and investment boom in the outer world. One-third of the 1956 exports consisted of timber, iron, and steel. If these were hit by a sharp decline in demand, Austria might still be faced by the need for considerable structural adjustments in order to overcome internal and external imbalances which, so far, have remained hidden. Since traditions die a slow death it is not at all unlikely that when such a recession comes, and when other nations will (quite rightly) turn their thoughts to full employment problems, to the internal and external implications of full employment, and to the wider issues of the capitalism versus socialism (marketing versus planning) question, many Austrians will once again pay excessive attention to size, regarding it as the main source of all evil.

III. THE LESSONS

The twofold experiences of Austria after 1918 and 1945 give us a rare opportunity to test some of our ideas on the influence of (small) size on development. It is, of course, not easy to isolate this influence and to give proper weight to the numerous other economic and historical factors influencing growth. But some tentative conclusions may be drawn.

(1) It is obvious that the *change* from one size to another involved some very real and difficult adjustment problems not unlike those that follow from fundamental changes in demand. The change problem was much more serious in post-1918 Austria than in post-1945 Austria, when far less change was required and when it was possible to build on the actual structure and the experiences of a small pre-war Austria.

(2) The change problem can obviously be solved much more easily in an expanding than in a stagnating or contracting world economy. This is another reason why Austria's readjustment experience has so far been much more favourable than after 1918. It is less certain whether there is an intimate relationship between the problem of size as such (apart from *changes* in size) and depression effects. The experience of the 'thirties does not indicate any clear-cut connection between the two. Of course, a small state will hardly be able to pull itself out from the economic mess by its own boot-straps. But, for that matter, very few big countries are nowadays in that position. There is, however, the very real danger that the trend towards greater self-sufficiency usually connected with international recessions hits a small country's economy harder than a big one. For a small home market

will become a serious limit for certain production methods which were quite feasible when world trade was functioning.

(3) If one leaves aside disruptive influences (*changes* in size, depressions) it is doubtful whether — as far as practical policy is concerned — size is really an important economic concept. Nations have historically grown to a certain size. This size, at any moment, is one of the structural characteristics of that country, just as much as the climate, the qualities of the soil, the wealth of resources. There are, of course, times when one may consider changing the size by customs unions, fusions, etc., just as one may consider evacuating areas where the climate is rough or the soil poor. Decisions of this sort will have far-reaching consequences for the whole way of life (including economic conditions and opportunities) of the population. Decisions on size are therefore major political decisions in which the economic argument is but one (and not necessarily the most important) aspect. Once the decision about size is made (by history or by deliberate action) the main problem seems to be not so much what the actual size is but whether the economy is properly adjusted to this structural element, just as a proper adjustment to other structural factors is essential for a balanced and dynamic growth. Switzerland, which went through a long and uninterrupted, peaceful adjustment process, and where doubts about the proper size and 'viability' of the domestic economy never existed, offers a good example of the possibilities for a happy marriage between small size and industrial structure.[1] Similarly, the continued survival of small and medium enterprises in big countries points to the fact that the size problem is decisive only for certain branches of production, but much less for others. Even with the advent of automation and the new techniques connected with it there seem to be no cogent reasons — given some reasonable regulation of international trade — why the size of a nation should become a factor of decisive significance.[2] If international and interregional exchanges can be made to function smoothly, in short, if the twin problems of full employment and proportional development can be solved, then the *economic* problem of the size of nations will, I believe, not play a major part.

[1] The frequent comparisons between Austria and Switzerland pointing out the better endowment of Austria with natural resources — correct as far as they go — usually neglect the importance of the psychological and the continuity factor.

[2] See the interesting remarks by S. Moos, 'The Scope of Automation', *Economic Journal*, March 1957, particularly pp. 27-30.

STATISTICAL APPENDIX

TABLE I

PROPORTION OF POPULATION LIVING IN THE CAPITAL AND IN
CITIES WITH MORE THAN 100,000 INHABITANTS
(Latest Census Data)

Country	Proportion living in the Capital	Proportion living in cities with more than 100,000 inhabitants (incl. the Capital)
	%	%
Austria	25	33
Belgium	2	11
Czechoslovakia	7	14
France	7	17
Western Germany	0·2	27
Hungary	11	15
Sweden	11	18
Switzerland	3	21
Great Britain	7 *	38

* Administrative county of London only.
Source : United Nations, *Demographic Yearbook*, 1955.

TABLE II

INDUSTRIAL PRODUCTION AFTER WORLD WAR I
(1921 = 100)

	Austria	Belgium	Czecho-slovakia*	France	Ger-many	Italy	Sweden	United Kingdom
1922	123	120		128	108	116	119	130
1923	123	133		138	73	126	132	148
1924	132	149	100	166	106	140	152	152
1925	154	149	106	167	125	154	155	150
1926	152	158	103	184	121	162	168	128
1927	164	175	121	176	150	156	177	163
1928	177	189	135	197	158	174	184	161
1929	177	195	139	209	158	176	210	172

* 1924 = 100.
Source : OEEC, *Industrial Statistics* 1900–1955 (Addendum);
for Czechoslovakia : *Statistical Yearbook of the League of Nations*.

TABLE III

UNEMPLOYMENT IN 1929
(In per cent of the Population aged 15 and over)

Austria	3·7	Hungary	0·2
Czechoslovakia	0·4	Italy	0·1
Denmark	1·7	Norway	0·9
Germany	3·5	Poland	0·6
France	*	United Kingdom	3·7†

* Less than 0·1 per cent.
† Including temporary stoppages.

Source : Statistical Yearbooks of the League of Nations. Only those countries were included whose unemployment statistics did not differ too widely in method.

TABLE IV

THE BALANCE OF TRADE POSITION IN 1929
(Percentage of Imports covered by Exports)

Austria	67	Italy	70
Belgium	90	Netherlands	74
Czechoslovakia	103	Norway	70
Denmark	94	Poland	90
Germany	97	Sweden	101
France	75	Switzerland	77
Hungary	96	United Kingdom	69

Source : *Statistical Yearbook of the League of Nations.*

TABLE V

INDUSTRIAL PRODUCTION AFTER WORLD WAR II

	Austria	Western Germany	OEEC countries combined	Austria	Western Germany	OEEC countries combined
	1948 = 100			Increase over previous year in per cent		
1949	134	144	113	34	44	13
1950	158	181	126	18	26	12
1951	180	215	138	14	19	10
1952	182	231	140	1	7	1
1953	185	250	148	2	8	6
1954	211	281	160	14	12	8
1955	239	327	175	13	16	9
1956	249	353	182	4	8	4

Source : OEEC, *General Statistics.*

TABLE VI

VOLUME OF EXPORTS

	Austria	Western Germany	OEEC countries combined	Austria	Western Germany	OEEC countries combined
	1948=100			Increase over previous year in per cent		
1949	124	185	120	24	85	20
1950	186	431	155	50	133	29
1951	203	608	175	9	41	13
1952	203	662	167	0	9	5
1953	270	769	182	33	16	9
1954	330	954	204	22	24	12
1955	368	1092	223	12	14	9
1956	433	1269	240	18	16	7

Source : OEEC, *Foreign Trade Statistics.*

TABLE VII

UNEMPLOYMENT IN THE YEARS 1948–56
(In per cent of the Active Labour Force,
employed plus unemployed) *

	Austria	Western Germany†
1948	2·3	4·2
1949	4·6	8·3
1950	6·2	10·2
1951	5·7	9·2
1952	7·7	8·4
1953	9·0	7·5
1954	7·9	7·0
1955	5·7	5·1
1956	5·5	4·0

* The percentage figures in this table are not directly comparable with those given in Table III.
† Without West Berlin.
Source : ILO, *Yearbook of Labour Statistics.*

TABLE VIII

THE STRUCTURE OF THE ECONOMICALLY ACTIVE POPULATION
IN AUSTRIA AND WESTERN GERMANY

Distribution in per cent of all economically active persons
(including unemployed)

	Austria			Western Germany †	
	1910 *	1934	1951	1939	1950
Agriculture and Forestry	39·0	36·1	32·3	27·1	23·2
Primary and Manufacturing Industry	31·8	35·5	40·8	41·9	42·3
Services	29·2	28·4	26·9	31·0	34·5
(of which : Domestic Service)	(7·3)	(5·3)	(2·3)		

* Present-day frontiers.   † Without Berlin.

Source : Österreichisches Statistisches Zentralamt, *Österreichs Bevölkerung*
(Vienna, 1953) ; *Statistisches Jahrbuch für die Bundesrepublik Deutschland*, 1956.

Chapter 11

THE PROBLEMS OF PORTUGUESE ECONOMIC DEVELOPMENT [1]

BY

L. T. PINTO
University of Lisbon

I. INTRODUCTION

IT is generally recognized that in the absence of foreign trade a large country can, *ceteris paribus*, develop more rapidly than a small one.[2] What difference does foreign trade make to this situation ? The classical or traditional theory of foreign trade leads to the conclusion that small nations derive greater benefits from foreign trade than do large ones. We may quote J. S. Mill, who says in his *Principles* : [3]

> It still appears, that the countries which carry on their foreign trade on the most advantageous terms, are those whose commodities are most in demand by foreign countries, and which have themselves the least demand for foreign commodities. From which, among other consequences, it follows, that the richest countries, *ceteris paribus*, gain the least by a given amount of foreign commerce : since, having a greater demand for commodities generally, they are likely to have a greater demand for foreign commodities, and thus modify the terms of interchange to their own disadvantage.

This form of analysis applies, however, to an imperfect market disposing of a given quantity of resources ; the analysis cannot easily be transposed into a developing economy. The classical conclusions would be valid in a dynamic process if the pattern of specialization adopted assured the permanence of short-period

---

[1] Translated from the French by Elizabeth Henderson.
[2] By a small country I mean in this context a country with a low *per caput* income and a small population. However, a country's size is not determined by these two factors alone ; cf. on this point François Perroux, *Europe sans rivages*, Paris, 1954, p. 335.
[3] J. S. Mill, *Principles of Political Economy*, Book III, Chapter xviii, § 9. (Ashley's edition, 1909, p. 604.)

advantages. But this implies the automatic transmission of growth from the motivating economy. Contemporary writers have shown, moreover, that national economies are capable of active behaviour and that domination and exploitation effects may upset the traditional view of the problems of the gain from trade and the size of nations.[1]

On these assumptions, let us try to analyse the experiences of Portuguese economic development and to examine as best we may its relation to the size of the nation. First of all, it is very hard to determine just what is the size of the Portuguese nation. If we retain the classical definition of a nation as an area beyond which there is relative immobility of factors of production, it is difficult to trace the economic frontiers of metropolitan Portugal in relation to the country's overseas territories. If, on the other hand, we consider all Portuguese territories as a whole, can we still speak of Portugal as a small nation ? Everything depends on the standard of measurement for the size of a nation.

Furthermore, developing countries are marked by the existence of 'controls', which are alien to the classical theory of short-period markets. Today, as in the past, government centres of decision play an essential part in the economic growth of the whole Portuguese economy and the formulation of long-term or medium-term development plans introduces the time factor in a manner neglected by the classical economists. All this makes it impossible or artificial to reduce the experiences of development to a purely economic and classical framework. For this reason we shall limit ourselves to describing the recent development of the Portuguese economy and to raising certain points which have proved of strategic importance in Portuguese economic expansion.

II. THE POVERTY OF PORTUGAL

The following global figures relating to metropolitan Portugal may serve to convey an idea of certain basic data and their recent trends :

(1) In 1955 Portugal had a *per caput* income of $200, which puts her, with Greece and Turkey, among the poorer European nations.

(2) The distribution of the working population and gross

---

[1] François Perroux has contributed much to this new kind of analysis.

national product among major sectors was as follows in 1955 :

TABLE I

DISTRIBUTION OF WORKING POPULATION
AND GROSS NATIONAL PRODUCT

Sector	Working population	Gross national product
	%	%
Agriculture	49	26
Industry	24	38
Services	27	36

The figures clearly show the low productivity and great pre-ponderance of the agricultural population and also the large share of the tertiary sector. If the overseas territories were included, overall *per caput* income would be still lower, seeing that these territories are far less developed than the mother country.

Thus it can be seen that on the basis of *per caput* income and of other indices Portugal is to be regarded as an under-developed region and a small country.[1]

As regards her external relations with other countries, Portugal's trade reaches a high proportion of gross national product. Exports consist of a limited number of products of which some are non-essentials (port wine, canned fish) and go to a small number of countries (United Kingdom, United States, Germany, France). The overseas territories are similarly, though less favourably, situated, because of the widely fluctuating prices of their export products. Finally, exports are almost entirely limited to products of the primary sector, the value added by industry to goods such as cork products or canned foodstuffs being almost negligible. By contrast, Portuguese imports consist of capital goods (25 per cent), semi-manufactures (28 per cent), and fuels (17 per cent) ; that is, of products essential for the Portuguese economy.

Thus Portugal is in a weak bargaining position and heavily dependent upon a few foreign economies. It is difficult to state the measure of that dependence without a detailed analysis of the structure of trade and market forms ; such dependence will obviously be greater to the extent that exports are sold to a government

---

[1] On structural economic problems of Portugal see F. Moura, J. Nunes, and Luis Teixeira Pinto, *Structure de l'économie portugaise* ; F. Moura, *Stagnation ou croissance de l'économie portugaise?* ; and L. T. Pinto, *Le Portugal devant l'intégration économique de l'Europe.*

department in a foreign country or to large international concerns.[1]

In the negotiations of commercial agreements since the war it has also become clear that Portugal's bargaining power is weak, although the difficulties in which some other economies, such as those of Great Britain, Germany, and France, have found themselves may have concealed the fact for some years.

III. THE REASONS FOR THE SLOW GROWTH OF THE PORTUGUESE ECONOMY

The relatively slow rate of growth of the Portuguese economy during recent years, despite certain highly productive investment, is shown by the estimates of the gross national product. Among the factors leading to this slow growth are the low level of income and saving ; the existence of a considerable amount of disguised unemployment ; the very limited diversification of production and exports ; the technical backwardness of much of industry ; the relatively high rate of population growth ; the insufficient integration of the metropolitan and overseas economies.

If we wish to apply the Harrod-Domar model, we must also take account of certain other conditions in an under-developed country. Thus we must start from the formula $G = \dfrac{s}{A_r}$, where G is the rate of growth, s the propensity to save, and A_r the capital/output ratio. In addition we should note the following among the many features characterizing under-developed countries :

(*a*) The limited scope of the accelerator and of the leaks due to the marginal propensity to import give rise to a certain amount of stability, which is, however, often disturbed by the impact of exogenous factors deriving from autonomous fluctuations in exports ;

(*b*) The absorption of disguised unemployment and the emergence of inflationary situations are largely due not to the propensity to save and the capital/output ratio, but to balanced growth of the factors of production.

Intervention is possible with respect to several constellations of variables, but the choice amongst them is a political decision.[2] Thus

[1] As regards such firms, cf. the original analysis by Maurice Byé, 'La Grande Unité inter-territoriale dans l'industrie extractive et ses plans', *Cahiers de l'I.S.E.A.*, Series F, No. 2, 1955.

[2] Extra-economic elements are of major importance today and we are far from the pure theory of international trade. See J. Weiller, *L'Échange international*, Paris, 1957.

the government has an *a priori* choice between the following alternatives :

(i) to adapt saving to the growth factors, particularly population ;
(ii) to adapt growth factors to saving ;
(iii) to fix a rate of growth and adapt the factors to that rate.

Portugal has most closely followed one or other of the two first methods. If the marginal propensity to save is 7 per cent and the capital/output ratio 5, we can readily calculate the rate of growth at 1·4 per cent. This means that national income grows approximately at the same rate as does the population. If the above assumptions are correct,[1] Portugal has made little or no economic progress during the past few years. However, we are fully aware of the fact that the use of aggregate figures, while not altogether useless, does greatly limit the scope of the analysis.

If we compare the development of Portugal's national product since 1950 and her population growth, we see clearly that the latter has matched or exceeded the growth of real income, thereby preventing any progress which might have raised the standard of living.

Of the various types of growth — spontaneous, transmitted, or planned — transmitted growth is shown to have been the most significant in Portugal. The expansion of the Portuguese economy was conditioned by the development of foreign trade and was thus subject to the influence of certain motivating economies and to the effects of cyclical fluctuations in the world economy.

The means of transmission — real and transfer flows, prices and terms of trade, and even expectations of prices — all played their part in Portuguese economic growth, though the influence of the terms of trade was small. In any case, Ricardo's and J. S. Mill's argument that a small nation benefits most from foreign trade because of the inelasticity of demand does not apply to the case of Portugal. It may perhaps better be said that greater specialization determines more favourable terms of trade.

As regards planned growth, it is to be borne in mind that actual investment has fallen short of the amounts envisaged in the latest development plan (1953–58). This is the more serious since this plan was not unduly ambitious and was more in the nature of a forecast of the employment of disposable funds.

---

[1] The reasons for the choice of these particular figures are explained in the author's thesis, *Aspects de la théorie de la croissance économique*, Lisbon, 1956.

IV. THE EFFECTS OF POVERTY AND
MARKET STRUCTURE

We shall single out market problems as among the other factors
which retard economic development. In Portugal, as in most
capitalist countries in process of development, the low level of
demand is to be regarded as one of the factors holding up expansion.
Consumers generally have very low incomes which have to be
devoted to the satisfaction of essential needs. Besides that great
mass of poor consumers, there is a more privileged class with larger
purchasing power, chiefly directed towards luxury goods, almost
invariably of foreign origin. Measured by purchasing power,
Portugal must be considered a very small nation, seeing that the
total population (including overseas territories) of 20 million is
equivalent, in terms of income and purchasing power, to a 'European'
population of less than 3 million.[1]

This situation has led most people to think that the problem of
Portuguese economic development is a market problem and this
point of view is reflected in the legal limitations placed upon new
entry into industry. Before setting up a new plant in almost any
branch of industry, entrepreneurs must make an application and
obtain a permit. This system is known as *condicionamento da
indùstria* and is designed to prevent harmful competition and waste
of capital ; in practice, it has sometimes contributed to strengthening
monopolistic and oligopolistic structures and to retarding technical
progress in industry. As a consequence, Portuguese industry is
characterized by the prevalence of monopoly or oligopoly and by
technical backwardness. Furthermore, lack of a spirit of enterprise
and the almost complete absence of a long-term capital market also
favour industrial concentration and self-financing. As a result,
investment is mainly in traditional or established branches of
industry : partly through mere imitation and partly because
capitalists are expert — and that sometimes to a limited extent —
only with those branches in which they have themselves been
engaged. The only alternative to reinvestment in the same industry
which Portuguese capitalists consider, apart from hoarding, is the
purchase of land or buildings. These factors together make for
unbalanced growth.

If we analyse the Portuguese market and its development during
the last few years, we also see that new firms tend to be set up in

[1] European in the sense of having a *per caput* income equal to the Western
European average.

sectors with an established market. Normally what happens is that entrepreneurs watch the volume of imports of a certain product, and if imports are large, an attempt is made to replace them by domestic production of the same goods. An application is then made for a permit and at the same time a claim for sufficient tariff protection ; if the entrepreneur obtains the latter together with his permit, he has a quasi-monopolistic position.

The new enterprise prospers, profits are earned and attract the envy of other entrepreneurs ; technical and organizational deficiencies pass unnoticed and stagnation sets in. If the first firm should be unable to prevent the entry of new firms, the market is divided after the first struggles typical of oligopolistic situations, and higher tariffs are demanded to meet foreign competition. Excess capacity is thus created, and thereafter new entry is not only prevented by the bargaining power of the group but by the argument that 'the productive capacity of the branch is greatly in excess of the market's consumption'.

It is obvious that in these circumstances firms produce for the domestic market and have no inducement either to introduce new techniques or to make any serious efforts to export. We may go so far as to assert that these circumstances completely invalidate the theory according to which technical progress is transmitted by virtue of the modification of the terms of trade. Moreover, the fact that the creation of a plant becomes profitable only if the product in question was already being imported in large quantities implies that, so far as current consumption goods are concerned, the poorest classes are made to pay for this type of development. A whole series of examples confirms that newly created industries have put a heavy burden on the poorest consumers.

Apart from this, there are a small number of goods which previously had established outlets but which were not produced domestically for reasons which have nothing to do with market problems. Striking examples are the production of iron and steel and oil refining. In both cases, the influence of foreign groups prevented or delayed the creation of domestic industries. This is to be regarded as the result of a domination effect holding up growth in less developed countries.

Given the characteristics of Portuguese industry, it will readily be appreciated that exports have not been developed of new products nor has Portugal benefited from abnormal foreign demand for any product. There has been no shock stimulant, such as occurred in Angola in the case of coffee, or as may occur for petroleum in Angola, or radioactive minerals in Mozambique. For the time being certain

Portuguese products still enjoy a foreign market, but the country's dependence on the Great Powers considerably limits the results of any efforts resting on an expansion of exports. This amounts to saying that it is much easier for the Germans or Americans to continue selling cars to Portugal than for the Portuguese to increase their sales of luxury beverages in the United States or in Germany.[1]

Technical progress and innovations may perhaps encourage the emergence of a set of conditions allowing for an acceleration of the rate of development in Portugal. Portugal is, for example, well placed in the field of atomic energy as a new source of power, because of the existence of deposits of fissile materials. But we must not forget that the countries of the Middle East, for all their oil resources exploited during the last fifty years, are still in a state of extreme poverty. Domination or power effects may contribute in a decisive manner to the perpetuation of a *status quo* which everybody refuses, or pretends to refuse, to accept. In any case, the example of Portugal shows that to be small is often an obstacle to growth.

---

[1] The degree of Portugal's dependence has, however, diminished. For example, the domination effect of the British economy is weaker today than it was before the war.

Chapter 12

THE SIZE OF THE ECONOMY
AND ITS RELATION TO STABILITY
AND STEADY PROGRESS: I

BY

L. TARSHIS
Stanford University

I. THE EVIDENCE OF STATISTICS

A CASUAL glance at National Income data for various national economies seems to provide all the evidence we need for an answer — though it is, perhaps, an unexpected one — to the question : 'How is a nation's stability related to its size ?' Comparing the record for the period beginning in the 1920s and ending in 1952 (with the war years and those immediately following omitted) for the United Kingdom, Germany, France, Sweden, and the United States, we find a reasonably clear-cut relationship : the greatest instability was found in the largest economies ; and vice versa. The United States, by any standard the largest of all, showed itself to be the most unstable, with its instability symptomized by the Great Depression which was deepest in that country ; Sweden, the smallest of the five, displayed remarkable stability, with a depression decline of only 9 per cent, or less than a third of that experienced by the United States. The United Kingdom, which also suffered a comparatively small decline in income, seemed to be only a little less stable than Sweden, while Germany and France showed less instability than the United States but much more than Sweden and the United Kingdom.

We can derive a somewhat more objective measure of each country's stability, first by making an allowance for the potential level of the national income over the period, allowing of course for growth, and then comparing deviations from the possible level of income. On the basis of these measurements, we find confirmation for our first impressions ; the coefficient of instability for each country is :

	%
Sweden	7·4
United Kingdom	6·6
France	16·0
Germany	14·6
United States	18·5

What should surprise us most about these results is that the most active trading economies of the five — the United Kingdom and Sweden — showed themselves to be more stable than the others; while the two, which by most standards were largest, displayed greater instability. At first glance, then, we should be inclined to answer that a small economy which was in active trading relations with others was most likely to be stable.

This conclusion is not the one we should expect, and our impulse is to distrust our findings. It is easy to feel distrust, because a demonstration of this sort is anything but convincing. Far too many factors which are quite independent of the economy's size could be called upon to explain the results. The relation may have been fortuitous, and certainly, before we dare accept such a statistical result as evidence, we must be assured that a cause-and-effect relationship between size and stability can indeed be operative. To consider the possible links between these variables is our main purpose in this paper.

II. THE EVIDENCE OF ECONOMIC ANALYSIS

At this stage in the proceedings, no point is served by examining in any detail the notion of the size of the economy. Presumably a large economy is one with a large population, a large area, a large variety of resources, and at least a moderately high level of income *per capita*. In such an economy the importance of foreign trade, as measured by its proportion to, say, the Gross National Product, is likely to be relatively slight, and the variety of products that comprise its exports, if not its imports, would be expected to be quite considerable. Likewise the variety of the products that make up its own output would also be considerable. These matters are all relevant to our inquiry.

The stability of any economy can be endangered by factors that are operative within it; it may also be impaired by factors that are at work outside, whose influence can be transmitted in any of a number of ways. It will be convenient to pursue our analysis with this classification in mind, considering first developments that could be expected in a closed economy, and subsequently those additional ones to which an open economy would be liable. In particular, we shall want to assess the relation between these various de-stabilizing factors and the size of the economy to which they relate.

Let us first consider the internal factors that might lead to instability or interfere with steady growth. We shall begin our analysis with a really large country, say the whole world, as our scene. Would there be any de-stabilizing forces in the world economy, considered as a unit? Here, of course, we abstract from all outside forces; we are dealing with a closed economy.

Clearly we should not be justified in expecting stability or steady growth. There are many reasons why the market for the world's output would not be stable, or better, why it would fail to grow at precisely the rate at which the supply potential grew. The buyers of capital goods, for example, may not find the inducements to purchase them strong enough to bring about an absorption of all that could be produced. It would scarcely be necessary to say even this much on the subject except for the fact that many seem to have rather over-learned the lesson taught by the last decade of prosperity; just as many others, ten years before the beginning of that decade, apparently over-learned the lesson taught by as many years of depression. Where depression once seemed inescapable, prosperity is now rather too glibly accepted as inevitable. But ten years is not the whole of history, and Say's Law, even though temporarily enthroned, has often before been forced into exile; certainly if such a change in status is possible, there is no good ground for anticipating stable growth over the long run. But what about stabilizing action on the part of government, you may ask. Even in our somewhat tentatively brave, new world, we could scarcely count on government to pursue the ideal offsetting policy — encouraging or discouraging buying to make up for forces that would otherwise give rise to depression or inflation; and I very much doubt whether either economists dressed up as government officials, or rules to take the place of human discretion, could secure stability, even in a single world economy. Some instability would be almost inevitable in the largest closed economy.

In any small region of this closed economy, the degree of instability could be expected to be somewhat higher than for the economy as a whole. Each region would be characterized by a unique industrial structure, reflecting its own resources availability, distribution of population, the peculiarities of its market, and so on. Shifts in demand away from or towards its characteristic products, the depletion or discovery of resources within its borders, or any of a number of other developments might lead to a swift decline or rise in activity, even when the economy as a whole was relatively stable. The more specialized is the region, the greater is the risk of such instability, since with a high degree of specialization there is only a small chance of offsetting movements. But working counter to this is the fact that inflationary or deflationary forces in one region tend to spread to others, even if these others are quite different in character.

III. EVIDENCE FROM RELATIVE INSTABILITIES OF DIFFERENT AMERICAN STATES

Some evidence on these matters can be found by comparing the instability in the level of personal income for a single region, in this case, a state, of the United States, and for the whole country. It will be observed that personal income for the economy as a whole was somewhat more stable than it was for some, at least, of the individual states.

We have computed our index of instability in exactly the same way as earlier — as the ratio of the root mean square of the deviation of the actual level of personal income from the potential level, to the mean value. The results follow :

COEFFICIENT OF INSTABILITY OF PERSONAL INCOME :
1929–40 AND 1946–54

	%		%
The United States	29·0	Wisconsin	30·0
Rhode Island	27·8	California	31·8
Vermont	29·2	Texas	30·1
New York	27·0	North Dakota	49·0
Ohio	33·4	Mississippi	34·0
Michigan	35·8		

We should note that the coefficient of instability for most states is higher than it is for the country as a whole ; however, the smaller regions — for instance, Rhode Island and Vermont — do not seem to be any less stable than the larger ones, such as Texas.

IV. THE SOURCES OF INSTABILITY

Looking a little more carefully at the sources of instability in any region, we see that they can be classified as those which have at least their proximate origin within the region, and those whose proximate origin is elsewhere, or in some other region. To illustrate the first of these classes : commercial building construction in one region may slow down because, for example, several years of intense activity have brought about an adequate stock of commercial buildings. To illustrate the other class : the output of, say, motor-cars may be curtailed because the level of income, not necessarily in the region in question so much as in other regions, has shown a decline and with that there has been a fall in sales. Moreover, just as one region may either initiate de-stabilizing forces, or instead import them from outside, so it can export these forces to other regions.

If we suppose that the region has very little control over trade, and capital movements between it and other regions of the same economy, then its control over the propagation of deflationary or inflationary forces will be practically zero. If other regions are experiencing a decline in income, very little can be done by the region in question to maintain the market for its own products ; it can do almost nothing to establish barriers against the import of deflation from outside ; likewise, if deflationary forces develop internally, it will be unable to do anything to increase the degree to which these forces are directed abroad and hence it can do almost nothing to reduce the deflationary pressures to which it is itself subject. To put this differently, the propagation of deflation or inflation will depend only upon the marginal propensities to save and to import of the various regions ; nothing can be done by any one of them to alter the functions themselves in such a way as to lessen instability. In this respect, certainly, we should expect a marked difference between the stability of the same region organized as a separate economy, since an independent country could be expected to try to limit its import of adverse forces from outside, and to stimulate its export of any such forces if they happen to be operative internally.

Now, let us consider once more the relation between the size of a region and its stability. We have already noted that a small region is likely to be specialized to one or a few types of economic activity ; from this standpoint, it is likely to show somewhat greater instability than a larger one. But its very smallness is also likely to mean that its marginal propensity to import will be high, and this will mean that, other things being equal, most of the effect of any de-stabilizing development that has its source inside the region will be passed on to other regions which will find their 'exports' changing.

The small region is likely to have a more severely restricted group of exports than a larger one. If the composition of its exports were random — some raw materials, some finished consumer goods, and so on — it would be especially liable to experience strong de-stabilizing impulses from developments in other regions of the country. But the character of a region's industries, and so its exports, cannot always be taken as random; it may, for example, produce items for which the income elasticity of demand is low, for instance, finished foodstuffs. Then its very smallness will protect it from most of the effects of any internal de-stabilizing development, and the nature of its characteristic products from most of the effects of any external development of this kind. It will show a high degree of stability compared even to a larger region, or to the whole economy. But without a good deal of empirical work it would be impossible to assert that the income elasticity of demand for a small region's exports is lower than for the exports of a larger one. But unless that is so, the small region would, as we have seen, tend to show less stability.

V. THE ANALYSIS APPLIED TO DIFFERENT ECONOMIES

The analysis so far has been cast in terms of different regions of a single economy. We must now extend it to cover the case of different economies. To do so, we might first determine what additional factors are to be considered when the separate regions of our economy are made into separate economies, each controlling its own monetary, fiscal, and trade policy, and having, of course, its own money. We must determine whether any additional de-stabilizing forces come into play, and, if so, how they are related to the size of the economies.

Our first step is to look into the level and stability of world income when the world consists of several separate economies. Since at the beginning we do not want to be concerned with questions of resource allocation, let us suppose that no barriers to trade have been imposed by any economy, and that capital movements are as free as they would have been had the separate economies been regions of a single economy. Transport costs, of course, have to be met, just as with interregional trade, but there are no other obstacles to trade. Each economy, however, is assumed to pursue its own fiscal and monetary policy, and each will, in formulating its policy, have to pay attention to its balance of international payments.

The breaking up of a single world economy into a large number of separate economies will bring about a change in the combined income of all only if it leads to a change in the amount of capital investment expenditure and government spending upon goods and services, or to a change in the consumption function. Certainly, such a result is not impossible. For one reason or another, to suggest one possible example, some of the separate economies may be induced to adopt fiscal or monetary policies which would have this effect. But except in the degree that developments of this sort occur, the mere fact that economies once joined are now separate is immaterial for our problem.

It might be argued that with net foreign investment in some countries positive, and in others negative, the effect upon world output of such a fragmenting of the world economy would be significant. But it must be remembered that one country's positive net foreign investment is another country's negative. One country may derive a positive stimulus as the market for its product is increased because of its trade relations with others ; but if it does so, other countries find themselves handicapped by these same dealings. But this, after all, is no different from the situation in a closed economy in which one region may find itself the gainer as it sells more to others than it buys from them ; and another region in contrast suffers as it finds the market partly dissipated by virtue of the fact that it buys more from the rest of the economy than it sells to it. In these respects the international and interregional situations are similar, and neither the level of overall activity nor the relative level of activity in each region is necessarily influenced by the breaking up of a single economy into several. It follows that, in some circumstances, the relation between the size of the economy and its stability will be no different from the relation, discussed earlier, between the size of the region and its stability.

VI. SOME ADDITIONAL COMPLICATIONS

This conclusion, however, abstracts from some of the most significant differences that exist between a situation in which there are several economies and one in which there is only one economy. For one thing, it overlooks the possibility of balance of payments difficulties and the effects these are likely to have upon policy : secondly, it abstracts from the problem of capital movements ; and, finally, it fails to take account of the possibilities of trade barriers. It is important to discuss each of these points in order to indicate its bearing upon our general problem.

First of all, when there are several separate economies, one or more of them may be faced with balance of payments difficulties ; by contrast, this kind of problem cannot confront any region of a single closed economy. A country in a deficit position may be compelled to employ measures that injure the interests of other economies, and perhaps of all combined. It may, for example, adopt a strongly deflationary policy even though aggregate demand is deficient to begin with. If its action were offset by other countries' policies of expansion, all would be well ; but a country with a surplus in its balance of payments is under far less pressure to respond to it in this way than is the country with the deficit. If, then, the countries with deficits in their balances of international payments should, say, raise taxes and tighten credit, and these actions are not offset by the other countries, there will be a net deflationary pressure on all combined. The countries in the deficit positions may, of course, make use of other remedies ; for instance, adopting a higher tariff, or depreciating their exchange. It should also be noted that a country which is faced with unemployment because of a decline in exports may employ either of the two latter policies.

Can anything be said as to whether a small economy will be more or less likely to run into these difficulties than would a large economy ? It seems to me that, as before, the answer depends emphatically upon the nature of the demand for the items that enter into trade. If the country's exports are highly income elastic, and its imports are not, the risk of serious difficulties, or for that matter of comfortable surpluses in its balance of payments, is high. In so far as a small country's exports are likely to consist of a relatively few products, and its imports of a wide range of items, this situation is likely to exist, though there are certainly instances in which the reverse is true.

On the whole, but with such exceptions as Portugal and Austria, the smaller is the country the larger is the proportion of its exports to its total output. This renders a small country especially vulnerable to changes in its exports, first, because a given percentage change in exports means a relatively large change in the market for its products ; and secondly, because the balance of payments deficit, if one comes into being with a decline in exports, is relatively larger — larger, it must be noted, not in relation to, say, reserves of gold or foreign exchange, but at least in relation to the volume of the country's output.

Difficulties in a country's balance of payments can lead to serious internal instability too. The instability will be heightened, of course, if the balance of payments deficit comes about as a consequence of a decline in the country's exports, for in that event aggregate demand may already be too low, and the effort to correct the external disequilibrium may lead to a further reduction. If a small country's exports are subject to serious interruption, either because they are particularly sensitive to changes in income in the rest of the world, or because they are a ready target for countries which are seeking to reduce their imports, its stability may be doubly endangered. This is perhaps the strongest case that can be made for the view that the smallness of an economy below a certain point can lead to instability. However, as already noted, so much depends upon the *character* of the country's exports and imports, and the relation between the character of a country's trade and its size is by no means obvious.

At this point it would be well to take explicit notice of a related matter ; I mean the sensitivity of a country's exports to policy moves by other countries. Once again, the character of the exports is perhaps the decisive factor, but account must also be taken of the likelihood of effective retaliation. In this respect a small country is in a less secure position. It will probably be a weaker economy from the standpoint of economic warfare, and consequently it is the best neighbour for the application of various kinds of beggar-my-neighbour remedies. For this reason, too, a small country's stability may be injured. In short, a small country may be in the situation in which its exports are especially important to it, and especially vulnerable to events abroad, including the policy decisions of others.

A country's stability may also be endangered if it is the recipient of capital movements which are liable to sudden interruption. It is hard to connect this with size, however, except in the degree that a small economy will probably have a somewhat narrower range of investment opportunities than would a larger economy. If, by some evil chance, its few industries no longer succeeded in attracting foreign funds, its balance of payments might be thrown into a severe deficit disequilibrium. In a larger economy, the probability of such an event is smaller, since when one type of industry becomes less attractive, another that attracts foreign funds may be found.

Mention must finally be made of the comparative abilities of large and small economies to adjust to damaging changes in the world economic situation. In one sense, the smaller economy has the advantage. Possessing fewer industries, it will probably be better able to formulate policy to facilitate, or at least to permit, the needed adjustment. In a larger economy with a wider range of industries, there are perhaps too many interest groups which stand in the way of the adoption of the right policy. But though the will to adjust may be somewhat stronger in a small economy, the ability to do so may be considerably less. With relatively few industries, there are likely to be greater gaps in the range of industrial experience and skill. Under pressure to reduce the scale of one industry, there may be no other like it to be expanded ; and the effort to build up a quite different industry may inflict grave difficulties upon the economy. Thus the reallocation of resources in a small economy may emphasize any tendency towards instability.

VII. SOME CONCLUSIONS

Adding these considerations together, it would appear that an economy below a certain size ought to be less stable than one somewhat larger. Yet, as pointed out at the beginning, this is scarcely what we find. Perhaps the explanation for this apparent paradox consists in the fact that policy has been somewhat more sensible in the relatively small economies ; certainly it seems clear that the United States, Germany, and France, in the inter-war years anyway, made almost incredible efforts to nourish any instability existing in their economies. But whether one can assert on this slim basis that a small economy is likely to have better economists is quite another matter.

Chapter 13

THE SIZE OF THE ECONOMY
AND ITS RELATION TO STABILITY
AND STEADY PROGRESS: II[1]

BY

G. LEDUC and J. WEILLER[2]
University of Paris

I. AN ATTEMPT TO FORMULATE THE PROBLEMS

THE subject which has been assigned to us is defined by the title
of this paper. But if any fruitful discussion is to follow this paper,
it would seem indispensable to try to define its purport more closely.
We find more explicit indications in the comments attached to the
Programme of this Round Table, where the problems are formulated thus: 'How far is a large nation more stable than a small
one: (a) in consequence of a smaller dependence on international
trade in general; (b) in consequence of a smaller dependence on
its ability to sell a small range of exported goods; (c) in consequence
of wider opportunities for adjusting its economy to changes in both
markets and technologies? . . . How far does a small nation have
an advantage in its capacity to adjust more quickly its policies to
changing conditions?'

It obviously remains for the Round Table discussions themselves to try to define valid criteria by which to qualify, and, if possible, to measure, the economic 'size' or 'dimensions' of a 'nation'.
But the spirit in which the programme has been drawn up leaves
no room for doubt: the dimensional factors are of a *geographical*
order (natural resources, usable area) and, above all, of a *demographic*
(size of population) and *economic* order (size of the 'domestic market').
In case of conflict between these categories of factors, the latter
group, and more especially the population factor, would seem to be
decisive in qualifying the size of the national economy under consideration. Thus we find (point 7 of the formulation) Canada and

[1] Translated from the French by Elizabeth Henderson.
[2] The views expressed in this paper are shared by both authors. Nevertheless
we would make it clear that Section IV, on the influence of external relations, was
written by Professor Weiller and the rest by Professor Leduc.

Australia grouped with Sweden and Switzerland under the heading of 'comparatively small nations'. The reason is no doubt these countries' small present population and certainly not their small area or low *per caput* income (all the four countries named are in the top group in this latter respect, with only the United States ahead of them).

The concept of a 'nation' as an economic unit also needs some more precise definition. Again we find that the formulation makes it sufficiently clear that the essential element here is of a *political* order. The nation is, then, here considered as a 'political' unit, a unit of action and also of analysis, in Simon Kuznets' sense : 'because the sovereign state is the vehicle for setting conditions and precipitating decisions which spell important determinants of economic growth, it seems to be the natural basic unit in the study'.[1] The distinguished author adds, however, and rightly so, that the importance of the concept of the 'nation state' is itself influenced by the size of the unit considered and that new complications arise from the fact that certain 'countries' (or 'territories') do not enjoy complete freedom of action, either because they are under the suzerainty of another 'country' or because they are subject to domination effects in spite of complete formal independence. On this point, as on many others, we shall do well to bear François Perroux's work in mind.[2]

The qualifications quoted were no doubt meant to be taken as given, and we can therefore immediately turn to the significance of the other elements to be discussed in this paper, that is, what we are to understand by 'stability' in combination with 'steady progress'.

Here again we feel we need not dwell at length on a question which must be well known to all, provided they are at all familiar with the views of the two authors already quoted and also remember the discussions at the First Congress of the International Economic Association, held in Rome in 1956.

Nevertheless some conceptual definitions do seem indispensable : should we identify progress with growth, progress with development, progress with expansion ? By what standard are we to judge presence or absence of progress and to measure its extent over a given period (having agreed on the 'indicators' (François Perroux) of such measurement) ? And what about the rate or rates of progress ?[3] How can we link, *ex post*, the evidence regarding the various possible manifestations of 'progress' with an analysis of the

[1] Simon Kuznets, 'The State as a Unit in the Study of Economic Growth', *Journal of Economic History*, 1951, pp. 25 *et seq.*
[2] His views are so well known that we can dispense with bibliographical reference.
[3] Cf. François Perroux, 'Les Mesures des progrès économiques et l'idée d'économie progressive', *Cahiers de l'I.S.E.A.*, Série I, No. 1.

extent to which this 'progress' (which may be limited to certain sectors or elements of the economy) has or has not taken place in a 'stable' (or at least relatively stable) environment and whether it can be described as 'steady' ?

Any definitions used here cannot, of course, be more than summarily elaborated to allow us to get quickly into our main subject, which may, as a first approximation, perhaps be formulated as follows : to what extent is steady progress (or growth) with — at least relative — stability facilitated or handicapped by the 'size' of the 'national' unit under consideration ? Is there any possibility of a scientifically valid analysis of the influence of 'size' in such matters ?

This leads us to make another point : it seems to us impossible to conduct any meaningful argument in terms of 'nations' politically and economically isolated from each other. Any such attempt would have an air of unreality about it and would not be applicable in practice to the world we live in. All the nation states into which the world's territory and peoples are subdivided today have relations with each other. They either co-operate or are subordinate one to the other in various ways which we do not have to examine here. Besides, the number and variety of these 'nations' keep increasing, largely by virtue of the contemporary evolution of 'colonial' or 'semi-colonial' status. These nations are basically unequal, both as regards natural resources (including 'exploitable' area) and human resources in quantitative and qualitative terms and as regards their present degree of 'economic development', the situation they have reached and the speed with which they have attained it in the course of a more recent or more distant past. And these inequalities exist in spite of, or perhaps because of, the interrelations which have made the separate evolution of each unit, at least to some extent, dependent on all others.

We are up against the question which Simon Kuznets (*op. cit.* p. 35) has so clearly formulated : 'The basic problem of economic growth is why, with the common background and with interrelations among various areas [we shall say 'states' or 'nation states'] of the world, there should be *inequalities in the rate of growth and differences in its structure.* This basic problem can be answered only in terms of the differences among the various state-units in the basic decisions made, which in turn lead back to differences in historical heritage, natural conditions and so on. We thus view the states as the focus at which differences in the rate and structure of economic growth precipitate against a common background provided by international flows and supranational factors.' [1]

1 Our italics.

We have to ask ourselves, then, to what extent and by what chain of causation these inequalities and differences are to be explained, at least in part, by influences which can be ascribed to the 'size' of the political and economic units considered. We shall do this here in a summary fashion only, in the form of quite provisional propositions, simply for the purpose of introducing the discussion.

It seems to us useful to begin with some reference to facts. We shall then be able to distinguish two groups of factors : those *internal* to the national units considered and those deriving from their relations with the *external* world.

II. A GLANCE AT THE FACTS

Having neither the time for detailed research on particular cases which we might have chosen as significant, nor access to the information necessary to do so, we shall use statistical evidence which has already been worked up and interpreted, notably by Simon Kuznets and François Perroux, whose pioneering work in this field remains fundamental.[1] Prior to these two authors' work we can find in the literature on economic development no explicit reference to any special features of development considered from the point of view of their connection with the 'size' of a nation. It is, for instance, almost impossible to discover whether small nations were more subject or less so than large nations to the cyclical and other fluctuations of the capitalist system during the nineteenth century and, let us say, the first four decades of the twentieth. Perhaps this conference will shed some light on this generally neglected aspect of comparative economics. It would be particularly interesting to hear the informed opinion of those of our colleagues who come from the group of 'small' nations, of whatever stage of economic development. Have the most advanced small countries such as Switzerland, the Scandinavian countries, and Belgium, to take our examples from Europe, had to purchase progress at the price of fluctuations greater than those of the 'large' countries, such as the United States, Great Britain, or Germany ?

As regards the comparative extent of 'progress' in the long period, we fortunately have some fairly precise knowledge on the basis of material assembled by François Perroux in the first section of

---

[1] See particularly the Statistical Appendix (unfortunately not included in the printed version) of Simon Kuznets' paper on the occasion of the 200th anniversary of Columbia University : 'Towards a Theory of Economic Growth', May 1954. Also François Perroux, 'Matériaux pour une analyse de la croissance économique', *Cahiers de l'I.S.E.A.*, Series D, No. 8.

the first chapter of his ' Matériaux pour une analyse de la croissance économique '. We see (cf. particularly the table on p. 43, which refers to Kuznets' statistics) that the rate of increase of real income per head of population (an indicator of economic growth which, it should be noted, the author considers as 'crude' and 'very incomplete'), in terms of ten-year averages over periods stretching generally from 1860 to 1950, does not seem to have been affected in any particular way by the size of any of the nations examined. The average ten-year rate of increase of real *per caput* income is 14·1 per cent for Switzerland and 17·1 per cent for Canada, while that of the United States is 16·8 per cènt. Sweden and Germany (1953 boundaries) are at the top of the list with a rate of 21·6. The Australian rate of increase, at 10·3 per cent, is smaller but close to the British rate of 10·7 per cent, although the reasons for the relatively low rate in the two countries are certainly very different : in Australia, the reason seems to have been the relatively rapid population increase during the first half of this century, in Great Britain a certain slowing-down of a process of growth which in the past was the most spectacular and the earliest of all the modern industrial nations.

France has a relatively low average ten-year rate of increase of *aggregate* real income (14·5 per cent between the periods 1840–49 and 1920–38), but this was not accompanied by any very markedly lower rate of increase of *per caput* income (12·6 per cent). This is quite obviously due to the pronounced slowing down of her population growth.

It would therefore seem that the 'size of nations' cannot be considered responsible for notable differences in the observed rates of growth either in 'new' or 'old' countries, in densely populated ones (Switzerland and, no doubt, Belgium), or in those which are still largely unpeopled (Canada and Australia) ; of large or small countries of 'early' development or of 'recent and rapid' development.

It is quite certain that small size (at least in the geographical and demographic sense) does not imply either slowness or irregularity of progress : witness the case of Luxemburg, which today enjoys real *per caput* income higher than that of France and even of Belgium, with which Luxemburg is associated within a very close economic union (Belgo-Luxemburg Economic Union).[1]

---

[1] The United Nations (*National and per capita incomes of seventy countries*, 1949) gives the following figures (in U.S. dollars) for average *per caput* incomes : 553 in Luxemburg, 582 in Belgium, and 482 in France. At the bottom of the international scale was Indonesia with 25 dollars per head, and at the top the United States with 1453 dollars, or nearly sixty times as much.
Average annual figures for net national product at factor cost are given by the

Nor, on the other hand, is small size a sufficient reason for rapid and steady progress. It is easy to find examples to the contrary, even without taking the extreme cases of the Republic of Andorra or of San Marino. Let us take at random the example of Haiti in Central America and Thailand in Asia — with, respectively, 40 and 36 dollars of average *per caput* income in 1949, according to the above-mentioned publication. At the other extreme of the scale of size, one need only point to the contrast between the United States on the one hand, and India or China on the other.

The question of inequality in the rates of growth has been the subject of some very interesting observations by François Perroux (*op. cit.* pp. 45 *et seq.*). He noted that 'for the developed countries on which we possess information, for a long series of periods, ten-year periods for instance, the rate of increase of the variables (such as total population, aggregate real income and *per caput* income) is *not* constant. Subject to numerous and precise further specifications, the first impression is that these rates first accelerate, and then slow down.'

The most remarkable thing about this statement is that it applies equally to the old densely populated countries such as Great Britain and France, and to the countries which were still relatively 'empty' in 1750, whether they be today regarded as 'large' nations, like the United States, or 'small' ones like Canada and Australia. The only notable exception is New Zealand, whose ten-year rates of growth from the initial period 1901–29 to the final period 1925–50 increased from 28·5 to 34·7 as regards aggregate real income, and from 3·3 to 19·6 as regards real *per caput* income, while the rate of increase of population declined from 24·5 to 12·5.

Should we conclude, after all, that development has its own ineluctable logistic·laws, irrespective of the size of the national unit considered ? We limit ourselves to raising this question, recalling with Perroux (*op. cit.* p. 46) that the above-mentioned statements rest on crude statistical procedures and on a limited number of countries. 'We must therefore be wary of vague generalizations such as : acceleration occurs at the beginning of industrialization, to give place to deceleration as that process continues. This statement requires thorough and most detailed research : we must define what we mean by industrialization and identify the timing of its phases much more precisely than has been done so far.'

It also seems proved — both for 'large' countries (United States,

United Nations in *Per capita National Product of fifty-five countries* — 1952–54 ; they are (at the official exchange rates) 890 dollars for Luxemburg, 800 for Belgium, and 740 for France.

Great Britain, Germany) and for 'small' ones (Sweden and no doubt other Scandinavian countries, Belgium, Switzerland, etc.) — that 'the acceleration of the rate of growth of population precedes that of the rate of increase of real *per caput* income.

Only when the growth of population has lost some of its impetus and when the rate of demographic increase has become more stable, and when industrialization is in full swing, only then does an acceleration of the rate of increase of real *per caput* income begin and gather momentum' (*op. cit.* p. 48).

Structural changes (changes in proportions and relations) which accompany economic growth also seem to follow similar patterns in all countries (notably the progressive transfer of manpower from agriculture to industry and later to tertiary activities) irrespective of their size. Certainly, to quote Perroux once more (*op. cit.* p. 52), 'the pattern of development varies greatly according to countries'; but it would not seem that differences of size could offer a valid explanation of these variations.[1]

Similar statements could be made about the relative differences, according to countries, in the amount of capital in its relation to economic progress — although here again we agree with Perroux (*op. cit.* p. 56) on the defects of capital as an 'indicator of growth'. But it does seem that the size of a nation has nothing to do with the relative order of magnitudes as regards either the ratio of capital formation to national product or the ratio of capital stock to national income (or product).

Neither the ratio between gross capital formation and gross product, nor the smaller ratio between net capital formation and net national income seem to be influenced by the size of the nation — witness the absence of any really notable divergences between Sweden on the one hand (as a representative of 'small' nations) and the United States or Great Britain on the other.[2]

[1] Thus the table on p. 53, which is based on statistical material furnished by Kuznets in his aforementioned study, shows for the period 1880–1930 a very marked decline of the percentage of the labour force employed in *Belgium* in personal services (from 20 per cent to 5 per cent), while during the same period this same percentage declined only from 17 to 12 per cent in Great Britain and rose from 9 to 11 per cent in the United States. In our view the significance of these opposite movements remains to be ascertained ; we do not believe that they have anything to do with size.

[2] Nothing more precise can be gathered from the relevant material furnished by Simon Kuznets in his study on 'International differences in capital formation and financing', in the volume *Capital Formation and Economic Growth*, Princeton University Press, 1955.

The statistical table on p. 60 shows for the period 1947–52 that the proportion of gross national product absorbed by gross domestic capital formation ranges from 10 per cent in Ceylon to 30·9 per cent in Norway. The figures relating to net capital formation and net product range from 6·8 per cent for the Philippines to 44·9 per cent for Southern Rhodesia (which is certainly an exceptional case).

As regards the ratio between net capital stock and net national income, this certainly does seem to vary considerably according to countries and also to be subject to changes on the precise measurement and significance of which the experts are far from agreed. This ratio seems to be higher in the 'old' countries than in the 'new' ones, which seems plausible enough. But both groups contain nations of all sizes : thus we find a coefficient of 3 for the United States as well as for Canada and Australia.

III. INTERNAL FACTORS

Seeing that we are still far from possessing a complete and valid theory of economic progress, we shall here limit ourselves to a few observations which may serve as a basis for discussion. We shall also neglect, or rather relegate to the subsequent section, those aspects of the question which are more especially international and which, we hasten to say, by and large are the more important the smaller is the size of a nation.[1]

We shall first briefly discuss the relation between the size of a nation and the danger of instability, the latter being understood in the purely business cycle sense of the term, that is, the greater or lesser extent to which the economy under consideration is exposed to the vicissitudes of fluctuations. Is that danger greater when the nation is small ? The answer depends in large part upon that nation's position in relation to outside domination or influences. This point will be taken up later.

As regards internal factors, the answer would seem to depend, above all, upon the degree of development, that is to say, upon the structure which the economy has already reached. Nations, large or small, which have not as yet got beyond the stage of subsistence economy are not much exposed to cyclical fluctuations. But the price of this safety is stagnation. As soon as the market sectors develop (and it matters little just how they are introduced) instability appears, and it is the more pronounced as these new activities are generally connected with foreign markets and specialized in the production of raw materials and certain foodstuffs. Size may have little to do with this.

But once a certain degree of development has been reached and

[1] We may recall the discussions of the International Economic Association's Round Table on Economic Progress, at Santa Margherita Ligure, September 1953, in *Economic Progress*, L. Dupriez, Ed., Louvain, 1955. See also Simon Kuznets, 'International Differences in Income Levels', Chapter 8 of *Economic Change*, New York, 1953, especially pp. 233-37.

the economy is more diversified and its internal structure progressively transformed, size may begin to play a less negligible part. However, it is difficult to say in what direction its influence works. A larger and more diversified economy offers more room to the complex operation of factors such as acceleration or the investment multiplier and the danger of instability thereby increases. On the other hand, a larger country has certain possibilities of spontaneous or induced redress, which are not open to smaller nations. No doubt substitution and compensation effects can come into play more easily in the absence of external constraints, by virtue of the diversity of resources present in an economy of a certain size. Witness the increased part played by the 'dependent territories' in the rehabilitation process after the Great Depression of 1929 in the countries which then had an 'empire' — notably Great Britain and France.

Let us now turn to the question of a nation's capability of steady and sustained economic growth. We have seen how disappointing the facts seem to be in this respect. None the less we can gain some knowledge, however fleeting reality may appear to be. It seems to us that three kinds of observation can find their place here, namely those relating to a nation's capacity to increase the productivity of its activities, to its capacity for innovation, and finally to the effectiveness of government action.

We shall treat the first point only very briefly, since it overlaps with questions which will have been discussed in an earlier session of the conference. Two of these questions seem fundamental to us and, moreover, interrelated : the determination of the optimum size of the firm on the one hand, and the size of the market on the other.

It is very likely that, at least for certain firms, there is to all intents and purposes no limit to the law of increasing returns (decreasing unit cost). As has been shown — notably by Tibor Scitovsky and Don Patinkin [1] — the combination of economies of scale and of external economies furnished to a national economy as a whole by the development of certain particularly influential activities, notably in the form of the reduction in the number of separate plants within a progressively growing single enterprise, certainly confers on nations with large domestic markets a marked advantage in the matter of steady progress. A country with a smaller domestic market could offer the same opportunities only if it could securely and permanently count on free access to foreign markets. But, as

[1] T. Scitovsky, 'A Reconsideration of the Theory of Tariffs', *Readings in the Theory of International Trade*, pp. 358-92 ; D. Patinkin, 'Multiple Plant Firms, Cartels and Imperfect Competition', *Quarterly Journal of Economics*, February 1947.

Kuznets has frequently emphasized, 'under existing and even past conditions of the world, such access is precarious'.[1] Kuznets adds that even for activities whose products cannot be replaced by imports and which therefore must necessarily be located within a country's frontiers, the reduced size of a nation (the indicator here is a small population) is very likely to lead to 'an uneconomic scale of operations in many industries'.

We should certainly also discuss innovations as an essential element of rapid (though perhaps, if we put our faith in Schumpeter, for example, irregular) progress. In this respect it seems to us that a large nation has advantages in so far as it disposes within its own frontiers, of a variety of potential human and natural resources on the production side, and, on the side of the market, of a large amount of disposable income or of funds which can easily be diverted from new uses appealing more to the tastes of the owners.

Perhaps small nations possess some more or less compensating advantages in the field of more effective government action on the general economic plane, particularly as regards the quicker adjustment of policy to changing conditions. This view seems to be shared by Kuznets.[2]

In a country of relatively small size — at least as concerns territory and population — general government action seems easier and more effective than it can be over vast areas and great masses of people. Perhaps economists would be well advised in consulting political scientists on this point. Perhaps, too, we shall have at this conference colleagues who can speak from experience. There is no doubt that forecasts are easier and intervention simpler on a small scale, but, on the other hand, there is a danger that the solution of many problems may take on a personal character which can do more harm than good from the point of view of the general national interest. Once again, we feel in no position to suggest any generally valid answer. It seems to us that this is a matter of interdisciplinary discussion.

IV. THE INFLUENCE OF EXTERNAL RELATIONS

The aforegoing observations plainly show that however much one may try to arrive at a rigorous definition of the terms *size*,

[1] *Economic Change, loc. cit.* p. 234.

[2] 'Also, it may be easier for a small state to achieve the degree of internal unity and cohesion of the population which so facilitates economic progress and prevents sharp internal conflicts from developing.' *Op. cit.* p. 235. The author also mentions greater opportunities of finding a favourable position in the 'interstices of the international economy'. We shall return to this point later.

stability, and *steady progress*, no even passably precise conclusions can be reached without recourse to a certain number of additional criteria. We return to our first common-sense reaction (knowing only too well that, particularly in a conference of this kind, our first business is to challenge common sense) : the conditions of stable economic growth appear much too indeterminate with reference to the sole criterion of size. What the contributors have to do is to classify methodically a whole series of hypotheses, as the problem appears more strictly defined by new criteria. Now the preceding part of this paper, while sharply limiting the field of action, does seem to show that internal factors are far from decisive. What, then, of considerations of an international order ?

The writer of this part of the paper,[1] over-specialized as he is perhaps, could not help a certain feeling of satisfaction at first at the idea that an examination of the external relations of any country — small, medium-sized, or large — might give us the key to the problem. He was thinking that such study should extend to the country's place in a network of international exchanges which could be larger or smaller and more diversified or less so, and also to the actual volume of the trade flows which link that country with others. But these hopes were soon disappointed. Everything seemed to become doubtful, *even our definitions of the nation and the size of nations*, by virtue of the mere fact of taking into consideration what, in French, is usually described by that very convenient expression : *les échanges extérieurs.*[2]

If we followed classical thought through to its conclusions, we would, at the end of a long and devious journey, find ourselves face to face with the same difficulties which often hold us up today. We may perhaps be satisfied with the idea that both small and large nations quite obviously 'gain' something from the development of their trade with other nations. But this is no longer the essence of the problem and we must also leave aside the interminable expert discussions of the comparative extent of the gain of small and large nations. We shall limit ourselves for the moment to the proposition that, in fact, both kinds of nation do gain from trade. By taking this proposition for granted, we could, so it would seem, define a set of problems.

[1] See footnote (2) p. 200. The author of this part of the paper is Professor Weiller [ED.].
[2] We have in French long used the expressions 'external trade' and 'external exchanges' rather than trade or exchange with abroad or with foreign countries. This has the great advantage, particularly in an economic discussion, of being able to discard everything which has to do with the development or the radical changes of relations of dependency or subordination of a political character. However, see below on this point.

We could, for instance, as a working hypothesis, assume the optimum size of any nation as given — not, of course, in any definitive sense, but with reference to historically known cases and to the continuous renewal of past adaptations. This optimum size would appear as the immediately desirable target and it would be a function of all the elements which have already been discussed. If then we suppose, for example, that a nation is smaller than desired, we could assume, on traditional lines, than an expansion of external exchanges should be capable of making up the difference, of closing the gap defined *a priori*.

We see at once that on this road we are bound, sooner or later, to encounter a whole series of difficulties. As is often the case, the logic of the classical demonstrations which are fully valid for an *initial stage* (and allowing only for more or less regular expansion) does not hold for a successive series of stages (in the course of which, incidentally, the nations will have become more or less closely integrated into complex exchange systems). We need only point out here that if we considered the problem as resolved, we would have to assume that international trade has, in fact, already produced revolutionary changes in the map of the world : nations which used to be regarded as small would not only have reached their optimum size from the point of view here under discussion (that is, from the point of view of stability and steady growth), but they would in effect have become large nations. Let us make the point clear : it is not a question of advance for the whole of the countries considered, but of a reclassification on the basis of actual performance in the development of external exchanges.

And this is where we have to think again about the validity of our definitions. Common language often more or less imposes itself on discussions of international policies and may perhaps do so, whether we wish it or not, even at this conference, and is it not the case, most often, in common language that the size of a nation or even our idea of that size is profoundly influenced by the nation's share in world trade ? Apart from any aspects of a psychological or sociological character and of the prestige acquired through growing international trade, we would have to consider also everything which in the course of that development has directly or indirectly contributed to making any country a large nation, and, inversely, everything which causes a nation exceeding a certain size to take a more active part in world trade.

Let this be as it may. In order to come straight to the realities of our present world, we think it is useful to compare a number of different maps : alongside the maps of plain geographical space, let us place those which reshape that space in function of the various countries' population (the distorted maps which Professor Leduc loves so much) and yet others which show the size of nations as a function of the volume of their foreign trade (these are the ones which interest us most just now).[1] We must say that at first sight the results surpass our expectations. These latter maps do indeed best reflect not only the traditional classification of 'small' and 'large' nations towards the end of the nineteenth century when Great Britain's leading part was uncontested, but they also reflect the nations' present order.

A certain flexibility is introduced according as we define a nation within the borders of its metropolitan territory or take in also the countries over which that nation has more or less firm political control or simply economic control within some regional union, currency area, or finally, perhaps, by virtue precisely of its position in world trade.

But it is always a mistake to try to prove too much all at once and we must, above all, avoid circular reasoning. To get away from it quickly, we shall deliberately think in terms of a sort of historical size. We do, of course, always have to remember the reasons why international trade plays an important part in this respect, but we should then not have to revise our judgement about the size of nations any more. On the basis of that classification, once established, we can go on to examine how, in the actual conditions of exchange relations, large or small nations can make new progress while maintaining such stability as is in any case necessary to consolidate the new progress over the long period.

We shall also continue to argue, in the traditional manner, as if the nation had, in fact, remained a major centre of decisions and were itself fully responsible for the development of its trade. We should, of course, though we cannot do so in this paper, take account of factors such as the part played by large multi-country firms, or situations of dualism or even pluralism within the boundaries of one national economy.[2]

As regards the past, the fact that countries like Tzarist Russia or the Soviet Union in the inter-war period, or India or China, participate less in world trade — and, which often is not the same thing, are less dependent on it — can in part be explained by these

---

[1] Cf., for example, the two weighty volumes by Mr. and Mrs. Woytinsky, *World Population and Production* (particularly the distorted map on p. 101) and *World Commerce and Government* (maps on pp. 126 *et seq.*).

[2] See particularly M. Byé, 'L'Auto-financement de la grande unité interterritoriale et les dimensions temporelles de son plan', *Revue d'Économie Politique*, 1957 (Report to the Congress of French-speaking Economists, Paris, May 1957).

countries' rich natural resources and opportunities of steady economic development of a comparatively autarkic character. Nevertheless the lag in these countries' entry into international trade, which was in any case also linked with a lag in economic development, was a contributory factor in their lesser importance in the concert of nations. They seemed smaller just because they were keeping more to themselves. It is also possible that the world was somewhat slow in recognizing that the United States had attained the status of a very large nation, just because her progress rested largely on her own resources and because her exaggerated protectionism, while not completely preventing a great development of external relations, did no doubt put a brake on the rise of the United States in the international field.

If we now want to appreciate (without getting into circular reasoning again) to what extent a nation's size can be influenced by its greater or lesser participation in world trade, we must first provide an answer to the related question of the political ties of subordination and dependence. The answer must, of course, be based on past history and on the enormous changes which are now taking place. From the strictly economic point of view this question to some extent coincides with the previous one. Should we say that Great Britain's ascendancy since the Victorian era was due to the fact that her real size was to be measured not by the frontiers of the British Isles but by those of a vast Empire ? Or is it not simpler to say that this was a case of a nation deeply engaged in a highly developed network of trade flows and dominating it by virtue of financial institutions, business connections, powerful firms, and so on ? It could be added that that nation was also able to become the centre of a network of complementary activities, and to guide the development of a 'development block' (in terms of Dahmén's and Nyblen's analysis). It can readily be seen how important this point of view could become through a series of successive steps stressing the institutional aspect of external relations : from colonial dependence one would go on to currency areas, customs unions, common markets, or free trade zones and all the modern forms of interdependence, including those of the fully planned economy.

But let us get quickly to the main point. Let us not stop to consider, for example, whether the progress made by Luxemburg should be appraised with reference to that country's size or to the Belgo-Luxemburg Economic Union (which has placed Luxemburg in a position similar to that of Brabant, or Flanders), or with reference to Benelux, or the European Coal and Steel Community, or finally to the whole network of Luxemburg's international trade.

This does serve to suggest, however, not only the danger of ambiguity, but also the advantages which relatively small countries may derive from trade development as well as the check which insufficient participation in world trade all too often imposes on nations which might long ago have come to be considered as very great.

   But where are we to look for the cause of what still seems the result of a series of highly diverse historical influences ? Here it becomes important to consider the conditions of stability or instability of exchange relations, according to the position of nations, large or small, in the network of international trade. The possible answers will obviously not be the same for today's world and yesterday's, nor for countries which still aim at a kind of expansion which is essentially national and which look abroad only to meet some temporary shortages or find additional markets, and, on the other hand, for countries for which international trade is the very condition of the level of economic activity or even of survival. In other words, we should abandon the notion of liberalization of trade with reference only to the conditions of the steady growth of national economies and their endogenous expansion factors. This was still the general basis of explanation during the first half of this century ; but now we must more and more adopt the perspective of integration into groups, which may be larger or smaller and have different structures, and where obvious importance attaches to the inequalities and asymmetries capable, according to circumstances, of encouraging or hampering steady progress.

   Whatever its size, a nation can, by appropriate policies, neutralize certain de-stabilizing factors and clear the way for new progress by judiciously exploiting its opportunities for extending its foreign trade. From this point of view, we must henceforth pay much more attention to foreign trade policies, and to the various countries' strategical record within a given zone or network of exchanges, than to the traditional teachings of the theory of international trade on the assumption of complete free trade and constant equilibrium in all countries. Indeed, if we ponder the lessons of a well-known article by W. Leontief,[1] even a modernized version of the classical theory itself enables us to point to very significant divergences between the old theory and the actual development of the structure of trade.

   Does this mean that the size of national economies becomes

---

[1] See W. Leontief's communication to the American Philosophical Society (*Proceedings*, September 1953) and his article in *Review of Economics and Statistics*, November 1956, as well as numerous other writings on the same subject.

directly relevant'? In many respects, yes. We may take as examples differences in capital intensity and factor proportions for various types of export products; differences resulting not only from the development of the terms of trade, but, more fundamentally, from the very large shifts in profits earned on the international plane in conditions of imperfect competition and on very diverse foreign markets. These questions merit attention, but they are too intricate to be studied here in the context of the problem of the size of nations.[1]

It is well known that the currently most widely accepted qualifications of the traditional theory of international trade do, at least in some respects, concern the problem of the size of nations. We can combine these more modern aspects of the theory with the previously mentioned elementary considerations concerning the stages of economic development, and so try to identify a few cases where size plays a relatively important part.

We shall no doubt be inclined to think that, *ceteris paribus*, a small country is initially in a better position than a large one to take advantage of the opening up of foreign markets and, above all, of the call for diversified imports. This would ensure those conditions of stability which a small country lacks by definition and which it needs for its growth. For this case we can reasonably retain the traditional demonstrations, though subject to important qualifications of which we shall have more to say. Similarly, though again with reservations, we can no doubt continue to think that small countries are better off than big ones with respect to their ability to use external aid in the 'take off' (to use Rostow's phrase) towards industrial growth. But what happens thereafter? Will not a small country be more sensitive to transmitted fluctuations? Will its growth not be at least slowed down in relation to the growth of its exchange partners by the fact that the small country is forced to adopt a strategy of adaptation, that it can offer less resistance to policies which it cannot control, whether it be the policies of large countries or large international firms?

The answer to these questions will be more or less confidently affirmative — or even negative — according as due weight is or is not attached to our reservations and, above all, to the condition *ceteris paribus*, and according as our definition of the term 'small country' (however ambiguous it remains) is or is not accepted. Not all the countries so described as small are what is generally called under-developed, but to our knowledge under-developed

---

[1] We shall be discussing the whole of this problem elsewhere. Cf. Jean Weiller, 'Échanges extérieurs, profits d'entreprise et gains des nations', to be published in *Économie appliquée*.

countries are always excluded by definition from the category of large nations. Now these under-developed countries run the greatest danger of instability : the advances of outside origin and the transfer of techniques and capital capable of ensuring the rapid transformations planned today (for demographic and political reasons no less than for economic and social ones) are certainly not such as to guarantee steady, or even continuous, progress. At best we can think of the success of one of those cases 'of growth intentionally induced by one nation in another' of which François Perroux spoke in 1956 at the International Economic Association's Rome Congress.[1]

Matters are rather different for advanced countries which, though small, will in case of success seem to be fairly high up in that order of size of nations which is so difficult to determine. Such a country need not have a position of leader or dominant economy within a zone or a larger network of trade. It can make its way as a 'brilliant second' with a rate of expansion both more rapid and more steady than that of the leader country, it can display its superiority in specialized productions or suitably differentiated lines of manufacture, its economy can compete with those of larger nations rather than being merely complementary to them, it can get export orders as a result of its own foreign investment, and so on. We can all think of numerous small and medium-sized European nations which answer the description. And what about those 'comparatively small' countries, as Canada and Australia are called ? Let us make only one additional point. In the nineteenth century — subject to very important reservations which are becoming increasingly clear — small countries orientated towards foreign trade could progress by the logic of the system of free enterprise and private profit ; but today we must put the main stress on the increasingly important rôle of the institutions, foreign trade policies, and general economic policies of these countries, which need to conserve a high degree of autonomy so as to retain their freedom of decision in this field.

We shall not dwell on the fact that a 'large country', even if it should by definition be capable for some time of economic growth in relative isolation if not autarky, must sooner or later resolutely engage on international expansion in the interests of growth. When

---

[1] François Perroux : 'On the Differences between Business Cycle Policies and Balanced Growth Policies', *Stability and Progress in the World Economy*, London, Macmillan, 1958. See p. 123, footnote (1), with reference to Leontief's description of the effects of the export of automated units to under-developed countries. As regards the conditions of instalment, self-financing, and more generally the policies of large firms, see also M. Byé, footnote (2), p. 212 above.

it does so, are its conditions of stability better than those of a small country ? Will the large country find opportunities of steadier progress ? There is no lack of controversy on this point. Isolationism has often been condemned in the past and imperialism is no less in disfavour ; but between these two temptations the large country must try to steer a new course — and the old colonial empires, after all, merely rendered explicit, from this point of view, the political ties capable of enlarging a nation into a much greater unit. Nowadays we have a fairly copious literature to give us guidance on the advantages, or at least relative advantages, which a very large nation can obtain by preserving a key position with respect to the control of economic fluctuations, and the dosage of internal and external investment. We should no doubt add : when that nation is in a position not only to maintain initiative and flexibility in the manipulation of its growth stimulants and protection of its economic and social structure, but also to exercise control through international firms, without the risk that the latter develop as non-integrated 'enclaves' in the national economy which is to enjoy steady growth.

But this would lead us into an abstract model rather than into the multiplicity of particular cases. The abstract model would be that of a very large nation having succeeded by superior strategy in making the most of its position in a network of international trade or even world trade as a whole. The particular cases revealed by empirical research are no doubt less seductive and the discussion should provide some information about certain peculiarities of certain great countries. There remains the question which model is the better for studying the conditions of greater stability and steadier growth, in connection with problems of foreign trade : this last model or one closer to the one we have suggested in connection with the more favoured 'small countries'.

In any event, it seems to us that in the twentieth century any model we use is bound to be rather different from those still resting on the classical theory of international trade. We have refrained from making even a necessarily brief incursion into the field of the relations between planned economies or of the development of exchanges between the latter and the rest of the world. We could nevertheless point to just one common feature as regards the conditions of stability and steady progress, particularly for under-developed countries. Given the instability which threatens that category of 'small' countries in international economic relations, we cannot evade the task of defining the economic policies most likely to ensure growth.

It is becoming more and more clear that when certain types of capitalist organization penetrate into a pre-capitalist society, there is a danger of undoing existing structures, indeed of a violent disruption of old social structures besides existing economic ones. And yet economic development appears as a pressing need of most 'small' countries (so much so, that we cannot help mentioning the problem). We are convinced that the penetration of the Soviet type of organization entails similar dangers. But this is a question which might lead us very far — as indeed perhaps it should, given the importance of the problem which arises not only for separate countries, but for extremely vast areas if not immediately on the world scale. Indeed we are coming to think that a 'small nation' should best be defined as one which is unable to resist outside influences and which must accept the worst of them together with the best ; the 'large nation' would then be defined as one which has enough autonomy and enough flexibility in its economic policy to provide a response to challenges from anywhere, so as to assure maximum stability and steadiness when decisive 'progress' has to be imported from abroad.

In conclusion, we would suggest that the discussion should turn to the ways and means open to various countries with a view to such strategies. The concepts we inherited at the beginning of this century are certainly being revised in every respect, whether they concern, for example, the monetary policies best apt to ensure day-to-day flexibility of adjustment, or national tariff policies which may, for various and often contradictory reasons, tend more or less to freeze at a certain level of protectionism. Between these two extremes, we can think of a whole scale of means of intervention, of a varied armoury of strategies of a more or less liberal or planning type. All of them would be designed to make national policies effective from three points of view : balance of payments equilibrium ; continuity of structural preferences at the level of government decisions ; ability to resist, better than others, the incidence of economic fluctuations transmitted within the various networks of international trade.

V. CONCLUSIONS

In the absence of any clear answer from the facts, we are constrained to attempt an abstract analysis, the results of which will no doubt be difficult to verify. Simon Kuznets has raised the question whether 'one should devise variants of a theory of economic growth for the many small national units different from those for the few large ones'; this does, perhaps, require no further answer than that which the same author has given himself : 'while the factor of size in and of itself may contribute to international differences in income levels, at the present stage of our knowledge and analysis, no great weight can be attributed to it'.

The difficulty of gaining greater knowledge lies in large part in the need to associate in one common explanation the, often contradictory, effects of the various elements which make up the overall or partial indicators of 'size'. If it were a matter only of geographical area, we would have to concentrate on the location of activities, although this would not suffice to give us a satisfactory explanation of the nature and rôle of the true economic 'spaces' (F. Perroux). If only population were involved, we would have to ask ourselves mainly how demographic expansion may set off or influence the steady and sustained growth of national output, either in aggregate terms or per head of labour force or per inhabitant (with all due reservations regarding the accuracy and significance of the statistical evidence).[1] We would have to work not so much with absolute figures as with comparative rates of growth. If, finally, the indicators of size were of a purely economic order, we would have to take up once more the much debated question whether or not the size of aggregate or *per caput* national product or again the degree of capitalization of a given national economy are factors affecting stability and steady progress.

As regards steady progress itself, can we, taking account of the past, say that its further development (in the short or long period) will be of a linear order, of an exponential order, or a logistical one, or some other which the mathematician's brain may devise ?

Finally, we must not forget that most national economies in the world are in communication with each other and that in this field the phenomena of transmittal are of the first importance, both in the case of more or less cyclical fluctuations and of long-term trends.

Let us beware of prophecies and humbly confess that we cannot conclude anything with certainty. But at least our task is clear. We must improve our tools of observation and analysis and we must get on with the work.

[1] The United Nations experts have tried to do this in Chapter XIII of their monumental work on *The Determinants and Consequences of Population Trends*.

Chapter 14

THE SIZE OF THE NATION
AND THE COST OF ADMINISTRATION

BY

E. A. G. ROBINSON

Cambridge University

I. INTRODUCTION

ANY consideration of the advantages and disadvantages of large size in their application to the size of nations would clearly be incomplete if it did not include some discussion of the effects of size upon the costs of administration of the nation itself as a nation, upon the costs of the provision of social services, and upon the costs of defence. Yet, so far as I can discover, this is an almost virgin field in economic analysis. If I have failed to find predecessors of whose writings I should have been aware, I apologize in advance. I have consulted others better informed than myself, and they would appear as unfamiliar as I with any substantial earlier work in this field.

In the circumstances I must depend to a greater extent than I would have wished upon *a priori* argument. There are, however, two sources of statistical evidence upon which I shall draw heavily. The first is a paper by Miss Alison Martin and Professor Arthur Lewis on 'Patterns of Public Revenue and Expenditure'.[1] This paper was not written with the immediate purpose of throwing light upon the effects of the size of nations ; its intention was to throw light on the relation of government expenditure to income per head and to the stage of economic development of different nations. But in preparing the evidence to analyse their own problem the authors have recalculated the public expenditure — central, regional, and local — of some sixteen nations under a uniform set of categories of expenditure, and have related the expenditure to the gross national product. Thus direct comparison of the percentage of gross national

[1] *The Manchester School*, Vol. XXIV, No. 3, September 1956. Perhaps I may be allowed to add that I tried to persuade Professor Lewis to come to Lisbon and take part in our conference, making use of his own material for the purposes for which I shall attempt to use it. It was only when he proved unable to do this that I ventured to undertake the task myself.

product devoted to different objectives is made possible, and can be used for the purpose which we have in mind.

The second source of statistical evidence is a study made by Milton Gilbert and Irving Kravis, entitled *An International Comparison of National Products and the Purchasing Power of Currencies*, prepared for the Organization for European Economic Co-operation in Paris. This study, which refers to 1950 but is projected for defence expenditure to 1952, covers naturally a more restricted number of countries than does Professor Lewis's study. The only countries common to both are the United States, the United Kingdom, France, and Italy. But the Gilbert-Kravis study permits what the Martin-Lewis study does not permit (indeed what that study rather deliberately avoids), a comparison of the absolute real expenditures of this more limited number of countries both in total and on certain broad categories of public services.

There are obviously exceptional difficulties in the way of any attempt to use statistical evidence to throw light on the comparative costs of providing public services in different nations with different characteristics of size, income per head, stage of economic development, and the like. There is not one definable and invariable thing represented by administration, education, defence, or whatever service one may consider. The quality and sufficiency of the service itself is a variable, and any full discussion must take account of the effect of size not only on cost but also on quality. I shall make some attempt to consider variations of quality below, but really adequate discussion is scarcely possible in the present state of knowledge and evidence.

II. CATEGORIES OF EXPENDITURE

It is convenient, following Professor Lewis, to distinguish various categories of public expenditure. His analysis (see Appendix) is made under twenty heads, which can, again following Professor Lewis, be summarized under two broad heads : basic expenditure, composed of administration, economic expenditure,[1] education, health ; other expenditure, composed of defence, public debt service (largely reflecting past defence), social insurance, food and agricultural subsidies. The latter group of expenditures reflects much more than the former the differences between nation and nation in regard both to income per head and to economic, political, and social policies.

[1] Rows 4-16 in Appendix.

The total expenditure on the two groups of services by the nine nations covered by the Appendix is shown in Table I below:

TABLE I

PUBLIC EXPENDITURE 1953–54 AS PERCENTAGE OF
GROSS NATIONAL PRODUCT

	Basic services	Other services	Total	Population (million)
United States	7·24	20·19	27·43	162·4
United Kingdom	11·52	22·48	34·00	51·1
France	10·79	14·97	25·76	43·0
Italy	12·79	11·79	24·58	47·7
Sweden	13·26	10·23	23·49	7·2
New Zealand	13·77	16·35	30·12	2·1
India	6·15	2·69	8·84	377·0
Ceylon	11·59	2·83	14·42	8·4
Jamaica	10·38	2·70	13·08	1·5

It will be seen that basic services vary substantially less between nation and nation as a proportion of gross national product than do the other services. The ranking of expenditure upon these is not widely different from the ranking according to population. But this correspondence is, when examined in more detail, illusory. Moreover, the measure employed in the above table is the proportion of gross national product spent on these services; the ranking in this respect is very different from the ranking in absolute real cost per head.

III. COST OF ADMINISTRATION

The cost of administration, narrowly defined, might reasonably be expected to be affected in a variety of ways by the size of the nation administered. On the one hand, a small nation will require to have much the same kind of central institutions as a large one. Where the institutions are democratic, the number of members of a central legislature and the services that need to be provided to them are dictated to a greater extent by the number of persons that can conveniently and efficiently take part in debate and by the workable size of a chamber than by any more basic principle of the desirable ratio of representatives to represented. Thus the number of members of the British House of Commons has been reduced from 658 in 1801 to 630 in 1957, while the population of the area covered (which in 1801 included all of Ireland) has risen from 17 million to 51 million. The present number of members of the House of Commons may be compared with the 594 members of the French National Assembly, the 590 members of the Italian Chamber of Deputies, and the 435 members of the United States House of Representatives.

Secondly, the size of the administration where it touches the external relations of a country is dictated almost as much by the number of contacts with the outside world as by the actual dimensions of the problems that may arise between that nation and other nations. A small nation will tend to have more dependence on other nations in proportion to its income, a higher ratio of imports and exports to national income, longer frontiers per million of population, and will thus tend to spend more in proportion to its income on foreign relations.

On the other hand, the administration of a large nation is, by the very fact of its size, likely to be more remote from the individual citizen. In a small nation, personal touch can exist between the governors and the governed. In a large nation, despite the radio and television, the two are increasingly distant from each other. This usually implies the necessity for some regional or provincial government to handle those problems which can be delegated to regional bodies. Increasing size also implies a lengthening and strengthening of the hierarchical chains and a multiplication of the civil service staff to co-ordinate action by an increasingly large number of subordinates.

At the same time large size of the area to be governed and increasing remoteness from the governed imply that issues must be more completely and exhaustively recorded and analysed on paper, and since those making final decisions at the centre have limits of possible numbers and possible time, more predigested and simplified. Good organization may permit a more effective use of staff up to a point, but anyone familiar with the differences between the immovable mountains of the administration of some of the larger nations and the small, intimate, and flexible administrations of some of the smaller nations must ask himself whether the advantages are wholly on the side of large scale.

With these ideas in mind, it is interesting to consider the actual proportions of gross national product spent on administration by different nations. The United States and the United Kingdom spent in 1953–54 almost the same proportion : 2·40 per cent and 2·36 per cent respectively. Ceylon and Jamaica, both countries with small populations and simple administrations, spent 2·77 per cent and 2·89 per cent. France and Italy spent appreciably higher proportions : 3·32 per cent and 3·76 per cent respectively. Sweden and New Zealand, with small populations but modern systems of government, spent 3·07 per cent and 2·92 per cent, much the same as India, 3·09 per cent, with a huge population, but a relatively thin administration.

TABLE II

CURRENT EXPENDITURE ON ADMINISTRATION 1953-54
AS A PROPORTION OF GROSS NATIONAL PRODUCT

	Administration as % of gross national product	Population (million)
United States	2·40	162·4
United Kingdom	2·36	51·1
France	3·32	43·0
Italy	3·76	47·7
Sweden	3·07	7·2
New Zealand	2·92	2·1
India	3·09	377·0
Ceylon	2·77	8·4
Jamaica	2·89	1·5

Before any attempt is made to draw inferences from these figures, it is well to see what they may or may not mean.

If there were no economies or diseconomies of scale, one might expect the cost of administration to be constant, given constant prices per unit of real resources employed, in one or other of two senses. First, one might expect the cost of administration per head of population to be constant. If police services are devoted to providing security to our persons, and if persons are no more valuable if they have larger incomes, police services will vary (disregarding economies of scale) in proportion to population. If police services are devoted to providing security to property, they will vary (again disregarding economies of scale) in proportion (if the capital/income ratio is fairly constant) to gross national product. But it remains necessary to ask how policemen are paid. If the pay of policemen increases *pari passu* with average gross national product per head, the cost of police services, which vary in quantity with population, will vary in cost with the gross national product, remaining a constant proportion of it. If, as income per head rises, more protection is required in proportion to income, and if the output of security per head of the police force is unchanged, police services will form an increasing proportion of gross national product.˙ It will remain a constant proportion of gross national product only if productivity of policemen rises *pari passu* with productivity of the whole economy.

I have set this out at length because I believe that it helps one to see the factors that lead to variations in the proportions of gross national product devoted to administration. While the civil servants of rich and efficient nations are undoubtedly in some cases more efficient than those of poorer nations, it is doubtful whether productivity differs as much as does productivity in the economy as a whole. There are, moreover, likely to be a number of services for which the need increases with higher income per head. Thus there are two reasons for expecting *a priori* a higher expenditure per head of the population, the higher is income per head, and as the outcome of the two factors working together, we might expect administration to involve, *ceteris paribus*, a higher proportion of gross national product in a richer country.

If we are to go below the surface in comparing expenditures on administration in countries of different income per head and different population, it is valuable if we can compare not only the proportions of gross national product which are shown by Professor Lewis's analysis, but also the absolute expenditures per head which he deliberately avoids. Some help in attempting such comparison is provided by the study made by Milton Gilbert and Irving Kravis referred to above. That study revalues in terms both of United States prices and of the prices in European national currencies the expenditure in the United States, the United Kingdom, France, and Italy,[1] not only the personal consumption in the countries concerned but also expenditure on administration, defence, and a variety of public services. The analysis relates to 1950 and is thus not directly comparable with Professor Lewis's analysis, but expenditure in this field does not fluctuate so rapidly as does, for example, defence expenditure. The definition of administration is, however, very much wider than Professor Lewis's and includes a number of what Professor Lewis has treated as economic services, such as expenditure on roads and transport, government services to industry, commerce, mining, and labour. Both alike exclude capital expenditure in the relevant fields.

It will be seen that per head of population the United States real expenditure on these public services was about the same as that in France and three-quarters that of the United Kingdom.

---

[1] The study includes Western Germany, which is not included in Professor Lewis's analysis and which I shall omit.

The United Kingdom with a gross national product about one-fifth of that of the United States employed for these purposes about two-fifths of the volume of resources, when measured at the same prices, and thus used just about twice the proportion of gross national product as measured at those prices. But since American

TABLE III

CURRENT EXPENDITURE IN 1950 ON PUBLIC SERVICES
OTHER THAN DEFENCE VALUED AT UNITED STATES PRICES

	Population (U.S.A. =100)	Real gross national product per head (U.S.A. =100)	Real gross national product (U.S.A. =100)	Real expenditure on administration per head of population (U.S.A. =100)	Total real expenditure on administration (U.S.A. =100)	Proportion of gross national product spent on administration	
						at U.S. prices %	at national prices %
United States	100·0	100·0	100·0	100·0	100·0	3·48	3·48
United Kingdom	31·5	62·8	19·8	130·2	41·0	7·22	3·94
France	26·5	53·5	14·2	101·6	26·9	6·60	5·47
Italy	29·4	30·3	8·9	82·6	24·3	9·49	3·75

Notes : (1) Real gross national product per head as calculated by Gilbert and Kravis, *op. cit.*, in terms of United States prices throughout. (2) Real gross national product calculated from Gilbert and Kravis estimates of relative gross national product per head at United States prices. (3) Real expenditure per head on administration is from data included in the Gilbert and Kravis estimates and is at United States prices and salaries. (4) Proportions of gross national product spent on administration are from data included in Gilbert and Kravis. The definition of administration is very much wider than that of Martin and Lewis and includes most of the economic services separated out by the latter. The first proportion is that of expenditure on general administration revalued at U.S. prices compared with the whole gross product revalued at U.S. prices. The second is the expenditure in the same field valued in national currencies compared with the gross product similarly valued, and thus is more nearly comparable with the Martin and Lewis figures. (5) It should be stressed that, by revaluing in all cases at United States prices, the possible effects upon the proportion of G.N.P. devoted to administration due to higher real incomes in richer nations for persons providing services of an unchanged character and quantity are automatically eliminated.

public servants are expensive as compared with other articles to be bought in America, and British public servants are, as compared with other articles to be bought in Britain, relatively cheap, the proportion of the British product valued at British prices devoted to administration was very much lower, and approached the American ratio.

The valuations at American prices are, however, the best indication of the relative absolute expenditures per head. It is clear that per head of population the British citizen pays for about 30 per cent more 'administration' than does the American or the French. The Italian pays for nearly 20 per cent less. Thus in absolute terms the largest country of the four falls mid-way between three countries of roughly comparable size, each between one-quarter and one-third of the size of the largest.

Measured in real expenditure per dollar of gross national product, that is to say, by the proportion of gross national product spent on administration, when both product and cost of administration are measured at United States prices, the largest country has substantially the lowest costs ; the other three are closer together, but with appreciable differences between them.

Thus the evidence is not inconsistent with there being some economies of size. But on the very limited data available it would scarcely be permissible to make any refined econometric attempt to attribute differences to size of nation and income per head respectively, since the quality and coverage of what is here defined as 'administration' is by no means uniform.

IV. SOCIAL SERVICES

There is no *a priori* reason for expecting that social services will cost either more or less to provide and administer in a large country than in a small country. It is, of course, true that both education and health services are more expensive to administer where the density of population is abnormally low than where it is high. But density of population is wholly independent of the size of the country. It is possible to provide examples both of countries that are small in aggregate population and have a low average density of population (like Australia) and of countries that are small in numbers but have a high density (like Belgium). Equally it is possible to provide examples of countries with a large aggregate population and a low density (like the United States) and of countries with large aggregate population and a high density (like India).

It would seem that costs of operation per head of social services are very much more affected by density than by size of aggregate population. Low levels of density may result in sub-optimum sizes of classes in schools, sizes of hospitals, higher administrative costs per unit of service. High levels of density of population may lead to the emergence of living conditions that require more elaborate and expensive health services. But these circumstances are quite independent of the problems of the economies and diseconomies of large and small nations.

If one turns to the statistical evidence, it throws little light on the problems of the relative costs of providing a defined standard of service. Table IV shows for 1953–54 the expenditures from public funds on education and health in the group of countries that are being compared :

TABLE IV

PUBLIC EXPENDITURE ON EDUCATION, HEALTH,
HOUSING, AND SOCIAL INSURANCE
AS PERCENTAGE OF GROSS NATIONAL PRODUCT, 1953–54

	Education	Health	Housing	Social Insurance	Total
United States	2·40	0·92	0·17	3·49	6·98
United Kingdom	3·47	3·28	0·69	5·84	13·28
France	1·97	1·62	0·11	3·51	7·21
Italy	2·99	2·08	—	4·33	9·40
Sweden	4·27	2·57	0·13	5·59	12·56
New Zealand	2·68	3·42	0·18	7·98	14·26
India	0·77	0·44	—	0·18	1·39
Ceylon	2·94	2·07	0·01	1·24	6·26
Jamaica	1·99	2·06	0·24	1·07	5·36

Notes : (1) Figures are from *Martin and Lewis, op. cit.* p. 233. (2) The comparisons are in terms of the ratio of the expenditures valued in national currencies to the gross national product valued at national prices and in national currencies. (3) Social Insurance includes all civil and military pensions, public assistance and social security benefits.

It will be seen that Sweden, the United Kingdom, and New Zealand all defray a substantial part of the total national expenditure on health and education from public funds. The United States employs in this way only about half the proportion of gross national product that do the others. India falls very far below the other nations analysed.

It is perhaps easier to appreciate the actual situation if the total expenditures on education and health from private as well as public sources are compared. While such a comparison is not readily available for 1953–54, the comparison has been made by Milton Gilbert and Irving Kravis for 1950 which consolidates all expenditure, private and public, in these fields, and in addition revalues it at United States prices, by calculating purchasing power equivalents in United States dollars for units of national currencies for a variety

231

of different types of personnel and services devoted to the objectives under consideration. The result of their work has been to estimate the comparative real expenditures per head of population in U.S. dollars for four of the countries concerned as follows :

TABLE V

COMPARATIVE REAL EXPENDITURE IN 1950 ON EDUCATION AND HEALTH FROM PUBLIC AND PRIVATE SOURCES COMBINED

	Real gross national product per head (U.S.A.=100)	Real expenditure on education per head (U.S.A.=100)	Real expenditure on health per head (U.S.A.=100)
United States	100·0	100·0	100·0
United Kingdom	62·8	61·5	68·0
France	53·5	66·0	55·5
Italy	30·3	56·9	9·7

It will be seen that the total real expenditure in the United States is about 50 per cent greater than in the United Kingdom both in education and in health, and closely reflects the difference of real gross income per head. Both France and Italy spend a relatively higher proportion of gross income on education. France spends about the same proportion of gross income on health ; Italy a very substantially smaller proportion.

It is very doubtful whether any conclusions relevant to the economies of size can be made to emerge from these figures. It is clear that, except so far as differences of the individual abilities of teachers and of the qualities of institutions can offset them, the richer countries can and do provide higher standards of these services.

V. ECONOMIC SERVICES

Economic services take a variety of different forms. Some reflect political policies and preparedness to subsidize particular types of activities ; included in these are expenditures on agriculture and especially on agricultural subsidies. Some, again, reflect the need for particular facilities, such as drainage, irrigation, land-settlement, and other public works ; these are understandably large in New Zealand, Italy, Ceylon, and India, but small in the United Kingdom and Sweden.

There is rather greater uniformity in the type of service provided in relation to roads and transport (though the latter includes any deficit on publicly owned transport services) and in relation to the public departments serving industry, commerce, and mining. It will be noted that, apart from India where low expenditure per head reflects low taxable capacity per head, the United Kingdom and the United States devote a smaller proportion of gross national product to roads and transport than do other countries. In the case of the United Kingdom this may be in part the consequence of underspending on trunk roads, but is primarily the consequence of relatively high income per head and high density of population in a small area. It would be difficult to argue from the expenditures on roads and transport that there are substantial economies of expenditure per head in a large nation. The real cost of roads per head in the United States is approximately the same as that in Sweden and New Zealand, about twice that in the United Kingdom or in France, about seven times that in Italy, and about ninety times that in India. France has nearly three times the real expenditure on roads per head of Italy with a very similar population.

TABLE VI

CURRENT EXPENDITURE ON ECONOMIC SERVICES
AS PERCENTAGE OF GROSS NATIONAL PRODUCT, 1953–54

	Roads and transport	Agriculture and agricultural subsidies	Industry, commerce, and mining	Public works, drainage, irrigation, water supplies, and land settlement	All other economic services	Total economic services
United States	0·90	0·87	0·03	0·11	0·08	1·99
United Kingdom	0·80	2·22	0·16	0·40	0·12	3·70
France	1·64	0·23	0·66	1·12	0·12	3·77
Italy	1·30	0·77	0·52	1·39	0·14	4·12
Sweden	1·50	0·81	0·23	0·47	0·30	3·31
New Zealand	1·90	2·41	0·22	1·73	0·08	6·44
India	0·34	0·41	0·27	9·77	0·06	1·85
Ceylon	1·34	0·47	0·24	1·52	0·27	3·84
Jamaica	1·50	0·72	0·12	0·94	0·04	3·32

Notes: (1) Figures from Martin and Lewis, *op. cit.* I have excluded expenditure on housing from economic services and have included it in social services, and have included here agricultural subsidies, thus departing from the categories of Professor Lewis. (2) Other economic services include labour and co-operation.

Size of Nation and Cost of Administration

It might not unreasonably be argued that small countries, being concerned about their defence and self-sufficiency, will (rightly or wrongly) tend to spend more on agricultural services and agricultural subsidies than larger and more naturally self-sufficient countries, with less obvious difficulties of war-time supplies. But the statistical evidence does not readily support this conclusion. The United Kingdom and New Zealand spend the largest proportion of gross national product on these objectives. But France, of similar population but with a larger agriculture, spends the smallest proportion of all. Sweden, Italy, the United States, and Jamaica emerge with very similar proportions, but with remarkably different populations.

The proportions of gross national product spent on industry, commerce, and mining might well be expected to show evidence of economies of size. The United States spends the lowest proportion ; the United Kingdom (apart from Jamaica with small concern about these matters) follows next ; France and Italy have significantly higher proportion. Sweden and New Zealand, small nations, have almost identical proportions, considerably below the French and Italian figures. The expenditure here clearly reflects the proportion of national resources devoted to industry and mining as well as economic policy in fostering these activities. It is not impossible on the basis of the evidence that there may be some economy of scale, but it is of very small significance in relation to the total value of the output of the nation.

Public works, including drainage, irrigation, water supplies, and land settlement may in principle yield economies of certain kinds to the large country. Where a river system, for example, lies wholly within one country it can be exploited more effectively and systematically, as practice in the United States and France, for instance, has demonstrated, than where, as in the case of the Indus, the Ganges, and the Jumna the head-waters are not under the full and exclusive control of the countries that principally depend upon them.

The statistical evidence, once again, is not inconsistent with there being small economies of scale. But it is doubtful whether any economies of these services are at all effectively measured by the actual expenditures. A better and more valuable service of land drainage or irrigation is not shown principally by the costs of providing it but in the effects upon agriculture and industries that benefit.

VI. DEFENCE

May I turn now to the costs of defence ? In this case it is particularly difficult to define when the effective service of defence can be said to reach a given acceptable level. And since different nations, because of differences of income per head, accept substantially different standards, or depend partly on defence provided by others, any statistical analysis of the relation of size of the nation to the costs of a given and consistent standard of defence is virtually impossible. All that is possible is to set out certain underlying determinants of the cost of a given defence.

In the first place, as every schoolboy knows, if one doubles the dimensions of any given figure — a circle, a rectangle, or any figure that is similar in the two cases — the circumference is doubled while the area is quadrupled. Thus if two nations have similar areas per head of population and shapes that are not widely dissimilar, if one has a population four times that of the other, the length of frontier will only be about twice that of the other, and the length of frontier per head of population will be about half that of the other. Thus so far as the cost of defence is proportionate to length of frontier to be defended, the larger country will be able to provide defence at about half the cost per head.

Secondly, again starting from the elaboration of the obvious, the proportion of the area of any country of given shape which is not within a distance of, say, one-quarter of the diameter of the country from the frontier, is constant whatever the area of the country. But if, as is more likely in the case of defence, one is concerned with the relative areas more than a given *x* miles removed from the frontier, the larger the country the greater the area. Thus again the larger country can be assured of a given standard of defence at smaller cost per head of population, or better defence for a constant cost per head.

Again, if two countries are of equal income per head, and if the average size of the productive unit is the same in both countries, the number of productive units will be larger in the larger country. The destruction of any one unit will thus represent a smaller proportion of the total productive capacity of the country. A larger country is thus not exposed to as great risks of the dislocation of production as is a smaller country, *ceteris paribus*. A larger and richer country may, however, owe its greater income to a greater concentration of its resources in industrial activities, and may, in practice, have its industrial activities concentrated in as few, or fewer, but much larger and more efficient units. In this case the larger and richer country may not impossibly require as large or larger a defence expenditure per head to assure that it is no more vulnerable than a smaller country in which industrial concentration in large-scale units is less advanced.

A small country is likely to depend to a greater extent than a larger country on foreign trade for the supply of essential food and raw materials. Thus effective defence is likely to require the maintenance of a flow of foreign trade even during war conditions, and the defence of the seas or land communications is necessary. In this respect also the smaller country is likely to be at a disadvantage as compared with the larger.

Moreover, it need scarcely be stressed that many of the actual problems of defence arise from uncertainty as to whether a group of allies can rely on the full mutual support of each other in case of danger. A large country possesses defence resources which it knows will be wholly available to it and which it can compare with the resources of potential enemies in complete certainty that they will be available. And since its forces are under its control and are

TABLE VII

EXPENDITURE ON DEFENCE, 1953–54

AS PERCENTAGE OF GROSS NATIONAL PRODUCT

	%		%
United States	13·90	New Zealand	3·74
United Kingdom	9·89	India	1·91
France	9·49	Ceylon	0·49
Italy	5·33	Jamaica	0·14
Sweden	3·74		

Note: The above figures are obtained by comparing the expenditure on defence, in terms of the current quantities of expenditure in each individual country and the prices of that expenditure in the currency of the country concerned, with the gross national product measured in terms of the prices and quantities of the country. This probably provides the best measure of the comparative burdens of defence in the countries concerned.

devoted to the defence of the whole of its territories, it can enjoy the economies of massed reserves to an extent that could not be achieved if similar forces were dissipated in an attempt to ensure the local defence of each individual segment of the territory.

Finally, there is good reason to think that there are economies of scale within defence expenditure itself. In the first place, a large part of defence expenditure is on overhead cost of research and development of new weapons, which can with advantage be distributed over a larger population. Secondly, in the actual manufacture of weapons there are large possible opportunities for obtaining the technical economies of large scale, and which almost certainly extend to scales larger than those achieved by most medium-sized nations. Some of these economies may possibly be secured by arrangements for division of responsibilities for research and manufacture among a group of allied nations, but it is doubtful whether this division yields economies fully equivalent to those that are possible to a single large nation.

If one turns from *a priori* argument to examine the actual expenditures on defence, it is at once clear that the richer nations, quite irrespective of size, spend very substantially more than the smaller nations. Table VII shows the very wide variations of expenditure as a proportion of gross national product.

The above figures do not, however, show the wide variations of real defence expenditure, which arise partly from differences of the percentages of gross national product devoted to defence, but partly also to differences of the gross national products themselves. Table VIII attempts to estimate, for the four European countries whose gross national products can be compared with that of the United States within reasonable limits of error as the result of the work of Milton Gilbert and Irving Kravis, the relative real resources devoted to defence and the real resources per head devoted to defence.

TABLE VIII

CURRENT EXPENDITURE ON DEFENCE, 1952

	Popula-tion (U.S.A. =100)	Gross national product (U.S.A. =100)	Defence expenditure as % of G.N.P.		Real expen-diture on defence (U.S.A. =100)	Real expen-diture on defence per head of popula-tion (U.S.A. =100)
			(a) at U.S. prices	(b) at national prices		
			%	%		
United States	100·0	100·0	14·6	14·6	100·0	100·0
United Kingdom	31·5	19·8	11·3	10·1	14·5	46·0
France	26·5	14·2	10·7	8·8	9·8	37·0
Italy	29·4	8·9	5·8	4·2	3·5	12·0

Notes : (1) the above figures are extracted or calculated from Milton Gilbert and Irving Kravis, *An International Comparison of National Products and the Purchasing Power of Currencies*, pp. 36-45. Since the figures come from a different source, it cannot be regarded as certain that the definition of 'defence' is identical in the Gilbert-Kravis analysis and in the Martin-Lewis analysis, but there is no reason to suspect substantial difference. (2) For purposes of comparison of the real expenditure on defence, all expenditure both on personnel and for other defence purposes has been valued at U.S. prices : 'the figures derived from United States prices are a significant measure of the real defence contribution measured by a common yardstick' (*loc. cit.* p. 44). (3) In 1950, before rearmament, the ratios as calculated by the same authors of defence expenditure to G.N.P., when valued by U.S. prices, were in all cases lower : U.S.A., 5·3 per cent ; U.K., 7·8 per cent ; France, 8·2 per cent ; Italy, 5·7 per cent. It is significant that at that date the United States ratio was the lowest of the four.

It will be seen that the United States devotes a very substantially larger proportion of a very much larger gross national product to defence than does any of the four European countries compared ; in consequence the real expenditure on defence in the United States is between seven and eight times that in the United Kingdom and about twelve times that of France. For this expenditure the United States gets about twice the real resources per head of population devoted to defence than does the United Kingdom. In view of the arguments of the previous paragraphs, the difference in the effective standard of defence is probably even greater.

It is clear that statistical evidence of the advantages from the point of view of defence that accrue to a large nation cannot be adduced from the relative expenditures of large and small nations. In the conditions of today the differences due to income per head dominate all else and provide widely varying effective standards of defence. It is clear, however, from the *a priori* arguments that substantial advantages lie with the large nation.

VII. CONCLUSIONS

The results of this first attempt to examine the economies of scale when applied to the operations of government are in a sense disappointing. It is clear that so far as one seeks to rely on statistical evidence, the outcome is inconclusive. Throughout the activities of government, the standards of service differ so greatly that it is virtually impossible to adduce evidence to show that a given and defined standard of government service is actually being provided more cheaply by the larger nation. For almost every service the cost per head is highest in the United States. But this is almost certainly because the United States, with a high income per head, has a fairly high income elasticity of demand for the services provided by government agencies. At the other end of the scale India has exceptionally low real expenditures upon almost all government services. But again this almost certainly reflects the low income per head of India rather than special economies of operating the public services of a nation of that vast size.

So far as *a priori* argument will take us, there seem to be relatively small economies, if any, in operating social services for very large nations rather than nations of medium or even comparatively small size, provided that the density of population is such as to permit the local units of operation — schools, hospitals, offices, and so on — to achieve their optimum sizes for economical working.

There may be some advantages in operating economic services for large populations rather than small populations. The difficulties of considering the economic relations of a small country to the outside world may well be greater and not less than those of considering the economic relations of a large country ; its degree of dependence on the outside world is likely to be greater ; the changes of the outside world are relatively larger and more likely to dominate the small economy. The small economy must distribute over a smaller population the cost of a service which in aggregate may require to be not greatly smaller than that of a larger nation if the standard of service is to be similar.

The two types of services in which economies of scale would seem likely to be large are those represented by general administration and by defence. The economies to be obtained under the head of general administration are somewhat uncertain, and probably do not represent more than 1 per cent of gross national product at most.

The economies to be obtained from better and cheaper defence are almost certainly more substantial, but the statistical evidence does not permit us to measure the gains obtained from a high level of security. In practice, defence expenditures reflect ability to pay for different standards rather than the economies of achieving a uniform standard. There are, however, good reasons for supposing that the economies of scale apply with considerable force to the field of national defence.

If one considers the problem as a whole, the economies of scale in relation to the administration, provision of public services, and the defence of a nation are probably on balance advantageous to a large nation, but, with the single exception of defence, are probably not of great significance.

Size of Nation and Cost of Administration

APPENDIX

CURRENT EXPENDITURE, 1953–54
AS PERCENTAGE OF GROSS NATIONAL PRODUCT *

	United States	United Kingdom	France	Italy	Sweden	New Zealand	India	Ceylon	Jamaica
Population (million)	162·4	51·1	43·0	47·7	7·2	2·1	377·0	8·4	1·5
1. Administration †	2·40	2·36	3·32	3·76	3·07	2·92	3·09	2·77	2·89
2. Education	2·40	3·47	1·97	2·99	4·27	2·68	0·77	2·94	1·99
3. Health ‡	0·92	3·28	1·62	2·08	2·57	3·42	0·44	2·07	2·06
4. Roads	0·63	0·70	0·78	0·55	1·05	1·18	0·22	0·51	0·82
5. Transport §	0·27	0·10	0·86	0·75	0·45	0·72	0·12	0·83	0·68
6. Public Works	0·03	—	0·82	1·01	—	0·94	0·53	0·55	0·50
7. Agriculture	0·23	0·24	0·23	0·61	0·72	0·54	0·41	0·43	0·58
8. Drainage	—	0·08	—	—	—	0·10	0·24	0·24	0·05
9. Water Supplies	0·08	0·32	0·05	—	0·23	0·14	—	0·16	0·09
10. Land Settlement	—	—	0·25	0·38	0·24	0·45	—	0·57	0·30
11. Co-operation	—	—	—	—	—	—	0·06	0·14	0·02
12. Industry	—	0·16	0·29	0·16	0·17	0·21	0·27	0·20	0·04
13. Commerce	0·02	—	0·37	0·36	—	—	—	0·02	0·07
14. Mining	0·01	—	—	—	0·06	0·01	—	0·02	0·01
15. Labour	0·08	0·12	0·12	0·14	0·30	0·28	—	0·13	0·04
16. Housing	0·17	0·69	0·11	—	0·13	0·18	—	0·01	0·24
17. Agricultural Subsidies	0·64	1·98	—	0·16	0·09	1·87	—	0·04	0·14
18. Social Insurance ǁ	3·49	5·84	3·51	4·33	5·59	7·98	0·18	1·24	1·07
19. Defence	13·90	9·89	9·49	5·33	3·74	3·74	1·91	0·49	0·14
20. Public Debt	2·16	4·77	1·97	1·97	0·81	2·76	0·60	1·06	1·35
Total	27·43	34·00	25·76	24·58	23·49	30·12	8·84	14·42	13·08

* For full notes, definitions, and sources (including sources of estimate of G.N.P.), see Martin and Lewis, *op. cit.* pp. 239-44, to which careful reference is strongly recommended. Estimates of population have been added from another source.

† *Administration* 'includes all administrative and legislative expenditure except the administrative expenditure of the education, health, and economic departments specified below. It includes tax collection and accounting, prisons, police, printing, fire service, and miscellaneous expenditure not elsewhere specified. Pensions are shown in Social Insurance.'

‡ *Health* 'includes hospitals, sanitation and medical services, but not health insurance '.

§ *Transport* 'includes railways, civil aviation, mercantile marine, harbours, posts and telecommunications. Current accounts include only deficits on those services, unless they are organised as separate agencies, in which case the administrative expenditures of the departments responsible for supervising them are also shown. Capital expenditures are shown only in so far as the budget provides for them.'

ǁ *Social Insurance* 'includes all civil and military pensions ; public assistance and social security benefits '.

Chapter 15

NOTE ON SIZE OF STATES AND COST OF ADMINISTRATION IN AUSTRALIA

BY

W. PREST
University of Melbourne

IN Australia, as in other federal countries, it is possible to compare the *per capita* cost of government services in states of various sizes. Such comparisons are made annually by the Commonwealth Grants Commission in the course of its examination of the claims of the smaller states for special federal grants.

These comparisons relate, of course, only to services undertaken by state governments, and therefore exclude defence, external affairs, and other federal government functions. Some state government services are not, however, strictly comparable from one state to another, *e.g.* mineral and agricultural services, the scope and nature of which varies with the natural resources of each state. Others, such as the maintenance of the legislature, involve relatively small outlays, and would not justify the work involved in preparing comparable data, particularly where state accounting procedures differ, as in Australia. There remain three large fields in which the Commonwealth Grants Commission has found statistical comparisons to be both possible and worthwhile. These are : (i) education, (ii) health and hospitals, and (iii) law and order.

Each year the Commonwealth Statistician prepares for the use of the Commission a comparative statement of twenty-one detailed items of state expenditure in the above three fields. *Per capita* expenditure in these fields in each state in 1955–56 is summarized in Table I.

The Commission compares, for each of the twenty-one services, the average *per capita* cost in the three larger states with that in each of the smaller states. In the light of its knowledge of the standard of service provided, and visits to schools, hospitals, and similar institutions, the Commission considers how far differences

241

Size of Nation and Cost of Administration

TABLE I

	New South Wales	Victoria	Queensland	South Australia	West Australia	Tasmania
	s. d.	s. d.	s. d.	s. d.	s. d.	s. d.
Education (10 items)	193 8	179 2	148 2	181 5	217 10	222 2
Health, etc. (7 items)	112 11	124 4	164 7	114 6	152 3	158 6
Law and Order (4 items)	48 6	45 0	57 4	42 5	51 8	60 5
Total	355 1	348 6	370 1	338 4	421 9	441 1

in costs can be accounted for by the effect of the following factors on administrative costs :

(i) size of population ;
(ii) sparsity of population ;
(iii) relative needs, and particularly the proportion of school children, which tends to be higher in states with small and/or scattered rural population.

Table II gives some data for 1953–56 illustrative of these factors.

TABLE II

	New South Wales	Victoria	Queensland	South Australia	West Australia	Tasmania
Mean Population	3,524,379	2,564,849	1,352,629	834,465	559,040	319,192
Persons per sq. mile	11·6	29·3	2·0	2·2	0·7	12·3
School children aged 6-13 as proportion of Population	14·97%	14·53%	12·52%	15·83%	15·78%	15·70%

In recent years the Commission has adopted overall margins of 6 per cent to cover the extra costs occasioned by the above factors in South Australia, and 12 per cent for such extra costs in Western Australia and Tasmania. Thus, in 1955–56 when the average cost of the services actually provided in the three larger states was 357s. 11d. per head, the same standard of services would, it is estimated, have cost 379s. 5d. per head in South Australia, and 400s. 11d. per head in Western Australia and Tasmania. The Commission has not published the details of its calculations, but it has stated that only comparatively small allowances have been thought necessary on account of sparsity of population (23rd Report, para. 48).

The differences between estimated costs of providing 'standard' services in the three smaller states (given in the preceding paragraph) and the costs of the services actually provided (given in Table I) are presumed to arise because the state governments chose to provide services below standard in South Australia, and above standard in Western Australia and Tasmania.

PART VI

FOREIGN TRADE AS AN ESCAPE
FROM SMALLNESS

Chapter 16

THE SIZE OF THE NATION
AND ITS VULNERABILITY
TO ECONOMIC NATIONALISM

BY

R. TRIFFIN

Yale University

I. THE CLASSICAL PRINCIPLES

ORTHODOX economic advice is once more being spurned by the statesmen. The common market treaty has already been signed, and negotiations on the establishment of a European free trade area are moving rapidly towards a successful conclusion. The spectres of discrimination and trade diversion have been unable to block the path towards regional liberalization and to push the nations towards the high-road of world-wide liberalization under the auspices of the General Agreement on Tariffs and Trade or of the International Trade Organization.

The economists, however, are gentle fellows who take such rebukes in their stride, and are quite willing — even anxious — to try to find belated economic justifications for the decision of their governments to do the opposite of what they had wanted them to do. Keynes did this in the 1930s and I suspect that we may have been assembled at this conference for a similar face-saving operation.

Let us not indulge once more in our favourite pastime and take the classical economists as the villains of the play. They cannot be blamed for our former misgivings and hostility toward preferential — or discriminatory — trade liberalization, customs unions, and so on. They were indeed remarkably silent on such topics, as well as on the broader theme assigned to us here : 'The Economic Consequences of the Size of Nations'. Their main contention was that any nation, whether small or large, has a selfish interest in pursuing free trade policies, irrespective of whether other nations wisely follow the same path or foolishly allow themselves to be lured away from it by protectionist fallacies. If, however, we were able to conjure up their spirits among us today and to ask them

247

point-blank to express an opinion on the 'economic consequences of the size of nations', I have little doubt as to what their answer would be. After having assumed everything else to be equal, they would probably point out that the larger the nation the larger the area over which free trade would be guaranteed by political organization in a world of nation states. They would also point out, I am sure, that if each nation state acted rationally and embraced free trade, little or no damage could be done by the existence of separate political sovereignties and that the size of nations would then be irrelevant to their economic prosperity.[1]

The adoption of protectionism by any one state, however, does damage to others as well as to itself, since it deprives them of opportunities for profitable exchange and specialization, based on comparative costs and advantages. Everything else being equal — once more — the smaller nation will be more vulnerable than the larger nation to the action of its neighbours, since its ability to concentrate on — and exploit to the full — the lines of production for which it is best fitted by natural advantages will be more dependent on its freedom of access to foreign markets for its exports and imports. Who can doubt that minuscule Luxemburg is more vulnerable to other nations' nationalism than the gigantic United States?

II. VARIOUS ASPECTS OF VULNERABILITY

This vulnerability expresses itself in a great variety of ways. A high level of foreign restrictions is the most familiar, but by no means the most important, of its manifestations. A second is the fact that the individual country is exposed at all times to sudden and unpredictable shifts in the level of these restrictions. This has become of paramount importance in a world in which the age-old — and relatively stable — techniques of tariff protection are now supplemented by quantitative trade and exchange controls, far more rigid in their incidence and subject to day-to-day changes of an administrative character, by-passing the slower channels of parliamentary decisions and re-negotiation of tariff treaties. A third is the growth of bilateral trade and payments techniques, in which naked bargaining power supplants price and quality competition as a determinant of each country's trade pattern. Finally, the course of economic events in a small country may be vitally affected even by the *internal* policies adopted by its trade partners. If it wishes

---

[1] Even then, however, the size of nations would still have been regarded as relevant to the mobility of factors of production.

to avoid recourse to trade restrictions or currency devaluation, it will be forced to adjust its own internal policies to theirs, or at least to eschew any faster rate of monetary expansion with relation to production and liquidity requirements than that prevailing beyond its national borders.[1] This may be regarded by outsiders as a desirable discipline, preventing the adoption of irresponsible inflationary policies, and it is sometimes pointed out that a small country enjoys in this respect a real advantage over a large country because of its inability to seek a practical escape from such discipline through protectionist restrictions and economic isolation. Its smallness thus protects it from the follies in which a larger country may indulge more easily ! This type of argument, however, is at best more convincing to outside judges than to the national authorities concerned. And it certainly glosses over the fact that the small nation may thereby be forced to adjust its policies to the inferior — as well as to the superior — wisdom and administrative capacity of other countries.

III. IMPLICATIONS FOR POLICY

The vulnerability of the small nation to economic nationalism still plays only a minor rôle in shaping the policy prescriptions of traditional international trade theory. First of all, it is often assumed — as already observed above — that each individual country will have a selfish interest in free trade anyway, no matter what other countries do. This might be true if other countries adopted, once and for all, a given and unchanging level of protection in their international trade relations. It may not be true, however, if other countries' policies exhibit frequent and violent shifts, making them highly unstable and volatile markets for the exports of their trade partners. Switzerland, for instance, might have a natural advantage in concentrating an even larger share of its productive resources on the manufacture of watches for export and in supplying a correspondingly larger share of its home requirements of other goods through imports rather than from home production. This advantage might not be decisive, however, and a certain degree of protection and insulation from world trade might well become advisable if, in fact, its export markets for watches fluctuate violently from year to year, and bring back recurrent waves of unemployment for highly specialized workers and equipment which cannot be shifted easily

[1] The emergence of balance of payments problems plays here a rôle similar to that of interbank clearings — and the inability of an individual bank to create legal tender — in preventing an over-expansion of credit by an individual bank relative to the pace of expansion of other banks, within the same country or monetary area.

and quickly into other occupations. One might presume, however, that these considerations would not go unperceived by private firms, although the spread of unemployment insurance schemes would tend to create divergencies between private and social calculations in this respect.

The second, stock-in-trade argument of traditional economics is that there is little that a country can do to influence the policies of others, and that in so far as such influence exists it only reinforces the argument for liberal trading policies. Protectionism tends to spread and invites retaliation, while liberal policies have also a tendency to spread and may be generalized and consolidated through the most-favoured-nation clause or through world-wide agreements of the ITO, or GATT, variety. The validity of this argument was far greater in the nineteenth century than it is today. It rested very largely indeed on the tacit assumption that all countries choose only between more or less *restrictive* policies, but do not resort to *bilateral* restrictions and discrimination. The situation became very different with the generalization of bilateral techniques in world trade and payments. Even a small country could now influence greatly the restrictions applied by other countries to its exports, depending on whether or not it agrees to engage in bilateral negotiations with them. The refusal of Italy to conclude a bilateral agreement with the United Kingdom in 1947, for instance, might have deprived that country of the bulk of its export markets for fruit and vegetables which the United Kingdom was in a position to buy elsewhere, or do partly without in accordance with the 'austerity' policy to which it was driven by its balance of payments difficulties. There were many economists in those days to recommend that Italy should put 'its own house in order', restore the convertibility of the lira, and refuse to accept payment for its exports in inconvertible sterling. If this advice had been heeded, Italians would probably have had either to eat their lemons and drink their Chianti, or to find substitute markets for them in the few hard-currency countries then in existence, and absorbing normally little more than 10 per cent of Italy's exports, or to accept severe unemployment, or to reshuffle fundamentally their production and export pattern to adjust it to generalized discrimination against Italian exports by the soft-currency areas — normally accounting for nearly 90 per cent of Italy's export trade. None of these solutions could be deemed very attractive or promising. In the short run, bilateral trading itself would result in a less wasteful allocation of Italy's resources than the very low levels of trade that would ensue at first from the adoption of such policies. And in the longer run the painful overhauling of Italy's trade and production pattern, necessary to maintain lira convertibility in an inconvertible Europe, would have had to be undone and reversed in order to readjust Italy's economy to the more normal conditions brought back by Europe's recovery.

Nineteenth-century techniques of trade negotiation were indeed attempted, and improved upon, during those days to deal with this kind of problem. But their success was very modest and the reasons for this cannot all be ascribed to temporary post-war dislocations. The liberal philosophy of limited interference by the government in economic life — internal as well as external — and the ignorance of modern techniques of intervention — such as direct controls, rigid inconvertibility techniques, bilateral trade and payments agreements — narrowly limited in former days the likelihood of large-scale divergences in the monetary evolution of the major trading countries and in their national price and cost levels. The harmonization of policies could be left, to a considerable extent, to the spontaneous interplay of market forces. The residual rôle left to international negotiation and agreements was a relatively modest one and could be handled by comparatively simple techniques, centring upon the conclusion of tariff treaties and their generalization through the most-favoured-nation clause.

The broadening of the horizons of economic policy — to include as objectives a maximum rate of employment and growth, the stabilization of prices, the improvement of working conditions, assistance to weaker economic sectors, and so on — and of the instruments of control or intervention at the disposal of national states have increased enormously the tasks that must be performed today by negotiated rather than spontaneous policy harmonization among independent economic sovereignties. The problems raised by such harmonization are basically different from those analysed by the classical economists, and cannot be handled or understood through the use of the traditional tools of economic theory. They refer to the reconstruction of the stable institutional framework for international trade and payments which the classicists assumed as a datum and a point of departure for their investigation, rather than as a problem for economic policy.

The reconstruction of such a stable framework involves essentially the acceptance by independent countries of certain limitations on their economic sovereignty, or — in less resounding words — of certain constraints on the manner in which they will make use of this sovereignty. It is a dangerous illusion to think that strict limitations on the use of *external* policy tools, such as exchange rate determination, tariffs, import restrictions, exchange controls, discrimination and bilateralism, can be effectively negotiated and implemented without parallel agreements of a more positive nature about mutual assistance, or escape clauses in case of difficulties, and even about a minimum of harmonization in the area of *internal* economic policies in so far as these have direct and important repercussions upon the countries' balance of payments.

The OEEC-EPU experiment, and the area covered by the more recent negotiation of the common market treaty, abundantly confirm this conclusion. They also make clear the reasons why success is more likely to be reached first by regional, rather than universal, organizations and institutions. The mere administrative burdens involved in continuous consultation and reconciliation of divergent interests and points of view are a first and immediate handicap to world-wide co-operation. The depth and comprehensiveness of feasible co-operation and commitments will, moreover, be in inverse relation to the number and heterogeneity of the participants in such discussions. The implication of these facts is obvious. While exploiting to the fullest possible extent the opportunities for world-wide agreements, we cannot neglect the greater potentialities opened up by regional agreements for more intimate forms of co-operation and harmonization of policies among countries highly interdependent, keenly conscious of this interdependence, and better prepared for such co-ordinated action by a common geographical and historical background and a relatively homogeneous stage of economic development. Various levels of economic integration are perfectly reconcilable with one another and may indeed reinforce one another. Agreements of the International Monetary Fund or GATT type can be complemented by closer and closer forms of association, ranging from those of the Atlantic Community, for instance, to intergovernmental agreements of the Organization for European Economic Co-operation and European Payments Union type, down to supranational groupings like the European Coal and Steel Community, economic unions *à la* Benelux, and finally the complete merger of sovereignty of the nation state.

IV. THE BOGY OF TRADE DIVERSION

This common-sense conclusion would indeed belabour the obvious, if common sense had not been strongly challenged and clouded over here by ingenious economic arguments stressing the dangers and pitfalls of customs unions and other 'discriminatory' arrangements among independent countries. Bizarrely enough, none of these economists appears to be disturbed by the discriminatory implications of national boundaries themselves, and none has followed his own line of reasoning to its logical conclusion and argued for the breaking up, in the name of non-discrimination, of national economic areas into smaller economic areas delineated by provincial, municipal, or even — why not ? — individual household boundaries.

The traditional argument against customs unions was formulated long ago and most lucidly, if succinctly, by Professor Viner. Customs unions may be good or bad depending on whether or not their 'trade-creating' impact outweighs their 'trade-diverting' impact. Let us suppose, for instance, that Germany can produce cars more efficiently than France, but less efficiently than the United States. A customs union between France and Germany would be good, according to Viner's concept, if it induced Frenchmen to shift from French cars to German cars, but bad in so far as it induced them to import from Germany cars that would otherwise be imported from the United States.[1]

Professor Haberler later made use of the same criterion to justify the ITO distinction between trade preferences and customs unions. The reduction of duties under preferential régimes is likely to be predominantly trade-diverting, 'because there is a natural tendency to reduce trade barriers only for those commodities which do not actively compete with domestic production'. On the other hand, 'a customs union will always be to some extent, possibly to a large extent, trade creating'. Yet Professor Haberler recognized that 'in Europe the policy of regional trade liberalization (implying though it does discrimination against the United States, Canada, Latin America, Japan, and others) has had some success and has gone beyond trade diversion, creating additional trade between the European countries. Fortunately, however, the discrimination against the United States, Canada, and Latin America has become progressively less severe because restrictions on imports from dollar countries have been reduced and currencies have become more freely convertible'.[2]

This latter observation illustrates, to my mind, the fact that the main argument for regional economic integration lies outside the scope of mere economic reasoning of a static character. The lowering of restrictions on imports from non-member countries and the gradual extension of currency convertibility may well be a by-product

---

[1] See Jacob Viner, *The Customs Union Issue*, Carnegie Endowment for International Peace, New York, 1950.

[2] *Foreign Economic Policy:* Hearings Before the Subcommittee on Foreign Economic Policy of the Joint Committee on the Economic Report, 89th Congress (Washington, D.C., 1955), pp. 501, 505, and 507-8.

of regional integration rather than an independent and fortunate accident. The trade-creating and trade-diverting effects of regional integration cannot be fully appraised by looking only at the immediate and direct trade concessions incorporated in a regional agreement. Indirect policy and incentives are far more significant for arriving at a broad judgement of the overall impact of the agreement on future trade patterns.

Let us first accept the Viner-Haberler argument at face value, and see whether we cannot make at least a tentative guess as to the probable balance of trade-creating and trade-diverting impacts in a concrete case. Continental OEEC countries, together with their overseas territories, absorbed in 1955 about 58 per cent of these countries' total exports. Sterling area markets absorbed another 16 per cent, making a total of 74 per cent, as against 8 per cent of total exports going to the United States and Canada, 6 per cent to Latin America, and 13 per cent to the rest of the world.[1] The proportion of EPU markets in individual countries' exports exceeded 70 per cent in all cases but three (Turkey, Italy, and Switzerland) and ran as high as 94 per cent in the case of Ireland (see Table I). Everything else being equal, therefore, one might expect that the area of trade amenable to 'trade creation' under the EPU type of regional liberalization is about three times as large as the area susceptible to 'trade diversion' under these arrangements.

Everything else was far from equal, however, in 1949. Restrictions on hard currency imports from non-members, and particularly from the dollar area, were about as stringent as they could be previous to the establishment of EPU. Imports from these sources were severely limited to essential goods and raw materials, for which there existed no substitute sources of supply within the EPU area. The scope for further 'trade diversion' was thus extremely narrow, while that for mutual 'trade-creating' concessions was enormous.

The same observation casts serious doubts on the practical relevance of Professor Haberler's common-sense expectations that preferential concessions — short of a full customs union — are likely to concentrate on 'those commodities which do not actively compete with domestic production'. In any case, the rapid expansion of trade liberalization commitments to categories of goods accounting for 50, 60, 75, and finally 90 per cent or more of total imports

---

[1] These proportions are practically identical with those of 1950, dispelling the notion that the OEEC-EPU system tended to isolate Europe from world trade and to result in a major distortion of trade patterns. Comparisons with 1937, however, show a substantial increase in Europe's exports to its overseas territories, at the expense of exports to the 'rest of the world', *i.e.* to countries outside EPU and the Western Hemisphere.

from other members, made it increasingly difficult to pick and choose these categories in such a way as to exclude goods competing with domestic production.

The trade-diverting argument is, moreover, open to broader objections and limitations on general grounds of economic theory. Let us, for the sake of concreteness, examine the implications of a preferential reduction of tariffs between France and Germany. Is it conceivable that France will be able to grant to Germany significant concessions leading to a substitution of German goods for

TABLE I

PERCENTAGE DISTRIBUTION OF OEEC AND
STERLING AREA EXPORTS IN 1955

	EPU markets			Other			
	Continental OEEC and Dependencies	Sterling Area	Total	Total	U.S. and Canada	Latin America	Other
Austria	62	9	71	28	5	4	19
Belgium	63	13	76	25	12	4	9
Denmark	43	37	80	19	6	4	9
France	68	11	79	21	5	5	11
Germany	59	13	72	29	7	8	14
Greece	60	12	72	29	13	1	15
Italy	47	15	62	37	9	10	18
Netherlands	55	21	76	24	7	5	12
Norway	43	29	72	29	10	6	13
Portugal	54	21	75	25	11	5	9
Sweden	52	26	78	22	6	6	10
Switzerland	49	13	62	38	13	9	16
Turkey	42	8	50	51	16	—	35
Subtotal	58	16	74	27	8	6	13
United Kingdom	27	48	75	25	11	4	10
Ireland	5	89	94	6	3	—	3
Sterling Area	24	49	73	26	11	2	13

Source : *International Financial Statistics.*

American imports rather than for French-produced merchandise? This would presuppose the existence of severe customs duties or other restrictions on goods which, in spite of these duties and restrictions, France herself still does not produce domestically. In other words, it presupposes a high level of *ineffective* protectionism by the French. Is it not far more likely that the highest duties will be encountered on goods whose home production can be stimulated thereby rather than on goods which France does not produce anyway ?

Restrictions may be imposed by France, however, for other than protectionist reasons, for example, for balance of payments reasons. In this case, trade-diverting concessions to Germany become possible. The *quid pro quo* of such concessions, from the French point of view, would be similar concessions by Germany opening the German market to additional exports from France. If, however, the French balance of payments difficulties are due to *overall* inflationary pressures, that is to say, to the financing of expenditures in excess of maximum production, the concessions obtainable from Germany would be of little value to the French. If their economy is already fully employed, an expansion of exports to Germany, accompanied by a reshuffling of import sources, but not by an overall increase in imports, could be effected only at the cost of a decline in French exports to other areas, or of an aggravation of internal inflationary pressures in France. Such a situation would create few incentives for mutual trade concessions of the 'trade diversion' variety.

These observations seem to me to restrict to a special case the Viner fears about the impact of preferential tariff reductions or elimination. They would be most relevant in a situation in which all partners suffer simultaneously from balance of payments difficulties and unemployment, arising from uncompetitive cost levels or exchange rates. They would have far less relevance to a situation in which duties and restrictions are prompted by protectionist motives or by balance of payments difficulties originating in *overall* inflationary pressures rather than in price distortions.

This distinction is all the more significant as the trade diversion argument loses much of its force in the first of the three situations distinguished above, *i.e.* in the case where balance of payments deficits coincide with unemployment. In such a case, trade diversion would improve both employment and the balance of payments of the partners to the preferential agreement. France and Germany, for example, would both reduce their imports from the United States, while keeping their *overall* import levels unchanged, and would export more to one another, without subjecting themselves thereby to shortages or upward price pressures susceptible of bringing a reduction in their exports to the United States.

The simultaneous abatement of unemployment pressures and balance of payments difficulties would then tend to reduce two major incentives to restrictions and discrimination against non-member countries. The trade-creating and trade-diverting impacts of regional integration cannot be fully appraised by looking only at the initial pattern of trade concessions incorporated into a regional agreement. Indirect effects and policy incentives must also be taken into account, including particularly the allocation of the balance of payments improvements resulting from trade diversion to the reduction of initial import restrictions against non-member countries.

V. THE BOGY OF THE SHELTERED HIGH-COST AREA

These favourable effects of trade diversion upon employment and the balance of payments would taper off, however, as full employment is approached throughout the territory of the participating countries. Further expansion of intraregional trade would then be accompanied by over-employment pressures, price increases, and a reduction of exports to the outside world. The union might develop into a high-cost area, increasingly cut off from world-wide competition by inflationary developments at home behind the barrier of higher and higher restrictions against imports from the outside.

Let us first remember, however, that the net impact of regional integration on the members' cost level will be the resultant of two contrary types of price pulls. Prices will be pulled upwards by trade diversion, but downwards by trade creation. The creation of competitive conditions throughout the European territory would expose each industry to competition from the most efficient producers in Europe. One suspects that, as of today, there exist relatively few categories of goods for which no European producer offers as strong competition as American production itself. The Belgian steel industry, the German electrical and chemical industries, watch and precision instruments in Switzerland, and so on, are as or more efficient than their American counterparts and would exercise powerful pressures for competitive readjustments in European cost levels. The mere elimination of bilateralism sufficed to reintroduce these competitive forces via the competition of exporters throughout the EPU territory. Excessive national cost levels had to be readjusted to preserve exports even before protective restrictions were themselves reduced under the OEEC trade liberalization programme. The dismantlement of protection will be carried out further under the common market and free trade area provisions. Progress will be slower in this respect — extending over a period of 12 to 17 years — but it is worth noting that the mere signature of the treaties will constitute from the start a powerful spur to the most efficient producers to increase their production capacity and develop their export markets, in the knowledge that such expansion will no longer risk being arrested by a sudden tightening of controls, but will, in fact, be assisted by the gradual elimination of existing restrictions.

In the longer run, the maintenance of competitive cost levels will depend, of course, on the comparative evolution of monetary, fiscal, and price policies within and outside Europe. The question should therefore be raised as to whether regional integration is likely to strengthen, or to weaken, monetary discipline in the participating countries.

Two possibilities should be sharply distinguished in this respect.

The first is that of a free trade area or customs union accompanied only by a minimum of monetary integration among the participating countries. I mean by this the type of monetary integration now embodied in the European Payments Union or the European Monetary Agreement. These arrangements are primarily designed to eliminate bilateral techniques in payment,[1] but leave each country fully responsible for the conduct of its monetary policy and the financing of its balance of payments deficits within Europe as well as outside Europe. Under such conditions, monetary over-expansion in any one country, relative to the others, rapidly leads to unsustainable balance of payments deficits and reserve losses, and forces the adoption of 'corrective' measures indispensable to arrest the drain on reserves. In the absence of a customs union, these measures may take the form of trade and exchange restrictions, behind the protection of which inflationary forces may be allowed to proceed to a considerable extent until their final impact upon export and import levels becomes economically and politically unbearable. The free trade area eliminates this possibility as far as regional trade is concerned, and authorizes only the tightening of restrictions on imports from non-members, that is, on a minor portion of the deficit country's total trade. The common market treaty goes even farther, since it involves the adoption of a uniform tariff which cannot be changed at the discretion of any single country.

Under such conditions, the deficit country will have no alternative left but to readjust its internal policies and cost level or to devalue its currency. Monetary discipline will therefore be far stronger than in the absence of regional integration. The participating

---

[1] Widespread alarm was expressed in 1949 and 1950 concerning the 'excessive' credit facilities of the EPU arrangements. These were totally unfounded and have been amply refuted by later events. See my book on *Europe and the Money Muddle*, Yale University Press, 1957.

countries will have to 'keep in step' with one another, and the pressures which will force them to do so will concentrate upon the more inflationary — or less deflationary — countries of the group.

The second possibility is that of closer forms of integration, culminating in a unification of monetary responsibilities and policies among the participating countries, and excluding exchange readjustments among them. The overall pace of expansion would, in this case, be determined by collective decisions, involving a greater or lesser degree of *a priori* centralization or *a posteriori* negotiations, rather than automatically by the policies of the more conservative countries in the group. Regional integration of this kind will make it easier for the group as a whole than it was for individual countries to isolate themselves from more deflationary, or less inflationary, policies followed in the rest of the world. Regional integration decreases the vulnerability of the participating countries to foreign shocks. It gives them the means of protecting themselves from the impact of other countries' follies or wisdom, increasing their ability to follow wiser or more foolish policies than those prevailing in the outside world. Whether acquiring such mastery over its own destiny would be a gain or a loss for Europe is a question on which statesmen are likely to feel the least need for the opinion of their economic advisers.

VI. THE BOGY OF THE LARGE AUTARKIC BLOCS

The various considerations outlined above seem to me to create a far stronger presumption in favour of regional agreements than that which might emerge from a purely static and exclusively economic interpretation of the balance between their immediate trade-creating and trade-diverting impacts. Yet it is still no more than a presumption, which may be strengthened or weakened by the concrete circumstances surrounding actual experiments in economic integration. If, for instance, regional integration tended in fact to divide the world into rival blocs bent on protectionist, autarkic policies, we would view it with much greater misgivings than if it created instead a large and stable area of freer trade, gradually drawing non-member countries into its orbit.

Post-war integration has clearly developed in the latter, rather than the former, direction. Formal co-operation among OEEC countries was extended through EPU to an area whose total trade accounts for nearly 60 per cent of world trade. Harmonization of this area's trade and payments policies with those of the United

States and Canada would cover about 80 per cent of world trade, and would be tantamount to establishing a universal framework for world trade and monetary settlements. The regional approach would blend, in this case, into the world-wide approach to economic co-operation.

Regional economic integration is indeed unlikely to lead to the formation of rival autarkic blocs for the simple reason that this would require a most radical upheaval in the world trade pattern. The formation of EPU was greatly enhanced by the fact that exports to the EPU area have long accounted for 70 per cent to 75 per cent of the total exports of most EPU countries. This was already true in pre-war days at a time when currency convertibility prevailed and discriminating trade and exchange restrictions were at a minimum over most of the present EPU area.

Trade patterns in other parts of the world are very different indeed. A Latin American union, for instance, would regulate only 10 per cent of the total exports of its members. Even a Western Hemisphere bloc would include only 53 per cent of the participating countries' exports, and substantially less than this (43 per cent) for the southern countries of the group, whose main export markets (47 per cent) are in the EPU area itself (see Table II). For reasons

TABLE II

REGIONAL DISTRIBUTION OF WORLD EXPORTS IN 1954

Exports from	Exports to			
	World	EPU Area	Dollar Area	Other countries
EPU Area	58	73	11	15
Dollar Area	27	34	50	16
Other Countries	16	51	22	27
World	100	60	23	17

Note : Exports to (first column) and from (last row) the world are given as percentages of world totals. The other data are given as percentages of each area's total exports to the world.

Source : Derived from GATT estimates in *International Trade*, 1955 (Geneva, GATT, May 1956), pp. 201-3 and 222-23.

amply discussed above, effective regional agreements are likely to be concluded only among countries closely interdependent on one another, and this would seem to preclude the duplication of EPU types of arrangement in other parts of the world.[1]

[1] This is not to say, however, that other countries might not find it useful to conclude different types of arrangement aiming primarily at strengthening their bargaining position in trade negotiations with non-member countries.

The impact of European integration on trade and payments arrangements in the rest of the world may indeed help us resolve a rather puzzling question. What is *international*, as distinct from *national*, convertibility ? One swallow does not make a summer. But how many swallows are needed to make a summer ? The preservation of convertibility by one or two countries obviously does not ensure international convertibility. Just as obviously, however, we would not regard the maintenance of inconvertibility by Paraguay or Honduras as a fatal flaw in the armour of international convertibility. Even the nineteenth-century gold standard rested essentially on the adherence of the United States, Western Europe, and its dependent monetary areas, but did not preclude various degrees of restrictions and protectionism by individual countries, and of exchange rate instability by many countries in Latin America and Asia.

I have discussed elsewhere the reasons why the elimination of bilateralism, rather than of protectionism, should be regarded as the primary criterion in definition of convertibility, if the latter is not to become confused with the old ideal of free trade.[1] The significance of regional European integration for international convertibility flows from this observation. European integration does not rule out protectionism in the rest of the world — nor indeed by Europe itself — but it greatly reduces the probable scope of bilateralism in the world at large.

No country has a direct interest in discrimination, in shifting its imports from less costly to costlier sources of supply, except as a means to extract from its trade partners similar discrimination in its own favour, or to protect its exports against unfavourable discrimination by them. The EPU Agreement, however, together with the non-discriminatory policies generally pursued by the dollar area, effectively safeguard against discrimination 85 per cent of the EPU countries' exports, and preclude the use of discrimination as a weapon for expanding these exports. All other countries together absorb only 15 per cent of EPU countries' exports, and their own exports account for only 20 per cent of total world exports (see Table II). This leaves relatively little room for discrimination, particularly if one considers that profitable discrimination requires in each case mutual action by at least two countries.

EPU countries have, moreover, an interest in avoiding discriminatory arrangements concluded with third countries at one another's expense. Recent EPU consultations have been dealing

---

[1] 'International Currency and Reserve Plans', in *Policies to Combat Depression*, Princeton University Press for the National Bureau of Economic Research, 1956, and *Europe and the Money Muddle*, Yale University Press, 1957, Chapter 7.

with this problem and have already led to a substantial contraction of credit margins in payments agreements with non-member countries, to a large decline in the number of such agreements, and to the adoption of transferable EPU currencies for settlements with inconvertible countries. The main concern underlying residual bilateral payments provisions is to guarantee debt repayment by the partner country rather than to promote a further expansion of exports through discriminatory trade and payment practices.

The increasing reluctance of EPU countries to perpetuate bilateral trade and payments agreements makes it correspondingly difficult for third countries to maintain such agreements with their major trading partners. Since the overwhelming bulk of their own trade is with the EPU countries, the United States, and Canada, the remaining opportunities for discrimination and bilateralism are becoming so scant as to be of little significance for world trade and payments in general. The essential point is that the broad direction of the international trade and payments system towards or away from convertibility is determined by the policies of the major trading nations. These can force their weaker partners into convertibility as well as into inconvertibility, but the smaller countries cannot exercise the same influence upon the larger ones.

This is why firmer, *de jure* arrangements among the latter are both necessary, under modern conditions, and sufficient to restore and maintain international convertibility. Trade and payments relations not covered specifically by these agreements will depend on the *de facto* policies pursued by the countries concerned, but will offer few opportunities, incentives, or pressures for discrimination and bilateralism, except as a protection of last resort against the international spread of deflation or restrictions.

Such a mixture of *de jure* and *de facto* convertibility may not be sufficient, of course, to ensure the continued progress of trade liberalization and exchange rate stability among all the countries of the world. Broader negotiations, within the framework of the Organization for Trade Co-operation and the IMF, will retain a major rôle in this respect, but it will be helped rather than hindered by the closer degree of co-operation and integration which may be achieved under regional agreements.

VII. CONCLUSION

Progress towards freer trade involves essentially the acceptance of specific limitations on the interference of political power in economic life, as a way to defend the interests — real or fancied — of the group subject to that political power. The acceptability of such limitations and their political feasibility have always depended in large part on the existence of other, alternative ways of achieving the same objective. Complete and irrevocable commitments to free trade are therefore hardly ever encountered historically except within areas subject to the same political sovereignty, *i.e.* within the confines of the nation state. The dismantlement of local barriers to trade followed indeed, rather than preceded, the withering away of local or provincial autonomy and the assertion of full sovereignty by national governments. The economists are prone to accept meekly, and sometimes unconsciously, these political developments as valid criteria for economic policy. A general rise in French tariffs against imports from foreign countries will be regarded as non-discriminatory, even though it implies a corresponding increase in existing discrimination between external trade and the trade of, let us say, Northern France with Southern France.

This is, of course, perfectly illogical and completely indefensible, on theoretical as well as on historical grounds. If various countries are ready to accept a partial pooling of their economic sovereignty sufficient to eliminate — or even reduce — national barriers to their mutual trade, the results of these arrangements cannot automatically be labelled as more discriminatory than those involved in the maintenance of separate *national* customs areas, merely because the latter rest on a full merger of political, as well as economic, sovereignty. The economic significance of national boundaries may change as a result of economic integration as well as of political integration among the participating countries.

Economic incentives to integration are closely linked with the degree of economic interdependence between various geographical areas and of awareness of this interdependence on the part of their residents and political leaders. These incentives, together with parallel political incentives arising from the awareness of political interdependence, must be sufficient to overcome the emotional and administrative obstacles to the acceptance of advance commitments to certain lines of action and policy or to collective procedures for the adoption or harmonization of later decisions. Both of these factors point in the same direction. The need for integration is greatest, the obstacles to integration are least, and integration is therefore most likely to be achieved among areas closely interdependent on one another, keenly conscious of this interdependence, and better prepared by geographic proximity and a common historical heritage for a sympathetic understanding of each other's problems and policies. Integration at the national level, within the political boundaries of nineteenth-century nation states, could serve reasonably well the needs of a world where *laissez-faire* traditions circumscribed narrowly the intervention of state authorities in economic life and minimized the chances for large-scale maladjustments in the international trade and payments pattern. The enormous growth of national interventionism in economic life has increased correspondingly the scope of such maladjustments while reducing or distorting automatic mechanisms of readjustment based on market forces. Conscious policy integration can no longer stop at the national boundaries, and cannot be approved or condemned on the basis of a narrowly economic appraisal of its trade-diverting and trade-creating impact. The fundamental dilemma of international economic relations in this twentieth century lies in the inadequacy of national sovereignty as a framework for policy decisions and their administrative implementation in an interdependent world. This dilemma cannot be resolved overnight through a sudden and radical transformation of our institutions and habits of thought. The days of a world government are not yet at hand. The mushrooming and overlapping of international and regional institutions since the Second World War are both bewildering and disappointing to the logical mind. This proliferation, however, merely reflects our persistent efforts to remedy the partial failure of previous, half-hearted gropings after new forms of political organization necessary to reach and implement collective decisions where their need is sufficiently felt to overcome old prejudices and inertia. The ambitious framework of universal co-operation, indispensable as it is in many cases, often limits feasible co-ordination to *ad hoc* — and often *ex post* — attempts to smooth out conflicts of views and interests on specific issues and proposals. Regional co-operation, on the other hand, is far more likely to succeed in developing habits of continuous consultation and negotiation over a broader range of governmental responsibilities ; and it may, if successful, gradually evolve towards the actual merging of areas too small and too interdependent on one another to preserve national welfare and security on the basis of national sovereignty exercised within present political boundaries.

We have long been familiar with the first problem, but we still fail to see clearly the full implications of the second for the reorientation of international economic theory as well as international economic policy.

Chapter 17

HOW FAR CAN FOREIGN TRADE AND CUSTOMS AGREEMENTS CONFER UPON SMALL NATIONS THE ADVANTAGES OF LARGE NATIONS? [1]

BY

G. MARCY

University of Aix-en-Provence

I. THE NATION IN CLASSICAL ECONOMICS

THE question posed by the title of this paper would have been meaningless for the classical economists. In their view the size of a nation did not matter and had no bearing whatever on international trade, provided the latter were completely free. In a famous example involving Portugal and Great Britain, Ricardo showed that it was always to the advantage both of a large country and of a small one to specialize and exchange their products. It is true that the classical economists abstracted even from the very existence of nations and that in their view 'the nation is never understood as an exchange partner nor as lending support to exchange partners. The nation never acts as a group possessing its own behaviour pattern or structural preference; it is void of sociological content. Foreign trade is carried on by isolated individuals who are, however, subject to special conditions through belonging to different nations.' [2]

These conditions are essentially three: first, the nation is considered as a 'closed factor area', 'that is to say it is surrounded by frontiers which the factors of production cannot cross'; second, 'the nation's pattern of specialization is unalterable'; third, 'the nation is characterized by a homogeneous and pliable price system which intercommunicates indirectly with other price systems'. In short, 'the nation is a set of arbitrary institutions which strictly condition [the individuals'] actions. It is not an organizational factor.' [3]

With the increasing recognition of political and economic reality,

[1] Translated from the French by Elizabeth Henderson.
[2] Michel Moret, *L'Échange international*, ed. Marcel Rivière, Paris, 1957, p. 40.   [3] Michel Moret, *op. cit.* pp. 41 and 42.

the existence of nations and of domination effects have been incorporated into economic theory. Politicians and economists have come to attach great importance to the fact that nations distinct from each other do exist and even more is made of the fact that they are of different size. It has become a widely accepted view that the world is divided into large nations and small ones and that the latter are always *a priori* at a comparative disadvantage. Hence there is a search for means by which equality between the two may in part at least be re-established.

II. SOME ADVANTAGES OF LARGE NATIONS

Other contributors to this Conference will no doubt define and list the characteristics of large and small nations. We shall here concentrate only on those which have a direct bearing on foreign trade. We shall be led to observe that the concept of a small nation is not an altogether unambiguous one.

The immediately obvious criterion of the size of a nation is its geographical area : a small nation covers a small surface, a large nation a large surface. This often means that a large nation possesses more natural resources than a small one. A geographically small nation is likely to have less agricultural land and there is a general presumption that its mineral resources are likely to be less varied and less abundant. Another possible criterion is size of population. This often leads to the same classification of the size of nations. Geographically small countries are often densely populated, but the fact remains that in absolute figures their population is usually small. By both these two first criteria Belgium, Switzerland, and Sweden are small nations, and the United States and Russia large nations.

But these criteria do not appear fully satisfactory if we are to accept the view that Australia and Canada must take their place among small nations alongside Sweden and Switzerland.[1] We must look for another criterion which, without neglecting the first two, enables us to place in one and the same category such vast countries as Australia and Canada and such tiny ones as Switzerland and Belgium, all of them having a relatively small population. So far as foreign trade is concerned, this additional criterion might be the degree of dependence upon foreign markets, with respect both to imports and exports. Countries like Switzerland, Sweden, Canada, or Australia have it in common that they depend much more heavily on foreign markets than do the United States or even France, both

[1] Point 7 of the Programme Committee's Formulation.

266

as regards outlets for their products and sources of supply of raw materials, food, and finished products.

In the case of old industrial countries of small area like Sweden or Switzerland, this dependence is due to scarcity of natural resources and limited population. These countries are thereby prevented from highly diversifying their economy and hence must rely heavily on imports, and their domestic markets provide insufficient outlets for production so that they must export a large part of it. In new countries like Canada or Australia dependence upon foreign markets is due not to geographical size but to the fact that industrialization has not yet gone far enough and natural resources are still far from being fully exploited. These countries produce a comparatively small range of products and must export a large part of their output in order to be able to import the many goods they still do not make for themselves.

If, however, we are to say that a nation is small when it depends heavily upon foreign trade for both imports and exports, we are up against the difficulty that Great Britain must undoubtedly be classed among the large nations and yet both her imports and her exports are relatively very large. We might get round the difficulty by considering not only the size of imports and exports in relation to national production, but at the same time also the diversification of the nation's foreign markets. We can then say that a nation is small when it has a high degree of dependence upon foreign trade and few markets for its exports. In such circumstances the nation must inevitably suffer a domination effect on the part of its buyers.

G. A. Duncan reached similar conclusions in his discussion of the components of one country's bargaining power in relation to another : 'The most important elements in the horse-traders' relative strengths are not mere size but the range of alternative markets open for the exports of each and the diversification of each one's production pattern'.[1] The more a country's exports are concentrated on one particular market, he argues, the more that country is susceptible to pressure from those who lay down the law on that market. Great Britain's predominance on many food and raw material markets enabled her to exercise pressure on her suppliers in 1931. The diversification of the production pattern, which Professor Duncan distinguished as the second element of a country's relative strength, is essentially dependent upon the variety of domestic natural resources and this is bound to be less in a small country than in a large one.[2]

---

[1] George A. Duncan, 'The Small State and International Economic Equilibrium', *Economia internazionale*, November 1950, p. 937.　　[2] *Ibid.* pp. 937–38.

Foreign Trade as an Escape from Smallness

The case of Great Britain obviously does not fit conveniently into such categories. Nor are Swedish and Swiss exports limited to just a few markets. In these circumstances it seems preferable to define a small nation as one which, while depending comparatively heavily upon foreign trade both for supplies and sales markets, makes only a modest contribution to the aggregate flow of international trade. We can summarize by saying that a nation is small from the point of view of foreign trade when its dependence on foreign markets is relatively great but its contribution to them small in absolute terms.

III. THE IMPRECISION OF THE CRITERIA

These criteria are even so somewhat imprecise. Expressions such as 'relatively great dependence upon foreign markets' or 'modest contribution to the flow of international trade' derive from the ordinal rather than the cardinal system of numbers. Perhaps it would be worth while making statistical investigations with a view to determining how large a contribution to international trade a country must make to secure a place among the large nations, and what is the minimum share of exports in national production for a country to be labelled a small nation.

It is clear that some countries cannot permanently be ranged among the small nations, whereas others have no hope of changing their status. Canada is on its way to becoming a large nation in the economic sense ; her population growth, the tapping of rich new natural resources, and rapid industrial development foreshadow a time not many years hence when economists will no longer be able to speak of Canada as a small nation. By contrast Sweden or Belgium have little hope of ever becoming large nations : the time is past when any country, large or small, had the prospect of enlarging the size of its economy by the acquisition of foreign territories.

The category of 'small nations' is thus not completely homogeneous, and all the less so because the dependence of a small nation upon foreign markets is a matter of degree. We readily agree with Professor Duncan that such dependence is greater when export markets are few : but we are bound to recognize also that the conditions of dependence with respect to foreign markets give rise to government intervention, that the relations are political as much as economic and that they may be closer or less close. Small nations are often subject to domination effects on the part of larger nations, but there is room for infinite variety in their mutual relations. First, the small nation may be a satellite under the political or economic sway of a great power. This is now the case in many countries of Eastern Europe in the Soviet orbit and was true of Central Europe and the Balkans in relation to Nazi Germany. Secondly, the small nation may be a member of a major currency area and be bound to its leading nation by multiple and varied ties of a political, economic, cultural, and sometimes emotional nature. Within one and the same currency area small nations may occupy different positions. Thirdly, the small nation's relations with a large one may be of a purely economic order, or at any rate more exclusively economic than in the preceding cases. The relations between the United States and Switzerland provide an example.

Finally we must be quite clear in our minds that no pejorative sense whatever attaches to the expression 'small nation'. The monetary, financial, and general economic situation of Belgium, Sweden, and Switzerland are infinitely better than those of some 'large nations', including Great Britain and France. The former countries' currencies and investment capital are much in demand. On the political plane 'small nations' have gained influence in the new international organizations based on the principle of national equality. Large nations are now obliged to court small ones in order to secure their votes in important decisions and the small nations' economic position may well be strengthened thereby. One can imagine a sort of bargain being struck by which a small nation would receive certain economic concessions in return for an appropriate display of 'understanding' in some international debate.

IV. ACCESSIBILITY OF LARGE NATION ADVANTAGES TO SMALL NATIONS

But when all has been said, the fact remains that, generally speaking, a large nation possesses certain advantages which a small nation does not possess. Among the large nation's advantages the following are the most common :

(*a*) By virtue of its geographical size and economic and political power it can exercise domination effects on international markets ;

(*b*) The size of its domestic market enables it to sell the bulk of its production at home and so to make the economy less sensitive to economic fluctuations originating abroad ;

(*c*) For the same reason it can take full advantage of the economies of scale deriving from mass production.

Foreign Trade as an Escape from Smallness

Are these advantages accessible to small nations ? The first two certainly are not. A small nation may, of course, exercise a domination effect on still smaller ones and occasionally even on a larger nation, especially if that small nation's products are highly specialized and much in demand ; but a permanent domination effect on a large nation is excluded.

The same is true of independence from economic fluctuations elsewhere. A small nation depends upon foreign markets both for supplies and sales ; it cannot hope to insulate itself to any significant degree against world economic conditions, especially since the only advantages within its reach, namely larger sales markets and economies of scale, can be obtained only through expanding foreign trade.

On the other hand, it should not prove impossible for a small nation to enlarge its outlets and benefit from economies of scale by expanding exports. Several distinguished writers [1] have recently developed this argument and it forms the basis of all the various current plans for a common market, free trade area, or economic integration in Europe.

In what conditions and in what measure can small nations obtain these advantages ? This is what we now propose to discuss in greater detail.

V. MEASURES TO PROMOTE CLOSER ECONOMIC RELATIONS

The problem is usually formulated as follows. Given the present conditions of international economic relations, small nations which are obliged to sell abroad any considerable proportion of their production find it very hard to do so. In a world economy which has still not got rid of the last vestiges of the Great Depression nor of the Second World War, all countries, large and small, practise all kinds of restrictive policies. Customs duties, import quotas, subsidies to domestic producers, and exchange control are all obstacles to the exports of these nations, and since their domestic markets are limited they must limit their production and cannot fully utilize their productive capacity, let alone think of new investment to

[1] J. Wemelsfelder, 'Some Problems Connected with the Establishment of a Common Market in Europe', *Economia internazionale*, August 1954 ; Franz Gehrels and Bruce F. Johnston, 'The Economic Gains of European Integration', *The Journal of Political Economy*, August 1955 ; Tibor Scitovsky, 'Economies of Scale, Competition and European Integration', *American Economic Review*, March 1956.

increase productivity and reduce costs.

The proposed solution is that these small nations should be integrated into a larger group within which there should be full freedom of movement for goods and services, and, if possible, also for labour and capital. Thereby these nations would have access to very large markets and could realize economies of scale.

It is not simply a matter of extending the liberalization of trade which has been going on since 1947 under the auspices of OEEC or GATT. If the proposed freedom of trade is to bear full fruit and if entrepreneurs are to make the efforts and accept the sacrifices involved, it is essential that none of the countries concerned should have the right to go back on its commitments. 'The severe and unstable restrictions on trade which have prevailed over the last three or four decades have unquestionably had a profound and lasting effect on the attitudes of business firms towards foreign markets. The capital formation for the purpose of serving export markets, the development of selling organizations, and other undertakings to serve foreign customers have been neglected in this long interim. If freeing of trade were to take place in the usual way, with each country having the right to reimpose restrictions at will, enterprises in the countries affected would be sceptical of the permanence of the agreement. While exports would increase, the desired reallocation of resources to export industries, particularly of capital resources, would be halting and slow. For this reason, the permanence of commitments to maintain free trade within the area would, in our view, lead to a more rapid and effective development of regional specialization.'[1]

Trade liberalization is no longer enough and a number of more far-reaching plans are being put forward. Firstly there are proposals for a free trade area : 'In such an area, as in a customs union, trade barriers (tariffs, quantitative import and export restrictions) between the participating countries are abolished, but each country retains its individual tariff in regard to countries outside the area'.[2] Secondly there are proposals for a customs union or Common Market in which, as in the free trade area, internal obstacles to trade are abolished and which has a common tariff in relation to non-member countries. Thirdly, these proposals for complete economic integration or union, which goes much further since it involves partial abdication of national sovereignty to a supranational authority. F. G. Gehrels and B. F. Johnston favour this solution to help Europe

[1] F. G. Gehrels and B. F. Johnston, *op. cit.* p. 281.
[2] *Report on the Possibility of Creating a Free Trade Area in Europe*, presented to the Council of the Organization for European Economic Co-operation, OEEC, Paris, 1957, pp. 7-8.

on to its feet again and to raise its economy to American standards. The essential features of such integration would include : agreement for gradual but complete elimination of tariffs, quotas, and exchange controls on trade among the member countries ; abandonment of the right to restore trade restrictions on a unilateral basis so long as the agreement is in force ; joint action to deal with problems resulting from the removal of trade barriers within the community and to promote more effective utilization of its resources ; some degree of harmonization of national policies that affect price structures and the allocation of resources (for example, social security and agricultural programmes), co-ordination of monetary and fiscal policies ; free, or at least freer, movement of capital and labour.[1]

This is not the place to discuss the conditions on which one or the other of these solutions might be adopted. All three of them imply full freedom of trade between member countries and this would enable small nations to expand their markets and to realize economies of scale. We would observe, however, that none of these proposals is in itself a universal panacea. The discussions among the potential future members will no doubt provide ample room for the play of domination effects between large and small nations and it is a moot question whether small nations do not stand to lose more than the others, at least in the immediate future. It is not a matter of indifference exactly which countries are to join any of these agreements : small nations only, or large and small nations, and in what proportions ? Or nations of all sizes ? Should the schemes be limited to neighbouring countries or extended to distant ones ? We limit ourselves to raising these questions without attempting any answer.

Let us assume, then, that there is durable freedom of trade within a group of countries which includes small nations. Will the latter be able to expand their trade and to make up by exports for the deficiency of their domestic markets ?

VI. CAN SMALLER NATIONS HOPE TO EXPAND THEIR MARKETS ?

Before attempting a reply to the above question, let us state precisely just exactly what is involved in freedom of trade within a free trade area, customs union, or economic union. Those who advocate these solutions have in mind a return to the true competitive spirit, getting rid of the idea that nothing must ever change,

[1] F. G. Gehrels and B. F. Johnston, *op. cit.* p. 277.

and eliminating or weakening domestic monopoly or oligopoly positions which are more or less encouraged by open or concealed government subsidies. This also means better organization of the distribution network and more anonymity in it. The most efficient firms should then prevail at the expense of the less efficient, whatever their nationality. Tibor Scitovsky recalls in this context the high mortality among firms in the United States, where the spirit of competition is much more lively than among many Western European firms.

In these circumstances the question arises whether the firms of small nations would be in a position to defend themselves and could hope to survive and indeed to expand their markets both within the free trade area and outside it. To keep its markets within the free trade area, a firm belonging to a small nation must produce at the same cost as firms belonging to larger nations. To expand its markets within the free trade area, it must produce at less cost if aggregate demand remains unchanged, or at the same cost if aggregate demand increases.

Let us elaborate certain points. Production cost means *ex-factory* cost plus transportation cost. The elimination of custom duties, quotas, and government subsidies puts all competitors on an equal footing, and any differences can be due only to the distance between the location of production and the point of sale. It is quite possible that initially the disappearance of protective measures will be felt much more painfully by the firms of the formerly most highly protected countries. It would therefore be interesting to know the present level of protection enjoyed by the firms of potential member countries; it would not be astonishing to find that the industries of small countries, which, as we have observed, are naturally drawn towards the export business, are less sheltered than those of large countries where the bulk of production is sold on the home market. If this really proved to be so, the small nation's firm could get off to a good start and immediately draw ahead by a few lengths.

It would, however, be a mistake to think that, things being as they are at present, only inefficient industries are protected and efficient ones are not. J. Wemelsfelder has recently shown that in the six countries of 'Little Europe' this is by no means true for quite a number of products and that some of the industries exporting most, and hence working under favourable conditions, are strongly protected.[1] The abolition of the tariffs protecting these industries would therefore not necessarily place the latter at a

[1] J. Wemelsfelder, *op. cit.* pp. 542 *et seq.*

disadvantage in comparison with foreign industries now enjoying less protection.

On the other hand, it is certainly no illusion to expect an expansion of the Western European economy. It may legitimately be hoped that an abolition of protective measures, a revival of the competitive spirit, and an improvement in distribution networks will cause a general reduction of costs and hence of prices and an increase in demand. If this should happen, the firms of small nations would be well placed to take advantage of the situation.

Firms which sell highly specialized quality products in inelastic demand will be in the most favourable position. Examples which come to mind are Danish agricultural commodities, Swedish iron and steel products, or Swiss watches ; these can surely be expected to sell better in a completely free trade area.

The next question is whether, after a while, small nations would not reach the limits of new expansion. Supposing a small nation specializes in agricultural products such as early fruit and vegetables or wine, or in livestock products ; is there not a danger that some day any further expansion of production will be impossible for lack of new land to exploit ? And will a small nation always have sufficient capital and, above all, labour to go on expanding production, whether in agriculture or industry ? These shortages might in part be made good by mobility of capital and labour within the free trade area, but the remedy would remain partial only, especially as regards lack of skilled labour. First of all it seems certain that the various nations are not yet ready to accept full freedom of movement for labour even within the free zone ; secondly, and this is more important, a small nation whose advantage rests on highly specialized and high-quality products needs very skilled labour — and this cannot be formed from one day to another, especially with foreign workers. It may be possible to economize highly specialized labour by improving productivity through new production techniques. This is a question for technicians, but in any case such a process would require additional investment. All in all, we can perhaps say that a small nation's industry which produces specialized and high-quality products for which there is a great demand has every prospect of improving its position and expanding its markets within the free trade area, but that further expansion may in the future be held up by lack of capital and, above all, by lack of skilled labour.

VII. WHAT WILL BE THE EFFECT OF INTEGRATION ON NON-MEMBER SMALL NATIONS?

It is quite another question what will happen to the markets of small nations which are not members of the group, whether this take the shape of a free trade area, customs union, or economic union. In all cases, we must think of possible trade-diverting effects, although we need not necessarily share Jacob Viner's pessimistic outlook and can recognize with J. E. Meade and with Helen Makower and G. Morton that the consequences may vary greatly in different cases.[1] But this is an aspect of trade liberalization which concerns large and small nations alike and which has been admirably analysed by the above-mentioned authors ; we do not propose to stress the point here. In any case, F. Gehrels and B. F. Johnston [2] have reached reasonably plausible conclusions with respect to the six countries of 'Little Europe'. Having stated that a customs union (the same could be said of an economic union or free trade area) gives rise simultaneously to the two kinds of effect discussed by Viner (the trade-creating and the trade-diverting effect) and that there is no *a priori* reason for expecting one to be stronger than the other, these authors go on to examine the economic composition of 'Little Europe'. They conclude that both in the sphere of agricultural production and in that of industrial production there are such significant cost differences that considerable expansion effects may be hoped for ; and that, on the other hand, sources of low-cost supply left outside the union are so few as to reduce to a minimum the harmful (trade-diverting) effects. 'These arguments lead to the conclusion that the increase in trade as defined earlier would be quite significant, while the diversion of trade from lower to high-cost sources of supply would be relatively unimportant.' It will be recalled that 'Little Europe' includes small nations.

But it is not enough to state this and to conclude that a small nation has every chance of increasing its total exports within a customs union or economic union. We must be sure that such a country's membership in one of these groups does not entail any diminution of its exports to non-member countries which would match or exceed the increase of sales within the group. A nation joining a free trade area retains control over its tariffs in relation to outside countries ; in a customs union or economic union all

---

[1] J. E. Meade, *The Theory of Customs Unions*, North Holland Publishing Company, Amsterdam, 1955 ; H. Makower and G. Morton, 'A Contribution Towards a Theory of Customs Unions', *Economic Journal*, March 1953, pp. 33-49.
[2] *Op. cit.* pp. 278-81.

members apply a common tariff to trade with outside countries. Is it too far-fetched to imagine that a small nation might find itself tied up with a union with such high tariffs that it might lose some of its outside customers, who might cease to buy either as a reprisal or simply because they can get the same product cheaper elsewhere ? Small nations could thereby lose some very important markets. Now who will fix the union's tariff ? The answer is no doubt : all the members together. So far so good ; but will the small nation be able to safeguard its interests in the preparatory discussions ? Is it not once more threatened by domination effects ? This is a very real danger if the members of a customs union or economic union negotiate on the basis of their own selfish and immediate interests. There must be some spirit of international co-operation and some willingness and ability to rise above the troubles of the day if the large nations are to appreciate that small nations have a greater need to keep their outside markets. Only then is there a chance of agreement on appropriate tariffs.

VIII. HOW FAR CAN SMALL NATIONS REALIZE ECONOMIES OF SCALE ?

Let us make the — by no means implausible — assumption that thanks to a free trade area, customs union, or economic union the small nation's foreign markets expand considerably. Will the small nation then be able to enjoy the economies of scale which are generally attributed to large nations ? All writers who have studied the effects of economic integration on the development of national economies make much of the potential economies of scale.[1] To say that small nations can realize economies of scale to the same extent as the larger nations, amounts to saying that a small nation's firms can realize these economies to the same extent as the firms of larger nations. Indeed, it is firms and not nations which encounter each other on the various markets.

There are two kinds of economies of scale : internal economies due to an increase in the size of the firm, and external economies due to a more favourable geographical concentration of firms. An increase in the size of the firm should lead to cost reduction, since it makes possible better internal division of labour and the use of more modern techniques. Large firms are also more capable of improvement than small or medium-sized firms and have easier

[1] In particular, Tibor Scitovsky, F. Gehrels, and B. F. Johnston, and J. Wemelsfelder, *op. cit.*

access to the capital required for development and modernization.

Tibor Scitovsky in analysing this aspect of the problem has especially stressed the concepts of optimal and sub-optimal investment. We would not presume to summarize this subtle study here ; but we should like to single out a few arguments which more directly concern small nations — as well as others often described as large nations.

At a given set of factor prices, it is possible to use several methods of production entailing different production costs. In a system of perfect competition where the market price is a datum for the entrepreneur, maximum profit coincides with maximum productivity. The entrepreneur has an interest in choosing the least costly combination of factors.

In the real world, the market is most often one of imperfect competition and the entrepreneur is not necessarily ruled by the coincidence of profitability and productivity. 'Different methods of production exploit economies of scale to different degrees. The rate of output, therefore, that minimizes unit costs of production is likely to be different for each method the higher the rate of output needed to reach minimum per-unit costs, or, to put it differently, the larger the optimum size of the plant. This fact would leave unaffected the entrepreneur's choice of a method in a perfectly competitive world, where no difficulties either of selling or of buying prevent his producing and marketing the output whose costs of production is the lowest. Not so in an imperfectly competitive world, where the entrepreneur faces a falling demand curve for his product and rising supply curves for his factors. Here, the price charged generally depends on the output to be marketed ; and if the more efficient methods require a higher rate of output for the full exploitation of their economies, then the output obtained by these methods is likely to be sold at a lower (and the required input of factors obtained at a higher) price. This, however, disrupts the simple correspondence referred to earlier between efficiency (minimum production costs) and profitability, because it lowers the profitability of the more efficient methods relatively to that of the less efficient ones. Hence the possibility that the limits to the entrepreneurs' markets will prevent — by rendering less profitable or even unprofitable — the adoption and use of the more efficient methods of production.' Typical cases are oil refineries or rolling mills : the full-time utilization of a single modern plant of optimum size yields a volume of output far in excess of the total domestic demand of the smallest countries of Western Europe. 'National self-sufficiency in these fields is uneconomical for the smaller countries and can only be achieved at the cost of using either relatively inefficient small-scale equipment or efficient large-scale equipment in an uneconomical way (*i.e.* on a part-time basis).'[1]

Whether the equipment be sub-optimal, that is to say, such as to preclude the least costly method of production, or whether it be optimal but only partly utilized, it is impossible to realize economies of scale. The author then shows that sub-optimal equipment is not only a current handicap for the firms but endangers their future position. It is to be feared that when demand increases new investment will also be sub-optimal since existing entrepreneurs may, for various reasons, including lack of a spirit of competition, not be anxious to try to expand their markets to the detriment of other firms.

In these circumstances, an expansion of the small nations' markets by complete trade liberalization within a sufficiently large area and a return to the competitive spirit should enable small nations to realize internal economies of scale — particularly if, as may be hoped, the creation of a free zone leaves room for expansion of all markets. Any firm which can hold its own in competitive conditions will be able to sell more cheaply by virtue of economies of scale, and lower costs will in most cases lead to increased demand and hence to increased production.

The chances of realizing external economies of scale are also adduced in support of proposals for customs unions, economic unions, or free trade areas. Geographical concentration of firms is said to hold out an immediate prospect of the development of certain service and supply industries, of improvement of transport facilities and lower transport costs, and of ample supply of skilled labour within a limited zone.[2]

Tibor Scitovsky also speaks of the better geographical distribution of investment which is to be expected. To our mind, this is also part of the external economies under discussion. Instead of being effected in the country where the saving originates, as has happened only too often in Western Europe, investment would then normally be directed to the most active regions.

IX. HOW MUCH CAN SMALL NATIONS EXPECT
FROM ECONOMIES OF SCALE?

It is an open question whether the member nations, and especially the small member nations, of an economic union, customs union,

[1] T. Scitovsky, *op. cit.* pp. 72-4.
[2] F. Gehrels and B. F. Johnston, *op. cit.* p. 284.

or free trade area would, in fact, be able to realize economies of scale to the extent that is generally hoped for. This can only happen on the assumption that, in fact, very many firms are now of sub-optimal size so that they cannot produce at the lowest possible cost. Is this really so ? No doubt it is true of some branches of industry, but perhaps of fewer than may be thought. This is, of course, conjecture on our part and the facts remain to be established by studies such as that which J. S. Bain has devoted to several branches of American industry.[1] His investigation is strictly limited to the United States and he is careful to point out that his results are valid only for the United States and for the industries considered. Never-theless Professor Bain's results are such as to give food for thought on certain points which do not seem to be alien to our subject.

Professor Bain's survey covers twenty very different branches of industry in 1947. At the risk of oversimplifying his very subtle conclusions, we believe the following lessons may be drawn there-from :

(1) Optimum plant size, which permits production at lowest cost, varies considerably from industry to industry. A flour mill may have optimum size if it contributes no more than 0·1 to 0·5 per cent to national capacity ; for a factory making tractors the percentage would have to be 10 to 15, and for a factory making typewriters 10 to 30. In nine out of twenty industries, the

TABLE I

RELATION OF PRODUCTION COST TO PLANT SCALE
IN SEVEN INDUSTRIES

Percentages of national industry capacity in 1 plant	Relative costs of production (Cost in an optimum plant = 100)				
	5%	2·5%	1%	0·5%	0·25%
Cement	100	100	100	115	130
Distilled Liquor	100	100	100·5	101	102
Petroleum Refining	100	100	102	104	107
Tyres and Tubes	100	100·3	103	104	105·5
Rayon	100	107	125	very high	
Soap	100	103	105	above 105	
Cigarettes	100	101	102	above 102	

[1] J. S. Bain, 'Economies of Scale, Concentration and Entry', *American Economic Review*, March 1954.

optimum plant represented less than 2·5 per cent of the total national production capacity. In only five industries was the percentage higher than 7·5 (motor-cars, tractors, fountain-pens, copper, typewriters). More generally speaking, economies of scale are small in the industries transforming agricultural or mining products, and much higher in the engineering industries.

(2) The economies of scale to be realized are really significant only when the plants have a very small capacity ; above a certain limit, which is low, these economies are not considerable. In the table, the relative cost of 100 represents the costs of an optimum plant.

(3) The economies of scale open to a multiple-branch firm are generally not large and the degree of concentration of the firms considered is generally greater than would be required by economies of scale alone.

If these conclusions could be extended to other countries and especially to European countries — which could, of course, only be done by means of a statistical survey — it might well become apparent that the number of industrial firms of less than optimal plant size is less than one thinks. If it is true that in many branches optimum size is reached at comparatively low capacity, have not a good many firms reached that point already ? We readily admit that there are certain branches of industry in which small nations are unlikely to have reached optimum plant size.

In the latter case, what are the chances that small nations will see plants of optimum size spring up in their midst ? Here again Professor Bain's study makes one feel doubtful. In nineteen out of the twenty industrial branches considered, the overall capital needed to found an optimum plant is considerable. Where are the small nation's firms to find such capital ? Some will be successful, no doubt, like Swiss firms — but what of the others ? The same considerations of investment cost will stand in the way of external economies of scale. Location specialists were quick to realize that the cost of displacing existing plants would be very high indeed. External economies will thus be within the reach only of new enterprises.

There remains the case of agricultural enterprises, which would deserve a special study of their own. It is difficult to imagine that there is much scope for economies of scale in agriculture. It is rather by improved methods of cultivation, and selective improvement of seeds and breeds, that Danish farmers, for example, seek to lower their costs.

X. WHAT CONCLUSIONS MAY WE DRAW?

With what very tentative conclusions can we end this study? It seems to us that if the various plans for freer trade which are now under discussion may be capable of making some of the large nations' advantages accessible to small nations, these advantages are less than many people are inclined to think. Only detailed surveys on a scale comparable with that of Professor Bain's work could bring all the required facts to light. Are such surveys being undertaken by the promoters of common markets or economic unions? It would not seem so.

Chapter 18

INTERNATIONAL TRADE AND ECONOMIC INTEGRATION AS A MEANS OF OVER-COMING THE DISADVANTAGES OF A SMALL NATION

BY

T. SCITOVSKY
Stanford University

I. THE SMALL ECONOMY

I PROPOSE in this paper to attempt a theoretical discussion, first of some of the factors that inhibit efficiency and growth in too small an economy, and second of the influence international trade and economic integration are likely to exert on these factors. Strictly speaking, the task I have been asked to undertake comprises only the second of these two. But to discuss the influence of trade and integration on the inhibiting factors, these latter must first be analysed ; also, the discussion of these factors and their influencing must be closely co-ordinated ; and at the time of writing I have no way of knowing the coverage and approach of the other papers. I can only hope, therefore, that this paper will not repeat too much of what has already been said and discussed at an earlier stage, and that whatever repetition it contains may not be too boring.

In discussing the sub-optimal nature of too small an economy and the factors that render it sub-optimal, it is useful to distinguish between technological and economic factors. Technologically an economy can be too small if its market is too small to provide an adequate outlet for the full-capacity output of the most efficient productive plant in a given industry. From this point of view, then, the minimum size of an economy is generally different for different industries ; and if we have an economy which is too small from the point of view of some but not of other industries, we have here right away a simple technological determinant of the composition of foreign trade that is completely neglected in the classical theory of international values. One must also note in this connection the complexities introduced by the existence of intermediate

282

products and industries. An economy, for example, that is large enough to provide adequate domestic market outlets for the output of at least one optimum-sized plant in all industries producing final products may still be sub-optimal if some of these plants need equipment, servicing, or other intermediate products, but provide too small a market outlet for some of these.[1] The technological optimum-size for an economy therefore may be very much larger than one might think at first.

In contrast to the technological factors stand the economic ones, all of which have to do with competition and its influence on efficiency. Economically, therefore, an economy is too small if it fails to provide the competitive conditions necessary to spur to utmost efficiency and to lead to the establishment of the technically most efficient plants. An economy large enough to absorb the output of at least one optimum-sized plant in all industries may still not be large enough to provide the incentive for the building of such plants. Thus, the technological optimum size of an economy is a necessary but not a sufficient condition to ensure the utilization of the most efficient means of production. In other words, the technological optimum is probably reached very much sooner than the economic optimum ; and this accounts for the often-held belief that small economies are more in need of central planning, while large economies, having more competition, can rely more easily on the working of the profit motive. There is some truth in this belief ; but it must also be remembered that the competition referred to here is a broader concept than mere market competition and therefore is not confined to an economy governed by the profit motive. This will be discussed in more detail later on, when I deal with the ways in which international trade and economic union stimulate competition and thus encourage efficiency and economic growth.

II. SOME CHARACTERISTICS OF EXPORT TRADE

Let us turn now to the ways in which international trade and economic union can offset the disadvantages of smallness in the purely technological sense. The days when international trade was believed to be just as good as domestic trade are long past. Today,

[1] This point and, generally, the fact that industrial interdependence renders very much larger the scale of output necessary for the full exploitation of economies of scale than would appear at first thought has been discussed in detail a few years ago in the pages of the *American Economic Review* ('Economies of Scale, Competition and European Integration', *American Economic Review*, March 1956, pp. 71 ff.).

the condition of efficient production is very often the large-scale production at a stable rate of a relatively few varieties of the product. In other words, mass-production methods to become profitable require a market outlet that is large, homogeneous, and stable over time ; and these requirements rule out reliance on export markets, except to a very limited extent. For export markets these days are regarded as highly precarious — liable to be closed off suddenly for political reasons or as a result of balance-of-payments difficulties ; and they are also the markets in which competition has highly undesirable characteristics, in the sense that competitors' behaviour is unpredictable on the basis of rational economic considerations alone, being governed by political motivation as well. In England — traditionally an important export producer — today's rule of thumb seems to be that it is not prudent to rely on exports for more than 20-25 per cent of a company's total market outlet.

There are means, of course, of eliminating or insuring against these disadvantages of export trade. International commodity agreements, long-term contracts between contractors and subcontractors are means of introducing long-term stability into international trade relations ; but the range of products to which they are suited is limited. It is no accident that commodity agreements are usually confined to staple foods and primary products ; long-term contracts between producer and distributor concerning industrial products are seldom feasible. Also, long-term agreements may be able to stabilize a situation already established ; but when it is a matter of a producer investing in mass-production equipment in the hope of *expanding* or *creating* a *stable* market, then the disadvantages and precariousness of export markets cannot be guarded against — and this, I suspect, is the really important case.

We may conclude, therefore, that if an economy is too small technologically — in the sense of providing insufficient market outlets for the output even of a single modern and efficient plant — then international trade is of little avail. Economic union would be better, provided it guarantees not only free and unrestricted trade but also complete stability of exchange rates among members of the union.

III. EXPORT TRADE AS AN ESCAPE FOR THE SMALL ECONOMY

Let us now investigate the way in which international trade and/or economic union can offset the disadvantages of smallness in the economic sense. First of all, what are these disadvantages ?

They all have to do with competition. Competition encourages economic efficiency and progress if the economic unit is large enough. It will fail to do this, however, when the economy is too small and competition in consequence is too personal and too weak.

There are several ways in which increasing the size of the economic unit or increasing contacts between different economic units leads to efficiency. One way — and one almost too simple to mention — has to do with differences in temperament and custom. There are tremendous national differences in temperament, work habits, commercial and industrial practices, economic imagination, awareness of opportunities to increase manufacturing efficiency and to exploit market possibilities ; and more contact and freer trade would be almost certain to effect not only a levelling of these differences but an upward levelling in the direction of greater industrial and commercial efficiency. Not only the more efficient but the economically and technically more imaginative, more pushing, and more ruthless would be bound to prevail over their more easygoing competitors and force these to imitate their customs and methods. That there is much scope, and unexploited scope, for such development is obvious ; and the great uniformity of economic temperament and practice in the United States, achieved despite great racial, climatic, and dietary differences, indicates the possibility of exploiting this scope — although, of course, such uniformity in the United States was achieved by more intimate interchange and intermingling than mere social contact and economic competition.

I am not at all certain that in purely human terms I would welcome such levelling and the elimination of national differences ; but its effects on economic productivity and output, as shown in the customary statistics of these quantities, are almost certain to be salutary. Let me add that these effects of competition are likely to be achieved by freer trade and economic union alike, provided they promote economic, social, and intellectual contact to a significant extent.

IV. FREER TRADE AND THE INTENSITY
OF COMPETITION

A second way in which freer trade or economic union can promote economic and technical efficiency is by rendering competition less personal and thereby more effective. There is far too great a tendency among some economists to regard the existence of many small firms in an industry as proof of atomistic competition and to identify this latter with the kind of competition that promotes technical efficiency and progress. This, however, is often wrong, and competition among many small firms is seldom of such a kind as to encourage efficiency and growth. For one thing, relations among the small producers composing an industry are often so close and friendly as to keep each of them from engaging in competitive actions that would hurt the rest. For another, in an industry composed of many small firms the problem who among them is to build a modern large-scale plant may be an insoluble one. To begin with, each firm may be too small to possess or have access to enough capital with which to build such a plant; secondly, to operate a large-scale plant efficiently and profitably, it might be necessary to encroach upon competitors' markets ; and each of the existing firms may shrink back from so ungentlemanly an action. Indeed, it is typical of many European industries that the first efficient, modern, large-scale plant often is built to cater to the export market — not because the internal market is not large enough to provide an adequate market outlet but because this is already being catered for by old-established small manufacturers whom it would be ungentlemanly to push out of the market. It can also happen, however (and probably often does), that the efficient large-scale plant is not built at all, because considerations of business ethics stand in the way of creating (by diverting from competitors) an adequate domestic market for it, and because the export market may be considered too precarious to serve as the main basis of mass production.

To what extent these problems would be solved by freer trade or economic union is difficult to tell. My feeling is that international trade, however free, would usually be considered too precarious to serve as the main basis for mass production, and that thoroughgoing economic integration would be required to solve these problems of too small an economy.

V. PROFIT MARGINS

A third way in which free trade or economic union might promote technical progress has to do with profit margins and turnover. An economy can be too small in terms not only of area or population but also of purchasing power. In many European countries it is said, especially of consumers' durables, that they cannot be mass-produced cheaply because low incomes preclude a mass market — on the other hand, the lower cost *and price* of such goods would by itself raise real incomes and thus go some way towards creating the mass market on which their cheap mass production hinges. In other words, there is here a *circulus vitiosus*, which may in some instances be quite important, and which may well be broken by increased competition brought about by freer trade or economic union.

How is this vicious circle brought about in the first place ? One of its causes may be, in the case of consumers' durables, inadequate facilities for hire purchase or its rejection on ethical or religious grounds (the Thomist condemnation of interest is still upheld by many catholics in the case of consumer credit). In this connection, the above-mentioned spreading of the most successful commercial practices through more economic and social contact may do much to break the circle. Another possible cause, and the one I propose to discuss in more detail, is the policy of high margins and low turnover.

It is a frequent comment of American business-men viewing the European scene that both European economies and European business-men would be better off if the latter tried to expand their markets by a lowering of profit margins and prices. Needless to say, this argument assumes that the price reduction would so much increase turnover as to yield new economies of scale and reduce unit costs of production (implying that prices could be reduced to a greater extent than profit margins), and that the higher rate of turnover would compensate or more than compensate business-men for the lower rate of profit per unit of output. Let us for argument's sake accept this view as correct and explore some of its implications.

The argument has often been advanced to European business-men ; and they have — most of them — rejected it. For one thing, high margin, low turnover, and catering for a small and intimately known market probably offer the business-man a quieter and easier life and more security and stability than a large and impersonal market with small profit margins, where he must ever be on the alert to keep his position and preserve his profits. For another thing, some manufacturers reject the principle of low margins and high turnover, because they realize that the adoption of mass-production methods usually involves a sacrifice of quality, workmanship, and finish ; and they are reluctant to make this sacrifice. To some extent such reluctance may be a simple value judgement and a rational choice ; to some extent it may also stem from a lack of realization that high quality can also be achieved (and in the United States is in the process of being achieved) with the use and through the perfection of mass-production methods. Also, European business-men often feel that they owe part of their market — especially their export market — to quality production ; and they may be reluctant to sacrifice this part of their market even if the additional market to be gained through price reduction promises to be larger and more profitable. This is a matter of preferring one bird in the hand to two in the bush. Furthermore, some European business-men may be reluctant to lower price for fear that the resulting rise in turnover would not be sufficient to justify the adoption of new and cheaper methods of production and would not recoup their profits. In this expectation they may be right or wrong — this, after all, is a matter of correctly estimating the price elasticity of demand.

There are a few conspicuous and well-publicized instances of highly successful attempts to introduce a cheap mass-product and create a mass market ; and they certainly seem to prove that business-men often underestimate the elasticity of demand of the market facing them. The success of cheap mass holidays in England, of a cheap refrigerator in Germany, of a washing-machine in France, and of paper-bound pocket books all over the world, are the first examples that come to mind. But this is a small sample and presumably a biased one (for success always gets more publicity than failure) from which no general conclusions should be drawn. For all I know, European business-men may often, perhaps mostly, be right when they insist that a price reduction would not stimulate turnover sufficiently to render the economies of scale of mass production feasible and profitable. I shall argue, however, that even in this case there may be truth in the American business-men's contention.

Assume an economy in which the average consumer's consumption pattern is fairly rigidly fixed by tradition or by his aspiration to emulate the consumption pattern of the upper classes, which in turn is largely independent of cost considerations. In other words, we are assuming an economy in which the average consumer's elasticity of substitution between different consumers' goods is low. In such an economy, a reduction in the price of a single consumer's good would not raise its sales very much, partly because the income effect of a single price reduction (the reduction, that is, in the price of a single good) is likely to be small, and partly because its substitution effect is — by assumption — also small. In such an economy, therefore, rational profit calculations might well prevent business-men abandoning a high-margin low-turnover policy, since a price reduction would probably fail to stimulate turnover sufficiently to render mass production feasible and profitable.

In this same economy, however, concerted action by many

business-men and the simultaneous reduction of the prices of a large number of consumers' goods could have a very different effect. For such a price reduction *would* have a sizable income effect and thus lead to a much larger increase in consumers' demand and hence sale of consumers' goods ; and this increase in turnover might well be sufficient to render price reduction and the transition to cheaper mass-production methods profitable.

Here, then, is an argument based on the simple notion of inter-dependence in consumption (or rather of pecuniary external economies due to interdependence in consumption) that shows the possibility of *profitably* expanding the domestic market and introducing mass-production methods through concerted action (central planning if you like) in a situation in which the same would not be feasible and profitable under atomistic conditions. The argument, of course, stands or falls with the assumption of a low elasticity of substitution in consumption ; and the realism of this assumption can only be ascertained by empirical investigation.

But whether or not this last assumption is realistic, the point is this. I have cited several possible reasons — and there may be many more — why entrepreneurs may retain their traditional policy of high margins, low turnover, and small-scale production under circumstances where the opposite policy would be not only socially more desirable but — in the sense and under the conditions just described — also more or at least equally profitable. I do not feel competent to appraise the relative importance of these different reasons ; but I do think that they merit attention and that some might be quite important. If this is so, then the increase in competition brought about by freer trade or economic union might well break the *impasse* and bring about a change in producers' thinking and policies. For increased competition would force prices down ; and a forced price reduction would be likely to eliminate *all* the above-cited reasons for the undue retention of the traditional policy of high margins, low turnover, and small-scale production. To begin with, a forcible price reduction would deprive entrepreneurs of their freedom of choice between high profits on the one hand, and pride of workmanship and quality or a quiet life and financial security on the other hand. For it would impose lower profit margins, and entrepreneurs, if they are to avoid losses, would be forced into a mass-production policy, the exploration of potentialities of market expansion, and the abandonment of the high technical standards and easy ways of life that small-scale production with high margins so often entails. Secondly, economic union or a general freeing of trade would bring about the all-around reduction of prices that would be necessary, according to our last argument, to create a mass market for certain consumers' goods (primarily consumers' durables and semi-luxuries) through a raising of real incomes.

VI. COMPETITION AND SECURITY

The above were a few examples — probably a very incomplete list — of the various ways in which competition may affect economic efficiency and technical progress — its absence inhibiting, its presence encouraging the adoption of the best methods known and a general staying alert and keeping up with changing conditions and requirements. In the traditional theory of competition it is customary barely to mention these aspects and to concentrate instead on matters of income distribution and static efficiency. These aspects, however, are important ; they would be among the most valuable consequences of freer trade or economic union — they would certainly be no less and perhaps more important than the latter's purely technological effects of the kind discussed at the beginning of this paper.

At the same time it must also be realized that if competition favours efficiency and progress, it does so at a cost. For these results of competition are achieved through the greater rewards it offers to those who have, and the worse punishment it metes out to those who lack, success — whether this is due to efficiency, alertness, and resourcefulness, or to adventurousness, ruthlessness, and luck. Such conditions undoubtedly make for the greater insecurity and precariousness of the economic position of the individual ; and it was partly to guard against such insecurity that competition was restricted. Freer trade and economic union, if they are to encourage efficiency, would tend to remove or offset these restrictions ; and I doubt if one can have their beneficial effects without paying for them the price of lesser stability and greater insecurity. Whether the advantages of greater efficiency and faster progress can also be had in other ways and at a lesser price is a subject that lies beyond the scope of this paper.

Chapter 19

THE INTRA-BLOC TRADE OF BENELUX

BY

P. J. VERDOORN

Centraal Planbureau, The Hague

I. INTRODUCTION

1. *Introductory Remarks* [1]

1.1 From the economic point of view the ultimate aim of a customs union is not to foster trade for its own sake, but to increase economic welfare by removing trade restrictions. No increase can, however, be anticipated without a change in the pattern of trade. An investigation of these changes in pattern is therefore necessary as a preliminary step before proceeding to estimate the welfare effects upon the countries considered or the world as a whole. Only the changes in trade pattern fall within the scope of this paper.

1.2 Since in the case of the Benelux Union the period of comparison lies before World War II, a study of the changes in commodity flows will inevitably reveal a number of facts that may — and perhaps may not — be attributed to the union. Likewise, these changes may — or may not — be considered as significant from the statistical point of view, depending upon the standards to be met in each particular case. As an econometrician the author feels compelled to apologize for this double inconclusiveness of the greater part of his findings to both the economist and the statistician.

1.3. *Summary of Conclusions*

Although, therefore, a fair amount of latitude must remain in the evaluation of the statistical results that will be presented, they nevertheless seem, in the author's opinion, to point to a number of

[1] I am indebted to Prof. P. de Wolff, director of the Central Planning Bureau, and several of its staff members, particularly Ir. J. Sandee, Dr. F. Hartog and Messrs. J. G. Kleve and J. A. Links, for their valuable advice. Also to Messrs. P. A. Neeteson, G. Podt, and G. J. Th. Vorstman, who between them shared the main burden of the statistical work and the computations involved. To Prof. W. Gorter, who kindly read the first draft of this paper, I owe many important suggestions.

Foreign Trade as an Escape from Smallness

relevant conclusions that can be summarized as follows :

(i) The maximum increase of the *value share* of Dutch imports of manufactures on the B.L.E.U. import market that can reasonably be attributed to the formation of the Benelux Customs Union is about 65 per cent (sec. 8.4).

(ii) The *volume-component* of this increase can safely be estimated at about 25 per cent, since two independent approaches point at an increase of this order of magnitude (sec. 8.3 and App. E, sub. 3). Moreover, this figure is within the range of one's theoretical *a priori* expectations (sec. 2.2.2).

(iii) A noteworthy feature of the development of mutual trade in the period considered (1938–55) is a substantial increase of the *price per volume-unit* as compared with the unit-values of competing imports belonging to the same branches of industry from non-member countries. For Belgian exports to the Netherlands this relative increase was on the average as high as 48 per cent ; in the case of Netherlands exports to B.L.E.U. it was 55 per cent (sec. 6.1). Although it is doubtful that the whole of this increase should be a direct consequence of Benelux, a relative price increase of 30 per cent, as compared with imports from outside countries, lies — as a maximum estimate — still within the realm of the possibilities (sec. 8.4). This suggests that a customs union tends to foster in most branches of industry the mutual trade in products of which the value added is relatively high.

(iv) As to *price competition* in intra-bloc trade, an analysis of 121 categories of trade mainly of manufactured products shows that in 1955 there was no systematic price difference between B.L.E.U. and Dutch intra-bloc exports (sec. 5.3). Given that Belgian labour costs were 29 per cent above those of the Netherlands, this seems to point to the fact that, at least under conditions of full employment, prices of Dutch exports to B.L.E.U. tend on the whole to adjust themselves to the relatively higher Belgian price level, as represented by Belgian export prices.

(v) Nevertheless, although the median as well as the average prices for these 121 categories were almost exactly the same for B.L.E.U. and for Dutch export prices, the standard deviation of the percentage difference between Dutch and B.L.E.U. prices was as high as 31 per cent. Since no statistical indications of a *division of labour as between categories of products* in the field of manufacturing between partner countries are to be found (sec. 5.2 and App. E, sub. 2), this considerable dispersion of prices confirms the view that specialization, if it did accompany an expansion of trade, is to be found *within* rather than *between* these categories of trade.

(vi) A statistical analysis of the same 121 categories further reveals that the share of total Dutch exports going to B.L.E.U. is much more equally distributed between the categories in 1955 than it was before the formation of the customs union. In as far as the pattern of total exports does still reflect the *comparative advantage* held by the exporting country over its competitors, this equalization of the shares of total exports going to the partner country may perhaps be considered as the establishment consequent upon the formation of a customs union of a new pattern of intra-bloc trade that corresponds more closely to the comparative advantage of participating countries (sec. 4.3).

(vii) As to *the impact of tariff reductions* upon intra-bloc trade, a price-volume elasticity of about -2.5 was found in the case of B.L.E.U. imports from the Netherlands. That is to say, a tariff reduction with one per cent of the price was, on the average, accompanied by a 2.5 per cent increase of trade (App. E, sub. 3). As a matter of fact this numerical relationship reflects only the structure of Benelux trade. It should therefore not be taken as representative for the consequences of the formation of other customs unions. Nevertheless this estimate makes it plausible that the price elasticity of substitutions between competing imports from different sources is, in the long run, much higher than one would expect when analysing short-term fluctuations in export demand (sec. 7.3). It corroborates, therefore, the findings of MacDougall, who suggests values for the elasticity of substitution of -4 to -4.5, whereas the usual estimates in the case of manufactures vary between figures as low as -1.5 to -2.5.

1.4 The material which underlies these conclusions and that will be analysed in the following, consists of three groups of related data, viz :

(i) The total commodity flows between partner countries themselves and with non-participating countries as described in Appendix C.

(ii) Aggregates for the trade in the products of the main branches of manufacturing. For these the computational details are given in Appendix D.

(iii) A sample of 121 more or less homogeneous products, mainly manufactures, for which trade figures are comparable not only for the two partners but also for the two periods to be studied (Appendix E).

As far as possible I have tried to preserve symmetry in data processing and to present results for the flow from the Netherlands to the B.L.E.U. as well as vice versa. But since even for a government agency time and manpower are scarce factors, the picture for the first flow is the more comprehensive of the two. For this I wish to apologize to our Belgian and Luxemburg partners in the union.

1.5 *Dramatis Personæ.*—The true heroes of the play are a_1 referring to B.L.E.U. exports to the Netherlands and b_1 the Dutch exports to B.L.E.U. Similarly a_2 and b_2 are the competing imports on the Dutch and B.L.E.U. import markets. $\tilde{a}_1$ and $\tilde{b}_1$ represent *total exports* of partner countries, $\tilde{a}_2$ and $\tilde{b}_2$ the same of competitors. B.L.E.U. *export prices* are referred to as r_1 ; Dutch export prices as p_1 ; competing prices as r_2 and p_2. $\hat{a}$ and $\hat{b}$ refer to *the share of total exports* of B.L.E.U. and the Netherlands going to the partner country. Capitals refer to *values*; lowercase type to *volumes*. *Lefthand suffix* $_0$ refers to the pre-war period; t to the period after the formation of the union.

Taking the B.L.E.U. import market as an example we have the scheme as given by Table 1.1.

TABLE 1.1

LIST OF SYMBOLS

B.L.E.U. imports	Dutch exports		Competing imports in B.L.E.U.
	to B.L.E.U.	Total	
Volume	b_1	$\tilde{b}_1$	b_2
Price	p_1		p_2
Value	B_1	$\tilde{B}_1$	B_2
Autonomous shifts of export supply	s_1		s_2
Import duties *	T_1		T_2
Elasticity of import demand †	α		α
Elasticity of import supply †	η		η
Share of B.L.E.U. in Dutch exports : $b_1/\tilde{b}_1$	$\hat{b}_1$		

* Measured as a decimal fraction of p.
† Assumed to be equal for b_1 and b_2.

Definitions:

Total B.L.E.U. imports : $b_1 + b_2 = m$.

Volume share of Dutch exports on B.L.E.U. import market :

$$q = \frac{b_1}{m}.$$

Value share of Dutch exports on B.L.E.U. import market :

$$Q = \frac{b_1 p_1}{b_1 p_1 + b_2 p_2}.$$

Ratio of p_1 to average import price :

$$R = \frac{p_1}{q p_1 + (1 - q) p_2}.$$

Ratio of Dutch to competing imports in B.L.E.U. :

$$H = b_1/b_2$$

Ratio of Dutch to competing import price :

$$P = p_1/p_2.$$

Ratio of B.L.E.U. share in Dutch exports after the union to the same in pre-war period :

$$g_1 = t^{\hat{b}_1}/{}_0 \hat{b}_1 \text{ and } G_1 = t^{\hat{B}_1}/{}_0 \hat{B}_1.$$

Finally, the last but not least important of the *dramatis personæ* : elasticity of substitution of import demand between b_1 and b_2 : ϵ.

II. THE 'EXPECTED' PRIMARY EFFECT

2.1   The establishment of a customs union affects trade in many ways. Apart from the effects attributable to the union there are a number of factors acting independently. Obviously, empirically the effect of the union has to be measured by comparing trade at two different points of time. If the intervening period becomes very long, as in the case of Benelux where 1955 has to be compared with 1938, the isolation of the net effect of the formation of the union becomes difficult indeed. The main factors to be reckoned with will be reviewed briefly.

2.2.   The Effect of Changes in Tariffs

2.2.1   As is shown in Appendix A, the two equations of import demand can be written as follows :

(1) $$db_1/b_1 = \{\alpha q + (1 - q)\epsilon\}\frac{dp_1}{p_1} + (1 - q)(\alpha - \epsilon)\frac{dp_2}{p_2}.$$

(2) $$db_2/b_2 = q(\alpha - \epsilon)\frac{dp_1}{p_1} + \left\{\alpha(1 - q) + q\epsilon\frac{dp_2}{p_2}\right\}.$$

Here changes in $m = b_1 + b_2$ due to other than price changes have already been neglected since we are mainly interested in alterations of the import share q.

We are, however, not free to assume away shifts in the supply curves of b_1 and b_2, since such shifts will tend to change the value of q. Hence the two supply equations are :

(3) $$db_1/b_1 = \eta \, dp_1/p_1 - \eta d'T + ds_1.$$

(4) $$db_2/b_2 = \eta \, dp_2/p_2 + ds_2,$$

where s_1 and s_2 represent the relative shift of the supply curves in the period $° \rightarrow t$ when prices remain constant.

2.2.2   This system allows already some important conclusions with respect to expected change in q (Appendix B) :

(5) $$\frac{dq}{q} = -(1-q)\,(ds_1 - ds_2 - \eta d'T_1)\,\frac{\epsilon}{\eta - \epsilon}.$$

In the special case $s_1 = s_2$ we therefore find :

(6) $$\frac{1}{q}\frac{dq}{d'T_1} = (1-q)\,\frac{\epsilon \eta}{\eta - \epsilon},$$

whereas the value share (Q), if subjected to the same condition, can be written as :

(6a) $$\frac{1}{Q}\frac{dQ}{d'T_1} = (1-q)\,\epsilon\frac{\eta + 1}{\eta - \epsilon}.$$

When deriving Equations (5) and (6) $_0p_1$ and $_0p_2$ have been put equal to one. Since T is measured as a decimal fraction of $_0p_1$ the result of a tariff reduction with 10 per cent of the price, *i.e.* $\Delta T = -\cdot 1$, is found by multiplying the right-hand side of Equation (6) with $\cdot 1$. Assuming reasonable values for the elasticities of demand and supply, *e.g.* $\epsilon = -5$ and $\eta = 5$, and $q = \cdot 1$ we find :

(7) $$\frac{dq}{q} = \cdot 09\,\frac{25}{10} = \cdot 225$$

and (8) $$\frac{dQ}{Q} = \cdot 09\,\frac{30}{10} = \cdot 270.$$

In this way it is possible to have at least an idea of the direct influence of the removal of tariff walls on intra-bloc trade.[1]   A tabulation for other combinations of η and ϵ is given by Table 2.1.

[1] A system applying to a tariff union between n countries assuming $\eta = \infty$ has been published in the author's paper for the 1952 meeting of the Dutch Economic Society.   Numerical estimates for a customs union between the OEEC countries can be found in *World Politics*, 6, July 4th, 1954, and in *Social Aspects of European Economic Co-operation*, Appendix III (Geneva, International Labour Office, 1956).

TABLE 2.1

EXPECTED RELATIVE INCREASE OF INTRA-BLOC TRADE AS A CONSEQUENCE
OF A TARIFF REDUCTION OF 10 PER CENT FOR DIFFERENT VALUES OF
ϵ AND η

$$(q = \cdot 1)$$

	Elasticity of supply (η)	Price-volume elasticities of substitution (ϵ)					
		-1	-2	-5	-10	-20	$-\infty$
Volume-share (q)	1	·045	·060	·075	·082	·086	·090
	2	·060	·090	·128	·150	·164	·180
	5	·075	·128	·225	·300	·360	·450
	10	·082	·150	·300	·450	·600	·900
	20	·086	·164	·360	·600	·900	1·800
	∞	·090	·180	·450	·900	1·800	∞
Value-share (Q)	1	·090	·120	·150	·164	·172	·180
	2	·090	·135	·192	·225	·245	·270
	5	·090	·156	·270	·360	·432	·540
	10	·090	·165	·330	·495	·660	·990
	20	·090	·172	·378	·630	·945	1·890
	∞	·090	·180	·450	·900	1·800	∞

Two comments are in order :

(i) For simplicity's sake it has been assumed that $_t T_2 = {_o T_2} = {_o T_1}$. This, however, does not necessarily apply to each of the partner countries, since $_t T_2$ has actually been fixed, as a rule, at the *average level* of the previously prevailing tariffs in both countries.[1]

(ii) The Equations (1)-(4) represent essentially a linear approximation whereas the numerical value of the elasticity of the price-volume substitution curve remains probably constant over a long range of the representative interval of the latter. It is therefore probable that Equations (5) and (6) and likewise Table 2.1 result in estimates of $\Delta q/q$ and $\Delta Q/Q$ that are somewhat too low. In the case of great numerical values of ΔT a better approximation will therefore be obtained by an exponential transformation of (5) and (6).

[1] The general principles followed when fixing the uniform tariffs are described by J. E. Meade : 'Benelux, The Formation of the Common Customs', *Economica*, August 1956, p. 205.

2.3. Other Factors affecting Trade

Schematizing the most important issues can be dealt with under four separate headings :

(i) The case of *prohibitive tariffs* cannot be treated with the method suggested in the last section. Actually the result obtained, *i.e.* $\frac{1}{q}\frac{dq}{dT}\Delta T$, represents a multiplier, the multiplicant being $_0q$. If, therefore, a tariff was previously high enough to be either effectively prohibitive or already sufficiently high to prevent partner countries from competing effectively with third countries, the corresponding import share will be infinitesimal or altogether zero. No matter how great the tariff reduction, its expected effect on intra-bloc trade will likewise remain zero or negligible.

This objection does not apply to already established flows of trade, but it certainly should be taken into account where supply is discontinuous. Here the exact shape of the export-supply curve of partner countries is decisive. It is clear, however, that apart from a discontinuous supply particularly high values of ϵ are required to bring q from nought to even a small value as say ·01.

(ii) *Quantitative restrictions* might have previously hit the imports from partner countries more severely than those from non-members. Also the few remaining restrictions still applied by Benelux might distort the picture.

(iii) Increased *promotional effort* will stimulate intra-bloc trade. If two small adjacent territories like B.L.E.U. and the Netherlands form a customs union one may reasonably expect some additional activity in the field of commercial organization of mutual trade. The reduced financial risks of establishing branch offices in partner countries and the greater facilities for subcontracting illustrate the point. Just as in the case of advertising,[1] these factors will primarily be reflected in a shift of the demand curve and hence in a shift of the price-volume substitution curve.

(iv) *Quality changes* are primarily a problem of aggregation. However, several qualities of the same kind of product fall within the same category of trade returns. For this reason there is no possibility of separating alterations in quality from price changes proper. A shift in the direction of better

---

[1] Compare for a recent contribution to the theory of consumer demand with particular reference to the influence of promotional effort : R. L. Basmann, 'A theory of demand with variable consumer preferences', *Econometrica*, Vol. 24, No. 1, Jan. 1956, pp. 47-58.

qualities (*i.e.* of higher value added per physical unit) will express itself necessarily as an increase of the unit-value while leaving the volume of imports the same.

Since weighted average duties will be used as the yardstick to evaluate the consequences of a tariff reduction by means of Equations (5) and (6) this again might present a certain downward bias of the expected effect. As a matter of fact, quality changes may — or may not — be due to the customs union. But one would expect tariffs to vary roughly with the value added of the product within the same main category. Therefore, since tariffs may be correlated with value added per physical unit, the value share, Q, will tend to rise faster than is compatible with Equations (6a), whereas q might behave according to expectations. Thus quality changes enter the picture as a separate factor.

III. DEVELOPMENT OF AGGREGATES

3.1. *All Commodities*

Tariffs between member countries were abolished as early as January 1948. Under the terms of the Pre-Union also quantitative restrictions disappeared at the end of 1949,[1] with the exception of those applicable to a number of agricultural products and a few others, such as coal. Nevertheless several years elapsed before the new pattern of trade was fully developed (compare Graphs I and II). For this reason 1955 has been selected as the 'post-union' year of comparison, whereas 1928 or 1938 will be considered as representative non-union years.

The influence of changes in world-market prices and to some extent that of cyclical conditions has been eliminated by presenting in Table 3.1.1 the shares of trade instead of absolute figures. (Complete trade-matrices in U.S.A. \$ for the years considered are given as Appendix C.)

Intra-bloc trade did certainly increase for each of the partners whether 1928 is used as base of comparison or 1938. The increase is the clearest for Dutch imports from B.L.E.U. and B.L.E.U. exports to the Netherlands $\left(\text{viz.}: \dfrac{a_1}{a_1 + a_2} \text{ and } \dfrac{a_1}{\tilde{a}_1}\right)$. It is less pronounced, at least when compared with 1928, for the flow in the opposite direction.

---

[1] A detailed account of the successive Benelux agreements is presented by J. E. Meade, *Negotiations for Benelux: An annotated chronicle 1943–1956* (Princeton, 1956).

Foreign Trade as an Escape from Smallness

Striking the balance by considering total intra-bloc trade as a percentage of all imports and exports of the B.L.E.U. and the Netherlands added together, the increase is as high as 50 per cent when compared with 1938 and 42 per cent as compared with 1928. In order to verify in how far this increase is due to structural changes of a more general character in the pattern of trade of Western Europe as a whole rather than to the formation of a customs union, comparable figures are given for the total intra-bloc trade of the OEEC (including Benelux).

TABLE 3.1.1

SHARE OF EXPORTS TO PARTNER COUNTRY AND OF IMPORTS FROM PARTNER COUNTRY (BOTH AS PERCENTAGE OF TOTAL EXPORTS OR IMPORTS)

	Exports	Imports
1928		
B.L.E.U.	11·8	11·6
Netherlands	11·4	11·2
Total	11·6	11·4
Intra-bloc trade *	11·5	
1938		
B.L.E.U.	12·4	9·0
Netherlands	11·0	11·5
Total	11·7	10·2
Intra-bloc trade *	10·9	
1955		
B.L.E.U.	20·4	13·2
Netherlands	13·2	18·1
Total	16·8	15·8
Intra-bloc trade *	16·3	

* As percentage of all imports and exports of member countries.

It then appears that the OEEC as a whole, with its fair degree of liberalization, had returned in 1955 to its pattern of trade of the late 'twenties, whereas Benelux intra-bloc trade showed an increase of somewhat more than 40 per cent.

Following a suggestion of J. J. Polak,[1] Table 3.1.3 gives also a comparison with the mutual trade between 5 medium-sized and smaller members of the OEEC. In this case mutual trade showed an increase of 20 per cent since 1938 as compared by 7 per cent for all members and 50 per cent for Benelux. The use of 1928 as year of comparison turns out less favourably for Benelux, since mutual

[1] J. J. Polak in *Economisch-Statistische Berichten*, Vol. 38, No. 1907, Dec. 10, 1953, pp. 1010-12.

trade of the 5 countries increased with 50 per cent against Benelux
trade with only 42. Averaging the results for the two years of com-

TABLE 3.1.2

PERCENTAGE INCREASE OF SHARES

		Exports	Imports
B.L.E.U.	1928–55	73	14
	1938–55	65	47
Netherlands	1928–55	16	62
	1938–55	20	57
Total	1928–55	45	39
	1938–55	44	55
Intra-bloc trade *	1928–55	42	
	1938–55	50	

* As percentage of all imports and exports of member countries.

parison we find an increase of 46 per cent for Benelux and of 33 per
cent for our control group.

TABLE 3.1.3

SHARE OF INTRA-BLOC TRADE AS PERCENTAGE OF ALL
IMPORTS AND EXPORTS OF THE COUNTRIES CONCERNED

	OEEC			
	Benelux	All members	5 members only *	
			†	‡
1928	11·5	46·3	9·0	59·3
1938	10·9	43·1	11·3	62·6
1955	16·3	46·6	13·6	60·8
Percentage increase 1928–55	42	0·6	50·8	2·5
Percentage increase 1938–55	50	6·6	19·8	−2·9

* Denmark, Italy, Norway, Sweden, Switzerland.
† Mutual trade as percentage of total trade.
‡ Trade with all OEEC countries as percentage of total trade.

It is clear that a part at least of the increase of Benelux trade
must be explained by the general tendency to greater interdepend-

ence among the smaller countries of Western Europe, rather than by the specific effect of a customs union.

3.2. Changes in the Main Categories of Manufactured Products

As can be seen from Table 3.2.1, the dominating feature of the development between the pre-war period and 1955 is the greater relative importance of the trade in manufactured products. Although total Dutch exports to B.L.E.U. showed the smaller increase of the two, the rate of growth of Dutch industrial exports is unquestionably the more spectacular. (Graph I.)

DUTCH AND GERMAN VALUE SHARES IN B.L.E.U.-IMPORTS

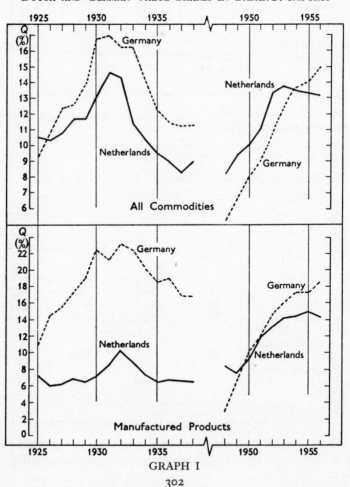

GRAPH I

For this reason the shift of Dutch manufactured exports since 1938 has been analysed more closely. In order to be less dependent upon specific years of reference, a regression analysis has been made for 11 categories of manufactured products. Since the volume

TABLE 3.2.1

COMPOSITION OF INTRA-BLOC TRADE *

(PERCENTAGES)

	B.L.E.U. to Netherlands			Netherlands to B.L.E.U.		
	1928	1938	1955	1928	1938	1955
Agriculture	14·0	8·5	5·2	52·1	45·4	21·0
Mining and mineral products	17·2	15·6	14·9	23·2	24·8	13·9
Manufacturing	68·8	75·9	79·9	24·7	29·8	65·1
Total	100·0	100·0	100·0	100·0	100·0	100·0
Total value in U.S. $m. (current prices)	121	89	580	103	70	375
Index 1928 = 100	100	74	479	100	68	364

* Categories of B.L.E.U. Trade Returns (1938) : Agriculture : I, II ; Mining and mineral products : III ; Manufacturing : IV-XXI.

share, q, appeared to be rather sensitive to changes in the unit-value ratio, R, and since next to R, cyclical conditions, y, proved to affect the volume share, the following equation was used to estimate the shifts :

(1) $$\log q = \zeta \log R + \gamma \log y + \beta D + \kappa.$$

Here D denotes the shift of the 'price'-volume substitution curve between the pre-war period as a whole and the period selected as representative after the formation of the union (as a rule, 1952–56, compare Appendix D where also the numerical values of the co-efficients are given). y denotes the percentage of total employment as an indicator of cyclical conditions.

It should be noted that ζ is a quasi-elasticity. As appears from the considerable changes in R (Table 3.2.2, column 4) during the pre-war period, ζ should be considered as a 'product-mix' elasticity rather than as a real elasticity of substitution. The fact that the values of ζ are equally distributed around unity [1] gives a good illustration of MacDougall's case number IV : 'Errors in logarithms of

[1] With a median value of – ·91 and an average of – ·97 (Appendix D, column 5).

relative quantity and relative price of equal magnitude but opposite sign'.[1]

Exactly for this reason, however, the shift, D, becomes largely independent of differences in the specific relative composition of imports before and after the union. D may therefore be interpreted as : *the increase of (the logarithms of) the import share as compared with the share that would have prevailed in the pre-war period at the same relative unit-value and under the same cyclical conditions.*

The shifts found for 11 exporting Dutch branches of manufacturing are given in Table 3.2.2.[2] The figures for the 6 B.L.E.U. branches have been taken by courtesy of the Netherlands' Economic Institute from a study by Marvin M. Kristein, who used a similar, although in some respects different, approach.[3]

3.3 A few conclusions as suggested by Table 3.2.2 may briefly be summarized as follows :

(i) For none of the 6 B.L.E.U. or the 11 Dutch categories has a negative shift been found.

(ii) The shifts appear to be significantly positive and quite substantial in all cases. For the B.L.E.U. exports it varies between 50 and 170 per cent of the comparable pre-war share, for Dutch exports between 40 and 675 per cent.

(iii) No clear relation is to be found between the estimated shift and the uniform tariff against non-participating countries, nor — as might be expected — between D and $\Delta R/R$.

(iv) Since the method used when estimating D corrects automatically for differences in R that did occur between the post-war and the pre-war period and, moreover, the average value of the quasi-elasticity ζ equals about unity, we have every reason to expect a rough correspondence between the weighted average of D and the actual change of the value share Q. As is shown by Table 3.3.1, the weighted average shift and the actual increase of Q both amount to about

[1] 'British and American Exports; a study suggested by the theory of comparative costs', Part I, *Economic Journal*, Vol. lxi, No. 244, December 1951, pp. 722-23.
[2] The series for R have been corrected for the tariff reduction in intra-bloc trade after the war. The values for βD as given in Table 3.2.2 and Appendix D tend, therefore, to underestimate the actual shifts as defined above. As the value of ζ, as a rule, equals about unity, the differences correspond roughly with the level of the common tariff. In most cases they remain, therefore, well within the 1σ limits of the present estimates.
[3] *Benelux. Its Effects on Belgian Exports to the Netherlands*, a report by the Division for Balanced International Growth of the Netherlands' Economic Institute, Rotterdam, June 1956 (available on request). In the case of two categories, viz. 'machinery' and 'iron and steel', new computations have been made in order to obtain comparability of results with the corresponding Dutch exports to B.L.E.U.

TABLE 3.2.2

ESTIMATED TOTAL SHIFT OF MARKET SHARES (1925–38 AND REPRESENTATIVE POST-WAR PERIOD)

Branch of industry	Price ratio R		Coefficient of variation of R 1926–1938	Import share q		Percentage difference pre-war–post-war		Percentage shift in share of import trade		Average duty (common tariff) % ad valorem
	1938	1955		1938	1955	R	q	Estimated	1σ Limits	
1	2	3	4	5	6	7	8	9	10	11
I. B.L.E.U. to Netherlands:										
Yarns	84	108	·134	44	61	29	39	53		1·9
Dyestuffs and paints	38	24	·199	20	33	-37	65	73		3·3
Machinery	56	103	·143	14	15	84	7	75	72–78	16·0
Iron and steel	79	82	·103	35	46	4	31	120	118–122	6·9
Clothes	74	95		14	67	28	379	135		18·6
Cloth	22	35	·109	62	144	59	132	172		
II. Netherlands to B.L.E.U.:										
Metals	37	55	·514	11	12	49	9	43	30–58	
Chemicals	94	163	·216	7	7	73	0	48	32–68	
Glass	27	56	·252	24	33	107	38	71	57–87	
Machinery	111	120	·239	6	10	8	67	105	91–118	
Foods (excl. agriculture)	75	87	·063	16	29	16	81	114	84–149	
Leather	68	91	·202	15	14	34	-7	124	64–207	3·7
Paper	127	102	·152	7	22	-20	214	160	138–183	5·6
Transportation equipment	24	92	·840	8	8	283	0	261	159–402	10·3
Textiles	44	111	·134	8	27	152	238	293	209–399	6·0
Wood	146	484	·370	2	1	232	-50	464	312–671	1·8
Wax and soap	79	87	·147	12	41	10	242	675	540–838	11·2

305

125 per cent. A figure of this order of magnitude appears therefore acceptable for the combined influence upon Q of all structural changes that intervened between the two periods under consideration.

SHIFTS IN IMPORT-SHARE (Machinery)

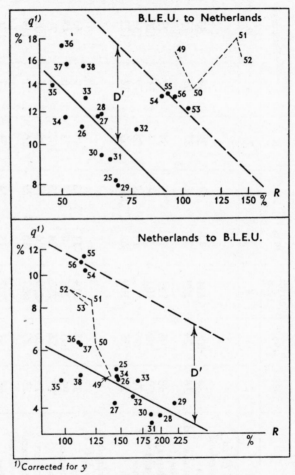

GRAPH II

TABLE 3.3.1

WEIGHTED SHIFTS AND ACTUAL INCREASE OF THE VALUE SHARE
OF DUTCH INDUSTRIAL IMPORTS IN B.L.E.U.

	Increase of import share %
Shifts weighted with :	
(i) 1938 import values	129
(ii) 1955 „ „	126
Average	127·5
Actual increase in aggregate value share— 1953–56 (average) compared with :	
(i) 1928	120
(ii) 1938	128
Average	124

IV. DIFFERENCES IN RATES OF GROWTH
BETWEEN HOMOGENEOUS PRODUCTS

4.1 To estimate that the import share increased by 125 per cent is one thing, but to explain an increase of this size is another. For this reason a sample of 121 categories, mainly of manufactured products, each as homogeneous as possible, was studied more closely (see Appendix E). Years of comparison were 1938 and 1955.

As to the more general tendencies governing the trade in these items two major conclusions are possible.

4.2 By far the most dominating factor appears to have been the rate of increase of total Dutch exports in the same category. By the use of multiple correlation the following — partial — relation is found :

$$(1) \qquad \frac{\Delta b_I}{\frac{1}{2}({}_0 b_I + {}_t b_I)} = \beta \frac{\Delta \tilde{b}_I}{\frac{1}{2}({}_0 \tilde{b}_I + {}_t \tilde{b}_I)} + \dots$$

where the coefficient β is a fair approximation of the elasticity between b_I and $\tilde{b}_I$. The value of β is about ·80, meaning that in this period there was a general tendency for the separate categories of b_I to increase at a somewhat slower rate than $\tilde{b}_I$. This lack of perfect proportionality is no doubt due to the fact that B.L.E.U. imports, as a whole, rose less than Dutch exports.[1]

The rather close correlation between b_1 and $\tilde{b}_1$ deserves attention, for it may mean that mutual trade — even between countries with a roughly similar structure of production — tends to conform to the overall changes in the export-pattern of the partners concerned.

4.3 Since total exports of the home country appear to be an important factor in the development of mutual trade, the 121 categories are classified in Table 4.1 according to their initial export share:

$$(2) \qquad {_o}\tilde{b}_1 = {_o}b_1/{_o}\tilde{b}_1.$$

The main conclusions to be drawn from this table are the following:

(i) As appears from column 4, the major part, that is to say, 59 per cent of the total absolute increase of Dutch exports to Belgium is due to items with an initial export share of 6 per cent or less.

(ii) This might be due to the removal of previously highly protective tariffs (the issue discussed in section 2.3 above), were it not that tariffs in these two first intervals as shown by column 4 were certainly not excessive. Particularly in the first class with the bantam-sized shares of 1 per cent or less of total Dutch exports, the increase of the share has been, it is true, a 24-fold (*vide* column 7). Nevertheless, the duties that should have been paid, if the original B.L.E.U. tariffs were still valid for Dutch imports, amounted to only slightly more than 4 per cent when weighted with the 1955 values of the additional imports. For this reason there is little occasion to attribute this huge relative increase to the customs union as such unless either quantitative restrictions hampered imports in this interval, or promotional effort as a joint product of the union did much to stimulate exports to Belgium.

(iii) The more striking feature of this table as brought out by column 7: $g_1 = {_t}\hat{b}_1/{_o}\hat{b}_1$ is the fact that the relative increase of the Dutch export share tends to become the smaller, and finally even negative, the greater the share, ${_o}\hat{b}_1$, of the product concerned previously was in 1938. On the one hand, this recalls the well-known genetic law that tall fathers will procreate children below their own size and vice versa. On the other hand, this reshuffling of export shares might be

---

[1] As is shown by Appendix C, the percentage increase of Belgian imports as measured in current $ was about 25 per cent less than the increase of Dutch exports.

TABLE 4.1

CHANGES IN DUTCH EXPORTS TO B.L.E.U., 1938–55, CLASSIFIED ACCORDING TO SIZE OF INITIAL SHARE OF B.L.E.U. IN TOTAL DUTCH EXPORTS

(SAMPLE OF 121 MAINLY INDUSTRIAL PRODUCTS)

(1)	Initial ratio of Dutch-B.L.E.U. exports to total Dutch exports (1938) (2)	Number of items (3)	Relative share in total increase of Dutch exports to B.L.E.U. † (4)	Average tariff ‡ on actual increase of imports (5)	Median of relative increase of Dutch exports to B.L.E.U. (6)	Median of relative increase of ratio of Dutch exports to B.L.E.U. and total Dutch exports (7)
I	<·01	18	22·4 %	4·2 %	999·00	23·62
II	·01–·06	22	36·4 %	15·8 %	12·30	3·39
III	·06–·15	22	9·9 %	22·7 %	3·16	1·10
IV	·15–·30	18	9·0 %	27·6 %	1·28	·20
V	·30–·50	23	5·8 %	15·0 %	1·14	–·13
VI	>·50	18	16·5 %	11·9 %	·91	–·27
	·146 *	121	100·0 %	15·6 % §	4·48 * 1·35 §	·36

* Median.
† Volume increase weighted with 1955 prices.
‡ 1938 B.L.E.U. tariff.
§ Average, weighted on the basis of 1955 prices.

representative of a tendency towards greater equality of export shares.

(iv) In fact, the dispersion of $\hat{b}_I$ as measured by the semi-interquartile range remains perfectly unchanged, viz. 9·3 per cent in 1955 as against 9·5 per cent in 1938. The median itself, however, shows an increase from ·146 to ·244. Hence the *relative dispersion* appears to have been reduced with 40 per cent. This means that export shares in 1955 were more equally distributed than in 1938.

(v) This is not to say that the greater equality of $\hat{b}_I$ is a necessary result of the customs union, although at least one argument can be given in favour of this view. Presuming free trade the composition of the total exports of a country (A) corresponds with the comparative advantage that each of A's exporting industries enjoys over industries which are on average similar in other countries (B, C, D, etc.). The trade barriers erected in any of these countries, say B, shelter, as a rule, B's least efficient industries. Mutual trade between A and B, therefore, no longer reflects the comparative advantage of A over B. Nevertheless, differences in relative efficiency between the industries in A are still roughly indicated by the composition of total exports of A. The pre-war exports of the United Kingdom and the United States as analysed by MacDougall point at least in this direction.[1] In so far as the comparative advantage of each of the industries of A over those of B is correlated with the actual composition of A's exports to all other countries (and in the present case the dominating influence just discussed of b_1 upon b_1 strongly suggests such a correlation) a removal of trade barriers between A and B cannot but lead to a greater equality of the percentage share of B in the different products exported by A.

V. DIVISION OF LABOUR AS REFLECTED BY TRADE

5.1 A customs union is intended to improve the division of labour between partner countries. It is therefore reasonable to expect that the shifts in mutual trade after the formation of the union will result in a fair degree of specialization of intra-bloc exports. The Dutch share of textiles on the B.L.E.U. import market, in fact, increased by about 300 per cent, whereas B.L.E.U., on a much higher base volume, still recorded shifts for clothing and cloth of well over the 100 per cent (see Table 3.2.2, column 9); for machinery the changes in mutual trade were 105 and 75 per cent; for other categories there were similar large increases.

[1] *Loc. cit.*

5.2 The degree of specialization as reflected by the mutual trade between two countries can conveniently be described by applying some measure of unequality to the ratios of the two flows of the same product for the different categories. The dispersion of the ratio $b_1 a_1$ will become larger if a process of growing specialization is started.

As might be expected, the dispersion of this ratio is considerable since b_I/a_I for the different items varies actually between 0 and ∞. Comparing 1938 with 1955, it appears, however, that the number of extreme values has been reduced, whereas the median showed an increase from ·176 to ·445.

TABLE 5.1

DISTRIBUTION OF THE RATIO b_I/a_I

(TOTAL NUMBER OF CATEGORIES : 121)

	< ·05	< ·10	> 5	> 10
1938	46	55	31	27
1955	30	37	27	21

5.3 It therefore follows that specialization, if it did accompany the expansion of trade, is to be found *within* rather than *between* the different categories of trade. Since price differentials of internationally traded goods on a small and almost entirely liberalized market such as Benelux are largely an indication of differences in kind of product or in quality, the existence of a large variance of the price differentials may be considered as symptomatic of a specialization within-categories-of-products.

Computing the price differentials between b_I and a_I, as : [1]

$$\frac{p_I - r_I}{\frac{1}{2}(p_I + r_I)},$$

we find for 1955 a standard deviation of ·31. This seems to corroborate the view that specialization of mutual trade between partners — if proceeding at all — as yet is mainly to be found within the same branches of industry.

Finally, the median and the average of the relative differences between Dutch and B.L.E.U. export prices are slightly positive, viz. ·01 and ·05, although Dutch prices have been taken f.o.b. and B.L.E.U. prices c.i.f. Nevertheless Belgian labour costs, including

---

[1] p_I being the Dutch, r_I the B.L.E.U. export price.

social charges and holidays with pay, were in 1954 still 29 per cent above the corresponding Dutch level.[1]

For this reason it is remarkable that the weighted average [2] of the price differentials also is slightly positive, viz. ·013. This, at any rate, rules out the possibility of a systematic price difference between mutual exports.

PRICE DIFFERENTIALS BETWEEN DUTCH AND B.L.E.U. MUTUAL EXPORTS

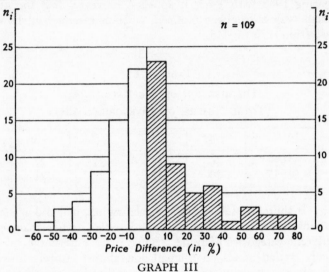

GRAPH III

VI. BEHAVIOUR OF THE UNIT-VALUE RATIOS

6.1 We see from column 7 of Table 3.2.2 positive changes of the price ratio (R) for imports from member countries to total imports are more dominant and sizable than negative ones. This holds for Dutch as well as for B.L.E.U. exports, although the Netherlands was a high-cost country before the war and became a low-cost country afterwards. Only in one of the 11 Dutch categories is the post-war price ratio lower than the pre-war one, whereas in 4 out of 11 cases the positive differences are 100 per cent or more.

As R does not present a reliable yardstick for the ratio between p_1 and p_2 — since R tends towards unity for increasing values of q

---

[1] *Social Aspects of European Economic Cooperation*, International Labour Office, Geneva, 1956, p. 33, Table I.
[2] The 1955 value of exports being used as weights.

(compare the formula on page 295) — the corresponding values of the ratio :

(1) $$P = p_1/p_2$$

are given in Table 6.1. The weighted average value of $\Delta P/P$ appears to be 55 per cent. The weighted average for the R's incidentally also amounts to 55 per cent.[1]

TABLE 6.1

RELATIVE CHANGES OF THE UNIT-VALUE RATIO * OF
INTRA-BLOC TRADE TO COMPETING IMPORTS
(1938–55)

B.L.E.U. to Netherlands	$\Delta P/P$	Netherlands to B.L.E.U.	$\Delta P/P$
Dyestuffs and paints	− ·61	Paper	− ·21
Iron and steel	− ·01	Wax and soap	·03
Clothing	·20	Machinery	·09
Yarns	·64	Foods (excl. agr. prod.)	·17
Cloth	2·36	Leather	·41
Weighted average: yarns, cloth, and clothing †	1·02	Metals	·52
		Chemicals	·82
Machinery	·98	Glass	1·02
		Textiles	1·75
		Wood	2·53
		Transportation equipment	3·13
Weighted average †	·48	Weighted average ‡	·55

* $P = p_1/p_2$.
† On the basis of the 1938 exports to the Netherlands from B.L.E.U.
‡ On the basis of the 1938 exports to B.L.E.U. from the Netherlands.

6.2 Two main conclusions seem to follow from this increase in P.

(i) A considerable part of the 125 per cent growth of Q (see section 3.3) is not due to the fact that greater quantities are traded between partner countries, but to the fact that the average price per quantity unit as compared with that of competitors has risen considerably.

(ii) Of course, at least some increase of P, when measured less of import duties, is to be expected on the condition that η does not approach infinity and ϵ remains negative :

$$\frac{1}{P}\frac{dP}{dT} = \frac{dp_1}{p_1} - \frac{dp_2}{p_2} - 1 = \frac{\epsilon}{\eta - \epsilon}$$ (see Appendix B, Equations 22 and 23).

[1] The 1938 values of exports being used as weights.

Assuming reasonable values for these elasticities, *e.g.* $\eta = -\epsilon$ $=5$, and taking into account that the tariff reduction was on the average about 10 per cent, only 5 of 55 per cent of the increase in P can be explained in this way.

6.3 For this reason it is doubtful that the whole price component of the increase of Q should be a direct consequence of the customs union. One is rather inclined to look for a common factor that would first connect the tendency towards equalization of the export shares with this rise in the unit-values and that could secondly tie in with the general increase of mutual trade between the medium-sized and smaller OEEC countries (see section 3.1 above). A relatively fast rate of industrialization, combined with a more even spread of new techniques of production, might be a possible factor, a hypothesis, however, that as yet has not been tested.

6.4 On the other hand, the customs union might have fostered a shift in the relative composition of intra-bloc trade so as to favour products with a high value added. The argument would then be that :

(i) tariffs probably vary with the value added of products ;

(ii) the weighted average tariff does not represent the real impact of a given tariff structure on trade ; [1]

(iii) quantitative restrictions in the 'thirties might have been imposed more heavily on those import items with a relatively high content of labour cost where partner countries had the comparative advantage.

VII. AN ASYMPTOTIC MINIMUM FOR ELASTICITY OPTIMISM

7.1 Attempts to determine the numerical value of the elasticity of substitution for international trade suffer, as a rule, from the fact that the unit-value is a poor indicator of price differences as such. As suggested by MacDougall, a certain bias in the direction of the unit-elasticity is inevitable, even when a cross-section analysis is applied.

7.2 A removal of tariff walls between two countries offers, however, a promising possibility to study ϵ without using unit-values as price indicators. As shown in Appendix B, the effect of a tariff reduction on exports can be approximated by the formula :

(1) $\dfrac{\Delta b_{\mathrm{I}}}{b_{\mathrm{I}}} = \dfrac{\eta\epsilon}{\eta - \epsilon}\left\{1 + q\,\dfrac{\eta}{\epsilon}\dfrac{(\alpha - \epsilon)}{(\eta - \alpha)}\right\}\Delta T_{\mathrm{I}}$ (see Appendix B, Equation 35).

---

[1] Compare : F. Lutz, 'Methoden des internationalen Zollvergleichs', *Magazin der Wirtschaft*, No. 4, 1928, p. 1207, and A. Loveday, 'The Measurement of Tariff Levels', *Journal of the Royal Statistical Society*, No. 92, 1929, p. 487.

As is easily seen, the coefficient of ΔT_I is always numerically smaller than ϵ since $\eta>0$, $\alpha<0$ and $0<q<1$.[1] In the special case that $\eta=\infty$ and $\alpha=0$, Equation (1) has the form :

(2) $$\frac{\Delta b_I}{b_I}=(1-q)\,\epsilon\Delta T_I.$$

For this reason, although the numerical values of α and η might be unknown, a regression analysis between the 121 values of $\Delta b_I/b_I$ and the corresponding values of ΔT_I, as contained in the sample mentioned already, will provide a *minimum estimate*, ρ, of $(1-q)\epsilon$:

(3) $$\frac{\Delta b_I}{b_I}=\rho\Delta T_I.$$

7.3 It is also possible to deduce the expected value of ϵ for different combinations of η, α, and q from an empirical estimate of ρ. The values for ρ actually found from this sample vary between $-2{\cdot}50$ and $-3{\cdot}40$, depending on the combination of explaining variables. Taking the lowest of these values as representative for ρ and a figure of $\cdot20$ as representative for the average q of this special sample, the following values are obtained :

TABLE 7.1

THE EXPECTED VALUE OF ϵ FOR DIFFERENT COMBINATIONS
OF η AND α $(\rho=-2{\cdot}50\,;\ q=\cdot20)$

α	η			
	3	5	10	∞
$-\cdot5$	$-\infty$	$-7{\cdot}57$	$-4{\cdot}30$	$-3{\cdot}00$
$-1{\cdot}0$	-141	$-7{\cdot}00$	$-4{\cdot}08$	$-2{\cdot}88$
$-2{\cdot}0$	-48	$-6{\cdot}20$	$-3{\cdot}71$	$-2{\cdot}63$

7.4 As can be seen from Table 7.1, the estimates of ϵ that correspond with higher finite values of η (*e.g.* 10) are well in agreement with the relatively high values as suggested by MacDougall's findings, viz. -4 to $-4{\cdot}5$.[2] A high value for η is acceptable in this case, since the share of a country's total exports going to a relatively small country is, as a rule, minimal. According to Table 4.1 even in the case of the Netherlands the median value of $_0b_I$ for the sample studied is as low as $\cdot146$.

---

[1] Presupposing, of course, $|\alpha|\langle|\epsilon|$.   [2] *Ibid.* p. 720.

7.5 The structure of the regression equation as used in Appendix E to estimate ρ is essentially that of a reduced-form equation. The estimate of ρ is, therefore, free from the bias that is to be expected if a demand relation is used. Nevertheless, one particular kind of bias might arise from the use of ΔT_I instead of prices as independent variable, since the weighted tariff may underestimate the real impact of the tariff structure upon the imports of non-member countries. But since the common tariff of Benelux is a moderate one, it seems improbable that this kind of bias will unduly affect the estimate of ρ.

VIII. THE NET PRIMARY-EFFECT: 1938-55

8.1 As is clear from the foregoing, any attempt to isolate the net effect of a tariff union from the other factors that govern trade must inevitably rely upon an arbitrary evaluation of the influences that are to be eliminated. For this reason the net effect, however computed, remains necessarily unreliable as a residaul-item. In order to show the uncertainties involved, an attempt is made below to quantify some of the factors concerned.

8.2 The gross shift of the value share of Dutch manufactured products on the Belgian import has been estimated at 125 per cent (section 3.3). In order to evaluate the net effect of the tariff union allowance will be made for the following factors:

A_I *Shifts in total export supply* to the Netherlands as compared with competitors. (The variable $(ds_1 - ds_2)$ of Equation (5), section 2.2.1.) The original shift of the supply curve is, of course, perfectly unknown. For our purpose, however, the difference between the export level (1938 = 100) of Dutch and that of competing exports at the world market prices of 1955 might be sufficient. The Dutch index rose to 236, the weighted average [1] of competitors to 210. It seems, there-

[1]

	Exports of manufactures	
	Total exports 1955 (1938=100)	Import share of B.L.E.U. (1938)
France	175	·19
Germany	224	·18
U.K.	134	·08
U.S.A.	305	·11
Total (weighted average)	210	·56

fore, only fair to make an allowance of $\frac{236}{210}$ or 1·12 for the relative change in Dutch export supply.

A_2 *The general increase of mutual trade* between smaller and medium-sized OEEC countries. Comparing 1955 with 1938 a relative growth of 20 per cent was found (section 3, Table 3.1.3). This percentage refers, however, to total trade. The percentage for manufacturing might have been higher. On the other hand, as between these countries a fair degree of liberalization as compared with 1938 has also affected trade. For this reason a percentage not higher than 20 or 30 might be acceptable. This leaves us with two alternatives : $_1A_2 = 1·20$ and $_2A_2 = 1·30$.

A_3 *The 'monopolistic' price-effect* due to a finite value of the elasticity of supply in the case of tariff reductions. In section 6.2 the possible magnitude of this effect has already roughly been estimated at 5 per cent, or $A_3 = 1·05$.

A_4 *The increase of the average unit-value.* According to section 6.1 the weighted average $\Delta R/R$ amounts to ·55 if 1938 weights are used. The use of 1955 weights shows a considerable higher rate of increase, viz. ·745. An exact estimate of the parts of the total value share of all manufactured Dutch imports that are due respectively to volume and unit-value changes would require a very complicated system of re-weighing of the separate $\Delta q/q$'s and $\Delta R/R$'s for the main categories. It is, therefore, assumed that an approximation of these two factors of growth can be obtained by taking the geometric mean of the average rate of increase of $\Delta R/R$ on the base of pre-war weights and that on post-war weights.

The average thus obtained amounts to ·65. This increase should, however, be corrected for :

(i) A_2 : the general increase of trade of the smaller OEEC countries. Here, the hypothesis formulated in section 6.3 has simply been taken for granted.
(ii) A_3 : the 'monopolistic' price-effect.

The remaining unit-value-effect is therefore reduced to :

$$_1A_4 = \frac{1·65}{1·05 \times 1·20} = 1·31,$$

or alternatively :

$$_2A_4 = \frac{1·65}{1·05 \times 1·30} = 1·21.$$

The problem what part of these residual increases should be allotted to the customs union remains, however, unsolved.[1]

[1] Compare sections 6.3 and 6.4.

8.3   Taking into account these four allowances the remaining *net volume-effect* appears to be :

	Value share (1938 = 1)	2·25
less A_1	Shift in supply	1·12
		2·01
less $_1A_2$	General increase of mutual trade	1·20
		1·67
less $_1A_3$	Monopolistic price-effect	1·05
		1·59
less $_1A_4$	Remaining increase in unit-value	1·31
		1·22
	Hypothetical net volume-effect :	·22

8.4   As to the *value-effect* two extreme alternatives are possible :

Alternative 1 : Choosing for $_2A_2$ and allotting no part whatsoever of $_2A_4$ to the effect of the tariff union.
Alternative 2 : Choosing for $_1A_2$ and attributing the whole of $_1A_4$ to the union.

	Alternatives	
	(1)	(2)
Value share (1938 = 1·00) less shift in supply	2·01	2·01
Less : General increase of mutual trade ($_2A_2$ resp. $_1A_2$)	$\dfrac{1·30}{1·55}$	$\dfrac{1·20}{1·67}$
Less : Remaining increase in unit-value ($_2A_4$)	$\dfrac{1·21}{}$	$\dfrac{1·00}{}$
Hypothetical net value-effect	1·28	1·67

8.5   As can be seen from the calculations just presented, an estimate of the residual net-effect is extremely sensitive to small changes in the assumptions.   Moreover, because of the increase of the unit-value ratios, the influence of the tariff union upon the balance of payments position is difficult to evaluate.

8.6   As to the *volume-effect*, a net increase of 22 per cent might perhaps be considered a reasonable estimate.   On the one hand, it does agree with the average influence of the tariff reduction as shown by the cross-section analysis of 121 trade categories, so that for the present purpose this analysis can serve as an independent estimate (see Appendix E, § 3).

On the other hand, it is not incompatible with acceptable values of the price-volume elasticity of substitution and the price elasticity of supply. According to Table 2.1 the absolute values of both, ϵ and η, would have to be of an order of magnitude of about 5 if q were to increase by 22 per cent.

In fact, a somewhat lower figure for ϵ might have been sufficient, since it is reasonable to assume that some additional promotional effort was invested in intra-bloc relations.

APPENDIX A: THE CROSS-ELASTICITIES OF EXPORT DEMAND

1. The Symbols used

Suppose that the imports of a certain product (b) from country Y in country X are studied. They allow for a certain degree of price-volume substitution by the imports in X of similar products from other countries. The notation of section 1.5 will be used.

2. The Partial Elasticities of Demand

Assuming a demand function for total imports of the product b of the form

$$(1) \qquad b_1 + b_2 = \beta \tilde{p}^\alpha$$

where $\tilde{p}$ is the average import price of b_1 and b_2. Approximating $\tilde{p}$ by the weighted geometric mean of p_1 and p_2 we get :

$$(2) \qquad b_1 + b_2 = \beta p_1^{\alpha q} p_2^{\alpha(1-q)}.$$

If the price-volume substitution relation is represented by :

$$(3) \qquad \frac{b_1}{b_2} = H = \gamma P^\epsilon$$

a set of simple expressions for the partial elasticities of import demand can easily be derived.

Differentiating (3) with respect to p_1, we have :

$$(4) \qquad \frac{dH}{H} = \frac{db_1}{b_1} - \frac{db_2}{b_2} = \epsilon \frac{dp_1}{p_1}.$$

Likewise, differentiation of (2) gives :

$$\frac{db_1 + db_2}{b_1 + b_2} = \alpha q \frac{dp_1}{p_1} + \alpha(\log p_1 - \log p_2)\, dq$$

and since
$$\frac{b_1}{b_1+b_2}=q:$$

(5) $$q\left(\frac{db_1}{b_1}\right)+(1-q)\frac{db_2}{b_2}=\alpha q\frac{dp_1}{p_1}+\alpha \log \mathrm{P}dq.$$

As $q=\dfrac{\mathrm{H}}{\mathrm{H}+1}$, dq in (5) can be written :

$$dq=d\frac{\mathrm{H}}{\mathrm{H}+1}=\frac{1}{(\mathrm{H}+1)^2}d\mathrm{H}=q^2\mathrm{H}^{-1}\frac{d\mathrm{H}}{\mathrm{H}},$$

and taking into account (4) :

(6) $$dq=q^2\frac{1-q}{q}\epsilon\frac{dp_1}{p_1}=q(1-q)\epsilon\frac{dp_1}{p_1}.$$

Finally, after elimination of $\dfrac{db_2}{b_2}$ from (4) and (5), by multiplying (4) with $(1-q)$ and substitution of dq by the right-hand of (6) we find :

(7) $$\frac{db_1}{b_1}=\left\{(1-q)\epsilon+\alpha q+\alpha\epsilon q(1-q)\log \mathrm{P}\right\}\frac{dp_1}{p_1}.$$

Neglecting the last term in the right-hand side of (7), as is permissible in those cases where either P differs but slightly from 1 — as we may expect for homogeneous products — or where the value of q is small, we finally find :

(8) $$\boxed{\frac{\partial b_1}{\partial p_1}\frac{p_1}{b_1}=q\alpha+(1-q)\epsilon}$$

Proceeding in a similar way, the following expressions can be derived for the other partial derivatives, viz. :

(9) $$\frac{\partial b_1}{\partial p_2}\frac{p_2}{b_1}=(1-q)(\alpha-\epsilon).$$

(10) $$\frac{\partial b_2}{\partial p_1}\frac{p_1}{b_2}=q(\alpha-\epsilon).$$

(11) $$\frac{\partial b_2}{\partial p_2}\frac{p_2}{b_2}=(1-q)\alpha+q\epsilon.$$

In the first place the formal analogy should be noted between the expression (8) for the price elasticity of import demand and Allen and Hicks's formula for the price elasticity of total demand for the product b :

(12) $$\frac{\partial b}{\partial p}\frac{p}{b}=q_b\phi+(1-q_b)\mathrm{E},$$

where q_b denotes the part of income spent on b, ϕ the income elasticity of demand, and E the elasticity of substitution between b and all other items of the consumers' budget.

Secondly, the set of elasticities as given by Equations 8-11 appears to be mutually consistent in so far as :

$$(13) \qquad \frac{\partial b_1}{\partial p_1}\frac{p_1}{b_1} + \frac{\partial b_1}{\partial p_2}\frac{p_2}{b_1} = \frac{\partial b_2}{\partial p_1}\frac{p_1}{b_2} + \frac{\partial b_2}{\partial p_2}\frac{p_2}{b_2} = \alpha,$$

whereas the requirement :

$$(14) \qquad \frac{\partial b_1}{\partial p_2} = \frac{\partial b_2}{\partial p_1}$$

remains satisfied as long as P equals unity.

APPENDIX B: THE NET PRIMARY-EFFECT

1. *The Primary-Effect as measured by the Share in Total Imports*

Here either the volume share (q) or the value share (Q) may be chosen. In the first case we find :

$$(1) \qquad dq = d\left(\frac{b_1}{m}\right) = \frac{mdb_1 - b_1 dm}{m^2} = \frac{db_1 - qdm}{m}.$$

In order to simplify computations, the initial values of total imports and prices can be put equal to 1 :

$$(2) \qquad \bar{b}_1 + \bar{b}_2 = \bar{m} = \bar{p}_1 = \bar{p}_2 = 1$$

and equation (1) reads :

$$(3) \qquad \boxed{dq = (1-q)db_1 - qdb_2}$$

With regard to the *value share*, Q, it should be noted that Q can be written as :

$$(4) \qquad Q = \frac{b_1}{m}\frac{p_1}{(b_1 p_1 + b_2 p_2)/m} = qR,$$

hence : (5) $\qquad dQ = Rdq + qdR$

and taking into account (2)

$$(6) \qquad dQ/Q = dq/q + dR.$$

As $\bar{p}_1$ and $\bar{p}_2$ have been put equal to unity, the expression for dR becomes :

(7) $$dR = (1 - q)(dp_1 - dp_2)$$

and substitution of (7) in (6) gives :

(8) $$\boxed{dQ/Q = dq/q + (1 - q)(dp_1 - dp_2)}$$

2. *A Simplified System of Import Demand and Supply*

Making use of the cross-elasticities as derived already in Appendix A and discarding further all irrelevant variables,. the demand equations for b_1 and b_2 can be written as :

(9) $$\frac{db_1}{b_1} = \left\{\alpha q + (1 - q)\epsilon\right\}\frac{dp_1}{p_1} + (1 - q)(\alpha - \epsilon)\frac{dp_2}{p_2}.$$

(10) $$\frac{db_2}{b_2} = q(\alpha - \epsilon)\frac{dp_1}{p_1} + \left\{\alpha(1 - q) + q\epsilon\right\}\frac{dp_2}{p_2}.$$

Assuming that the elasticities of supply for Y's exports of b and for competing exports are equal, viz. :

(11) $$\eta_1 = \eta_2 = \eta,$$

and besides that the uniform tariff as maintained against non-participating countries will be the same as the old tariff prevailing previously in X, so that

(12) $$\Delta T_2 = 0$$

the two supply equations become :

(13) $$\frac{db_1}{b_1} = \eta\frac{dp_1}{p_1} - \eta d T_1$$

(14) $$\frac{db_2}{b_2} = \eta\frac{dp_2}{p_2}.$$

Taking into account that $\bar{b}_1 = q$ and $b_2 = 1 - q$, $p_1 = p_2 = 1$ and writing A_1 and A_2 by way of shorthand notation for the two partial elasticities in (9) and B_1 and B_2 for those in (10), our four-equation system becomes :

(15) $$db_1 = qA_1 dp_1 + qA_2 dp_2.$$
(16) $$db_2 = (1 - q)B_1 dp_1 + (1 - q)B_2 dp_2.$$
(17) $$db_1 = q\eta dp_1 - q\eta d T_1.$$
(18) $$db_2 = (1 - q)\eta dp_2.$$

Solving (15) and (17) for dp_1 and dp_2, we get :

(19) $$dp_2 = \frac{\eta - A_1}{A_2} dp_1 - \frac{\eta}{A_2} d T_1.$$

Similarly from (16) and (17)

$$(20) \qquad dp_2 = \frac{B_1}{\eta - B_2} dp_1.$$

Combining (19) and (20) and solving for dp_1 respectively, dp_2, the following expressions are obtained :

$$(21) \qquad \frac{dp_1}{dT_1} = \frac{\eta(\eta - B_2)}{(\eta - A_1)(\eta - B_2) - A_2 B_1}.$$

$$(22) \qquad \frac{dp_2}{dT_1} = \frac{\eta B_1}{(\eta - A_1)(\eta - B_2) - A_2 B_1}.$$

Substitution of (21) in (17) and (22) in (18) gives :

$$(23) \qquad \frac{db_1}{dT_1} = q\eta \frac{\eta A_1 - \alpha\epsilon}{(\eta - A_1)(\eta - B_2) - A_2 B_1}.$$

$$(24) \qquad \frac{db_2}{dT_1} = \frac{(1-q)\eta^2 B_1}{(\eta - A_1)(\eta - B_2) - A_2 B_1}.$$

3. *The Volume-Effect*

The derivatives of b_1 and b_2 with respect to T_1 as given by (23) and (24) is all that is required to establish a relation between the volume-effect and the structural coefficients of supply and demand. Substituting (23) and (24) in (3), we find :

$$(25) \qquad \frac{dq}{dT_1} = \frac{(1-q)q\eta\{\eta(A_1 - B_1) - \alpha\epsilon\}}{(\eta - A_1)(\eta - B_2) - A_2 B_1}.$$

As is easily verified, the different combinations of A_1, A_2, B_1, and B_2 appearing in Equation 25 can be written as :

$$(26) \qquad A_1 - B_1 = \epsilon.$$
$$(27) \qquad A_1 + B_2 = \alpha + \epsilon.$$
$$(28) \qquad A_1 B_2 - A_2 B_1 = \alpha\epsilon,$$

and Equation 25 takes the form of :

$$(29) \qquad \boxed{\frac{1}{q}\frac{dq}{dT_1} = (1-q)\frac{\eta\epsilon}{\eta - \epsilon}}$$

Here T_1 is measured as a decimal fraction of p_1, the initial value of which has been put equal to zero. If T_1 did previously amount to 15 per cent, the right-hand side of (29) should therefore be multiplied by $- \cdot 15$ in order to show the expected relative increase of Y's import share in X.

4. The Value-Effect

When applying formula (7) it should be remembered that p_1 and p_2 refer to prices measured after import duties have been levied. If measured at the frontier, *i.e.* less duties as happens to be the case in trade statistics, Equation 8 should be written as :

$$(30) \qquad dQ/Q = dq/q + (1-q)\{d(p_1 - T_1) - d(p_2 - T_2)\}.$$

Since $\qquad \dfrac{dT_1}{dT_1} = 1$ and $\dfrac{dT_2}{dT_1} = 0$ we have :

$$(31) \qquad dQ/Q = dq/q + (1-q)(dp_1 - dp_2 - 1).$$

Substitution of Equations 21 and 22 in 30 gives, after replacement of $B_1 + B_2$ by α :

$$(32) \qquad \boxed{\frac{1}{Q}\frac{dQ}{dT_1} = (1-q)\frac{(\eta+1)\epsilon}{\eta - \epsilon}}$$

5. The Influence of Shifts in the Supply Curves

Assuming that changes in export supply will result in a horizontal shift of the export-supply curve and that at every price the percentage change (s_1 and s_2) of supply is the same, an additional term, ds_1, should be inserted in the right-hand side of (13) and a term ds_2 in (14).

As is easily seen, this introduction of shifts in the supply curve leads to the following equation for dq/q :

$$(33) \qquad \frac{dq}{q} = -(1-q)(ds_1 - ds_2 - \eta dT_1)\frac{\epsilon}{\eta - \epsilon}.$$

6. Tariff Changes and the Level of Exports

Remembering that $\hat{m}$ has been put equal to 1 and that consequently $_0\hat{b}_1 = q$, Equation 23 reads after replacement of A_1, A_2, B_1, and B_2 by the original structural coefficients :

$$(34) \qquad \frac{\Delta b}{b_1} = \frac{\eta\epsilon}{\eta - \epsilon}\left\{1 + q\frac{\eta}{\epsilon}\frac{(\alpha - \epsilon)}{(\eta - \alpha)}\right\}\Delta T_1.$$

APPENDIX C

INTERNATIONAL TRADE OF THE BENELUX COUNTRIES *
(U.S. $M., C.I.F. AT CURRENT PRICES)

Importers	Exporters				
	B.L.E.U.	Nether-lands	Benelux	Other countries	Total imports
1928					
B.L.E.U.		103	103	786	889
Netherlands	121		121	957	1078
Benelux	121	103	224	1743	1967
Other Countries †	902	800	1702	—	—
Total Exports	1023	903	1926	—	—
1938					
B.L.E.U.		70	70	710	780
Netherlands	89		89	689	778
Benelux	89	70	159	1399	1558
Other Countries †	631	565	1196	—	—
Total Exports	720	635	1355	—	—
1955					
B.L.E.U.		375	375	2457	2831
Netherlands	580		580	2627	3208
Benelux	580	375	955	5084	6039
Other Countries †	2266	2462	4728	—	—
Total Exports	2846	2837	5683	—	—

* Sources : 1928 and 1938 :. Foreign Trade by Areas 1928, 1937–53 (OEEC, 1954) ; 1955 : Foreign Trade, Series I (OEEC, 1956).
† The c.i.f.-value of exports to other countries excluding OEEC has been estimated by adding 10 per cent to the f.o.b. value as given by trade statistics.

APPENDIX D: REGRESSION EQUATIONS FOR MAIN BRANCHES OF MANUFACTURING *

Class-number of Belgian trade statistics (1938)		Branch of manufacturing	Representative post-war period	Coefficient of correlation	Unit-value elasticity of market share (ζ)	Influence of economic conditions (γ)	Shift (βD)
1		2	3	4	5	6	7
I. Netherlands to B.L.E.U.							
XII	2	Paper	1952–56	·980	−1·44 (·36)	−1·31 (·52)	·414 (·037)
XIV	3	Glass	1950–56	·957	−1·29 (·52)	1·31 (·94)	·234 (·037)
VI	4	Wax and Soap	1953–56	·954	−·91 (·52)	−3·52 (·94)	·889 (·083)
IV	6	Foods	1952–56	·860	−·88 (·50)	−1·69 (·61)	·330 (·066)
XV	9	Metals	1951–56	·910	−·84 (·18)	−1·52 (·69)	·156 (·042)
V	11	Chemicals	1953–56	·868	−1·33 (·21)	1·31 (·50)	·172 (·052)
VII	12	Leather	1952–56	·660	−1·22 (·46)	−3·49 (1·06)	·351 (·136)
XVII	13	Transportation Equipment	1953–56	·898	−·79 (·28)	−4·76 (2·01)	·557 (·144)
X	14	Wood	1952–56	·914	−1·43 (·22)	−1·31 (·84)	·751 (·136)
XVI	15	Machinery	1954–56	·970	−·53 (·14)	−2·74 (·35)	·310 (·029)
VIII	16	Textiles	1952–56	·980	−·10 (·27)	−2·02 (·58)	·594 (·104)
II. B.L.E.U. to Netherlands							
		Iron and Steel	1952–56	·946	−1·02 (·35)	−2·83 (·64)	·342 (·035)
		Machinery	1952–56	·971	−·96 (·38)	1·41 (·35)	·242 (·078)

* Standard errors are given by the figures in small type below each coefficient.

APPENDIX E: A CROSS-SECTION ANALYSIS FOR
121 HOMOGENEOUS PRODUCTS

1. Selecting the Sample

Actually, the term 'homogeneous' implies a gross overstatement. As used here it merely indicates that, wherever possible, the sample includes only the narrowest categories of products as found in trade statistics. The design of the sample is as follows :

(i) To begin with, any category is accepted that according to the finest classification of B.L.E.U. or Netherlands trade statistics of 1938 or 1955 for at least one of these years surpassed a certain limit in one of the two countries.[1]

(ii) Rejected from this sample are those categories which still were subjected to trade restrictions (some agricultural products and coal) in 1955.

(iii) Likewise rejected are the categories for which it is impossible to obtain comparable figures of the other partner country in 1938 (in 1955 both parties used essentially the same S.I.T.C. classification) or where differences between the 1938 and the 1955 classification rules out any link.

(iv) Finally, in order not to reduce unduly the number of observations, instead of discarding non-comparable categories of minor importance, in a number of cases two or more categories are combined.

In this way a 'sample' of 121 more or less homogeneous products is obtained. Nevertheless important elements of heterogeneity are still present as is shown by a standard deviation as high as ·31 of the relative price-differentials in mutual trade (see Section V and Graph III). Further, it should be noted that the method of selection is certainly biased in the direction of the more important items of trade. This bias is, however, mitigated, for a category, that is selected because of its surpassing the 20 million francs boundary as set for B.L.E.U. exports in 1955, may still remain well below the other three limits of acceptance.

Finally, the percentage of total Dutch exports (excluding coal) thus covered amounts to 54·8 per cent in 1938 and to 48·5 per cent in 1955. Excluding the agricultural and mineral items of the sample, the coverage of corresponding total industrial exports is 52·0 per cent in 1955.

2. The Choice of the Variables

In order to analyse the direct influence of the removal of tariffs on intra-bloc trade, a reduced form relation, such as Equation 35 in Appendix

[1] Limits as actually used :

	B.L.E.U.	Netherlands
1938 :	5×10^6 frs.	3×10^5 Dfl.
1955 :	20×10^6 frs.	1×10^6 Dfl.

B, is used. Since trade for each separate item is measured in physical units the spurious influence of quality changes on unit-values is avoided.

The regression equation tested has the following shape : [1]

$$(1) \quad \frac{\Delta b_I}{\frac{1}{2}(_o b_I + _t b_I)} = -\rho \frac{_t T_I}{100 + \frac{1}{2} _t T_I} + \beta \frac{\Delta \tilde{b}_I}{\frac{1}{2}(_o \tilde{b}_I + _t \tilde{b}_I)} + \gamma \log \ _o \tilde{b}_I + \kappa.$$

By expressing rates of growth in this way, infinite values of the variables, due to zero-exports in the base year, are avoided. At the same time, as is easily verified, the coefficients correspond closely with elasticities.

Since a reduced-form equation is aimed at, the introduction in (1) of a term with,

$$(2) \quad \frac{\Delta \tilde{b}_2}{\frac{1}{2}(_o \tilde{b}_2 + _t \tilde{b}_2)},$$

representing Δs_2 would only have been logical. Since, however, the classification of the greater part of the competing importers on the Belgian market after the war has been changed, the difficulties involved would have been enormous.

Similarly, as (1) is concerned with variations in b_I and not in q, an indicator for the shift in total import demand might have been expected to appear as an independent variable. One of the aims of the present study is, however, to investigate the impact of division of labour on the pattern of trade. No variable reflecting immediately the shifts in import demand has therefore been used. Instead, some experiments have been made with variables representing changes in the comparative advantage of the different products of B.L.E.U., either with respect to the world as a whole (use being made of a function of $\Delta \tilde{a}_I$), or with respect to the Netherlands (by the use of a function of Δa_I). The reasoning behind these attempts is that for categories where B.L.E.U. exports have gained considerably, this comparative advantage must necessarily hamper imports from the Netherlands. In no case, however, a coefficient with a significantly negative sign is found.

Some negative influence, however, is to be found for $_o \hat{b}_I$ — or rather log $_o \hat{b}_I$ — thus confirming the tendency towards equalization of export shares.

3. *Numerical Results*

Shifts in the supply curve, as represented by total Dutch exports, appear to be the most important factor in the rate of growth of b_I. After that come tariffs and the initial export share. The part of the standard deviation of the dependent variable as explained by these three factors is respectively 64, 17, and 14 per cent.

An indirect and certainly not conclusive opportunity of checking whether or not a value of about -2.50 can be considered as realistic is

[1] See for notation the list of symbols on p. 295.

TABLE E.1

NETHERLANDS-B.L.E.U. EXPORTS *
(109 CATEGORIES ; 1938 AND 1955)

	R	Independent variables †		
		ΔT_I	$\Delta \bar{b}_I$	$_0\hat{b}_I$
	1	2	3	4
I	·462	− 7·27 1·33	—	—
II	·727	—	·96 ·09	—
III	·754	− 3·43 1·07	·85 ·09	—
IV	·768	− 2·64 1·11	·84 ·09	− 29·95 13·08

* Since in this set of equations the log of one of the variables appears, again 12 observations, this time with initial zero-exports, had to be excluded.

† Only the relevant element of the actual variable as used in the analysis. The coefficients represent elasticities except in the case of $_0 b_I$. Figures in small type are the corresponding standard errors.

given by the residual estimate of 22 per cent for the net volume increase (see section 8.3).

Since
$$\rho \sim \frac{d \log b_I}{d \log (1 + T_I)},$$

and ΔT_I is about ·10, we find :

$$\rho \sim \frac{·097}{− ·041} = − 2·40.$$

But here, as in fiction, any resemblance might be accidental.

PART VII

REPORT ON THE PROCEEDINGS

REPORT ON THE PROCEEDINGS

SUMMARY RECORD OF THE DEBATE

BY

DOUGLAS HAGUE

FIRST SESSION

Wednesday morning, September 11th, 1957

THE DISCUSSION OF PROFESSOR
SVENNILSON'S PAPER

Chairman : PROFESSOR LINDAHL

Professor Robinson, as chairman of the programme committee, introduced the programme of the Round Table. He felt that the subject needed little apology since it was of great immediate importance at a time when many nations were considering economic integration, common markets, and free trade areas. We were to discuss the validity of arguments in favour of measures to increase the effective size of nations, and it was important to examine these. What were the real economic advantages of a large nation ? There was very little economic literature on the subject, and in the immediate post-war period many arguments of very doubtful validity had been used to justify European economic integration. The connection, if any, between size and wealth needed to be demonstrated rather more rigidly.

Professor Robinson then turned to Professor Svennilson's paper, which was the subject of the morning's discussion. Professor Svennilson had tried to answer the question : Why is the nation important in economic analysis ? His answer was that it was the unit of political authority and of central decision making. Various discontinuities arose at national frontiers, and one could divide these discontinuities into two kinds. First, there were discontinuities which could not be removed by economic policy — those arising from fundamental factors such as language, culture, or educational background. There was also the discontinuity in the sense that certain groups of people had a feeling of common loyalty, being willing to make sacrifices together or to be taxed together. These were not unchangeable discontinuities, but were equally not the direct consequence of economic policy. Second, there were discontinuities that were the consequences of institutions. Professor Robinson himself put first the currency area and the consequent existence of one banking system, a single budget and a single tax system. How far, as countries moved nearer

333

together, could they continue to have separate monetary, financial, and budgetary policies ? One of the difficulties in Europe at the moment was Germany's greater success in dealing with the problems of inflation ; the rest of Europe was under strain as a result. Could one have two budgetary and financial policies within an area that was trying to work together as a single unit ? A second group of important institutional factors lay in the labour market. Some of the obstacles to mobility were artificial, the consequence of government or trade union policy. Some were inherent in differences of language, background, and so on, and could not be wholly got over by free movement. Then came the fact that the nation was the unit of the welfare state — a term used very broadly by Professor Svennilson to include full employment and financial policy as well as social services — for differences in social security systems and the like led to a discontinuity. Finally, obstacles to the movement of goods, geographical or institutional, led to discontinuities, but this was a question for later discussion.

Professor Robinson said that the second part of the paper (pages 3 to 9) puzzled him. He shared Professor Svennilson's dislike of extreme political nationalism, but he did not know how far Professor Svennilson was trying to take us. Chauvinism was an emotive word, and we did not want to import emotion or moral judgements : we should not condemn those who regarded the nation as the unit of economic action. But what exactly was Professor Svennilson condemning ? Illiberal policies between nations ? Or the reluctance of small nations to be absorbed into super nations ? His own prejudices were in favour of the small nation. He thought it good that small groups of people with a long political tradition should have the right to make their own laws and decide on their own policy, and he would like a world where small nations could be as economically efficient as possible without having to join in vast super nations. If to want this was to dream of the past, he wanted to be persuaded that it *was* a dream. On integration, too, his prejudices were to be reluctant. Could we not have co-operation instead of absorption ? We must, however, be morally neutral and look at the problem as scientific economists.

Professor Svennilson said he would like to explain that on page 4 of his paper his intention had not been to condemn anything but merely to explain what factors lay behind modern nationalism — to show that economic nationalism was founded more on social attitudes than on politics. The ideas of the welfare state seemed to be of major importance. These ideas had perhaps emerged first where socialism was dominant but had now penetrated into most political systems and were accepted by liberals as well as conservatives — by entrepreneurs as well as by labour. He had mentioned Chauvinism in this context only to show that it was of minor importance in economic nationalism. He had not condemned it, although he was sceptical of some of its manifestations.

Professor Edwards suggested that national identity might have economic significance for two reasons. One was that, in the development of various sorts of internal service, the size of a country might be relevant in that bigness might keep costs down, as it did in big industrial plants. The second reason covered all those characteristics of nations which raised obstacles to the free movement of goods and resources. If states worked towards the freer movement of goods and money across frontiers, the significance of the nation would be reduced. Our present Conference would have had much less significance before 1914, when the general most-favoured-nation tariff policies, the gold standard, and the smaller degree of direction of investment through government policy, probably meant that there was less economic significance in the differences between big and small nations.

Professor Scitovsky fully agreed that both national loyalties, and an increased understanding of economic processes, might be serious obstacles to economic integration of the West European type. An integrated capital market was needed to allow the transfer of one country's savings to help in developing resources in another. There would probably be much opposition to this, as there would to a co-ordinated employment policy. For example, a local depression in the Detroit area could be met by concentrating orders there and one would find no opposition from, say, New England ; but there might be objections to such anti-depression measures on an international scale.

M. Duquesne stressed the importance for economic integration of cultural links and the discontinuities arising from them. Since cultural ties were so important, he could not conceive of a process of integration which took place without some *rapprochement* of cultural backgrounds. Integration might be easier if it started with the regional integration of countries with similar cultural backgrounds. M. Duquesne also wondered how far the national welfare state could enter an integrated area without having to abandon some of the prerogatives of a state. Was a 'middle of the road' solution possible ? Or was a super-national welfare state needed ? Some experience had been gained during the negotiations for the European Common Market, but different methods of financing the welfare state might cause problems. Were there any ways of financing it without causing distortions ? M. Uri had shown that two kinds of distortion were possible. First, there could be a general distortion where all prices in a country were raised by the same percentage. Such differences in price levels need not be insuperable obstacles, for they could be corrected by changes in foreign exchange rates. It followed that big differences in general tax rates need not prevent integration. But there might be specific distortions ; for example, if state A decided to tax a particular commodity only, the production of that commodity might then have to be abandoned, and this could lead to serious dislocation.

Professor Baudin had found that one point in the programme shocked his Cartesian mind. The title of the Conference was 'The Economic Consequences of the Size of Nations'. The word 'nation' had been defined, but not so 'size'. Everyone had defined size in a different way ; not only were there different interpretations of the word, but there were different categories of thought. Size for some authors meant geographical extension — area (Professor Jöhr for instance). Others insisted on demographic aspects ; a nation was large or small according to its population. Again, there was a combination of area and population — some authors made a direct link (Professors Kuznets and Marcy) — and this was an oversimplification. The size of market was also used, for instance by Professor Fabricant, and the nation's purchasing power by Professor Scitovsky and Dr. Marsan. *Per capita* income and even the 'development potential' of a country were used. These were different criteria and led to the paradoxical conclusion that Brazil and Australia were small countries.

Qualitative factors, like psychology and prestige, elements outside the field of economics, were used by two authors (Professors Leduc and Triffin). Hence came the idea that the size of a nation might indicate its ranking among a group of nations, or a criterion of dependence. There were, therefore, many ideas, and this without mentioning the difference between real and imaginary size — the size a nation was and the size it thought it was. Professor Baudin felt it essential to reach agreement on definitions, especially because of the problem of French translation. In French, according to *Littré's Dictionary*, the meaning of 'dimension' was merely a physical dimension, yet in Professor Fabricant's paper we met the phrase 'the dimension of size' — which seemed untranslatable. All this was very complicated indeed. What did we mean by size ? A debate on this would clarify our future discussions.

Professor Robinson accepted Professor Baudin's criticisms. In formulating the problem for discussion, the programme committee had been thinking largely but not exclusively in terms of population. For example, what were the advantages of being a member of a country of 150 million people rather than 50 or 15 million ? He did not think one could usefully discuss income per head without also considering area per head.

Professor Leduc agreed that we had to decide what we meant by 'nation' and what we understood by 'size'. First, 'nation'. Was a nation defined by its population, its territory, and the existence of a government taking basic decisions on economic life ? He thought we were thinking in institutional and juridical terms and that most people would agree on this. Within a nation, there had to be sufficient unity to allow the adoption of certain policies, for example monetary, tariff, immigration, or welfare policies. We might, therefore, define a nation in terms of the institutional mechanism which allowed it to live in a given area. Clearly, the United States was a nation, so were Brazil and Belgium. But what happened when one went down the scale ? Andorra was perhaps a nation, but he was less sure about Monaco ; and what of San Marino ? Yet even if one concentrated on the clear-cut cases, it was evident that the economic action of nation states was not unfettered. There were differing degrees of economic domination and dependence, for example, between Italy, Ghana, and Morocco. Nor was the system static ; the pattern was always changing.

Then there was 'size'. Could we agree on the criteria by which to measure size ? Population was not a very satisfactory criterion since it might be arbitrary. Should we take population, plus geographical size, plus certain economic criteria — for example, average *per capita* income ? But then Switzerland and Belgium would be large and Brazil small, and he was not at all happy about this. Perhaps we needed a mixture of criteria.

Professor Weiller still wondered what really was meant by 'size of nation'. In the nineteenth century, the main factor was supposed to be the density of population. But some countries with a low population density, like the United States, had had two major advantages. First, they had had a great deal of disposable land so that costs were low in agriculture and consequently in industry ; a distinction should be made between output per man-hour and output per square mile. Second, from a dynamic viewpoint this had been linked with the advantages of an *increasing* population — and, for a long time at least, the availability of land had allowed immigration.

Professor Jöhr warned against giving undue weight to definitions. The nation was the unit of political decision — unitary or federal. There was no need to define size but we must consider all these aspects. The decisive thing was to compare the concept of the region with that of the nation. Even if there were free movement of goods, capital, and labour under a gold standard, the nation would still have considerable importance in providing for the common defence, law, and so on. This could be shown by differences between Liechtenstein and Switzerland. For traffic in goods and capital, there were no frontiers between Switzerland and Liechstenstein, but they had quite different tax systems and Liechstenstein had no army, which had important consequences.

Professor Hoffmann wondered if one should introduce a distinction between static and dynamic aspects. If the size of a nation were defined by income per head, the difference between India and Switzerland was important. How could the size of a nation be changed ? By creating the necessary conditions of growth within a country, or by integration. Integration should mean a common economic policy, pursued by common economic institutions, between different nations and creating a new 'internal market'. Under the hypothesis that growth conditions were more favourable within the new common market than within each separate country before, integration was a way of increasing income per head. Co-operation merely on the basis of a liberal policy between nations did not necessarily have the same effect.

Professor Stigler suggested that, while Professor Svennilson's emphasis on deliberate political action was proper in the short run, in the long run more emphasis should be put on transportation and on the movement of people. In 1850 the United States did not have an effective economic unity. Transport costs were high and there was not one single market. The price of wheat in some areas was three times as high as in others and income differences between states were two or three times as big as they were now. Progress in transport had made this geographically large area a real unit; the same progress might have reduced the advantages of small nations in developing both goods and ideas.

Professor Vakil wondered how far the concept we were discussing was applicable to under-developed countries. Most of the illustrations given so far were taken from developed areas. In South-East Asia there were both big and small countries. Ceylon was small and India big from the point of view of area, but population density must surely be considered. Again, most of these countries had only recently become independent and he suggested that they were not yet *established* nations in the Western sense. They lacked some of the essentials of nationhood, and were still struggling to become real nations, with many unfamiliar problems arising in the process.

If one applied the concept of size of nation to these countries, one found that they were simultaneously struggling to achieve political and economic nationhood as soon as possible and impatiently trying to skip not decades but centuries of progress. In that process of economic growth under political difficulties, many different forces worked against integration, for the process of integration ran counter to many of the new forces acting in these developing nations.

Professor Patinkin said he would comment on page 10 of Professor Svennilson's paper, where it was argued that there was a budget restraint from an international point of view which did not exist within the nation. Did this mean anything in real terms? In such terms a restraint must exist even within a nation. Perhaps what Professor Svennilson had in mind was the absence of a restraint in *monetary* terms — due to the ability of a nation to print domestic money, but not foreign exchange.

Dr. Rothschild made three points. For him, Chauvinism meant a very particular kind of nationalism, one which was imperialistic and unwelcome. Perhaps Professor Robinson's kind of nationalism — group loyalty — had economic advantages, as every form of decentralization had. It meant that people could understand economic policies. On definitions of size, Dr. Rothschild agreed with Professor Jöhr that we should not give these undue emphasis, but we should certainly not include economic aspects in size; if we did, we began to beg the whole question which the Conference hoped to solve, namely whether size had economic consequences. Finally, Dr. Rothschild doubted whether Professor Svennilson was right (on page 12) where he suggested that large countries had many different exports. The more *industrialized* countries had more exports, but this was not a function of size, it was a function of development.

Professor Scitovsky wanted to emphasize Professor Svennilson's point that the risk factor made the size of a nation relevant. The riskiness of selling in foreign markets was the most important risk in an age when changes in import quotas and foreign exchange rates were frequent. Mass production depended on a certain stability of market, and this might be a factor determining in part the efficiency of large and small nations. It was linked to what Professor Robinson had said about the nation as possessing its own monetary unit, exchange rate, and so on.

Hague — Summary Record of the Debate

Professor Svennilson, closing the discussion, said the purpose of his paper had been to draw attention to the relativity of the concept of a nation. The debate had further illustrated this. The concept of a nation depended partly on internal conditions and partly on the external framework. There were possibilities of federation, of varying degrees of development towards a welfare state, and of greater and less internal integration. The external *milieu* made the nation a very relative entity, one reason being the mobility of factors of production. As Professor Stigler had pointed out, improvements in transport altered the relative position of each nation. Among various discontinuities at national frontiers, he agreed with Professor Robinson that the currency question was the most important, and, as Professor Robinson had also pointed out, this currency position had its consequences for the budget and for the tax system. A nation must pay its way.

Professor Patinkin had pointed out that the importance of the budgetary position depended on capital movements. What distinguished relations between the areas within a given nation from relations between different nations, was differences in credit facilities and in the freedom of movement of capital. At present, with little international capital movement, the balancing of external accounts was important.

Professor Svennilson felt that we should come to no real conclusion on whether large or small nations were the more efficient. Our answer would be that it depended on internal and external factors, and that one could not judge large and small nations in isolation. There were three possibilities for proceeding. First, one might use models of isolated nations and discuss their efficiency. This was not a fruitful approach. Second, one might adopt a static approach, and take nations just as they were with their internal structures and their international setting, and compare their efficiency. Even there any conclusion would be difficult. Finally, the most useful approach was the dynamic one ; how did big and small nations react to changes in the internal and external conditions for development ? Perhaps the Conference would find it most useful to alternate between these three possible approaches.

SECOND SESSION

Wednesday afternoon, September 11th, 1957

THE DISCUSSION OF DR. FABRICANT'S PAPER

Chairman : PROFESSOR ROBINSON

Professor Scitovsky, opening the discussion, said he felt too much in agreement with the paper to lead an attack on it. He was in sympathy with Dr. Fabricant's concern over the shortage of statistical data and over the spuriousness and complexity of the statistical techniques concerned, but he did not share his dislike of output per man-hour as an index of efficiency. Dr. Fabricant had suggested using an index of the output of labour plus other resources. Clearly, if one took all the resources used the result would be a tautology. He preferred a measure of the output of one resource only, and if only one were taken, then that should be the worker. We were vitally concerned with standards of living, which were very closely correlated to output per man, but we should remember the importance of other resources. The distinction between natural resources and reproducible capital was important ; the great riches of the United States in terms of natural resources must represent a great part of the explanation of higher output per man in the United States.

As for intangible capital, he would be even more cautious than Dr. Fabricant. He had no idea how to measure it. He had once tried to list French scientific inventions, later exploited not in France but in other countries, inventions which ranged from tar dyes to frozen foods in plastic bags. No doubt these were minor instances, but were we really sure that the intangible capital represented by scientific knowledge was greater in the United States than elsewhere ? On the economies of scale, Dr. Fabricant had concentrated on the scale of output of the industry and had shown that there was a low correlation between scale and costs. He could see the importance of this, but he suspected that the individual plant was really more important than the industry, especially for achieving maximum production. This had not been considered. Nor was even the plant everything ; the scale of the individual investment in a co-ordinated plant was also important. If investment took place in small steps, a large factory might be built piecemeal and hence fail to exploit economies of scale.

Dr. Fabricant had complained that factor mobility in the United States was high, but not so high as it might be. As a European, Professor Scitovsky felt that labour mobility in the United States was already very high. This was a question of relative versus absolute standards. On the question of greater variety or greater standardization, Dr. Fabricant had suggested that they were irreconcilable opposites. He did not agree. There was a larger number of industries in the United States than in other countries, but within each American industry there might well be greater standardization. Moreover, there was more information on standardization than Dr. Fabricant had suggested. European productivity centres had collected much data on, for example, nuts and bolts and consumer goods, and all of this showed greater standardization in the United States than in Europe. He sympathized with Dr. Fabricant's argument that the greater standardization in the United States had been made possible because the rapidly increasing population led to a high proportion of *nouveaux riches* with more flexible tastes. Consequently, manufacturers rather than consumers held the initiative in planning new products.

Dr. Fabricant had said that Americans were easily persuaded to use the most economically produced and effective goods. This was a good point, but it was also a treacherous one. If it were true that consumers could be persuaded easily by advertisements, this automatically raised various problems in welfare economics. Finally, there was the greater enterprise of Americans, which could perhaps be equated to greater ruthlessness in competition. Did this mean that in order to obtain more rapid economic progress we had to pay a price through more ruthless competition ? If so, it would be a high price in social terms.

Dr. Fabricant pointed out that he had tried to list questions and to indicate some of the reasons why he thought that they were questions. If asked whether the United States was rich because it was big, he would answer 'yes and no'. 'Yes', because he thought size was one factor. 'No', because there were other things which were more important, for instance, the availability of natural resources. Nor was it only a question of how size led to efficiency. One needed also to know the reasons for the large size of the United States ; we must explain its population size as well as its income per head.

On particular points made by Professor Scitovksy, he came first to the question : How did we measure efficiency ? In the paper, he had merely been raising the point, and he could quite see that there was a considerable advantage in using output per head — or output per man-hour. He agreed that output per head was correlated with output per man-hour, but we still had to take account of such things as capital input. What determined output per man-hour ? Natural resources, reproducible capital, and intangible capital, all more or less distinguishable, were involved. Natural resources here meant no more than *potential* resources. Such resources were man-made quite as much as, say, steel ; the coal now being mined was there in 1491 and yet in a way it was not. How to measure intangible capital was, of course, a major question, but so was how to measure tangible capital. Efforts to measure tangible capital on Goldsmith's basis had been worthwhile, but in measuring intangible capital should we, in Professor Scitovsky's example, credit the French inventors with having produced the intangible capital ? His own view was a more or less Schumpeterian one, that we should regard invention as only the first step in developing technology. Dr. Fabricant also wondered whether national product per head might be a good measure of efficiency ; national income per head, which took account of terms of trade, had some attraction too. Also, a country was somehow efficient if it *generated* capital, but this did nothing to simplify the problem. There was the question of timing. In the past the United States had somehow created the capital which it was now using. He agreed that capital and labour were both very mobile in the United States, but how much more than in other countries ? We wanted even greater mobility, and must apply absolute, not relative, standards.

Dr. Fabricant said it was true that statistical work on the relative efficiency of industries in the United States and in Britain had been done, but it was insufficient. Nothing at all had been done on individual firms and plants. He regretted, for example, that neither Frankel nor Rostas gave information on the absolute size of the industries which they studied, except in unusable terms. Industry A might be three times as big in the United States as it was in Britain, and yet remain minute. Absolute size had to be considered too. A study of the relative efficiency of different industries in different countries ought also to use averages over longer periods than a single year, and to include more countries, for example, Canada. Output per man-hour should be defined more exactly in terms of quality, variety, and so on, and local industries needed studying more explicitly.

Professor Jewkes suggested that in trying to find complicated reasons for differences in efficiency we should not overlook simpler explanations. If one said that output per head in America was higher than in Britain because Americans worked harder, there was at least a possibility that this was true. On measurements of labour mobility, Professor Jewkes felt we must not forget that there was a great deal of mobility in the United Kingdom and that this was one of the results of an inflationary situation. But up to now it had been short-distance mobility. Finally, we had been warned that to say that the United States was large and also efficient left us with no way of deciding between two possibilities. Was America efficient because it was large ; or was it large because it was efficient ? But even if it was more efficient now than in the past, the fact remained that when it was small it had possessed inherent powers of expansion. It followed that it was extremely difficult to separate cause and effect. Dr. Fabricant had argued that output in America was high because America was more competitive. Was this true ? Was a competitive economy really more efficient ? Up to 1936, German industry had been astonishingly efficient, yet it was an industry of large units with a highly monopolistic structure.

Professor Stigler contended that it did not matter whether one used a measure of efficiency which was itself inefficient, provided one took all other factors into account. For instance, one could use the area of an attractive woman which was not covered by clothing as a measure of the temperature, instead of using a thermometer. What he did not like was a measure which only considered the output of one factor — labour.

Professor Scitovsky held that efficiency should be defined from a normative point of view. If we wanted to show increasing efficiency, which index would show it best ? If we were concerned with the standard of living, surely output per man was what we wanted to study ? But if we then discovered that in the United States there was a higher output per worker, we must proceed to consider all the possible explanations of this and we could not do that by our choice of a measure.

Professor Jewkes wondered why only one index was suggested. Why not use one index of output per man and another one of output per unit of capital ? The results of the two could then be compared.

Professor Scitovsky agreed, but he would still say that in the United States one reason for the higher output per worker was the greater amount of capital used.

Professor Jöhr noted that Professor Fabricant had said that we should measure output per worker in a country taking into account the input of raw materials and the amount of land at its disposal, so that we knew what each country had available and could measure how well it had done with the resources it possessed. This could not be achieved by just measuring output per head ; we must measure output per unit of the original factors of production, which would require some common denominator of labour, land, and raw materials. If such a revised basis could be constructed and were accepted, Switzerland, with its great scarcity of land and raw materials, might come out even better than the United States.

M. Duquesne wondered when American industry had become more efficient. Work had been done by V. Paretti and G. Bloch [1] to compare the rate of expansion of output per head in manufacturing industries in OEEC countries and in the United States. If we excluded the war and immediate post-war years, the rate of expansion was similar. It followed that part of the difference in efficiency between Europe and the United States was a result of time lost during the wars and not made up in times of peace ; the rest sprung from the initial difference of efficiency in 1913.

Professor Robinson suggested that this was a crucial point. When *did* the American economy become more efficient ? Rothbarth's famous article had shown that the American economy was the more efficient as far back as the 1880s, long before it embarked on large-scale output of manufactures. This led one to think that we should perhaps look to simpler explanations, as Professor Jewkes had suggested. Perhaps one of these explanations was not the scale of output in the United States, but the American worker's energy, rhythm of work, and so on.

Dr. Fabricant thought we should add to this some truly economic factors, for instance, the ruthlessness of competition. This was fostered by Congress, and by the state governments before 1890. It would be very interesting to discover the comparative efficiencies of the United States and the United Kingdom in 1850. He himself would guess that national income per head in the United States was higher than in Europe by 1870, and that it might even have been higher in the years 1800–50. For the higher standard of living in America was surely one of the reasons why migrants went there. A good deal of American national income in those years went into investment and this did not get into the ordinary figures. The early history of farming in the United States showed how much income came from what seemed to be increasing land values, but was really the ploughing back of capital. On the check to European growth caused by war, this was really Professor Jewkes' point — the need to look for simple factors. On the other hand, war was not really a simple explanation. How many years did the effects of the Second World War cover, and what about other periods which were unnatural ? The 1930s was one. Again, America herself had had wars, like the Civil War. We

[1] 'Industrial Production in Western Europe and the United States 1901 to 1955', in *Banca Nazionale del Lavoro Quarterly Review*, No. 39, Dec. 1956 — Rome.

certainly ought to look for simple explanations, but to establish their importance was a quite different problem.

Professor Scitovsky pointed out that the Rostas comparison had a forerunner. Taussig in the 1920s had compared productivity in Britain, America, and Germany in 1912 and in the late 1890s. This study had shown the same disparity then as Rostas had established for 1936.

Professor Weiller thought M. Duquesne's point raised the question of spatial and temporal discontinuities : war was clearly a discontinuity through time. In Professor Svennilson's paper we had seen that at a later date *spatial* discontinuities for Western Europe were reduced by world trade. On the other hand, alterations in political and economic structures also caused *temporal* discontinuities which might bring 'structural' disequilibrium in world trade. Our evaluation of the 'steady progress' in small and large nations was linked with such a question.

Professor Ellis thought that the distribution of leisure between the United States and the United Kingdom was important. The services of housewives were not included in the Gross National Product, though those of domestic servants were ; yet the real effort of housewives must show in the economy somewhere. Again, there was the age of retirement. In America, it was a disgrace and not an ambition to retire early, in Europe, it was the opposite. Similarly, holidays were less frequent in the United States than in Catholic countries. Do-it-yourself was another factor. It meant the disappearance of leisure, but made a contribution to the economy by increasing the real flow of goods and services. These differences in attitudes to leisure were not correlated in any way with the size of the nation.

M. Duquesne summed up this part of the discussion by saying that we seemed to agree that American superiority went back a very long way, and that the over-population of Europe in the early nineteenth century probably gave rise to this early advantage.

Professor Gudin said he would take advantage of the presence of experts and ask for an explanation of the Leontieff paradox — namely that the United States imported capital-rich goods and exported labour-rich goods. He himself had suggested to Leontieff as an explanation that one million dollars worth of machinery in the balance sheet of an American corporation was probably more efficient than in Europe because of the more rapid amortization and replacement of the obsolescent equipment in the United States.

Dr. Fabricant said we were now back at the problem of how to measure physical capital. Professor Leontieff had only considered information about American capital and had not taken account of capital embodied in goods imported into the United States.

Professor Hoffmann thought that in considering these productivity problems, we discussed global figures too much. If we compared the productivity structure within countries, we should see that this structure was independent of the size of nation ; the ratio of productivity between industries — textiles, chemicals, metals, cars — remained relatively stable. If there was this tendency towards constancy that was independent of size, we should exclude it.

Professor Stigler suggested that in the United States size and efficiency might follow a chicken and egg sequence. Were there economies or diseconomies of size ? This was the Conference's problem. It was not an insoluble problem in principle though it might be in the present state of the available statistics. If one related output to the amount of labour and other resources used in various countries, it should be possible to estimate the extent of increasing or decreasing returns.

Professor Robinson explained he had just finished a research project in Cambridge, during which he had tried to get round differences of size and of product by studying the experiences of several big international companies producing identical goods in different countries. The results showed a cost advantage of about 1·5 : 1 in favour of the United States and not the 2·8 : 1 which Rostas had shown. He had also found that much of the explanation of this difference lay outside of pure scale and of differences in technical methods. Over the whole of industry there was a big unexplained advantage to the United States, which seemed to arise from the fact that the average American firm was more efficient (with identical equipment and scale) than comparable firms in the United Kingdom or in other European countries. Was this part of the answer ? He also believed that Dr. Fabricant had left out the biggest thing of all — differences in natural resources — and was taking just a little too much credit for the ability of the United States to invent natural resources. There were far greater difficulties in mining coal in Europe than there were in America. We must surely consider natural resources more carefully than Dr. Fabricant had done.

M. Duquesne wondered whether there was a significant difference, in Professor Robinson's study, between the size of the European establishment and that of the others.

Professor Robinson replied that in most cases differences in size were not important. His experience was that most of the plants displayed some differences of scale but small differences in method. There was a number of cases where the large plant differed from the small in that it multiplied the same basic processes rather than showed fundamental differences of method. For instance, razor blades were made by an almost standard method, and production was increased just by installing more machines of the same kind, though there were some small economies in administration when output rose. Professor Robinson felt that too much of modern economics was written in terms of the abnormal conditions of the motor industry.

Professor Scitovsky said that a case study had apparently shown that an American oil refinery in England, managed by Americans, was more efficient than an identical British plant with British managers. One of the reasons adduced for this was the greater ease of communication between labour and management at all levels in the American company.

Report on the Proceedings

Professor Verdoorn suggested that differences in production methods between America and Europe lay not so much in the size of the firm or of the plant, as in the length of the individual production run. The diversity of technical processes carried out in the same plant was much smaller in America than in Europe. Apart from static effects on productivity, the length of the production run also had a dynamic influence. According to the 'learning' or 'manufacturing progress' curve, productivity per man-hour increased as a function of total accumulated output since any process started. Many processes showed a 20 per cent gain in productivity if accumulated output doubled. The diversity of processes in an American plant was much smaller than in Europe so that, even with equal total output per firm, the length of the average production run would be much greater. This fact might well account for a considerable part of the differences in productivity.

Professor Baudin recalled that almost all productivity missions had blamed low French productivity not on the size of the firm but on the way in which workers behaved and thought. American experts in a Belgian mine had tried to raise productivity by American methods and had failed. It followed that in some contexts behaviour, and not size, was the critical point in determining economic effects and that was a psychological factor.

M. Duquesne said that, although Professor Baudin was right, in this Belgian case the failure was due less to psychology than to the different physical conditions under which coal-mining took place.

Professor Edwards suggested that perhaps people in the United States were allowed to work harder. If competition did have any effect in America, it was not only through business laws. In the American economy it was easier to change processes to suit the changing scene. New centres of production and population had been appearing and these had destroyed business and labour monopolies. The law had helped and supplemented this work, and where America had failed to prevent monopolies, the failure had been only local. There were apparently some 1400 price rings in the United Kingdom, and he thought it would be hard to find so many in the United States ; they were so much more open to attack. This had been true until recently on the labour front as well. Much of America's productivity existed because people had been allowed to be very productive.

Professor Leduc wondered whether American economists would not agree that one major reason for the greater efficiency of the American economy was that, for psychological reasons, inefficiency was not tolerated but was pitilessly crushed. Yet in a country like France, inefficiency was quite respected, if not positively encouraged. It was considered with favour by trade unions and by the government, for the French liked what was small and disliked what was large, and it was therefore thought to be in bad taste to try to lower costs and push less efficient firms out of business. It was better to help them to continue. The newcomer was pushed out if possible, but once he was in, everything was done to help

346

him to stay in. There were psychological reasons for these non-competitive features of French industry.

Professor Weiller had one small point of difference with his colleague. Since past and present records suggested that the average was very often not so bad, he would like to pay tribute to those who had contributed to the increase in the *general level of productivity* in France. There had been considerable productivity increases in the 1890s and the 1920s, as well as in the years since 1945. A comparison between different parts of the country showed great *regional disparities* ; for example, there was a considerable contrast between the North and South-West. One had to remember the French attachment to the established way of life, which might be one of the mitigating factors calling for tolerance over the alleged inefficiency of the South-West.

Professor Robinson felt we must remember the American genius for designing simple things which were easy to make. Many goods in this world were produced on a large scale because they were cheap, not vice versa. It was the fact that American goods were cheap, and therefore suited to a large market, which permitted them to be produced on a large scale.

Professor Edwards went on to say that it was strange to American ears to hear price cutting discussed as though its chief aim was to drive rivals out. In the United States prices were cut in order to expand sales and often made room for more firms.

Professor Scitovsky pointed out that Hawtrey had written about Professor Robinson's problem. To be suitable for mass production, a product must be designed in a special way and that was impossible if products were ordered by a merchant who held the initiative. The passing of the initiative in design to the producer himself was the fundamental change needed to make mass production possible. It was interesting, for example, that when the American forces had designed munitions during the war, industry had commented that changes in design would be needed in order to make mass production possible. In America, the initiative in product design had lain with the producer for a long time.

Professor Patinkin, however, pointed to an opposite trend in American automobile production in recent years. The process of mass production was now so arranged as to allow individual requirements to be catered for by assembling standardized parts in different ways.

Professor Prest felt that once again we had paid too much attention to industry, and suggested that the efficiency of agriculture was important. Here, America was not superior to the rest of the world. Australia and New Zealand both produced wool and dairy products more efficiently than America, and the Americans kept these products out by tariffs. Why, Professor Prest asked, did the American advantages not work in this field ? Was there not the same opportunity for large-scale production and management of labour ? And if this was the case, had that fact a bearing on the issue ?

Dr. Rothschild closed the general discussion by saying that economists often spoke of the advantages for industries, themselves not large, which arose because they were in a big economy — the supply of relatively cheap machines and so on. He would have thought that this problem could be overcome for the small country by foreign trade. Going on from this, why could not research findings be made more widely available ? Was it because they had to be tailor-made ; or was it because secrecy was too important to make firms willing to share their knowledge ? If so, that was a disadvantage smaller nations could not overcome, because it meant that they could import machines, but not solutions to research problems.

Dr. Fabricant said he had started by trying to summarize what he felt and he agreed that many questions remained open. The discussion had confirmed that these questions *were* still open. We all had ideas, whether simple or complex, about the sources of American efficiency and the relative rôle of national size, but we could not claim to have any definite conclusions until we had carried out much more analytical and statistical work. We talked of competition as a factor ; the word had various meanings and we should not regard it too narrowly as mere anti-trust policy. His own opinion was still the same. If pressed, he would say that the size of the United States was one rather modest factor in explaining the high level of her national income per head.

Dr. Fabricant added that there were obstacles at national borders to the movement of machines, knowledge, money, and men. These obstacles were not insuperable, but they existed. French industry might use American machinery to make bread but it would be dearer bread. International trade could solve some problems, but not all. Size was a factor contributing to American efficiency, even if only a modest one.

THIRD SESSION

Thursday morning, September 12th, 1957

THE DISCUSSION OF THE PAPERS BY PROFESSOR JÖHR AND M. DUQUESNE, AS WELL AS THE PAPER BY PROFESSOR KUZNETS WHICH HAD BEEN CIRCULATED

Chairman : PROFESSOR BAUDIN

Professor Svennilson, who introduced the papers, began by commenting on some statistical points. First, there was the table on page 22 of Professor Kuznets' paper which tried to show that the imports and exports of small countries were more concentrated than those of the larger ones. This illustrated Professor Baudin's point about the measurement of size. Professor Kuznets had used Dr. Hirshman's indices and had chosen to introduce a dividing line at a population of 10 million ; this led to strange results, not the least being that the United Kingdom and Portugal were classed in the same group as large countries. The considerable trade of the United Kingdom meant that she dominated the group of 'larger' European countries so that an unweighted index told one little about the structure of trade. There was also a mixture of types of economy in both the larger and smaller countries, some specializing on raw materials and others on manufactures, and this affected the statistical results as well. Second, the table on page 55 of Professor Jöhr's paper was unreliable, especially in its estimates of the purchasing power of the various currencies on their domestic markets (column 2). Quite apart from the inevitable problems in calculating such figures, these were based on a Swiss budget. If one used another system of weights, the results might change. He was reminded of a study of living costs in Stockholm and Copenhagen. Based on a Danish budget, this showed that the standard of living was higher in Copenhagen ; a calculation based on a Swedish budget showed that the standard of living was higher in Stockholm! Because of this, Professor Svennilson would not be willing to draw any conclusion from the figures in column 5 unless there was a productivity difference of at least 15 to 20 points. It followed that only two countries quite definitely had lower productivity than Switzerland, namely Italy and Austria.

Professor Leduc was surprised to see the Netherlands and Portugal included among large countries. As Professor Kuznets had told us elsewhere, they numbered less than 10 million, but since Professor Kuznets was not present, we could not discuss the question.

Professor Patinkin commented on the meaning of Professor Kuznets' table. Perhaps Hirshman's study had not been using the 10 million population criterion, or perhaps it was based on 1938 when populations were smaller. So far as exports were concerned, one could take the various classifications, and ask if the grouping was meaningful. Here there were three classifications, two geographical — Europe and Latin America — and one institutional — the British Commonwealth. All three gave the same result ; all showed a higher concentration of exports in smaller countries. This was not a chance occurrence, but had a definite meaning. On the other hand, the information about imports was the opposite of what Professor Kuznets had stated in his paper. Only in one case was there greater concentration in the smaller countries. Professor Kuznets had evidence on the export side but not for imports.

Professor Robinson intervened to make it clear that Professor Kuznets' paper had not originally been written for this Conference, but for the opening of the Kaplan School in Israel. The fact that the paper had been written for an audience in Israel might well have influenced Professor Kuznets in the measure of size which he had chosen, though Professor Robinson agreed that the 10 million dividing line was far too low for our purposes and 15 million was better. We wanted to be able to regard Belgium and the Netherlands as moderately small economies. Professor Robinson suggested that the Hirshman figures of imports reflected only the imports of the primary country of importation. Where primary products were sent first to the metropolitan country and later exported across the world, they would still show as imports for the metropolitan

Report on the Proceedings

country. Yet, in many cases, goods sent from, say, the British Commonwealth to London had very different final destinations.

Dr. Fabricant suspected that in the Hirshman table the boundary was not at a 10 million population, but at that level which would divide the nations into two equal parts ; in other words, the division was at the median. We were discussing complicated matters and we needed to follow Professor Kuznets in trying multiple correlations. Here we had a three-variable scheme, but a four-variable one might be even better. Some of the indices we were dealing with were not of a type which behaved simply.

In Professor Jöhr's paper the index of industrialization (page 62) gave very peculiar results ; the United States was shown to be less industrialized than Switzerland, Belgium, the United Kingdom, and Sweden. Industrialization was a process during which the percentage of wage and salary earners in building and manufacturing increased up to a certain point and then decreased. Most industrialized countries had a smaller percentage of their labour force in manufacturing than some less industrialized countries — a process which involved the transfer of labour into the tertiary, or service, industries. Dr. Fabricant thought it was always better to use numbers, if they were reasonably precise. The 10 million line of division was, at any rate, specific. To talk of stability without implying that it meant a certain correlation coefficient was useless. We always needed some measure. For instance, the fact that the correlation coefficient for output in two successive periods was greater than 0·4 meant something. It enabled us to be sure what we were talking about.

Professor Baudin suggested that when Professor Kuznets said (on page 16) 'most of the nations that are small in population are also small in area', this was quite wrong. It was especially untrue of five countries of Latin America which had between 1 and 9 million people, and areas of 400,000 to 1,300,000 square kilometres.

Professor Jöhr explained that his collaborator Doctor Kneschaurek could not be in Lisbon because of military service. He himself was aware of the margins of error which Professor Svennilson had pointed out. We could say, however, that the welfare and productivity of Switzerland was, at any rate, not less than for other countries in Europe, and that was what was relevant for our argument. The table in question did take into account some of the peculiarities of Swiss spending habits, for example, the importance of chocolate.

Dr. Fabricant recalled that the problem of comparability had been raised when the United States Bureau of Labour Statistics tried to measure relative quantities of food consumed in various countries in the 1920s — during prohibition and therefore with no alcoholic liquor included. The conclusion seemed to be that the French were starving to death when wine was eliminated from the basic expenditure.

Professor Weiller pointed out that similar problems had faced the International Labour Office in the 1920s. Statisticians had then evolved some simple 'tricks' which meant that they were able to avoid the particular predilections of particular countries. But it was not so easy to decide whether a preference for veal rather than mutton, for example, was a matter of taste alone, or whether it reflected economic factors which showed themselves in relative prices and discrepancies in standards of living.

Professor Svennilson then turned to Professor Jöhr's welfare index in the final column of Table I which was based on Gross National Product per inhabitant. There were, of course, some fundamental problems here, for instance, how to distinguish between private incomes and gross business profits. In some countries a high share of business profits led to a high rate of savings and to rapid progress. Was this the case in Switzerland ? There were also problems in interpreting differences in personal income distribution between countries. Professor Svennilson proceeded, basing himself on I.L.O. statistics of hourly wages including fringe benefits, to give some further figures which could be compared with Table I. For 1954 (Professor Jöhr had been concerned with 1955) and with Switzerland as 100, real earnings in the same categories were 88 in the United Kingdom, 128 in Sweden, and in Italy, for industrial workers only, 73. If the purchasing power of money were taken into account, the welfare index based on *wages* was (Switzerland still 100), United Kingdom, 100, Sweden, 122, and Italy (industrial only), 98. This showed that a welfare index based on wages gave a very different picture from Professor Jöhr's. This difference might help to explain the high rate of progress in the Swiss economy.

Dr. Fabricant pointed out that these wage statistics were based on workers in manufacturing, but Professor Jöhr's figures covered the whole economy. One would obviously expect a different measure for part of the economy as compared with the whole. He thought that if one took a particular sector, college professors for example, the United States real income would be much lower than in Sweden.

Professor Svennilson replied that he had not intended to point to any very profound conclusions. He merely wanted to show that different results could be obtained by using other methods, and that these results might show that the distribution of income was different in different countries ; that might explain varying rates of growth.

Professor Jöhr said his welfare index was national income divided by number of inhabitants, and not gross national product, but Professor Svennilson's point was nevertheless important. It was quite possible that the income distribution in Switzerland might favour the entrepreneurs, and especially those with small firms.

Professor Robinson agreed that we all knew the perils of these statistics, but asked why there should be a bias *in favour* of the small nations. The general impression was that living standards in the smaller European nations were just as high as in the '50 million' nations : France, West Germany, and the United Kingdom. Could we not take the statistical difficulties as read and go on to discover the causes of the wealth and productive efficiency of small nations ?

Report on the Proceedings

Professor Svennilson then went on to his third point. Professor Kuznets had pointed out, on page 28 of his paper, that because of smaller populations and closer internal ties, small nations could more easily make the social adjustments needed to take advantage of the possibilities of modern technology and shifting market conditions. It might, however, be more important for their social flexibility that they were more specialized, that therefore their foreign trade was more important and that consequently they were forced to adjust by international competition.

If one looked at particular cases, it was clear that, having few natural resources, the Swiss had concentrated on developing specialized skills and on building up capital — intensive industries which did not use mass production. Similarly, Belgium depended on a favourable geographical trading position and had specialized on the simple transformation of imported raw materials. Sweden had resources of forests and iron ore and on these had based manufacturing industries which enjoyed comparative advantages. All these economies had a high share of international trade. This meant taking great risks, and all had suffered in the 1930s from growing protectionism in other countries. These countries had shown flexibility, but perhaps not because of their social structure. The main explanation might be that since so much of their output was exported they had been forced to make changes.

Professor Hoffmann wondered if we should expand our view to cover the whole world. He agreed that the larger a market was, the higher, in a general sense, was the degree of specialization. This might be correct, but the actual situation depended on the structure of the whole economy, and we must remember the greater importance of agriculture, and the consequently lower incomes, in other parts of the world. Our comparisons here were between countries in the same region. Flexibility in agricultural economies was necessarily very much lower, and that was the reason why many under-developed countries had problems. Flexibility in turn was low *because of* low productivity. We should bring, say, Latin America into our discussion.

Professor Patinkin said that the question whether specialization in foreign trade was a function of size was being considered in a study that was being carried out at the Hebrew University by Dr. Micha Michaely. The International Monetary Fund statistics of foreign trade had been broken down into 150 categories. Nations had been classified as large or small on the 10 million basis, and as developed or under-developed countries on the basis of a $300 *per capita* income. The study covered 44 countries which carried on 80 per cent of world trade. The conclusion was that, if one took all the large countries together and all the small countries together, there was not much difference between the concentration of exports in the large and in the small countries. The classification meant that one was taking under-developed and developed countries together in each group, and their characteristics cancelled out. But differences did appear if one distinguished between developed and under-developed countries. Among the large developed countries, there was a much smaller index of concentration for exports ; the concentration on commodity categories was twice as great in the small developed countries. On the import side, the difference was not significant, the index of concentration for large countries being only slightly smaller. With under-developed countries, there was a higher index of concentration for the exports of larger countries than for smaller ones, though the difference was not great. This seemed to indicate that the distinction between large and small nations was only economically significant if one also distinguished developed from under-developed countries. In the under-developed countries, the imports of the smaller nations were slightly less concentrated than those of the larger ones, but the difference was not statistically significant.

Professor Weiller suggested that one might be able to interpret Professor Patinkin's statistics rather more easily if one considered the nature of the goods exported. Larger countries generally had a wide range of products ; the classification of these in the trade statistics also tended to be broken down. But the larger under-developed countries not only had fewer basic exports, there were also fewer distinctions in customs classifications. These countries produced cotton, jute, or oil, but, for instance, when that oil was refined it would yield many different products. When America had been less industrialized, she had exported oil. Nowadays, she exported a wide range of products all derived from oil, but belonging to many different product groups. He therefore suggested that it was partly because of the way products were classified in trade returns that we had diversification appearing as countries became industrialized.

Dr. Rothschild thought that the discussion had shown that size was only one factor in economic efficiency. There were others too. We had tried to start too much from an abstract idea and had taken too little trouble over laying bare actual historical and geographical conditions. Professor Kuznets had given three reasons for the slow progress of small countries. One was their smaller area and fewer natural resources. This was too abstract. It assumed that natural resources were randomly distributed over the earth's surface, and this was obviously not true. Resources such as climate, transport, and coal were highly concentrated. So when travel on the Mediterranean had been the main means of moving goods, size had been less important than being on the Mediterranean, as Venice had been. Similarly, when the Atlantic grew in importance, it was Spain and Portugal which developed. We *must* start from the actual conditions, and not from abstract ideas, for the latter led only to a list of exceptions to all the principles which we tried to establish.

Professor Robinson felt that the papers being discussed in this session were almost the most interesting of the whole Conference because they were so disturbing to one's preconceptions. If one gave a beginning student of economics the job of making a list of the conditions which, if satisfied, would keep national income per head as *low* as possible, he would give just that list of the characteristics of the Swiss economy which Professor Jöhr had given — few raw materials per head, small firms, cartels, and tariff protection. Why would the list be wrong ? Were all the things in the list, after all, the unimportant things ? What were the advantages of Switzerland ?

First, there was the high degree of industrialization. Dr. Fabricant had pointed out that Professor Jöhr's measure of industrialization was misleading ; the measure misled because it left out tertiary industries at one end and agriculture at the other. According to most English economists, the United Kingdom in the nineteenth century had had a high income per head, because there had been few people in agriculture where incomes were low. The high income per head in Switzerland occurred because agriculture, though protected, used a small proportion of national resources. What features of the Swiss economy *were* important ? The high level of education and a high level of energy and application to work ; it was these things which seemed to be the important ones.

Professor Robinson thought he would have found Professor Jöhr's paper more interesting if it had included a table explaining which were the sectors of the Swiss economy where there was high productivity. Was a large part of the national income generated in tourism ? If Swiss mountains *were* an inbuilt natural resource of that industry, then we could not, after all, dismiss the Swiss natural resources as unimportant. How much of the Swiss national income was generated in tertiary industries, in commerce and banking, and in the sale of the services of a country with a strong and sound currency ?

We had been suggesting in the Round Table, so far, that lack of diversification in a nation was a handicap. Yet an earlier generation of economists had said that a high income per head was the direct result of a high degree of specialization. Lack of diversification might well be a handicap, but in the case of Switzerland she clearly made up for this by specialization. If nations could find industries for whose output the world *would* pay, and specialize on them, all was well. Switzerland's most interesting characteristic was the remarkably high percentage of exports which some of its industries had achieved. These achievements threw great doubt on the springboard theory, that one needed a large home market to prosper in world trade. They also challenged the theory that welfare was diminished if a nation concentrated on exporting those things in which it had the greatest comparative advantage, as, for example, Lancashire cotton had done in the nineteenth century. A small, efficient country had everything to gain by doing much trade and by specializing very highly in fields where it held a comparative advantage.

Professor Edwards suggested three further reasons for the efficiency of the Swiss economy. First, the lines of Swiss specialization, especially in exports, were in products which other growing economies would use — precision instruments, etc. Second, Switzerland's long-established policy of neutrality had meant that, in time of trouble elsewhere, Switzerland attracted large amounts of refugee capital. Swiss laws made this capital welcome and gave it advantages. Third, the Swiss chemical industry had *not* started under a patent system, but by imitation of German technology that could not be patented in Switzerland. There might be less truth in the assumption that industrialization necessarily came through a patent system than was often supposed.

Professor Jöhr, replying to Professors Robinson and Edwards, said he was glad that Professor Robinson had come back to the list of factors in his paper and had put so much weight on Swiss education and Swiss energy. Yet this habit of hard work had its disadvantages — less leisure in life, and the less attractive side of the Swiss character. He was sorry about the absence of tables showing productivity indices for different sectors, or the main sources of Swiss income, but he could say a little. The 'mountains', or tourism, were not really such an important branch of the economy as foreigners usually believed. Tourism added 600 million Swiss francs (net) to the balance of payments on current account in 1956. The gross receipts from foreign tourists in 1956 were 1100 million Swiss francs, which represented only 4 per cent of national income. Tourism had been suffering ever since it reached its peak in 1913. There had been severe losses during the wars and the Great Depression, and tourism was only now starting to recover. The season, or rather the seasons, were short and productivity was not high. The net receipts for the balance of payments from transport were about 120 million Swiss francs, and from insurance business about 100 million Swiss francs. It followed that none of these could explain the high economic welfare of the Swiss economy, which must be ascribed to Swiss industry.

The tertiary sector was smaller than in either the United States or Germany, and Switzerland was more industrialized because industrial goods were her chief exports. She gained a lot by specialization, and even customs barriers did not play such a considerable rôle as they might have done with mass-produced goods. Professor Jöhr wondered whether Professor Edwards was right in saying that Switzerland exported goods to expanding economies. In the nineteenth century textiles had been her chief export and she had been slow to change to scientific instruments, watches, etc. The embroidery industry had suffered terrible losses after 1920, and his own town of St. Gallen had not yet fully recovered from the shock. So far as capital from other countries was concerned, the answer seemed to be that assured peace *was* a natural resource. Capital certainly came in. He did not know about the patents mentioned by Professor Edwards, but he did know that patents were less important in the pharmaceutical industry because development was so rapid. Research was very important and much was spent on it.

M. Duquesne said that Professor Robinson had described the problem of the small country very clearly. How could it increase income per head ? It must develop those sectors where productivity was greatest, and this meant that a small country had more important decisions to take than a large one. He agreed with Professor Robinson that the advantages of specialization must be emphasized. Why should a small country, more than a large one, try to specialize ? One reason was the uneven distribution of natural resources. For example, Kuwait *had* to develop

oil for it had nothing else. By contrast, Switzerland, Belgium, and
Sweden all specialized in types of production which were not so much
the result of the possession of natural resources, as of a careful choice
which .ad made comparative advantage pay. Admittedly, national policy
had determined the choice of textiles and basic metals for Belgium, but
some specialization had to take place one way or another ; a small country
could not have a sensible structure unless the size of its main export
industries was adequate. So, a choice of strategy had to be made and
the risk here was that the choice might be the wrong one, as perhaps in
Denmark, where there had been a conscious choice in favour of agricultural
production which now had insufficient outlets. Foreign markets were too
small, and this led back again to flexibility.

Professor Svennilson said he agreed with Professor Robinson that there
were advantages of specialization ; for instance, external economies in
the industries in which one specialized. But at the same time one lost the
external economies of having a full set of industries. There was also the
risk of setbacks in international markets. To survive in a world economy,
a country had to produce a stream of innovations in order to maintain
export activity and to allow her to produce new products as her traditional
ones were taken up by other developing countries. The pressure towards
innovation was greatest in small specialized countries with economies
directed towards exports. The overhead costs of research and development might represent a heavy burden for small countries.

Dr. Marsan felt one should not overlook the fact that the small rich
countries being studied were already far advanced in industrialization and
capital accumulation before 1914. He thought that before 1914 discontinuities between home and export markets had been much smaller
and the dangers of specializing consequently less. The minimum capital
investment for a low cost production unit was also much smaller then.
These countries had therefore been able to build on an already high level
of income and of accumulated savings. Again, Switzerland and Sweden
had both avoided many of the effects of both world wars, though Belgium
had, of course, been involved. Yet the main question was not one of the
past, but of the future. What was the outlook for the small non-industrial
country today ?

Professor Baudin thought that Professor Kuznets' paper had been very
much attacked but insufficiently defended, perhaps because he was not
present. Was this because the report had a fairly general title but was
directed to the specific case of Israel, and was Israel rather different
because it was so new ? Perhaps Professor Patinkin could help us here.

Professor Patinkin said that perhaps the fact that the paper had been
prepared for delivery in Jerusalem might explain why countries of only
10 million people were classed as large ; Israel had a population of under
2 million. Apart from this, no specifically Israeli problems were studied
in the paper. The argument was intended to be quite general. It was
too early to say whether the Israel situation reflected the influences which
Professor Kuznets had described. The first nine years of Israel's existence

had been dominated by two special events — her huge defence expenditure and the vast growth of population through immigration. Conditions in Israel were exceptional, but could they teach us anything about the general problems of new nations ?

Israel's exports were concentrated on citrus fruits, and her only real natural resource was a climate favourable to citriculture. She had no other natural resources, except perhaps the chemicals of the Dead Sea. Practically all sources of energy had to be imported, and fuel oil accounted for 99 per cent of energy used. Agriculture provided 18 per cent of her net national product. This development of agriculture came, in part, because of the tradition of agricultural fundamentalism, and, in part, because the country had to provide her basic needs for security reasons. In Israel the example most often quoted was Switzerland, with her stress on light industries that used a largely skilled labour force. Israel wanted to take advantage of the specific qualities of her own skilled labour to solve an acute balance of payments problem. The population structure had changed and the mass of migrants was now made up of Jews from North Africa, Iraq, and Iran, with lower education levels than the earlier population. The problem of education was a fundamental one, but there was a common underlying cultural tradition. There was little heavy industry in Israel ; only one automobile *assembly* plant, for example. A steel mill had been built in the last few years, but industry was mostly small scale and light.

The final part of the discussion resulted from some questions asked by *Professor Jöhr* about Belgium and the Netherlands. They had been among the richest countries in the sixteenth and seventeenth centuries. Was this early start of any importance in producing their present standards ? Were harbours and shipping important ? And had their colonies increased income per head ?

M. Duquesne replied that Belgium had been the foremost industrial country in Europe in the fourteenth and fifteenth centuries. The wars of Louis XIV initiated a long decline which brought the standard of living down throughout the eighteenth century. Belgian ports were closed to navigation, there was a situation of maritime blockade for a whole century, and on the other side of the country, France erected high tariff barriers. Only after the union with the Netherlands in 1815 did the renaissance begin. M. Duquesne thought Belgium's colonies were as unimportant as tourism in Switzerland in raising *per capita* income. Income from capital invested in overseas territories made up only 1 to 2 per cent of national income, though the income from trade with overseas territories represented 5 to 6 per cent of total national income. Income from shipping was small.

Professor Leduc thought the influence of a colonial empire was an interesting aspect of this problem. What happened when an empire was growing or shrinking ? Was it true that before the war, when the Netherlands held Indonesia, the resources originating in Indonesia represented only 6 per cent of the national income ?

Professor Verdoorn replied that there were several estimates of the percentage of Dutch national income generated by Indonesia before the war. The highest estimate was 14 per cent and the lowest 6 per cent. The 14 per cent estimate was no longer accepted since it assumed very high multipliers. A figure somewhat below 10 per cent would now seem a reasonable overall estimate. There were, however, certain disconnected advantages from the possession of colonies ; they had, for instance, stimulated the manufacture of textiles in the nineteenth century.

Professor Baudin closed the session by saying that the morning's discussion had made it clear that 'small', when applied to a nation, had no pejorative meaning, and that small nations might be among the greatest ones.

FOURTH SESSION

Thursday afternoon, September 12th, 1957

THE DISCUSSION OF PROFESSOR JEWKES' PAPER

Chairman : PROFESSOR AMZALAK

Professor Stigler (United States) introduced the paper by saying that, in a sense, the question was too easy. Of course, economies of scale were not unlimited ; only the desires of consumers and of tax-gatherers were infinite. The Conference as a whole was mainly interested in the behaviour of returns to scale for the whole economy ; but not Professor Jewkes. He had been set the task of concentrating on the firm and the plant. We needed to know two things. First, did economies of scale diminish with size and finally vanish ? Second, were there marked differences in the average costs of enterprises according to whether they were large or small ? One way of trying to answer these questions was to discover the average size of the company and measure trends in it. He himself had rejected this technique for elementary statistical reasons. All censuses had a 'cut-off point' at the bottom, for example, where the value of annual output was below, say, $5000. This meant that a large number of very small enterprises was ignored. These firms had little effect on aggregate employment, but a large influence on the number of enterprises, and that could upset results very badly. Professor Stigler had, therefore, not used the average size measure, but Darwin's method — the survivor method. One set up classes of firm, and calculated whether, as time passed, more output was coming from some particular classes. If a particular size class was producing a steadily diminishing share of output, it must be relatively inefficient. He had used this test to investigate steel, petrol, and cars in the United States, and obtained different results from those of Professor Jewkes. In each case, the smallest efficient size of enterprise had been growing in absolute terms, but the *relative* size of the efficient enterprise had not grown. He had also found that, in general, for a wide range of enterprises, there was no perceptible effect on costs from being at a rather larger or rather smaller size ; the largest efficient size was about five times the smallest. He had more confidence in this survivor technique and accepted its broad conclusion. With the possible exception of automobiles in the United States, there were no advantages from continuous expansion in the industries he had studied. In steel or petrol, a plant producing one-half of one per cent of the industry's output was sufficiently large to guarantee the lowest possible level of costs.

Professor Fabricant felt that, so far as Professor Jewkes' remarks (on page 98 of his paper) about the trend in the average number of workers per establishment in the United States were concerned, he would here read an upward trend — though not a steep one.

Professor Hague raised two points. First, there was a danger that Professor Jewkes' statistics might be used to prove whatever one wanted to prove, and there were clearly many special and particular influences which should not be overlooked. For example, in Great Britain the number of people employed in textile establishments was shown as declining between 1950 and 1955. Had the mild recession in the textile industry during that period been the reason ? Again, had the growth of the British rayon industry reduced employment in the traditional textile-spinning trades and led to a concentration on weaving, where the number of workers per establishment was relatively small ? One could find all sorts of specific reasons for not taking any particular figures too seriously.

Second, he was just a little disturbed that Professor Jewkes had paid so much attention to supply and so little to demand. He pointed to the letter from Marshall to Flux in 1896, in which Marshall had commented that even efficient firms possessed 'unexhausted internal economies'; and Marshall's 'typical' establishment produced in conditions of imperfect competition. Might there not be industries where firms were technically able to produce even more cheaply than they were doing, but could not expand their output in order to do this because the market was not big enough ? Where Professor Jewkes' conclusions were based on statistical evidence, they might very well depend on the fact that demand was very imperfect and that it was the smallness of their markets, and not purely technical factors, which limited the size of firms. One could not say, merely by looking at statistics of numbers of workers per establishment, which of these two possible explanations was the right one.

Professor Hoffmann said that West German figures for 1950–56 showed that net output per establishment and also the number of employees per establishment was increasing in all industries, but especially in auto-mobiles, chemicals, and tobacco.

Professor Robinson suggested that we should now move on from what Professor Hague had said about the logic of things to ask what was the smallest possible size at which one got reasonably near to the exhaustion of internal economies. In other words, were the unexhausted economies discussed by Professor Hague big or small ? His own view was that firms exhausted a large proportion of the major economies at a reasonably small scale of output and that they then reached a large zone of virtually constant costs. He thought this was more realistic than the textbook model where one moved rapidly from a point where one had not exhausted all major economies, to a point where one ran into diseconomies — at the optimum size of the firm. After this long 'plateau' stage, one came to the monsters which were too big to handle. He believed that the monsters *were* too big to handle, but in a changing rather than a static context. In emphasizing the logic, it was all too easy to suggest that big and important economies in production often remained to be secured by larger output. But did they? All his evidence showed that the major economies of scale, even in the large-scale industries, were exhausted at a relatively modest level of output, with, say, 4000 to 5000 people per firm. If that was so, even small countries could still sustain firms of the minimum efficient size.

Professor Scitovsky commented that it had taken economists fifty years to realize that the size of the firm was not the same thing as the size of the individual plant. There was now further confusion, and it was suggested that even the size of the plant was not the main factor, but the scale on which each single product was produced. He wondered how far one achieved production economies by producing more than one article in the same or related plants.

Professor Edwards while he was sceptical about logic, was not persuaded by experience either. The Federal Trade Commission had condemned price discrimination, but left the possibility of justification if cost figures were produced. Two things had struck him when he had been on the staff. First, even relatively specialized firms usually produced many diversified commodities in various shapes and sizes, for many types of customers. Second, they did not use their cost records to produce breakdowns of costs which would justify their prices. There was no sign that firms had figures of their own which were being currently collected and used by management. Either they began to collect such figures after the F.T.C. had challenged them to do so, or else the figures they did have were so bad, or covered such broad categories, that firms could not tell whether or not they were losing money on particular parts of the business. In one firm, the cost figures, which the controller gave to the President after a special study, showed that about 40 per cent of the firm's output was not even covering direct costs.

It was obvious that if a firm survived its total receipts must be covering its total costs, but prices might not cover the costs of each individual product it made. Some of the profitable products might be covering the losses on others, but these latter parts of the business might still be carried on because of ignorance of actual cost conditions.

Professor Robinson wondered if it helped if one tried to distinguish two sorts of production economies — first, the economies of organizing large quantities of resources ; second, the economies of long *runs* of output of a standardized product. In many cases, the latter was much more important than the former. In a large economy like the United States with, let us say, six times the real national income of the United Kingdom, it was much easier for a firm to achieve a long production run of a moderately standardized product. The problem was that, in order to organize a largish quantity of resources in a country of the size and technical development of the United Kingdom, one must have a multi-product firm. All the productivity teams since the war had contrasted the degree of standardization of product in the United States with that in Europe. We could go further. One essential feature of scale of production was that it was two-dimensional — a rate of flow over a period of time. In the United States there was a larger instantaneous flow which might continue over a longer period of time. But some of the American gains from a larger instantaneous flow might be swallowed up in more frequent changes in product, and perhaps we in Europe made up for our lower *rate* of output by producing over a longer period. Was there any empirical evidence on this particular point ?

Dr. Rothschild explained the difficulties of standardization in smaller countries. It would often be possible to produce standardized goods on the necessary scale, and yet factories did not do this. In the Austrian radio industry, for example, each factory made the whole range of sets and of components for security reasons. A second problem was, who called the tune ? In the shoe industry, for example, the producers made a number of types, and each shopkeeper seemed to have his own views, so that special shoes were made for him. Yet before the war, other countries had been able to standardize.

Professor Stigler said that the Royal Commission on Canadian Economic prospects was troubled by this problem. In textiles they were concerned about change-over costs. He wondered whether we should think of costs for the individual enterprise at various levels of output, or of those for a whole industry. People were inclined to say that the economies of scale for the whole industry were unlimited in extent, though not necessarily in magnitude.

Professor Weiller said that since we were now considering many countries, he wondered whether there was a 'demonstration' or a 'domination' effect even between small and large countries. In women's fashions, for instance, those countries which followed the leadership of another could not have the same economies of scale as the leader nation itself. For the latter built up a pattern of industry in accordance with its own situation and perhaps some types of article could not be imitated by others. There was also the dynamic aspect of change, the leading country keeping the lead in new products for quite a long period.

Professor Scitovsky pointed out that even so, in fashion goods, the economies of scale were achieved by America rather than France, in the manufacture of French model dresses in New York.

Professor Lindahl raised a new point. It was generally agreed that the optimum size of plant was soon reached, but that thereafter, under certain conditions, there might be advantages from increasing the size of the firm. He could see no theoretical limits to the size of the firm provided it had managerial capacity. But, in fact, if one inquired whether firms were trying to increase in size or whether they were satisfied with their present size, he believed that in Sweden most firms were trying to become still larger. There were no limits to a firm's *desire* to increase. All firms wanted to become large, but if one looked at the statistics, the firms in the real world were not large. So perhaps we should accept a more dynamic explanation ; perhaps we should study the lives of different firms and try to find the cause of their smallness. In many cases, medium-sized firms had been built on a basis of good, personal management. When the able manager died or retired, there might well be a decline. In giant firms, the length of life of a manager was not so important, but it still mattered in medium and small firms.

Professor Hague was pleased to hear that Professor Lindahl was becoming a good Marshallian, propounding Marshall's idea that the 'life cycle' of the one-man firm was the factor which prevented many firms from exploiting the available economies. Of course, as Marshall had admitted, the growth of joint stock firms had probably invalidated this theory. But no one had produced a new theory. It was interesting to ask whether perhaps we had not yet lived long enough with these giants to discover whether they too had a life cycle. British Celanese was one example of a giant which, now that those who had developed the firm in the 1910s and 1920s were getting older, had been bought up by Courtaulds. The giant firm was a very recent phenomenon, and perhaps only after 100 years should we be able to say for certain whether the life cycle did, or did not, apply to it — in a modified form. However, there was no doubt that nowadays many modern joint stock firms *did* become very large and also showed every sign of having long and active lives before them. It followed that, although Professor Lindahl's remarks applied to the many small and medium firms which still existed, we could not laugh off the economies of scale of the very large firm.

Two reasons why large firms might be able to survive despite their managerial problems were suggested. On the one hand,

Professor Hoffmann had visited a German steel company — the largest in Europe, despite the advantages of other countries. He had tried to analyse its organization and costs, but could not explain why the firm was so big. Perhaps it was a matter of psychology or sentiment ; it was certainly difficult to find a purely economic explanation. There was a tendency to concentration nowadays, and firms were growing, at least to some extent, independently of the economies of scale. Perhaps the answer was that the big business did not respect the economies of scale. This did not mean that firms were behaving irrationally, but only that other factors, not related to costs, were at work.

Professor Scitovsky, on the other hand, stressed the fact that the large firm could buy the best management. Was this not an important point of difference between the United States and Europe ? In the United States some firms, when they brought new men into management, paid much attention to their special abilities, but in many other countries there was greater interest in keeping management within the family or the controlling financial ownership.

Professor Robinson wondered if he could provoke Professor Jewkes. It was surely going too far to say that firms could not grow because they had not enough time to do so. The British nationalized industries, he believed, were definitely too big to be run as single organizations. In fact, they had reached the stage of having one organization nominally, but were really a group of imperfectly decentralized organizations.

Professor Jewkes commented on the first part of the discussion. If he had written this paper a little later, he would have mentioned two very interesting books on this topic — Professor Kaysen's book, *U.S. v. United Shoe Machinery Corporation*, and Professor Bain's book, *Barriers to New Competition*. The United Shoe Machinery Corporation study was especially important. That company controlled over 90 per cent of the United States market and was in a dominating position in other countries. It was technically efficient, and seemed to be the perfect case for large-scale operation. Yet Professor Kaysen had doubted whether the company was, in fact, getting economies substantially greater than those of other much smaller companies competing with it. Professor Kaysen seemed to be denying the virtues of large-scale operation, even in the kind of case which he himself would be prepared to accept. On the other hand, Professor Jewkes said he was not quite sure what to make of Bain's book. In particular, he was uncertain how reliable the evidence, in the form of answers to questionnaires, really was. How reliable were business-men's answers when they were asked how big they would like their firms to be ?

On points raised in the discussion, Professor Jewkes said that he agreed with all the statements about the difficulty of interpreting existing statistics about the size of plant. He would be quite happy if economists were to adopt a self-denying ordinance to stop using such statistics. But if they did, they would also have to drop all the old, sweeping generalizations about economies of scale. Professor Jewkes recalled that his task had not been to discuss why firms grew ; but since the point had been raised, he would say that he believed there were all sorts of reasons, quite apart from the efficiency associated with large scale. For instance, the size of firms in the British steel industry had little to do with economies of scale. Firms in many countries expanded without regard to the effects of expansion on costs, because of factors such as prestige and because of misconceptions about the true relation between size and efficiency. They also expanded in the hope of attaining monopoly power. But we must remember that all this had nothing to do with our question : how much growth was inherently associated with efficiency ? On the economies of long runs, Professor Jewkes said we needed to know much more about the cost of stopping and starting machines, of changing models, and so on. When he had been on the Cotton Working Party, figures for the Lancashire cotton industry showed that, even where fairly frequent changes were made, there was only a 5 per cent reduction in cost to be achieved through standardization of production and the consequently longer production

Report on the Proceedings

runs. He agreed with Professor Scitovsky that we should be talking about the efficiency of whole economies, but as we moved from measuring the relative efficiency of different plants to the efficiency of different economies, we were moving from the relatively simple to the undoubtedly complicated.

M. Duquesne thought it was obvious that in some cases the technique of production itself dictated a minimum efficient size of enterprise. In the electricity industry, plants must have capacities of at least 120,000 kw. hr. This minimum capacity changed as time passed, but at least we knew what it was in our time. Again, in the nitrogen industry the economies of scale were limited only by the possibility of producing sufficiently large machinery, and this became easier as new metals were developed. In other industries, size was governed by purely human factors. In the Belgian haberdashery industry, for example, bigger firms usually represented the creative work of one man. When this man died or retired, the firm declined. A study of these different firms consequently gave no clear relation between profitability and size ; the minimum optimum size was probably connected with managerial capacity, and the optimum size itself might increase with the growth of managerial capacity. Firms were frequently managed by skilled technicians who had no ability in management. The relation of this to the size of nations was that if an industry was efficient enough to expand into foreign markets, national frontiers did not represent a discontinuity any longer. But if such expansion was difficult, then national limits might restrict the size of the firm, with bad effects on productivity.

Professor Baudin broadened the discussion by pointing out that the question : 'Are economies of scale unlimited ?' should be asked about all sectors of the economy, including agriculture and commerce. So far as the scale of agricultural production was concerned, the main obstacles to expansion in France were connected with the provision of managerial skill. Supervision became difficult with a larger farm, so that the manager decided on empirical grounds where workers were becoming inefficient. There was also the problem of incurring the hostility of one's neighbours, which was likely to happen in France if one's farm became big. In commerce the factor limiting any increase in size was progressive taxation. The only way out in both sectors was through innovation and invention. In commerce there had been the introduction of 'fixed price' stores, 'open door' department stores, and so on — the results of the inventiveness of small entrepreneurs. It followed that individual inventiveness led to bigger firms and to bigger farms.

Professor Jöhr also wanted to get away from talking about industry alone. In industry the huge firm began with, say, 10,000 workers. In other sectors, the big firm was much smaller than this. In the retail trade it was often a great advantage to the consumer to be able to go into a small shop, and the same could be said of repair businesses. In building, too, there were still many small firms, though, ultimately, prefabrication might change the picture. In the hotel industry, Swiss experience showed that small hotels, with, say, sixty beds, could overcome difficulties of trade fluctuations better than bigger ones. The same might also be said of service industry, and we had already agreed that the tertiary sector would increase in importance with economic progress, and that this would tend to keep down the size of the enterprise. Could we learn something of the limits to the scale of the enterprise from this ? Could increased managerial knowledge overcome these obstacles to increased size ? And had the technique of operational research increased the possibility of efficient management in big firms ?

Professor Leduc extended what Professor Baudin had said to the industrial sector of the French economy. In some countries, some entrepreneurs developed firms beyond their optimum size for reasons which Professor Jewkes had explained. The opposite was true in France. Business-men kept their firms below the optimum size, partly because of taxation but partly because of the French aversion to bigness — to economic strength. The smallness of firms was also connected with the attitudes of entrepreneurs themselves. He had asked entrepreneurs why they were not willing to increase output if that would lower costs. They had replied that they were not interested in increasing their gains. They were doing quite as well as they wanted to do ; being larger would only mean greater strain. How could this attitude be overcome ? Could we increase competitiveness ?

Professor Robinson wondered whether these French industrialists who were content to stand still were, in fact, standing still. Most English business-men would say that you could either go forward or backward, but *not* stand still. He would say that these French industrialists were, in fact, going backwards and were complaining about the decline of business. Was it really so easy to stand still, as Professor Leduc suggested ?

Professor Weiller said he would qualify Professor Leduc's remarks, which gave a brilliant caricature of J. B. Say's entrepreneur. If this type of industrialist prevailed, it would be hard to explain French industrial progress ; it was this type of entrepreneur whom we liked to exemplify. The others were less well known to us, since they lived in climates where it was less pleasant to rest and to fish than in the South or the South-West. There was another France, producing iron and steel, chemicals, electrical goods, motor-cars, and aircraft. There was also French agriculture in the Beauce and other parts. Some of the achievements of France's nationalized industries, like electricity and the railways, were spectacular. Finally, we should not give too much prominence to Professor Leduc's 'average' industrialist ; it would be better to think in terms of a dualist economy. There was a big difference between the corporation and the family business.

Professor Marcy gave two examples of old and established French industries where small and medium-sized firms had been trying to achieve economies of scale. In the French textile industry 150 small firms had recently left the industry and their disappearance had allowed the remaining firms to increase output and improve their production methods. Similarly, in the Marseilles oil industry, instead of forty small family concerns before 1939 there were today three large ones linked in a cartel, plus some small firms which were under contract to the big ones.

Professor Jewkes, closing the discussion, said that he had expected to be more roughly treated in the discussion, but he would try now to be pessimistic about the small countries in order to link what had been said with what would be said in later sessions. The basis for his pessimism was that aircraft, chemical, and motor industries were, in the main, not found in small countries, however defined. Yet he hoped that these small countries could be economically viable and consoled himself with the importance of the Swiss chemical industry. Nevertheless, chemical industries did not generally exist in small countries.

In the motor-car industry, General Motors seemed to spread itself everywhere but did not collapse under its own weight. Perhaps the economies of scale were considerable here, or perhaps the particular form of decentralization which General Motors used was part of the explanation. But again, most small countries did not possess a motor-car industry. Finally, there was the aircraft industry. Nine-tenths of the civil aircraft in the world were produced in America. Why was this ? Technical progress in aircraft had not begun in America ; the early developments were in Italy, France, and Germany. Nor had the American aircraft industry been particularly progressive and inventive ; for instance, the jet engine was British. America was not technically dominant, and this was not a mass-production industry. How was it that the American aircraft industry was so dominant ? Here was a case where a new and important industry had established itself only in the largest countries.

Professor Jewkes hoped he was wrong about all this, and that smaller countries might at least be able to enter the production of parts for some of those articles which had to be produced on a large scale. As matters stood at the moment, however, there were grounds for pessimism.

FIFTH SESSION

Friday morning, September 13th, 1957

THE DISCUSSION OF PROFESSOR
CORWIN EDWARDS' PAPER

Chairman : PROFESSOR GUDIN

Dr. Rothschild opened the discussion. He said that although Professor Edwards had kept well within his limits of length, so much was condensed into his paper that it was hard to summarize. He would therefore confine himself to a few main points. The paper had three sections. First, an introduction where Professor Edwards showed the ambiguity of our terms ; second, an economic analysis of the interdependence of these terms ; and third, a discussion of the social effects of competition in general.

The stimulating feature of Professor Edwards' paper was that it represented a different approach to some of the problems already considered in the conference. Up to this point, the nation had been taken as a fixed and given area within which the firm's fate was mainly decided. Professor Edwards started with the international firm, and nations and frontiers now became the flexible units ; the size of the market was a function of business policy. This change occurred largely because Professor Edwards was mainly concerned with big international firms and cartels and it was vital for us to remember the important part that these played. Dr. Rothschild did wonder, however, what were Professor Edwards' ideas about the outlook for local industries in competitive environments in big and small nations respectively. International firms could certainly set up enterprises in almost every country and national boundaries played a small part. But was it not still likely that the big international firm would *begin* its life in a larger country, with the latter's sizable domestic market providing at least a starting-point ? If this were true, some of its subordinate companies would surely settle in big countries as well. Here, the discussion linked up with Professor Jewkes' earlier remark that there was no good reason why these big firms should not have subsidiaries in small countries. Even if international companies did regard the world as their playground, it might still be true that they concentrated their activities in the bigger domestic markets.

Dr. Rothschild found Professor Edwards' data on diversification surprising and very interesting. He at least had not known previously just how important diversification was, and perhaps we economists tended to overestimate the importance of specialization. If the diversified firm really was the typical firm, that fact raised many problems for economic theory, because economic analysts had usually ignored it. It was also important, as Professor Edwards had stressed, to realize that bigness was desired, not to allow economic efficiency only, but because it strengthened the firm's bargaining power and gave it the hope of earning monopoly profits. We had hitherto concentrated on the size of the firm needed for technical efficiency and had not given sufficient attention to these other benefits flowing from bigness, and in which it was obvious that the large country had an advantage. If it were true that bigness was an advantage, quite apart from its technical consequences, we should expect smaller nations to stand at a disadvantage. Their firms could not have the same financial strength in oligopolistic fights. It was also likely that in big countries a diversified firm led to more competition than in smaller ones. Dr. Rothschild wondered how far Professor Edwards' American examples were typical of other countries. Was the strategy of American firms typical of European and other countries ? It would be interesting to know, yet the position was dominated by American material, of which so much more was available.

Dr. Rothschild said that Professor Edwards had assumed that more competition was desirable. We might all agree so far as the welfare argument was concerned, but if we were thinking of economic development, we must at least consider Schumpeter's views. Was the special efficiency of American industry the result of the *blend* of monopoly and competition which existed in the American economy? America was quoted as a country possessing both the biggest monopolies and the most aggressive competition. Surely these were both characteristic of the American economy. If the blend was the important factor and was partly due to the size of the American market, would a big market in Europe produce similar results? Clauses in the treaty for the European Common Market sounded well and seemed anti-monopolistic, but would the American-type mixture ever appear in Europe? Would there not be a European cartel-type of system? In conclusion, Dr. Rothschild said that Professor Edwards' paper had given us some important new ideas, but it led to similar conclusions to those of the other papers; size played some part in the economic efficiency of a nation, but it was not a very big part, and it was one whose importance was very hard to discover.

Professor Scitovsky felt that Professor Edwards' paper, especially the sociological part, was so effective that for him it answered some of Dr. Rothschild's questions. We had all been guilty of looking at competition in a static framework, and asking merely whether it eliminated profits. If one looked at it from the point of view of the extent to which it led to expansion and to the building of more efficient plants, this led to quite a different answer. It was also important to remember that Schumpeter was often concerned with the advantages of large size rather than of monopoly, even though he used the word 'monopoly'. Professor Scitovsky thought that the question : 'Would an integrated Europe have American-type competition?' had been answered by Professor Edwards' point about diversity. The kind of competition which was conducive to growth involved stepping on competitors' toes, and European competition was far too gentlemanly. The heterogeneity of the American economy was ideal for ensuring that competition was less gentlemanly and more conducive to growth.

Professor Jewkes suggested that a highly cartelized industry might well know what competition was. Foreign competition could have a big impact on an industry in a small country, even if that industry was highly cartelized. The Swiss watch industry was a very good example of this.

Professor Leduc made two points. On the first part of Professor Edwards' report which considered the effect of the size of the national market, he did not think it right to say that there was a specific size of firm which could secure all economies of scale. Was there really a minimum size of this kind — a 'threshold'? Research in France, carried out by engineers and economists, had shown that diminishing costs and increasing returns occurred in all firms up to a certain size. This was certainly the case with firms making washing machines and refrigerators and with railway rolling stock. Second, Professor Leduc turned to the effect of the national market on the character of competition. He agreed that probably a large country experienced more competition than a small one, but he believed that competition was influenced more by policy and psychology than by the size of markets. Professor Marcy had explained that in the French cotton industry and the Marseilles oil industry, there had been considerable reorganization as the result of strong economic pressure. The cotton industry was mainly an exporter and was one which got little government support. Similarly, the development of Senegalese oil processing and the consequent pressure in overseas markets had caused the difficulties of the Marseilles oil industry. In France the state usually supported existing interests. This explained why price theory was approached in terms of competition by American economists, but in terms of monopoly by Frenchmen, for example, Cournot.

Professor Hoffmann thought it essential to distinguish between the existing value system and education in fostering 'competition mindedness'. That the value system was a function of religion, sociology, and so on had been shown by Max Weber. But German experience showed the importance of the education system. Under Hitler, German manufacturers had forgotten how to calculate prices because of the long period of government control. Since 1945, with education and persuasion, entrepreneurs were learning that market phenomena were not fixed and immutable. There was little relation between the size of a nation and its competition-mindedness — the latter depended on its value system and/or its education. This fact was important for under-developed countries.

Professor Hoffmann also wondered what advantages were to be gained from a distinction between competition in goods and in services. In many countries there was competition in the pricing of goods, but not in the pricing of services. Especially where there was a relatively static social structure, competition in the service sector was much more difficult to achieve.

Professor Svennilson found Professor Edwards' argument so subtle that it was hard to summarize, but the trend of thought at the end seemed to be that small countries were likely to be culturally more homogeneous and that competition was therefore likely to be keener in small countries.

Professor Edwards replied that he was trying to say that because there was more cultural homogeneity in a small country there was more likely to be mutual forbearance from competition.

Professor Jewkes said that, in other words, Professor Edwards' argument was the exact opposite of Dr. Fabricant's, which was that it was easier to make changes in small countries.

Professor Scitovsky said there was a seeming contradiction in having the advantages both of heterogeneity and of homogeneity; but, in fact, there was no contradiction. For it was the homogeneity and standardization of products that facilitated low-cost production; whereas it was the cultural heterogeneity of a society like the United States that promoted competition and the standardization of products. In small countries, a high degree of competition was sometimes assured by imports; but in the domestic market, sheltered from outside competition, cultural heterogeneity might well be an important condition for competition.

Dr. Fabricant said that if there were any correlation between the size of a country and its lack of homogeneity, he would say that the United States was an exception to this, being one of the more homogeneous countries in the world.

Professor Svennilson noted that Professor Edwards also argued that small countries had fewer resources to invest in change, so that change would be slower than in large countries. If we took hypothetical model countries, for instance, the United States with little foreign trade and the others with much, we should reach similar conclusions. We had already decided that small countries were more specialized and also had a larger share of foreign trade. For example, in Sweden 30 per cent of textile output was imported and competition in the Swedish market depended both on Swedish producers and on producers in many other countries. Homogeneity did not play the same rôle in Sweden as it did in Professor Edwards' paper. We could not say that these overseas competitors were homogeneous — yet there was fierce competition in the markets of small countries. What was cultural homogeneity? Would a free European market be more culturally homogeneous than the American market? Professor Edwards' large countries had more resources to invest in change, but small countries specialized and that advantage tended to disappear.

Professor Baudin wanted to separate economic and sociological arguments ; the sociological point of view was instructive, especially if considered from a dynamic angle. The capacity for receptivity in cultural groups could change ; Professor Hoffmann had mentioned the possibility of education. In some countries a loss of personality by the individual was now taking place, thanks to instruments of standardization like the political party system, the press, the radio, and television. The individual was lost in the mass and would follow the leadership of someone who had all the characteristics of the mass. With this mass psychology, in the future, competition would weaken and disappear in a de-personalized world. It might be true, as Professor Hoffmann suggested, that in underdeveloped countries education could prepare the way for greater competition. But what would happen in our more developed countries ?

Professor Robinson returned to the more economic problem. He had been fascinated by Professor Edwards' views on the relation between the size of a nation and the diversification of the firm. Professor Edwards had made it clear that one must expect more diversification in a smaller country with a smaller market. There were a number of reasons for the multi-product firm, and one found two main types of such a firm. First, there were giants like I.C.I. or English Electric. These were really holding companies with many specialized plants. Their success could be explained by several factors. There were those characteristics of the capital market which helped the big firm to raise money more easily. There was its ability to break into new parts of the market. Again, many big firms were good innovators ; they had scientists who were expert in carrying out developments from the laboratory to the plant-building stage. The big firm had all sorts of advantages as compared with the new entrant.

Second, one had the rather smaller firm, making a variety of goods inside one factory and using standardized machinery which could produce alternative products. Such firms would sell the output of their machinery and management in whatever market was profitable at the moment, and they had advantages and disadvantages. Certainly lateral expansion was easier than with less specialized plant, and the British firm of this type could expand quickly in any unworked market ; but these firms did not have the advantages enjoyed by the specialized American firms of standardization and of long production runs. The British firms were very sensitive to an increase in the profitability of a particular line and moved quickly into it. The American specialized plants might behave differently here. If the product was not going well, the American plant experienced great pressure to bring the price down and to tailor the product to the market. One therefore had more intensive technical competition where firms concentrated on a narrow range of products. Another form of diversification previously mentioned by Professor Jewkes, was the vertical disintegration of industries in which some stages of production were passed back to specialized firms. With a larger market and with bigger and more efficient specialist firms, there was more vertical disintegration and the central firm could concentrate on being more competitive.

Dr. Rothschild could not quite see why the small multi-product firm which moved on to a more profitable line was contrasted with the specialist who held on and tried to lower costs. Was there any distinction ? Both were simply adjusting to their market.

Professor Robinson said we were all using the word competition in different senses. He was concerned with pressures to become more efficient and to reduce costs. He felt there should be a maximum pressure to lower costs ; to change the product was one answer, but to become more efficient was surely the ideal.

Professor Jewkes commented that General Motors had shifted into making aeroplane engines, but, though not very successful, they would not move out again. The reason was prestige ; they would struggle on and ultimately succeed.

Professor Verdoorn was glad that Professor Robinson had made his distinction between the giant multi-product firm, working with a separate plant for each different process, and the small one. The latter was typical of a small country, as shown by many branches of industry in the Netherlands. One reason why we might expect this, and one which had not been mentioned before, was the fact that the length of the production run was not determined only by costs of production, but also by selling costs. However, selling costs per unit were determined by the share of the market rather than by the total volume of output. For this reason the selling costs incurred in attaining the optimal production run (as seen from the production point of view) tended to be prohibitive in many cases where the home market was small and exports were hampered by tariff walls abroad. Here, of course, the competitive position of a small country could not but be inferior when compared with that of the larger country.

M. Uri suggested that we should also distinguish between different types of cartel, since there was a danger of over-simplification. Should we increase competition, or merely make cartels more effective if we brought nations together? In Europe the main incentive lying behind the creation of cartels or of large firms had been to enable them to bring pressure on governments. The cartelization of small-scale industry in France, for example, had had the aim of obtaining government protection rather than of increasing efficiency. In a broader market, should we have more effective pressure from industry on each of the governments, or would it be frustrated? M. Uri thought it was clear that we still had competition, even in the large firm, for such a firm was not moved only by immediate considerations. If there were a sudden shift from high to low activity, forbearance broke down and competition appeared. There was fear of possible competition even if this competition were not present all the time. In considering the cartelization which might occur in a European market, we must distinguish between international cartels and the internal cartels which might exist alongside them. There was a change in the attitude to internal cartels where, before the breakdown of frontiers, everyone's share of the market was maintained whatever happened. Such national protection disappeared overnight and there was a danger of international competition. The attitude of the national industries had previously been, 'let us not exceed the size of the market, let us produce less rather than more'. This attitude could not be maintained because, if it were, some other country would immediately take the opportunity to step in and take part of the market.

Professor Hague had been glad to hear Dr. Rothschild's view that a blend of competition and monopoly was the ideal for progress, having reached this same conclusion in a study of the British man-made fibre industry. Up to the present, the man-made fibre industry in Britain had been an efficient one and this efficiency had resulted from competition. But it was not the result of competition from within the British man-made fibre industry, nor even in international trade. It resulted from the fact that man-made fibres were in close competition with natural fibres. The effects of such competition from right outside the industry should not be ignored or under-rated. Indeed, Professor Hague wondered whether the French man-made fibre industry was not more efficient than the firms in other trades mentioned by Professor Leduc. For no amount of mono-polization of the man-made fibre industry within France could free it from the competition from cotton, wool, and silk which had kept its British counterpart on its toes.

Professor Leduc said that the rayon industry in France had indeed reduced its prices because of competition from cotton and wool. Although he had no clear idea of the structure of the French rayon industry, he believed it to be strongly monopolistic and controlled by a group with headquarters in Lyons.

Professor Jewkes was perplexed by our casual use of the word com-petition. Perfect competition had been mentioned and also competition-minded business-men. The theoretical model laid down nothing about the mentality of business-men, who merely had to work in the market. The model of perfect competition had nothing personal about it. Again, the Swiss watch industry, which exported 90 per cent of its output, therefore experienced keen competition. Were we arguing that it would be better to break the cartel down ?

Professor Edwards commented on the discussion up to this point and said that it had ranged far beyond his subject. His paper had been based not only on American experience, but also on as much as he knew about European industry through investigation of international firms. His generalizations, he thought, were quite widely applicable. Dr. Rothschild had suggested that big specialized firms started in big markets, and, when they became international firms, moved into big markets elsewhere. His own view was that the large market for standardized products in the big economy held back the diversification of large firms and slowed down the movement of big firms into international markets. The growth of such big firms seemed to him to come, in countries smaller than the United States, by diversification and by international growth. He doubted whether such firms often moved into big markets. They tended to move into small countries where they would not meet such strong competition from local industries. For example, international firms like Imperial Chemical Industries and Philips were slow to move into the American market.

The type of diversification which Professor Robinson had described tended to increase the size of the firm. He only had quantitative information for the United States. There, though the small concerns did diversify, they did so over a much narrower field than the giants. He agreed with much of what Professor Robinson had said, and differed only in that he did not think diversified enterprises, especially the small ones, knew much about their own costs. Perhaps, partly because of this, they did not quickly abandon their bad ventures but often allowed the good ones to carry the losses of the bad. There was no doubt that the well-being of the economy was promoted if both diversified and specialized firms were present.

Professor Leduc had commented on the economies of scale. He did not doubt that there was a minimum size of firm below which efficiency was low and the French studies were concerned with the relation between efficient technology and size. Some American figures suggested that production economies at the factory level continued even after dis-economies at the administrative level had begun. We must take that into account.

Professor Edwards said he believed in the general desirability of competition, but did not think that his points were acceptable only to people who shared this particular view. He had not used the concepts of monopolistic or of perfect competition in his own thinking for years. He was using the word in the different sense elaborated in his book *Maintaining Competition*. He merely assumed that there were sufficient concerns to give people on the other side of any market a reasonable number of

Report on the Proceedings

firms to choose from. If one had a blend of competition and monopoly in America, the monopolistic part of the blend would look after itself, but the competitive part might need protecting.

Professor Edwards agreed with Professor Jewkes that much competition was impersonal, but thought there was a great deal in Professor Hoffmann's idea of competition-mindedness. If there were few firms, the character of competition was affected by the personalities and relationships of a few managers. He believed that competition-mindedness could be produced by education, but more through events and policy than by exhortation. In the United States it was a recurrent experience to see business-men shift away from a belief in competition and then snap back into it. The discovery of the potentialities of competition was not always willingly made, but it *was* made when experience forced it upon people.

Professor Edwards then moved on to consider Professor Jewkes' comments on the Swiss watch cartel. He was not accustomed to use the word cartel in the European sense. Europeans spoke of cartelization in the sense both of 'competition in restraint of trade' and also of innocent trade association activity. There was little restrictive impact on consumers in some European cartels. Professor Edwards said he was in favour of the Swiss watch cartel being dissolved *if* the cartel gave effect to restrictive business practices. Competition from elsewhere was not enough. But he had not seen the Swiss documents for some time and was therefore uncertain how the cartel now worked. On the relation between competition and development, according to Dr. Rothschild the progress of the United States might be due to monopolistic elements in the industrial structure. He agreed that Schumpeter was more concerned with praising bigness than monopoly, but, though a large concern was clearly capable of financing and organizing systematic research, it did not follow that we should rely solely on large concerns for bright new ideas. The danger in doing so was clearly shown in the United Shoe Machinery Corporation case. This firm was skilled and progressive technically, as the judge had stressed in an anti-trust decision. Yet two or three small competitors were started on the basis of inventions which United Shoe Machinery Corporation had rejected, and these firms were successful despite the Corporation's power. It therefore seemed that important opportunities would be lost if technical progress depended on concerns possessing monopoly power.

Professor Svennilson's points on the relation between bigness and research were well taken. Specialization did do something to offset the greater resources of the larger country, but did not offset them completely. There were two reasons for this. First, in a diversified country one industry could make use of research discoveries in other industries, and such chances were lost if the industry in a country were specialized. Second, in opposition perhaps to what Professor Robinson had said, the aggregate *did* matter. In the United States there was a large number of universities with a large number of people working on ideas which would eventually become available to industry. A thousand chemists working

374

over fifty years would unearth more bright ideas than ten similar chemists working over the same period.

Professor Edwards said that as for cultural homogeneity, which had been dubbed sociological, he thought it belonged in economic discussion if it helped explain economic phenomena. If asked whether the European Common Market would have a similar scope to that of the American market, he would reply that all comments in this field were inevitably mere prophecy. If the Common Market idea were carried out as planned, it might create a non-homogeneous area of activity with intensification of competition, but there was still a danger in the existence of self-conscious national units with their own traditions. Territorial allocations along cartel lines might be established at national boundaries, creating discontinuities similar to those of the tariffs which had been removed.

Professor Jöhr said that in the Swiss watch industry the cartel was one in Professor Edwards' first sense ; it operated price fixing, product control, restriction of entry, and so on. It was a system of many cartels and a product of the Great Depression. It was now often suggested that it was hindering progress, but the industry, though cartelized, remained in competition with the watch industry of the rest of the world. Competition between cartelized industries in different countries could be very effective and our classifications of competition must allow for cartelized industries which competed with each other, and brought about a consequential reduction in the effects of monopoly practices. It could also be pointed out that while cultural homogeneity in America was very high, the opposite was true in Switzerland ; yet there were many cartels.

Professor Jöhr pointed to Professor Edwards' view that the influence of democratic institutions was to ensure competition-mindedness (footnote p. 130). This was not the experience in Switzerland. The Swiss view was that the cantons, towns, and traditional industries all had a right to continued existence and was thus similar to Professor Leduc's view. The use of a referendum was clearly democratic ; but it operated against competition. Laws were referred to the popular vote and support for them could be assured only if there were a compromise between the various groups. For example, a referendum had supported the continuance of import quotas to protect some 100 Swiss cigar producers. This was the effect of democracy. Professor Hoffmann had spoken of education to produce a spirit of competition-mindedness and Professor Leduc had said this was not strong in France. Yet in France, the spirit of competition was very highly developed in schools. Was the answer that people became so tired of competition at school that they wanted no more of it afterwards ?

Dr. Rothschild felt there was not much difference between his views and those of Professor Edwards. Any difference was merely a question of terms. He had meant by 'monopoly enterprises' firms so big that they possessed some element of monopoly power. He had spoken of international firms setting up enterprises mainly in the bigger countries, and he still thought there was something in this. European business-men were afraid to enter the United States market, but that was a special case. Big American companies had set up factories in Germany and in the United Kingdom and not in smaller countries. They looked for a country large enough to have a profitable market.

Professor Weiller said we had been speaking about competition and monopoly ; but we must bear the historical background of these in mind. First, there might not be much competition in an industry of small firms like baking ; at a higher level, with fewer firms there might be more competition, and we could have a more precise idea of it. But if there were a strong tendency towards monopoly we might rapidly reach an optimum structure from an economic point of view, if firms were not to grow beyond a certain point. We should then need, somehow, to encourage competition or to use such bodies as the Federal Trade Commission to check further growth. Only in this way could we be sure that the economy would reach its highest efficiency. Second, Professor Weiller pointed out that during the war it had been discovered that many important American firms had cartel connections with European firms whose existence had not been known. Finally, we had discussed *market homogeneity*, but what of the *political homogeneity* of the economic policies of a given government ? That was difficult to discover. But it seemed that in the field of economic policy, more complete homogeneity might be achieved in a Union where the centre of authority had power.

Professor Robinson agreed that it was a large *aggregate* expenditure on research in the big countries which gave them their advantages. There had recently been two studies of expenditure on research, one in the United States and the other by the D.S.I.R. in Britain. The ratio of total expenditure on research and development to gross national product was apparently very nearly the same in the United Kingdom as in the United States, but the American gross national product was six times bigger, and the *total* spent on research and development in the United States was therefore vastly greater. Statistics were, however, difficult to interpret because it was very hard to distinguish research from development, especially with aircraft and the costs of producing a prototype. It was interesting, however, that well over two-thirds of British expenditure on research and development went on defence, and the figure was very similar in the United States. The wastage of research ability during cold wars was immense. This was perhaps very relevant to the Swiss economy, since Switzerland was obviously not wasting anything like so much money.

Professor Gudin wondered whether mass research was as usual in the United Kingdom as in America.

Professor Robinson replied that there was mass research in the big firms like I.C.I. and the electrical firms. There was also some in the co-operative research associations, a great deal of which was 'semi-mass' research carried on to obtain some of the economies of large-scale research.

Professor Jewkes surmised that since defence research was subsidized, it would therefore be carried out in a most wasteful way.

Professor Robinson, on the other hand, wondered how much industrial research money was wasted because firms wanted to get very quick results, especially where research between firms was very competitive.

Professor Edwards wondered whether it was not a fortunate fact that the administrative controls of large governments were sufficiently ineffective to allow much 'defence' research to be carried out which was only remotely connected with defence.

Professor Robinson thought this was less true in Britain than in the United States.

M. Duquesne thought it would be interesting to study how far, so far as scientific research for defence expenditure was concerned, its by-products could be used for civilian purposes, for this might counterbalance some of its waste. For example, the motor-scooter in Italy had been evolved as a by-product of research expenditure on defence. Similarly, atomic energy for peace was a by-product of its development for war.

Professor Robinson was sceptical over whether a significant fraction of defence research expenditure came over into civil life.

Professor Patinkin suggested that if money were wasted in getting research results quickly, this was surely an inevitable feature of competition.

Professor Jewkes said that his complaint was that *subsidized* research tended to be wasteful. The other type of waste in research needed much more careful analysis. Military research in Great Britain and the United States had been conducted through organizations which tended to be wasteful, though he felt that the subjects actually studied had usually been the right ones.

Professor Robinson said that in the United Kingdom the total costs of university research, both commissioned and self-instituted, were within the margin of error of the total — only about 5 per cent of the whole.

SIXTH SESSION
Friday afternoon, September 13th, 1957
DISCUSSION OF THE PAPERS BY PROFESSOR VAKIL, DR. MARSAN, DR. PINTO, AND DR. ROTHSCHILD
Chairman : PROFESSOR HOFFMANN

Professor Prest introduced the papers. He explained that one thing which had interested him in Dr. Marsan's paper was the question of definition. We had considered whether we should define size in quantitative terms with a population of 10 million as the dividing line ; but Dr. Marsan regarded Italy, with a population of 40 million, as a small nation. This was because its low standard of living meant that it had a small market. Another question was the effect of the size of a country on its economic viability and the extent to which this might be increased by some measure of integration. Dr. Marsan had a great deal to say on the ways in which Italian economic conditions might be improved by her membership of a European Free Trade Area.

Dr. Rothschild had dwelt more on the effects of disintegration than of integration. He showed how, twice in the present century, Austria had been torn away from a larger area, and concluded that, although adjustments in such a situation were difficult, they were not impossible. Austria's problem was easier on the second than on the first occasion because of the higher level of activity in the world at large. This did not, of course, answer the question whether the Austrian standard of living was as high as it might have been if Austria had been part of a larger economic unit.

Professor Prest said that the paper by Professor Vakil and Dr. Brahmananda dealt in more general terms with the question of economic adjustment in the case of a developing country. It distinguished a number of cases of economic integration. First, it studied the integration of countries with large areas and a high density of population. This would cover some, at least, of the European members of the Economic Union. Second, it considered countries of large size but with a low population density; third, came under-developed countries which were small in size compared with their populations. Benelux would fall into this last category, though the paper had only considered under-developed areas.

One question which Professor Prest would have liked to hear discussed was the other example of disintegration, namely the splitting of Pakistan from India and the effects of this on the economic life of each. He also wanted to hear something about the Indian attitude to the European Free Trade Area. He had gathered when he had been in Delhi some months previously that the Indian government was alarmed about the Free Trade Area, but he was not sure why.

Finally, Dr. Pinto's paper illustrated another case altogether, that of a small country with a relatively low standard of living, but which had colonial territories attached to it. The question here was the effects that integration might have on such a country.

Professor Patinkin wanted to ask Dr. Marsan to spell out one explicit assumption he had made, namely that an export market was more risky than a domestic market. In what sense was this true ? Risk clearly arose because one was dependent on tariffs, import controls, and foreign exchange restrictions which a foreign government might impose. But was this the only risk involved, or were there others ? In what sense could it be more risky for an Italian manufacturer to sell in Germany or France than for a New England manufacturer to sell in Texas ? Surely the manufacturer could maintain the necessary contact with the customer in both cases ?

M. Duquesne was concerned about this point too. In Belgium there was the paradox that it was the export industries which complained most bitterly of difficulties in selling on foreign markets ; yet those very industries which complained were also the most successful in the long run. Could one suggest that, other things being equal, there really were greater difficulties in selling in a foreign market, just as Professor Patinkin had said, but that if the choice were between selling in a small domestic market or in a large but risky export market, the foreign market was obviously the one to choose ?

Professor Robinson felt that Professor Patinkin's own answer was obviously the main one, but there was a further point. In an internal market, inflation operated on both demand and supply, but in export markets inflation at home might affect the supply side but not the price at which one could sell one's output.

Professor Patinkin agreed that this was a valid point, though governments were often ready to provide export subsidies.

Professor Verdoorn suggested another possibility. As a rule, a firm's market share was smaller in the international market than in the home market, so that the elasticity of demand on the international market was probably the greater of the two. The resulting tendency towards dumping must contribute to the special risks incurred by the exporter so long as his home market was protected by tariffs.

M. Uri thought we should make a distinction between exports of goods which were *not* produced by the country to whom the exports were sent and those which were. In the first case, changes in tariffs, etc., were the main danger. In the second case, however, imports might represent only marginal consumption in the importing country. The difference between these two cases could be seen from the minor United States recession in 1949. Tin was not produced in the United States and tin imports declined only in proportion to the change in American demand for tin. But imports of copper fell to zero because it was domestically produced.

Professor Scitovsky wondered if we could summarize the issue by saying that the difference in risk was this. There was always an economic risk in catering for any market, but in catering for a foreign market there was also the political risk that the country might impose restrictions to solve its balance of payments problems. Competition in export markets might well appear fierce, especially because third countries exporting to these markets could practise dumping for balance of payment reasons. Finally, if one were catering for a variety of foreign markets there might be greater heterogeneity among customers.

Professor Jöhr said he wanted to support what M. Duquesne had said about Belgium. The Swiss export industries were more successful than industries catering for the domestic market, but, of course, they made specialities which the world liked and in which other industries did not have the same comparative advantages. Professor Jöhr thought it right to distinguish between economic and political risks, but even within business risks he thought one should separate off business cycle risks, which were much greater in the world at large than in the domestic market. The value of world exports was reduced by two-thirds during the 1929–33 depression.

Professor Patinkin said he could not dispute the empirical statements which had been made, but he found it difficult to understand them from a theoretical viewpoint. The existence of keener competition in a foreign market had been given as a possible reason. But consider the position of a country which *could* at the moment gain an export market but did not do this because it feared stiffer competition in the future. Why was this not also important in the domestic market? Were we bringing in a political element? Was it that tariffs would be raised if foreign firms started selling in the home market? He was also puzzled about the remarks on marginal quantities. The marginal unit was every unit. Why should the marginal unit not be from Utah? Why from Rhodesia? Surely there was nothing but a political influence at work even here.

M. Uri thought there might be a theoretical mechanism which explained why imports represented marginal output. If, in the United States, the delivered price included a large element of duty and of transport costs, and if the price then dropped, it was imports from abroad which would be cut off first. The tacit assumption lying behind what Dr. Marsan had said was that to export it was essential to have a home base. But was this assumption valid? Once more we must distinguish between different industries. The clearest case in its favour was the movie industry, which wrote off most of its production expenditure in the home market. The Luxemburg steel industry was the exact opposite and exported 99·9 per cent of its production.

Professor Jewkes thought this was the common case. The goods which Lancashire manufacturers exported were the things they would not normally sell at home.

Professor Verdoorn thought there was not only a political risk, but also a sociological one — loyalties between producers and consumers were strongest in the home market. If business conditions became worse, it was the foreign supplier who had to abandon the market first.

Professor Weiller gave an answer along the same lines as that of Professor Verdoorn. As already mentioned by M. Duquesne, there was a 'threshold' to be crossed before it was possible to enter a foreign market. Some degree of adaptation was necessary before goods could be exported. Professor Weiller said he had been fighting for twenty years against the habit of reasoning as if we actually lived in a free trade economy, as if the pattern of trade had not already been influenced by past economic policies. One had a given economic structure and a long-term preference for maintaining it, or for determining progressive changes in it. Adaptations were made in all circumstances from this already-selected, preferred structure, in spite of cyclical disturbances and with the desire to avoid discontinuities, major crises, and unemployment.

Professor Jewkes did not think there could be any theoretical answer to Professor Patinkin's question, only a set of speculations. It was conceivable that a domestic market might be so unstable, and the relevant export market so stable, that all the advantages were the other way round. All these so-called theoretical arguments were really generalizations based on experience, and the risks we were thinking about were risks of unpredictable change. There might be a change in consumers' demand; but this was easier to foresee at home. Or there might be a change in the intensity of competition, where the dangers were greater in the export market. A third risk arose from government action, and here he was in great doubt. One could argue that a manufacturer was less capable of predicting the actions of foreign governments than of his own government, but he was not at all certain that this was true. He recalled that, in the recent past, British motor-car firms had suffered five changes in purchase tax rates, three changes in hire purchase regulations, and two in investment allowances. A timidly anti-inflationary policy of a home government might be far more damaging than any policy of a foreign government.

Professor Verdoorn said that risk came to the same thing as unpredictability. Because of cyclical fluctuations, sales on the home market were already unpredictable. Since import elasticities with regard to national income were well above one — in the case of the Netherlands about 2·0 — the risk involved in exports was *ipso facto* much greater.

Dr. Marsan wondered if there was not economic justification for his argument. Italian experience, so far as agricultural products were concerned, was that this risk was mainly a question of tastes ; foreign consumers' tastes were less homogeneous. With manufactures, there was the high cost of marketing abroad — for instance, the need to create a whole new marketing system in another language could be very important. There was also the fact that one could only maintain a stable volume of exports if one could achieve and remain in the lead technically. If research was, in fact, handicapped in a small country, this was one diseconomy of being a small country.

Professor Robinson switched the discussion to a new topic. He felt the important topic for this session was how far a small economy with few exports, and those possibly declining, was a more vulnerable economy, and therefore more difficult to pull out of a decline, than a large one. Was it easier to induce development in a large economy than in a small one which concentrated heavily on a few industries ?

Professor Hoffmann thought vulnerability depended on the *distribution* of exports between countries, while *M. Duquesne* thought that if, in a small country, there was a certain amount of industrial concentration, this automatically brought it fairly close to monopoly conditions. The difficulty could be overcome. For example, Belgium had virtual duopoly in the cement industry. No disaster sprang from that, but other firms did not expand as far as they might because they were afraid of being accused of being monopolistic.

Professor Jöhr's view was that in the 1929 depression the two countries most severely hit were the United States and Germany. Switzerland was less affected, as were most of the smaller European countries.

Dr. Fabricant thought this should remind us that a large country was extremely vulnerable to depression if a serious mistake was made by one of its central authorities, say, the Federal Reserve system, while *Professor Weiller* argued that we should exclude the United States from

Report on the Proceedings

this particular discussion because that was where the depression started.

Professor Verdoorn pointed out that, despite her small size, unemployment in the Netherlands' manufacturing industries approached 30 per cent in the 'thirties.

Professor Edwards suggested that, if he had correctly interpreted what little agreement we had achieved, the consensus of opinion was that small countries had narrow industrial bases, and also depended strongly on export markets. It would therefore seem that, in less than universal depression, they would be vulnerable in varying degrees, and this seemed to fit in with what had been said.

M. Uri turned to another question. He said one thing in the papers had struck him very forcibly; this was the influence of the policy a country followed on its rate of development. There was no direct link between size and the level of development reached, but we must consider each time the way the problem had been tackled. In Belgium, development had been governed mainly by monetary policy. In Italy there was the error of thinking along purely liberal lines that the South would catch up with the North. The picture was now changing considerably since deliberate action had been taken.

Professor Robinson thought an important issue was the adjustability of economies — the dynamic change of economies of different sizes. If one had a large economy, and here he took Italy as a larger economy, the problem was of intense poverty, especially in the South. In general, the government was drawing people, and not pushing them, out of agriculture and into other expanding activities, but one could work from both ends because the economy was fairly large. He knew less at first hand about Indian problems, but both India and Pakistan were trying to deal with dynamic problems within the framework of a large nation where the ratio of imports to gross national product was relatively low. We were here a little nearer to a closed economy, where one could organize, within the economy itself, expansion to deal with those sectors which were contracting. This had to be contrasted with other examples, such as the sugar islands where sugar had declined and the rest of the economy was too small to allow the introduction of an expanding activity to replace what was contracting. This led us to the question : Had the large economy an advantage in its diversity which enabled it to maintain, on average, the fuller use of its resources, with ups and downs averaged out ? The same kind of contrast occurred between Lancashire and South Wales. In Lancashire the quite extraordinary decline in cotton had been balanced by an expansion in engineering. In South Wales it had been much more difficult to set up new industries locally, and the problem of decline had been solved by drawing labour out to expanding areas. He thought the solution to the problems of the decline of those industries which did decline was more easily discovered in a large economy. On the other hand, the smaller economy was perhaps more quickly acting, with its smaller unit of decision. Professor Robinson wondered if the Portuguese economists thought the advantages of Portugal as a small, vigorous, and

382

active economy were offset by its obvious shortage of specialist firms which could take up new products.

Professor Edwards said that in a large country like the United States any shift in the balance of industries was usually accompanied by a shift in industrial location. People had to move from the old industrial centre to the new. If national boundaries were major obstacles to population movement, these industrial shifts would obviously be more difficult in an area of a given size, which was split up by national boundaries, than in one of the same size, where there were no frontiers. But this disadvantage of the small country seemed to be declining as industry became more, scientifically based. Location was still decisive in industries with heavy transport costs, but in scientific and precision industries it was now possible to choose the location wherever one wanted to live. For example, especially in New England, industries were growing because people wished to live there and location was not decisive. The more industrialized a country was, even though it was a small country, the less difficulty it experienced over this kind of adaptation.

Professor Leduc agreed that the advantages of the small nation were centred on its ability to make quick decisions in the field of economic policy. Luxemburg explained its prosperity by precisely this reason, but that also had its disadvantages. Everyone in Luxemburg knew everyone else, and the government could not take its decisions anonymously. Since such decisions immediately affected so many other people, it was hard to say which type of economy was better.

Professor Baudin commented that when one was considering the rapidity with which political decisions were made, the political régime was fundamental. One could have remarkably quick decisions in a dictatorship.

M. Duquesne thought that, if one wanted rapid decisions, the element of cultural homogeneity was important, as well as the size of the country. Belgium had two languages, and also far less cultural homogeneity than other countries, and that might slow down decisions. If one had great cultural homogeneity, decisions would be rapid, but people would all want the same solution and there would be no truly alternative choices. Where there were different cultures, there would be different solutions to the same problem, and this might lead in the end either to agreement or to deadlock.

Professor Patinkin suggested that the advantages of diversification in nations were similar to the advantages in diversified industrial firms. In the United States there was a growing diversity which sprang from a desire to reduce risks. We might find a similar development with nations. This led to another possibility. If the rate of changes in tastes and in technology was greater now than it had been in the nineteenth century, did this not mean that the disadvantage of being a small country had increased during the last century? There were, however, difficulties if one tried to generalize from historical facts, for one could then find examples of all the cases that one wanted.

Austrian flexibility was not a function of size, for Austria had recovered much more quickly in 1945 than in 1918. Again, the Swiss had changed from textiles to precision instruments, making a rather strong adjustment to changed demand. The British case had been mentioned by Professor Robinson. Again, in 1939–45, Palestine had moved over from growing oranges to war production. All these small countries had made rapid adjustment to changing conditions. One could also think of big countries which had made rapid changes, despite their size. Russia, for example, had made extremely swift changes. On the other hand, Italy and France had faced serious problems of adjustment, and had accomplished this adjustment slowly and only with very great difficulty. It followed that there was no such thing as a uniform, historical experience ; one could not find a simple relationship between size and flexibility.

The final part of the session was devoted to a discussion of Portugal.

Professor Pereira said he would make a few comments on behalf of Dr. Pinto about his paper, though he did not wholly agree with Dr. Pinto's conclusions. Dr. Pinto had not sufficiently stressed some very important facts. First, it was difficult to know whether Portugal was large or small. On a map of Europe it was certainly small, but with its overseas empire, and in a world context, Portugal was definitely not small. One could not understand the African economy without studying the rôle played by Portugal. The Conference had often taken a population of 10 million as the dividing line between big and small nations. Portugal now had 9 million people, and would soon have 10. Professor Robinson had asked if it was preferable to be large or small for making decisions. Portugal was small from the point of view of area, but her decision-making power was particularly great. Professor Baudin had already analysed this from a political point of view and we seemed to agree that decisions were taken very easily in small countries, for rapid decisions needed full knowledge of the problems which might arise in particular parts of the economy. It was obviously hard, for example, to take rapid decisions in Brazil and in the United States. Portugal gained here.

Professor Pereira said that Portugal, although small and having a weak economic structure, did possess important attributes, being in a geographically central position. Also her possession of African territory made her assistance essential to other parts of Africa. Again, Portuguese lead and tungsten had played an important rôle in World War II, but it also meant that the Portuguese economy depended on the policy of the American government over tungsten prices. Supplies of uranium had been discovered, and Portugal was the fifth biggest producing country for fissile material, with a massive export trade.

Professor Baudin said that Professor Pereira had given us some very necessary information about Portugal, but he would like to add to it. On page 187 of his paper, Dr. Pinto had said that the Portuguese economy was dominated by monopoly or oligopoly ; yet, since 1953, Portuguese industry had been free except for key industries like chemicals. Nor did he agree with Dr. Pinto's view (on page 189) that, in some cases, foreign influence had slowed down development. Portugal needed much foreign capital and had been given great assistance by France in developing her mining industry, her railways, and even the Lisbon underground.

As Professor Pereira had said, the concepts of size of nations here reached their highest degree of ambiguity. The attributes of a nation were clearly hard to define, but if a nation were characterized by a close unity between the men who composed it, Portugal was a nation to the utmost. Portugal had a better ethnic mixture than any other country in the world. Nevertheless, she needed great technical changes to improve her efficiency. These would take time, and the authorities intended that change should not lead to inflation. He was glad to see that in this way the Portuguese were trying to escape the troubles which France had suffered.

Professor Amzalak said that during the previous thirty years Portugal had made unspectacular but real and tangible economic progress. The administration had been in office for a long period, but, for thirty years, there had been no budgetary deficits, and Portugal had been able to invest where investment was most necessary. Her people enjoyed a modest life, but a tolerable one. With a growing population, Portugal was paying much attention to housing and to improving the quantity and the quality of food. Her currency was as stable as any other. But capital from abroad was very welcome, and the oil-refining industry had profited greatly from such help from the very beginning.

The authors of the papers under discussion then summed up.

Professor Vakil said that he had been asked about the problem of disintegration in 1947. Along with the splitting up of the country into India and Pakistan, there had simultaneously been the *integration* of the old Indian states with the rest of the country. They had represented one-third of its area, and one-quarter of its population. The economic consequences of these events would take too long to discuss, and his own book, *The Economic Consequences of Divided India*, written in 1949, remained the standard work on it. Professor Prest had asked about the Indian attitude to European Customs Unions. If India was against these ideas, it was because, so far as her foreign trade was concerned, her main exports and imports went to and from the United Kingdom. If this relation were seriously disturbed by the creation of a Free Trade Area, there would be repercussions for both the United Kingdom and India. India's currency and foreign exchange systems were both linked to sterling, and all her economic planning depended on imports which had to be paid for in sterling, many of which came from the United Kingdom. If European integration disturbed Indian planning, her opposition to it would be justified. So far as adaptability was concerned, there had been a sudden upheaval in 1947. Indians had now adapted themselves to partition and should be able to adjust themselves rather more easily to any ill effects of a Customs Union. Professor Vakil concluded by saying that he thought that there was more diversity than homogeneity in India. However, India had adopted democratic economic planning, which meant slow decisions, but trying to progress as rapidly as possible.

Report on the Proceedings

Dr. Marsan explained why he thought that Italy was small. The problem of dynamic adjustment was such that, with her population and shortage of natural resources, the Italians could not solve the problem by themselves. A huge movement away from agriculture was needed, and this implied a corresponding expansion of employment in secondary and tertiary industries. As Italy had few raw materials, sustained growth coupled with external balance was only possible with a rapid expansion of the exporting sectors. This was one reason why Italy's future, as well as that of other Western European countries, lay in the chemical and engineering industries. In these industries, technical and economic factors favoured the large-scale organization · of either production or research, or both, which explained in a large measure the monopolistic structure of Italian heavy industry: All these reasons made it wise for her to favour integration.

Dr. Rothschild wondered whether Austria's standard of living would go up if she became part of a large area. He could not produce an authoritative answer. It was a question here of good or bad decisions, rather than of slow or rapid ones. That was where his doubts about integration lay. With an integrated trading area, the centre of decision shifted, and regional problems might become much more important. One could not separate purely economic problems from political ones. Nations were political units and could not be discussed without considering policy decisions. He would come out himself in favour more of co-operation than of integration, with sufficient decentralization to allow each nation some control over its own future. He did not quite agree with Professor Patinkin's views on the impossibility of deducing anything from history. To draw an analogy from the firm, we could say that, despite the great differences between the histories of various firms, there was nevertheless something valuable in constructing a theory of the firm. He thought the same could be said of making generalizations based on the history of large and small nations.

SEVENTH SESSION

Sunday morning, September 15th, 1957

THE DISCUSSION OF THE PAPERS BY PROFESSOR TARSHIS AND PROFESSORS LEDUC AND WEILLER

Chairman : PROFESSOR VAKIL

Professor Triffin introduced the Leduc-Weiller paper, saying that it was the most modest, and at the same time the most ambitious, of the Conference. With truly Gallic logic, they wanted us to define terms before we started ; terms like nation, size, stability, progress, and growth. If we insisted on knowing what we were talking about in this way, it was very hard to know what to say. The authors had quoted Professor Perroux' laws of growth. Professor Perroux had claimed, first, that there would be acceleration in the initial stages of growth, followed later by a slowing down, irrespective of the size of the nation. Second, Professor Perroux had said that the acceleration of population growth must *precede* the growth of income per head. Finally, he had postulated a shift in the pattern of the economy, first from agriculture to industry, and then to the service trades.

Professors Leduc and Weiller extended these conclusions by examining internal and external factors separately. Within the economy, they said, size had little to do with stability in the early stages of development. This part of the paper was not easy to follow, but it became more positive when its authors moved on from stability to progress. The capacity to increase productivity was seen as increasing with size as firms got bigger and more external economies became available. But, so far as effective government action was concerned, the authors seemed to say that a small nation was better placed.

On external relations, Professors Leduc and Weiller returned to definitional questions and presented the rather paradoxical view that size was influenced by the degree of participation in world trade. Here they raised a crucial theoretical point, namely, the economic criterion for being a nation. Was the size of Luxemburg defined by the size of Luxemburg itself or that of the Benelux Union? Similar questions could be asked about the gradual movement towards integration in Europe since 1945 and about the proposed Common Market and Free Trade Area. The authors had stressed policy problems and the ability of nations to use policy decisions to neutralize some of the de-stabilizing effects of small size. The development of such policies was much more important than size itself. We should ask ourselves what could be done to overcome the disadvantages and to exploit the advantages of small size.

Professor Baudin wanted to ask three questions of the authors, though he was not sure which of them since they formed a 'tandem'! First, he thought that size and development were related in a strange way in the paper. Nobody would deny that some small nations were developed (for example, Switzerland), but the authors claimed that under-developed countries were never large nations (p. 215). Must we describe Brazil and India as small countries? Second, size was measured in terms of the dependence created by international relations as determined by the structure and behaviour of the nation (p. 218). It seemed, therefore, a question of the nation's personality itself. This was an interesting idea which should be developed. Each individual, according to Sartre, would play in life the part which he had assigned to himself. The same thing must be true of each nation. He felt that he was translating the idea of the authors in saying that size, in their minds, was defined by a combination of the elements of force which determined the position of a nation in the world scale of nations. In this case, size would be a sort of coefficient, analogous to the hierarchy quotas determined by the International Monetary Fund and the International Bank for Reconstruction and Development. Third, there were statements on the effects of domination. Domination might play a part, but a part which must not be unduly emphasized. The relation between dominating and dominated countries could often be the reverse of the apparent one. For example, Great Britain had dominated world trade in the nineteenth century, but she had also depended on it and was greatly afraid of being blockaded.

Professor Marcy thought that the degree of economic development and the economic structure of a nation were basic principles. Economic history suggested that countries were more dependent on world trade if they exported raw materials and food than if they exported manufactures. Recent experience seemed to confirm this, but how far did it fit in with the theory ?

Professor Robinson agreed that the Leduc-Weiller paper was most interesting and stimulating, and that it opened up many questions. First, there was the relation of size to rate of growth. The authors had shown clearly, through the Kuznets/Perroux statistics, that the rate of growth of small nations was at least as great as that of big nations. But if one thought about it, one might expect such a result. If one took any big nation — the bigger the truer — its rate of growth approximated to the average rate of growth of the whole world. There would be much greater disparity between the rates of growth of small regions within that large nation. For instance, one probably had a staggering rate of growth in California. The same applied to small nations as to small regions, so perhaps we ought to think of the *average* achievements of small nations, and not of the staggering expansions of some few of them ; it was easy enough to quote the spectacular. So far as the rate of growth of income per head was concerned, Kuwait's might well be the highest in the world, and other small nations which had occupied favourable positions during the last few decades had expanded at a terrific rate. Ghana had grown as quickly as any country in the last thirty years, and Kenya and Uganda were planning on the assumption of a rate of growth of 10 per cent per annum. Such small countries in favourable positions were bound to show high rates of growth. Before we concluded that size had nothing to do with rates of growth, we must think not only of them but of the average of small nations. Had the *average* rate of growth of small nations been higher than the average rate of growth of large ones ?

Professor Gudin thought the problem presented too many variables to be considered at the same time. The size of a country by itself was economically meaningless. What about its resources ? Or the *quality* of its population ? Or the 'moment of inertia' in a country with a large population undernourished and under-educated, where a small minority had to work to improve the whole ? It was very difficult to establish anything useful on the basis of so many variables.

Professor Vakil said it was easy to see that, from the point of view of size and population, India was a large country; he did not see how it could be put in the category of small nations unless it were on the basis of *per capita* income, and that was circular reasoning.

M. Uri made three points. First, he thought one should distinguish between large nations and great powers. A nation could not exist until it had reached a certain stage of development, but we must be careful to avoid a vicious circle. Efficiency could not be included in a definition of size. Second, M. Uri thought we should be cautious when we talked of rapid expansion. In many cases, the rapid growth of small nations might be dependent on resources coming from large nations. The small nation might expand because of massive imports of capital from, or exports of, valuable primary products to a rapidly growing large country. The advantage of being a small nation was not that it was small but that it had large nations alongside. M. Uri thought two alternatives were thrown up by the title. Was stability connected with growth, or was the alternation of expansion and recession necessary for the most rapid growth ?

Professor Leduc considered this point on the relationship between stability and progress. Such a relationship was implied by the title of the paper and it was the Programme Committee which had deemed it advisable to link the two. The English term 'steady progress' had not been quite rightly translated. It was not quite *progrès regulier*. On page 202 he had pointed out that the relation between stability and progress must be considered, and he doubted whether a reasonable rate of progress was compatable with complete stability.

Professor Jöhr thought that the subject itself made it necessary to speak in concrete and not general terms. A distinction had already been made between small primary producing nations and small industrialized nations. In considering world stability, however, the most important country was the United States. Was it right to say that the United States was the dominating economy from the point of view of world stability ? Was it either the source of cycles or at least the place where they reached their greatest amplitude ? He would say yes, and Professor Tarshis seemed to agree. This led one to ask what was the effect of an American depression on other nations. Was a depression starting in the United States intensified in small countries ? Or was the opposite the case ?

Professor Hoffmann said there were difficulties in international comparisons of growth rates. Did we not assume, when considering the whole world, that the growth rate followed a straight line on a half-logarithmic scale ? If one sacrificed this idea and assumed that the growth rate followed a logistic curve, then we could only split up growth into specific structural phases. If one then compared the growth rates of large and small nations at the beginning and at the end they would be very different. For the United Kingdom and the United States, of course, the long-run growth process was not following a straight line, and there were breaks in any case for world wars. This showed how hard it was to make international comparisons of growth rates. Professor Hoffmann was also interested in the relation between the rate of growth and the amplitude of the cycle. Was it true that the lower the rate of growth was, the greater the amplitude of the cycle, or vice versa ? And could this relation be established ?

Professor Weiller said he had no specific reply to make to Professor

Hoffmann, but wanted to clear up one or two points of principle. The paper had spoken of steady progress and had laid emphasis on the statistical notion of progress. Steady progress was not 'balanced growth'. The authors had not been discussing the rate of progress and were not concerned to know when progress was most rapid. On the other hand, the paper had mentioned Professor Perroux's views on growth, but had not assumed that his arguments were directly under discussion.

Dr. Fabricant said that when comparing rates of growth in small and large countries, he would not worry over the fact that growth was non-linear. He would want to take an average of the rates of growth of small countries over, say ten- or fifteen-year periods, and to compare that average with the average for large countries. Any systematic differences between small and large nations would then show up. Like others, he thought it would be very useful to get some idea of differences between the performances of particular small countries. But we were interested in the random element, and it was not a matter of chance that some countries did better than others.

Professor Scitovsky suggested that size of the market was an important determinant of the rate of growth. He agreed that the rate of growth was one determinant of the size of the national income, and that the size of the national income determined the size of market which, in turn, determined the rate of growth. But, while this was a circular argument, it was not a dangerous one to use. A similar circularity occurred in the Keynesian multiplier, where income determined consumption and consumption helped to determine income, and where this interaction was used to explain the leverage effect of the other determinants of income. Here, too, the circularity merely gave the other determinants of growth a leverage effect, and we should not be afraid to say that the size of the market had something to do with the size of national income. A country's endowment with natural resources was also vital, and this was certainly not part of the circular argument.

Dr. Rothschild said we all had qualms about these comparisons. Professor Tarshis' paper began with the statistical argument leading to one result and then used an economic argument leading to the opposite conclusion. It followed that size was not the only factor at work. How much did these figures mean ? And was an averaging process the way out ? We had too few long-term figures for too few countries for the average to be reliable. Even Switzerland had only recently published national income and production figures, and the figures for some other countries were bound to be less reliable — if they existed at all. So the statistics might not lead very far, even though we believed that size did have something to do with rates of growth. Little had been written on size, so we had all done the same thing. We had all compared figures for large and small countries and had all ended up in the same position of getting very little from the figures, or else finding that they conflicted with our logical conclusions. For the influences at work were so complex and so many. He therefore wondered if we should not rather study single nations very intensively, and try to decide what would be the difference in their rates of growth if they were larger or smaller.

Professor Svennilson could not quite understand Professor Robinson's views on the growth of big nations in relation to general world trends. It was certainly true that what happened in the United States would dominate world statistics, but growth in the United States was still fairly independent of what happened in the rest of the world. Even complete stagnation elsewhere might not hold back growth in the United States. Indeed, it might even encourage growth by improving America's terms of trade. Small countries were more dependent, for expansion, on their foreign trade, especially in their main export lines. If a small country had one major export good, then the character of this particularly dominating good was very important. The development of exports and also internal expansion would depend on what happened to that particular export product in the world as a whole. It was also clear that what happened to the prices of goods like cotton and oil depended on technical advance in the rest of the world — on the development of man-made fibres, for example, or of new uses for oil. Transport costs for some primary products were such that they had to be sold in the neighbourhood of the small country. For instance, Danish agricultural products depended on markets in the United Kingdom and in Germany.

With industrial goods the situation was partly different, because there was no homogeneous world market. One possibility for a small specialized industrial country lay in shifting the direction of trade. For instance, Swedish high-quality steel had formerly been sold in the European market, but when that market was stagnating Sweden had adjusted to the needs of other expanding parts of the world. This kind of change in markets might develop new products, and new specialization might well mean alterations in the nature and direction of exports.

Professor Robinson replied to Professor Svennilson that when he had spoken of the United States in relation to rates of development he had only meant that any large country was already an average if there were a large number of regions within that country. It was not that America dominated the world. Even in India, Calcutta and Bombay were averaged with other Indian areas that had much slower rates of growth. Professor Robinson said we had spent a lot of time on definitions. Was this not a linguistic difficulty ? When French participants spoke of definitions, they were really saying that there were a number of different concepts which were all relevant. First, size in terms of population ; second, small or large gross national product ; third, moving on from gross national product, there was average imports per head and the extent of the nation's trade. The Anglo-Saxon tradition was to think of these problems as functions of a series of variables, sometimes with one more relevant and sometimes another. One did not overcome the problem by saying that there was only *one* correct definition. For all that, we must be clear which concept we happened to be dealing with at any given moment.

Professor Prest said that Professor Svennilson had drawn a distinction between small countries exporting primary products and those trading in manufactures. He had said that the latter would find new outlets for their goods more easily, but it was possible that these producers of manufactured goods had an advantage on the supply side as well as on that of demand. They could transfer their activities more easily to other fields, as indeed the Swiss had done when they changed from textiles to watches. Changes were much easier where the major factor of production was human skill. On the other hand, there was rigidity in a small country exporting primary products. What could be done with the Australian outback, except to use it to produce wool ?

Professor Patinkin said that statistical arguments involving the rate of growth in Kuwait and Bahrein showed how important it was to choose our period correctly. When considering the growth of Kuwait, we should get a tremendously high rate if we started from a year just before the discovery of oil. On the other hand, if we took a base one or two years after the discovery of oil, the results were less startling.

Professor Edwards said that the discussion had illustrated the ease with which a wrong variable crept into any analysis. It was true that small countries were more specialized on some segment of activity and one therefore had a dispersion of rates of growth among them. But it was equally true that regions in a large country were more specialized than the country as a whole, and, if we studied these regions, we should get similar results. However, when we had analysed all this, we should still only have demonstrated the misleading character of statistics. What we were really trying to do was to find whether a particular specialized segment of the world would tend to be more or less stable if it was, or if it was not, crossed by national boundaries. Professor Prest had thrown light on the kind of question which was crucial in his discussion of a shift of markets. There was also the question whether a large country subsidized outdated activities more or less readily than a small one. We must focus our attention on points such as these if we were to learn of anything more than the fallibility of statistics.

Professor Scitovsky thought one should expect greater variations in incomes between regions of a large economy than between several small and separate economies. The advantage of a large economy was that resources could move between its various regions much more easily than between different small countries.

Professor Svennilson also commented on Professor Edwards' views. He felt there was a correlation between the trend of a dominating export industry in an area, and other industries in that area. Denmark, for example, had an agricultural export trade which was not expanding, and, as a result, a lack of external viability that prevented other Danish industries from growing at a satisfactory rate. In Sweden, where the wood pulp trade was going ahead rapidly, an internal economic climate was created that favoured a rapid growth of other industries. If Denmark and Sweden were to integrate, Danish industries would benefit from expansionary economic climate that would be created, thanks to the expansion of Swedish export trade in wood pulp.

Professor Leduc replied to the discussion on his part of the paper. He said that Professor Baudin had raised the question, which of our concepts were most useful in practice. There were many different ways in which one could take account of the influence of size, and it would be interesting to see how the concept of size of nation had been interpreted in determining the contribution of different countries to the IMF and the World Bank. Professor Perroux's notion of domination was perhaps most interesting in its implication of irreversibility ; yet some French economists had said that this worked both ways. We should try to see how the principles of domination worked, and whether there was an inexhaustible dominating tendency at the bottom. Professor Marcy had said we should distinguish nations on the basis of their structural characteristics, and if size had any effect on the rate of progress we should clearly study this. Professor Leduc agreed that nations exporting primary products were much more sensitive to booms and slumps than other nations, but this phenomenon was quite separate from size. Brazil, for example, was a big country, yet it was very sensitive to changes in trade because of its dependence on coffee. Professor Robinson's views on the statistical comparison of groups of large and small countries were very interesting. Development in the different regions of the United States had been extremely unequal, and to compare the United States taken as an average with a single small nation might not give a very valid comparison. Some of us were indeed very doubtful of the validity of this sort of statistical argument. There was little to be learned from a comparison of developments between groups of nations, whether small or big, for was not the kind of grouping we used an irrational one ? Professor Hoffmann had raised the problem of statistical technique. Professor Leduc said he agreed that, in the existing state of statistics, we could not show whether small or large countries possessed a more or a less steady rate of growth. As he had said in his paper, we must improve our techniques. Professor Leduc agreed that the United States was the dominant economy, and also with Professor Jöhr's views on the transmission of fluctuations so far as Switzerland was concerned, but he was not sure that it was true that American fluctuations led to similar but smaller fluctuations in, say, Holland.

Professor Weiller, also replying to the debate, said that Professor Robinson's problems over terminology might sometimes simply arise from problems of *translation*. He could not clear up that question on the spot, but he wanted to say that all French economists were not agreed on concepts. Did not the usefulness of the papers lie mainly in the fact that they pointed towards different sets of concepts, and put forward different assumptions ? When he had read Professor Leduc's contribution to the joint paper, and also the paper by Professor Tarshis, his reasoning had run as follows. First, he had tried to see how we could avoid circular arguments, for instance, by taking a nation which had already increased in size by some process or other, perhaps through international trade or through acquiring overseas possessions. A further stage occurred when that nation or these territories began to develop as independent units. Could we think in different terms of the 'size' of that nation and of these territories if trade was continuing along something like the previous lines ? Was not trade itself the most important factor, or, more exactly, trade policy in connection with leadership or flexibility in adapting to world economic fluctuations ? The next question he had considered was whether a country which had once been small but had now grown, by some means or other, could adapt itself rapidly enough to ensure steady growth. As for Professor Tarshis' paper, we could note that all the countries discussed there were large and their instability was connected not with size but with other elements. The remainder of Professor Tarshis' paper suggested the need to study different regions *as* regions and then see what difference it made when these regions had been divided into separate nations.

Many speakers had referred to the effectiveness of political adjustment. We should think mainly in terms of economic policy. Certainly the regions in any country had different rates of development, but they also had a common national strategy combining different economic policies. It might be that the ability to use monetary, fiscal, and trade policies would allow countries like Switzerland to avoid de-stabilizing factors. His own view was that the effectiveness of such policies depended to a large extent on problems and policies in the realm of international trade.

Professor Triffin closed the discussion. He said that progress and stability depended on many things besides size, but we must narrow down the field if we were to achieve results. If we were interested in size, irrespective of policy, we could do what Professor Tarshis had done, and obtain an answer which was itself merely a result of statistical techniques. Was it not clear that an average was more stable than its component parts ? In speaking of the size of nations and not of regions, we had to introduce political questions. The world was one where evolution depended on frontiers and on agreements leading to integration. Professor Triffin thought size might be better defined in terms of some criterion like the percentage of gross national product devoted to the export trade. The large nation was less dependent on external trade, its fate was much more in its own hands, and so whatever could be done to reduce political division in the world was highly desirable.

EIGHTH SESSION

Monday morning, September 16th, 1957

THE DISCUSSION OF PROFESSOR
ROBINSON'S PAPER

Chairman : PROFESSOR JÖHR

Professor Edwards said that Professor Robinson was exploring new territory with unfailing ingenuity, skill, and good sense, asking the question, Do large countries spend more or less on government services than small ones ? He had used two methods of study. First, he had made use of the limited statistics available. At most these were inconclusive, but at least they did not *disprove* the existence of economies of scale in government services. Second, he had argued on a logical basis, concluding that large countries might well enjoy substantial economies in administration, defence, and social services. Professor Edwards said he would like to ask one basic question, but in different aspects. This question was whether the activities of different governments were so unlike as to make such comparisons invalid. He was uncertain for several reasons. To begin with, government expenditures were very confusingly classified, and for that reason not comparable. The figures had been, so far as possible, reduced to nearly comparable categories by their compiler, but three virtually inescapable differences still remained.

First, principles of classification differed in the various countries. For example, in the United States the control of restrictive practices came under judicial expenditure, while in European countries it more often came into the expenditure of a Ministry of Economics. Second, Professor Edwards thought there was a strong tendency to lump together unlike activities. For example, the United States spent money on mosquito control, and 'mosquitoes' as a technical term was found to include rats, lice, and so on. The third problem was that, in order to get their budgets through Parliament, governments tended to give to expenditures whatever title the legislators were most likely to support. For instance, American economic aid was now called defence expenditure. It followed that anyone doing what Professor Robinson was trying to do needed to be intimately aware of the character of every item of expenditure in order to be sure that the broad categories of expenditure under consideration were comparable. This was one major difficulty. However, if we assumed complete comparability, a second problem then arose. Was there sufficient difference between the national positions of governments for us to need special classifications of governments themselves, according to these positions ? First, there was location. Argentina's geographical position probably had a great deal to do with the size of her defence budget by comparison with, say, Sweden. Second, there was the stage of development. If capital accumulation had not gone very far, there might be few private fortunes and no well-organized private capital market to facilitate development, so that most such expenditure had inevitably to be met by the government. Where private resources were much larger and the capital market better organized, private spending might be more important for development. Again, differences in the stage of development might mean that one country regarded the extension of literacy at a very elementary level as the main task of education, while in another, university and technical education were very important. Such differences probably made necessary some sub-classification of the task facing the country.

Third came the problem of structure. Quite apart from its size, it was likely that a federal country with written constitution would undertake more paper work than a parliamentary government. Fourth, there was the problem of how big an existing burden of debt a country had already incurred because of its past wars, and how that burden had been modified by subsequent inflation. The burden of the national debt could vary greatly. Finally, it made a great deal of difference whether government outlays took the form of annual grants or of something different. American expenditure on education had originally been supported by land grants, as had a substantial amount of railroad construction. These grants did not appear in the federal budget, but they could not be ignored. It followed that, in considering large and small countries, one probably needed a classification carried out in the light of the various factors which had to be taken into account before comparability could be achieved.

· Professor Edwards suggested that a third major problem was that governments differed in their notions of the proper scope for government activity, some differences being the result of ideology and others of convenience. One striking fact emerging from Professor Robinson's paper was that expenditure on education and health differed considerably. In the United States it had been assumed that most such expenditure should be private. In France, Italy, and the United Kingdom, governments spent much more on health and education than in the United States. This suggested that perhaps Professor Robinson should have classified nations so as to segregate those with similar concepts of governmental tasks. Further, countries had also to decide on the *intensity* of performance of these governmental tasks. For instance, Professor Robinson had said that police activity was likely to vary with population and with gross national product. But Professor Edwards thought there were considerable variations between the various countries in how much policing was thought necessary. For example, there were more police in rural Spain than in rural America. Was this connected with the acclimatization of a country to bureaucracy? 'Parkinson's Law' was thought to apply in England; perhaps it also did in the United States. The degree of policing needed also depended on whether people who disagreed with each other lived closely together. If members of a new race came into an urban area in America, it was usually wise to increase the number of police. Similarly, if the rich and the poor lived very close together, one needed more police in order to guard against theft. The tradition of obedience to law had much to do with policing too, and it was also affected by technical change. For instance, there had been a great change in the amount of work which one policeman could do in an urban area since the advent of radio cars. Policing certainly did not seem to lend itself to simple comparison between nations. And if this kind of factor was important where policing was concerned, it was surely important also for other kinds of state activity.

These were Professor Edwards' doubts on the comparability of government activities between countries. He now turned to Professor Robinson's analysis of the problem of defence. Professor Robinson's main discussion had been concerned with the possibility of economics of scale in defence production, and the position of a large country compared with a small one in the general field of defence. Professor Edwards thought the major defence expenditure now arose from the division of the world into two power groups, so that the defence expenditures of those on one side of the Iron Curtain would depend on the achievements of those on the other. Within each group, the amount of any nation's share in defence outlay was greatly affected by the fact that it was a member of a larger organization and that its spending therefore depended, to some extent, on its ability to pay. It followed that the defence capacity of a country with a fairly small gross national product was not to be measured by its own expenditure ; nor was the defence expenditure of large countries what they would have to pay if each of them stood alone. Defence expenditure depended only partly on location, but partly also on a country's position of leadership or followership.

If this were true, some of the segregated analysis needed to be modified. Professor Robinson's contention that a large country had an advantage in the development of new weapons was impeccable, provided that each country developed the weapons merely for itself. But if the larger country shared weapons with its allies, that was to say with a number of smaller countries, these latter acquired the weapons without development expenditure. Admittedly, this was a half truth ; but it supplemented the partial truth of Professor Robinson's analysis.

Professor Robinson replied immediately and said he would like to do so at some length. He agreed that the question of comparability was a most difficult one. It was quite extraordinarily difficult to say anything at all on this subject. It had been suggested in the past that the power of economists to say anything declined as the cube of the number of economists present. The only hope of agreement was where only two were present — the author and his conscience. In the end, since he was very interested in this question, he had decided to overrule his conscience, and had tried to say something.

Professor Robinson said he agreed wholeheartedly with all Professor Edwards' doubts. One way to deal with the classification problem was, of course, to get all the classifications exactly right ; the other was to reduce the number of frontiers between classes. He did not think that any of his arguments really hung very much on the difference between mosquitoes and lice. It was true that whether control of monopoly was classed as legal expenditure or went under an economic department was relevant, for one might be administration and the other economics. His way out had been never to deal in sub-classes, but to keep the groups rather large. There were, of course, a great many variables in addition to size, and perhaps he had overestimated the importance of not attributing to size things which were directly attributable to income per head. His own view was that income per head was far more important than size, and that density of population was very important indeed in the case of services like health, education, and also the police. Indeed, he believed that the density of population was much more important than the absolute population. Quality of service came in too, and he thought he had emphasized it. He agreed that if one considered central administration it made a big difference whether one had federal or unitary government. It was likewise quite clear that ideological views about public versus private expenditure were very important.

Professor Robinson said he shared completely in the view that this was a very complex subject and that size was only one factor involved, and not the most important one. The question was whether the difficulties were so insuperable that it was better to close one's eyes to the problem as a whole. Despite all the difficulties, he thought the question was sufficiently interesting and important for us to attempt to consider it. The problem was certainly not one in which the refinements of statistical technique could carry us very much further. He wanted, therefore, to apply a mixture of the historian's approach and that of keeping relevant factors in mind while proceeding to disentangle what were the important factors. With few exceptions, size measured in terms of population seemed to be one of the unimportant factors. On defence, Professor Robinson agreed that the part played by the big countries in leading groups of allies was very important, but that did not deprive him of the possibility of *a priori* reasoning about what would happen in a world of small war-like nations which could not batten on large ones.

Professor Edwards summed up the position, saying that if there was a difference between Professor Robinson and himself, it might lie in the choice among procedures. Professor Robinson had chosen to group expenditures in groups large enough to let him hope the differences would not be very important. His own approach required classifying expenditures more fully in order to make them more comparable.

Professor Jewkes thought we were considering two separate things. One was the efficiency with which a service of a certain standard was provided in countries of different size. The second was whether a service, by being amply or only partially provided, might influence the efficiency of the economy in another way. Medical services in any country, for example, were, to a certain extent, producer services in the sense that they increased output per head, through providing spectacles for those with poor eyesight, etc., thereby keeping up output. But these health services normally went much further, and in the end became consumer services, keeping alive people whose economic usefulness had ended. Medical services were now largely devoted to prolonging the lives of people who had already reached the end of their economic usefulness. It followed that these services might be tending to decrease the efficiency of most nations.

After this general introductory debate, the discussion turned to more specific statistical points.

Professor Vakil, for example, wondered whether, in the figures he gave on page 233, Professor Robinson had included India's development expenditure, for development expenditure in India had barely started by that date. Now the administration had taken up so many other activities that this expenditure needed a new name.

Professor Robinson replied that he was dealing with current expenditures ; capital outlay in the Indian development plan was not included.

Professor Vakil went on to say that rightly or wrongly developments in India meant that capital outlay was dominating the budget so greatly that taxpayers could not be sure which was current and which was capital outlay. He wondered whether it would not be wise, in a study like this, to group countries into the developed and under-developed, and also according to the scope of their activities. Would this bring us nearer to clear conclusions about the influence of size ?

Professor Robinson did not think the distinction between developed and under-developed countries would help us here.

Dr. Rothschild said that the Statistical Appendix showed that the country most like the United Kingdom was New Zealand, though in size and population they were countries which were as different as they could be. Yet they did have heavy expendures on health, agricultural subsidies, and public debt. It was therefore obvious that economic and social philosophy was an important determining factor, and this was the one really striking fact which emerged from the statistics.

Dr. Fabricant suggested that if one interpreted philosophy in an unphilosophical sense, one important question was the relation between the level of income and the kind of goods and services which people expected the government to provide for them. So perhaps we were still dealing with an economic problem. He also felt that there was no doubt that statistics of government expenditure were quite as inaccurate as those for consumer expenditure, and just as badly classified. There were all kinds of errors in these figures. Nevertheless, something could be learned about the costs of governmental activities ; and something already had been learned. He agreed that the dominant variable was income and the standard of responsibility to which a given level of income led. A second factor was density of population. Population size was not important in itself, though in some way it was related to density.

Dr. Fabricant said he agreed with Professor Robinson's conclusions, not merely on the basis of *a priori* reasoning or of statistical analysis, but because there was some coherence between the two. In the United States a statistical and theoretical analysis of the public expenditure of the forty-eight states had been made, and reasonably clear-cut results obtained. There was a distinct indication that the level of income and the density of population were both very important factors. When income rose, government expenditure rose ; when density rose, these expenditures fell.[1] A recent report on trends in public employment in Britain had made a comparison between the United Kingdom and the United States. The results were not conclusive, but showed that something could be done.[2]

Professor Jewkes asked what was meant by the correlation between

[1] See Solomon Fabricant, *The Trend of Government Activity in the United States since 1900* (National Bureau of Economic Research, 1952).
[2] Moses Abramovitz and Vera F. Eliasberg, *The Growth of Public Employment in Great Britain* (National Bureau of Economic Research, 1957).

expenditures in the various states of the United States. Was the relation one between size and spending per head ? Or did efficiency come in too ?

Dr. Fabricant agreed that this was a serious difficulty. One could not really measure government *output*, only government costs. He did not see how one could arrive at either a quality factor or an efficiency factor, though primitive attempts had been made in the United States to set up standards for making comparisons between American states and American cities. Dr. Fabricant said that the study made by the National Bureau of Economic Research into the trend of government activity, to which he had already referred, suggested that government costs per head had risen as a percentage of national income, and also that government output had very probably risen as a percentage of total national output. On the question of what happened to government expenditure standards as wealth increased, the answer was the standards expected rose as well as the government's capacity to provide them.

Professor Prest suggested that it might be interesting to compare what Dr. Fabricant had said with Australian experience. The same problem of inter-state comparisons arose in Australia, and he was himself a member of a Federal Government Commission which compared the budgets of the various states in detail to determine how much higher costs were in the smaller states. His Commission had recommended grants on the principle that in smaller states the administrative cost per head of providing services was 12 per cent higher than in the bigger ones.

There were some qualifications to this. We were talking here of really very small states — the comparison was between states with under one million people, and ones with between two and three million — and the conclusions might not hold if extrapolated for larger units.

There was also a problem of statistical classification. Even in the same community, where states presumably operated on similar general lines, there were different systems of auditing and classification. The only fields where strictly comparable activities could be studied were education, health, and law and order.

Other factors were associated with size, for instance, density of population. Australian experience showed that states with a low absolute population also had low population density. Though population density was found to be relatively unimportant for government costs, the ratio of school children to total population was extremely important. Small states in Australia seemed to have high birth rates, and so heavy social costs. For Australia this question of comparability was a practical problem, whatever its difficulties.

Dr. Fabricant asked if it was a statistical analysis which showed that the density of population was less important than its size, to which *Professor Prest* replied that the Commission was comparing the budgets of states. The question was how much more did a state spend because of its size as distinct from the density of its population.

Professor Robinson wondered if the investigators distinguished between economies of administration and economies of operation. For example, some of the expenditure on education would be in the schools themselves, and some on a central administrative system. Did the figures show that both types of expenditure cost less in a larger state ?

Professor Prest explained that there were separate figures for each of these and that the figures showed economies in both of them in the larger states.

Professor Scitovsky raised a new topic. He suggested that in countries with a high general level of labour productivity, professional and personal services were bound to be relatively dear. How did Professor Robinson allow for international differences in the prices of such services ? Valuation at American prices would give an indicator of physical quantities of the various services ; at national prices, this would represent an index of the burden of the cost of providing the services.

Professor Robinson said that in his Table III, the last two columns, the first of these two columns was at American prices and the second at national prices. He agreed with Professor Scitovsky that national prices gave the best indicator of the burden on the rest of the community, while the figures at American prices were better as an indicator of quantity. In Table V, he had been trying to measure comparable physical amounts of the various services.

Dr. Fabricant suggested that if relative prices differed, and to the extent to which this difference reflected differences in quality, it would be reflected in the price differences ; the services would *not* be the same. The Gilbert-Kravis method assumed equal quality in the various countries, and he did not know how much quality differed between, say, France and the United Kingdom. He also thought there was a high degree of correlation between the level of government expenditure per head, government capital expenditure, and total government outlay. Such problems of classification, therefore, mattered little.

Professor Patinkin took the opposite view ; to bring in capital items would *increase* differences between countries, because the size of these items depended so much on government policy. The capital budget in Israel financed a large proportion of investment in Israel, and if it were added into total government expenditure one would get a much bigger government expenditure in countries like Israel and perhaps India also. It followed that if one wanted to show the effects of size alone, and not of political philosophy, capital items should be excluded.

Professor Prest suggested that government capital expenditure out of revenue should be kept distinct from expenditure out of government loans, while *M. Uri* thought that in a budget like Israel's one must distinguish between investment expenditure on public services like schools, and the development budget where the government was making investments which in other economies might be made with private capital.

Professor Robinson said that Martin and Lewis had (so far as they could) excluded all capital items from public current expenditure and had used these capital items in a separate study of the capital expenditure of governments. His paper had not mentioned this second study at all.

Report on the Proceedings

Professor Leduc said it might be assumed that capital expenditure could replace current expenditure. It seemed to him that it was much more likely that capital expenditure would, at a later stage, lead to bigger current expenditure, and this kind of problem was very important, for example, in planning the French North African territories. Capital investment by France immediately generated a large current expenditure.

Professor Vakil explained the Indian situation. A certain percentage of development expenditure was rapidly becoming part of ordinary administrative expenditure, and taxes were being used quite deliberately both by the states and by the central government to finance development expenditure. Items which could not be financed in this way were financed by loans, and so counted as capital expenditure.

Dr. Marsan pointed out that in Italy the problem of comparability was complicated by the existence of state-owned industries. In other European countries the government helped to cover state industries' expenditure, but in Italy state-owned industry financed itself almost entirely from the capital market both for current and development needs. Any state contribution was exceptional and this might well create a problem of comparability.

Professor Robinson said that this part of the debate turned on Professor Svennilson's point about the substitution of capital for current expenditure. Such substitution certainly affected the comparability of the statistics, but did not alter the figures so drastically as to make any conclusion meaningless. On the Patinkin-Marsan point, he had decided that to include capital expenditure would only confuse the issue. In any study of capital expenditure, the complications of differing ideologies were almost overwhelming in considering the public sector. In India, public utilities were in the public sector ; in Italy, investment in state industry was in the private sector ; in the United Kingdom it was very difficult to draw the boundary lines at all. There was a class of state-owned corporation in the United Kingdom which was neither fully in the private sector nor yet in the public sector, but somewhere between the two. He had therefore decided that we should add nothing but confusion if we tried to discuss the amounts of public investment in the various sectors when differences were almost entirely a result of ideology. He agreed with Professor Vakil's points, but we were here measuring expenditures and not considering how these were financed. We were therefore not concerned with the extent to which investment expenditure was financed by budget surpluses. Those cases lay right outside the analysis of current expenditure.

M. Duquesne raised a point on the Appendix. Was *all* administrative expenditure, including that related to other expenditure, lumped together in Item 1 ? Or did the administrative expenses in the fields of health, housing, etc., appear under other heads ?

Professor Robinson drew attention to Note 4, which explained that where there was a separate ministry dealing with a particular service, the administrative expenses of that service were included in the figure for the service itself.

Professor Leduc then suggested that the figures in the Appendix relating to France should be checked. There must surely have been big outlays under Item 17 in view of the very strong protection of French agriculture, and in 1953–54 considerable sums had gone on agricultural subsid'es. Professor Leduc also felt that the figure under Item 18 must be too low and that one must adjust the figures to allow for the particular French conditions, which meant including the whole social security scheme and not just the benefits under it.

Professor Triffin wondered whether on agricultural subsidies the answer was that there was a different form of help to French agriculture, such as a tariff, which was very important economically but could not be called a subsidy.

Professor Robinson said he was anxious not to mislead in an attempt to defend figures which he had not himself compiled. On the agricultural subsidies point he would, however, say that there were more ways in which one could impose costs on a nation than by collecting taxes and paying out through government accounts. His table had considered a subsidy as a cost, but had ignored a tariff. However, he had certainly been very surprised to find the figure for French agricultural subsidies to be zero and he suspected it. He agreed with Professor Leduc over the treatment of figures in the French social services. Martin and Lewis had included the government contribution and excluded the contribution of industrialists and workers themselves.

Professor Triffin said that where there were disguised subsidies to agriculture in the shape of a tariff, the amount received from the tariff would be spent by the government in one way or another and there would be little difference in total.

Professor Jewkes suggested that if in any one country expenditure on, say, roads was low, and if, in consequence, the costs of transport rose, we should allow for that.

Professor Robinson said he half agreed. It was just another illustration of his previous points. There were many ways in which government expenditures contributed to the whole efficiency of the economy, but there were all sorts of reasons for low expenditure on roads. One might, for example, have low expenditure because one lived in a small island and all heavy goods went by sea.

M. Duquesne thought the main problem arose from the way in which the figures were broken down. We did not know the nature of a particular expenditure even if we *did* know its purpose. If one considered health, for example, was the spending on wages of those employed in the service or on salaries or on equipment ? We needed much fuller information to show us this.

Professor Edwards thought the crucial point was that we had no measure of government output in this field and therefore had to assume that it was somehow measured by the government's input of expenditure.

Professor Patinkin raised a further point. He suggested that Professor Robinson had a certain model in his mind all the time — that of an independent, self-reliant nation belonging to no blocs and having no allies, and all of whose members possessed a common view or ideology. The study that Dr. Fabricant had mentioned — of differences between the states of the United States — might be a more fruitful basis for studying our hypotheses than the actual study of real nations — with the exception that one could then say nothing about defence. In studying actual nations, it was extremely difficult to get away from these differences of social philosophy — ideology was too strong a word. There were large differences over policies that required expenditure by the government. Was price control, investment control, and so on a proper function of the government ? If a government performed such functions, its expenditure would be high whatever its size.

On defence, too, Professor Robinson used his basic model again, and assumed a degree of contiguity between nations. All were within striking distance of each other. He went on to analyse military expenditure on the basis of war as we had so far known it, with land armies and the length of a country's perimeter therefore very important. But area became important with air warfare and one of the diseconomies of small size thus disappeared. Another diseconomy of small size was that a large country had land reserves. It could retreat 500 miles without facing complete defeat, and so did not have to maintain such a high degree of readiness.

One specific instance of a saving for a small country was that it did not have diplomatic representatives in all the other countries ; there were great variations in sizes of consulates and embassies, and one could adjust one's expenditure overseas to suit the size of one's country.

Professor Hoffmann was very sceptical of there being any relation between size and government expenditure. Since states differed in their functions, was not the only possible way out to say that if we limited the state's function to a minimum, the larger the size of a nation was, the bigger was the need for decentralization and the higher the cost of bringing central and local governments together ?

Professor Triffin wondered if we could not try, still using statistics, to increase comparability. We might concentrate on groups of countries which we believed to be fairly homogeneous, or another plan would be to start from the figures in Professor Robinson's Appendix and leave out the less comparable ones. The general progression then seemed plausible. Defence outlay was 6 per cent of gross national product for the United States and 10 per cent for New Zealand with a regular progression in between. Similarly, the figure for India was 5 per cent compared with Jamaica's 8 or 9 per cent. Another different method might be to look again at the conclusions we wanted to reach in order to determine the shape of the question. We were not interested in comparing larger and smaller nations in the abstract, but in seeing what policy conclusions emerged. Perhaps we should analyse the experience of the Zollverein as an example of a merger of nations and the Scandinavian Union as an example of a dissolution. We could then compare conditions before and after the change. Such a study would not be easy, but it would be much simpler than our present statistical analysis.

Professor Scitovsky said that at one time he had tried to study the Zollverein. The cost of collecting import duties had been high ; the administrative cost of collecting these customs duties at an immense number of points on the frontiers of small states had in some cases been higher than the revenue from the duties. But surely the Zollverein was a rather special case.

Professor Edwards pointed out that the United States produced an annual budget statement of huge thickness and detail, as did other countries. One would work on such budgets, select meaningless items and compare these between different countries. There would still be many difficulties and many problems, but at least one might overcome the problem of differences in public policy.

Professor Jewkes thought the other way would be to compare costs in countries which ran comparable services but where size varied, as, for example, in the health services of Britain and New Zealand. One might then establish a direct link between efficiency and size.

Professor Lindahl believed that if one were to look at the cost of government only from the point of view of size, one might expect some economies of large scale. Scandinavia, for example, had three kings ; a union would save two of them. Similarly, the health scheme in a large country could produce spectacles and false teeth in large quantities and this argument applied to other items in the public budget, though not to defence. Professor Robinson's table did not contradict these conclusions.

On administration, Professor Lindahl thought income per head was not important, and here we had an interesting problem. Public expenditure was increasing in all countries, and it would be interesting to learn from other countries trends in the cost of public administration. Did experience in countries like the United States and the United Kingdom, with their relatively high income per head, show that when national income per head increased it was possible to reduce the proportion of expenditure on administration ? The figures said nothing in either direction.

M. Uri suggested another approach which would avoid the problems caused by differing degrees of development. Quite irrespective of the level of development, we might consider input and output of some public services which had an essentially measurable output, for example, miles of road built or numbers of children educated. If we did this, it would give us an opportunity of measuring costs.

Professor Robinson summed up. He had found the discussion very interesting. At an earlier stage he had wondered whether the programme committee had been rash to include a discussion of this paper in the Round Table at all. He now thought that it would have been foolish *not* to do so. Economies in expenditure on defence was one of the major arguments for the integration of Western Europe and, without some study of it, the discussion would have been incomplete.

With all that had been said of the perils of statistics, he would agree, though he did not think the problems were as difficult as M. Duquesne had suggested. He agreed with Professor Triffin that it would be useful to compare basic services where ideological differences were small, and to separate off the social services where they were bigger. Similarly, it would be useful to take the minimum functions of a state and see how the expenditures of different nations compared. We should find that differences attributable to size were unimportant. On the other ways of making this study, especially the suggestions by Dr. Fabricant and Professor Prest that greater use might be made of comparisons of regional expenditure in federal nations, he wished more material was available. Indeed, he hoped that the morning's discussion would encourage someone to do more work in this field.

This led to the question of what was the right way of going about all this — Professor Patinkin's point. Professor Robinson said he had been content to use very simple models. He agreed that this was a complex subject where a complex model was wanted ; but any model which took into account all the complexities was not a model at all, it was the real world itself. We had to use models in order to concentrate our attention on a few simple points, but he hoped that others would use slightly more complex models and achieve something half-way between the complexities of the real world and his own over-simplifications. Professor Patinkin had been interesting on the small nation's ability to escape expenditure on some embassies and on international organizations. In Britain, for instance, the problem of keeping up with the American example in the field of international discussion was very great.

Professor Robinson wondered where the morning's discussion had taken us. It seemed to him that the original conclusion from the statistics was little modified. If one left out defence, economies of scale really were rather small. One could occasionally economize by having fewer kings and fewer parliaments, but the economies of parliaments were limited. Other things were rather more important, but economies of scale in government expenditure other than defence were clearly not of great significance in any discussion of the advantages and disadvantages of small and large nations.

NINTH SESSION

Monday afternoon, September 16th, 1957

THE DISCUSSION OF PROFESSOR TRIFFIN'S PAPER

Chairman : PROFESSOR JEWKES

Professor Weiller opened the discussion. He said that Professor Triffin's report dealt with a number of problems which troubled him, and, indeed, with many of his interests, but the title was slightly misleading. It stressed problems of the relation between the size of nations and their vulnerability to economic nationalism, and was mainly concerned with the current discussion of common markets. It was therefore best not to discuss the title of the report, but what was in it.

Professor Weiller considered that some concepts of size which had been discussed earlier were also relevant to the argument in Professor Triffin's paper, especially the discussion of how countries could influence each other's policies. He himself found the use of 'distorted maps' interesting. One could have such a chart to show national importance based on population ; for a country like India this was of great importance. Again, one could classify on the basis of the various countries' importance in international trade. This would not be connected with political power or population and here India, for instance, would come out badly. She was a great power, a member of the sterling area, but played a relatively small rôle in international trade, and it was with this that Professor Triffin was mostly concerned. Then we might have other charts.

He himself would like to see a chart on the basis of different existing national (or possible supernational) economic policies though he did not believe it was possible. One participant had mentioned the flexible trade policies of small nations ; it would be interesting to use such charts to study how the emergence of a common market, which we should be discussing tomorrow, affected these policies.

Professor Weiller said that Professor Triffin's first section compared the present situation with the pre-1914 world. Yet we should be concerning ourselves with mere mythology if we thought of the pre-1914 period as if there had been no deliberate policy before 1914, but only free trade and a system of automatic adjustments. We had a convention in our minds about that free trade period and forgot that we could be guilty of compartmentalized thinking. For most of the countries the issue in this period was not of choosing in an abstract manner, as in the text-book, between free trade and protection. The pre-1914 era of so-called free trade was one of national strategies — combining monetary, financial, and commercial policies — and of *bilateral* agreements. (These were subsequently multilateralized by the most-favoured nation principle.) It was not a question of choosing at once between protectionism and free trade but of progressing from the one to the other. In this progression, foreign investment played a rôle by promoting liberalization. There were also possibilities of intervention through the direction of investment abroad, and these also had not produced the same results as free trade. We could not say that before 1914 nothing was ever done deliberately. Professor Triffin had made much of the automatic process of adjustment, but surely even he would agree that it was investment by London or Paris that made these adjustments possible and this investment was not influenced only by the market.

Professor Jewkes said that, as Chairman, he proposed to take Professor Triffin's three sections in order, beginning with the first of Professor Triffin's three bogies, the bogy of trade diversion.

Professor Scitovsky thought it might help if he were to say something about his attempt to estimate the economic loss caused by trade diversion. Professor Verdoorn had estimated the effects of customs union on the trade matrix of Western European countries. He had obtained estimates of the resulting increase in intra-European trade and of the reduction in Western Europe's overseas trade due to trade diversion — to the tendency of these countries to buy from each other goods formerly bought from outside.

From Professor Verdoorn's figures, Professor Scitovsky said he had concluded that the trade-creating effect would lead to a saving in costs of some $70 million at 1952 prices, equal to one-twentieth of 1 per cent of the national income of these countries. Trade diversion would lead to a loss of about the same amount, and there would also be an improvement in Western Europe's terms of trade with the rest of the world — to the tune of half a billion dollars. He had decided at the time, that these estimates, indicative at best of orders of magnitude, showed the changes to be very small and insignificant. This judgement, which also applied to the bogy of trade diversion, suggested that the advantages of a customs union would be reaped in other ways.

Professor Verdoorn said he could find no fault with this conclusion from his calculations. The losses due to trade diversion might be even smaller, for there might be a positive correlation between import elasticities and the level of tariffs. Apart from this, his calculation referred only to the primary effects of a customs union. We might well expect that with changes in the pattern of trade, overall productivity in member countries would rise, bringing with it a greater demand for primary products from the outside world.

Dr. Rothschild said that we were told there would be little trade diversion arising from the free trade area, while European countries were being told at the same time that they would lose catastrophically if they stayed outside it. Was there not some contradiction here ?

Professor Scitovsky replied that he was simply trying to arrive at some orders of magnitude. He had concluded that trade diversion would be very small, but had said nothing about the effects of staying outside a customs union. The Common Market would have many other effects not covered by this narrow category of trade creation and diversion.

Professor Gudin asked Professor Scitovsky to give the reasons why he thought that the terms of trade for Europe would improve, and *Professor Scitovsky* explained that trade diversion would mean a reduction in Western Europe's imports from the rest of the world by $146 million. Her exports would rise by $611 million. If exchange rates remained fixed, trade diversion would therefore result in improved balance of payments with the outside world. But this figure could also be interpreted as showing what appreciation of currencies would be made possible. The gain in the terms of trade which he had mentioned was the result of this hypothetical raising of exchange rates.

Professor Robinson said one must obviously make some assumption about the earnings of the EPU area in the outside world. If one assumed that with a larger EPU area some industries would become more efficient than before, Western Europe's earnings from the rest of the world might well increase. It might therefore be increasing its imports from the outside world, or changing their composition as a way of taking its benefits.

Professor Scitovsky agreed ; but his own calculation was entirely a matter of primary effects with total output unchanged. If output rose and the demand for food and raw materials also increased, that was another question.

Professor Weiller said we were thinking already in terms of fiscal policy and trade policy. He had intended to say that we could not go back to something that did not exist before. The Common Market was not so very different from what had existed before 1914, though we sometimes thought it was. Professor Triffin had started with an analysis of the possibility of trade diversion which was based on a study of balances of payments. If we looked back to the period 1946–47 with the big dollar deficits, we recognized that if all the countries out of balance with the dollar area could have increased their trade with each other, they would have improved their joint balance of payments with the United States.

Professor Weiller suggested that what we needed was continuity in progress from one stage to another. What was the situation today ? We were still in a position where changes in structure would be needed to create trade and enlarge the relations between the United States and the rest of the world. Perhaps, then, we could avoid the bogy of trade diversion by moving to a situation where Europe's total trade was bigger.

Professor Triffin said he agreed with everything that had been said and hoped others would understand if he devoted all his attention to Professor Weiller's remarks. Perhaps stress had been laid on a nuance of difference. He agreed that before 1914 the situation was not one of perfect automatism and free trade, but he would be tempted to keep our minds on the differences between the position before 1914 and the position now. Techniques of international trade had not been those of today, despite the kind of trade negotiation that Professor Weiller had mentioned. We now believed more in bilateralism and in quantitative restrictions, but perhaps the most important differences were in internal policy. Changes in the foreign exchange system allowed the possibility of interference by the political authority, with its inevitable effects on balance of payments. We could not have even the limited degree of automatism which had existed before 1914.

Professor Jewkes suggested that it was now time to move on to consider the bogy of sheltered high cost areas. If a country with high costs was prevented from employing tariffs, did it need to make more use of monetary policy ?

M. Duquesne said that some ideas had been suggested to him by the closing lines of this section of Professor Triffin's paper. For a small country there was great advantage in being in a 'milieu' of countries with well-co-ordinated economic policies. Professor Triffin had outlined Italian policy at the time when she had concluded a bilateral agreement with the United Kingdom, and had determined to adopt an economic policy aligned to that of the United Kingdom. Belgium had faced similar problems both during the Great Depression, at a time when monetary policies were very different, and again after the war. Especially in 1947–49 and 1951–52, there had been a serious divergence of demand between European countries and the United States. Belgium had then been in an uncomfortable position, being in deficit with the United States and in credit with European countries. She did not want to follow the United States too closely for fear of European discrimination against her exports. But neither could she align with Europe for fear of losing price stability and thereby harming her exports to the United States. It therefore seemed that, for a small country, it was a great advantage to belong to an area of a reasonable size and with a highly concerted economic policy.

Professor Hoffmann wanted to support Professor Triffin's mention, on page 257, of an integration effect — the effect on investment when entrepreneurs found integration within sight. This effect should not be underestimated. In Europe, the first incentive would be to move capital and labour around the Common Market. Leading business-men in Europe thought that integration would, in fact, take five to six years rather than twelve. They were already discounting in advance the effect of lowering tariffs and anticipating the competition which would exist in five years' time. Therefore the integration effect would be speeded up. Professor Hoffmann wanted to disagree with the assumption that there might be a minimum of monetary integration. There had to be some integration of monetary policy, or one could not reduce tariffs. It was a pity we could not pick out a single policy instrument, but if integration were complete, monetary integration could not be kept at a minimum.

Professor Verdoorn liked Professor Triffin's remark in the last paragraph of page 257 of his paper. There would be powerful pressures for competitive readjustment as a consequence of the creation of a customs union, and he thought this the most important effect. Professor Robinson had already discussed the small multi-product firm, and his own view was that its prevalence hampered the increase of productivity in the smaller European countries. With integration in Europe, these firms would be forced to reduce the number of items they produced to those in which they were most competitive — they would have to specialize.

Professor Scitovsky did not quite agree with Professor Triffin on the influence of monetary factors on costs. So far as price effects were concerned, he did not think prices would be pulled up by trade diversion. European prices could not exceed those outside Europe by more than the amount of the tariff.

Professor Triffin said he had not considered this, in order to limit the length of his paper, but if the revenues from tariffs decreased other forms of tax must be imposed.

Professor Weiller differed from Professor Triffin over his step-by-step analysis. Though Professor Triffin often mentioned monetary policy, he only considered it *after* the common market had been set up ; yet even when economies were considered to be liberal, they were pursuing different economic policies. With the introduction of a common market or a free trade area — and during the transition period — these policies would become all the more necessary. Another point was that we must not think only in terms of monetary policy, but also of the other forms of intervention determined by the economic structures and community preferences of particular countries. Finally, we must remember that the rates of growth of various countries were different : a common market or a free trade area must change the structure of the economy of domestic investment, etc. Policies would be needed which would control the rhythm of that change. This made it impossible to speak solely in terms of monetary policy, as we had to think in terms of 'structural policy' too. We could not change the whole structure of a country except in a progressive way, and we needed to take the available resources and the possible rate of growth into account as a limiting factor.

Professor Weiller thought there was another limiting factor. Countries did not, apparently, want to concentrate their efforts on trade within a common market or any other area and there would always be keen competition between projects to stimulate exports to the different markets and areas of the world. Fortunately, therefore, it was probable that not too much trade diversion would occur, under such pressure as a Common Market would bring, since the same structural differences of aim would remain and these other objectives could not be discarded.

Professor Jewkes felt one could rightly say that if a country was unable to employ tariffs it must either use monetary policy or devalue, and unofficial devaluations, if frequent, would be as disturbing as official ones. What about the 'rules of the game' here ? Did we want to create a sort of European international monetary fund ?

Professor Triffin said he agreed with M. Duquesne and would like to stress the point that, even worse than the effects of the domination of large nations over small ones, were the effects of incoherence in the policy pursued by big powers. To Professor Hoffmann, Professor Triffin said he would like to say that uncertainty and instability over policy was far more disturbing than any degree of restriction. What was more, he would expect much uncertainty in the first stages of the Common Market, however long they lasted — eight, ten, or fifteen years. Professor Triffin did, however, agree on Professor Hoffmann's second point. He had not tried to suggest that there were two separate possible policies — total lack of co-ordination on the one hand and total integration on the other. He had only been indicating the consequences of particular possible lines of action. The first policy, total integration, would wreck the agreement. His own point was purely academic, except that in the absence of some agreement over monetary policy, there would clearly be complete breakdown. Everyone was concerned with the necessity of gradualism in the introduction of the Common Market. He was himself seriously worried about the *speed* with which the Common Market might come into being. He was less worried than many about the probable disturbances that might follow from rapid integration. We already had experience of integration from the European Coal and Steel Community. If the European economy were expanding rapidly in any case, quite apart from the common market, the dislocations caused by the latter would be swallowed up in the general disturbances throughout Europe.

Professor Triffin said he had been interested by Professor Jewkes' last question. He himself was very interested in a reform of the European Payments Union which would increase its importance. He was thinking in terms of a system which would create some kind of Clearing Union among common market countries — like Keynes' 'bancor' — with reserves separated from current dealings. But he did not see that we could expect totally automatic re-lending. The automatic re-lending of creditors' deposits would be impossible if the only criterion which the borrower had to satisfy was that his balance of payments was in deficit. We should need enough harmonization of internal policies to maintain a considerable degree of stability in balances of payments, though this harmonization need not extend to other sectors.

Professor Jewkes asked if there were any comments on the last bogy — the fear of large autarkic blocs.

Professor Weiller thought there was something rather optimistic about Professor Triffin's assumption here. He neglected the whole Eastern bloc, though it was rapidly developing. He also ignored South-East Asia with its population pressure. As a result, such figures as he gave would change completely in twenty or thirty years.

Professor Robinson said that Professor Triffin had provided a useful introduction to all the papers for the next day. He had given a good run to the idea that certain attempts to close economic systems might be trade creating as well as trade diverting. Much could be said for closing an economic system and thereby reducing the barriers inside it. Having said that, however, he could not help feeling that we must balance trade diversion against trade creation, and that the extent of each must depend on the circumstances of each particular case. For example, he was not convinced by the Scitovsky-Verdoorn calculations which represented averages for whole areas.

On page 252, Professor Triffin had surely said something profoundly untrue when he wrote : 'Various levels of economic integration are perfectly reconcilable with each other and may indeed reinforce one another'. There might be one case in a hundred in which this was true. If there was any state of affairs in which polygamy was quite impossible, it was in the membership of preferential regions. One could not pledge undying preferential faith to a series of areas ; one had to choose a partner and stick to one's promises. The United Kingdom could not keep faith with both the Common Market and the Commonwealth, and the political problem was which partner was preferable. The United Kingdom was already a member to a greater degree than most of a world economic system — more so, for example, than Belgium or the Netherlands. When we looked selfishly at the advantages of abandoning the world and joining

Western Europe, it was difficult to balance the advantages and the disadvantages. There was only one way in which consistent promises could be made to both areas, and that was to include all countries in the area to which one was making promises. It would indeed be wonderful if we could include the Commonwealth in the Common Market and Britain could admire the ingenuity with which the French had been able to include their colonies. But if one started enlarging the area in order to suit all the members of it who were also in a nearly world-wide system, it would become the whole world with only a small area left out. Then the whole thing began not to make sense. Was there not more to be said for GATT than for any widely defined regional system ? Professor Triffin's argument applied quite well to a group of small nations already trading closely with each other and with little outside trade which could be developed. But it did not apply anything like so well to countries with large foreign trade. He did not feel we were anywhere near proving that the advantages of enclosing oneself within a small region exceeded those of being part of a world system.

Professor Edwards thought Professor Triffin had spent most of his paper studying a closed system which was not really closed. The danger with a closed system was that there might be more than one of them — leading to the emergency of rival blocs. What did Professor Triffin think about this ?

Professor Scitovsky explained that when he said the effects of trade diversion and trade creation in the Common Market would be small, he was thinking only in terms of savings and losses in production costs, and had assumed that there were no balance of payments problems. If there were catastrophic changes, of course, the position became quite different.

M. Duquesne wondered why we should talk at all about closed areas. So far as he knew, Professor Triffin had been arguing about integrated areas, but was not implying that these should be closed. They were open to external trade with other parts of the world. M. Duquesne said that in his conclusions on page 264, Professor Triffin recognized the necessity for integrating national policies as an outcome of government intervention on a national level. He felt that the more intervention there was, the more the various national economic policies would conflict with each other. Economic policy in a general way had become all-pervading. He was not suggesting that it had ever been possible to fail to co-ordinate economic policy, but in former times co-ordination had not been consciously organized through deliberate planning. Now a much more conscious process had become necessary and we needed to co-ordinate economic policies in the world as a whole. This left room for varying degrees of integration in economic policy. Where nations fitted together more closely in an economic sense, we needed as nearly as possible a complete integration of policy ; but where areas only had a small amount of trade, one need have integration only on general lines and not in detail.

Professor Hoffmann suggested that any kind of integration would make sense if the rate of growth of the integrated area were greater than the weighted average of the growth rates of the individual members now being integrated, otherwise the whole process made no contribution whatever to world trade. He added that the fact that politicians made this kind of statement was no argument against it. To Professor Robinson, Professor Hoffmann asked whether the alternatives really were to marry either Europe or the Commonwealth. That decision had only to be made if integration failed. If integration succeeded, and gave greater incomes to both Europe and the United Kingdom, then other countries would be forced to strengthen their links with the Common Market.

Dr. Fabricant said that, on Professor Hoffmann's first point, he would agree that integration would seem sensible if growth was faster in the integrated area. Yet world integration would only really make sense if the least successful countries were made to grow as rapidly as the weighted world average of today.

Dr. Marsan suggested that the condition that the average rate of growth of the union should be higher than the rate of growth of the consisting parts before union was not enough. As in nineteenth-century Italy, growth might be badly distributed. The condition we needed to satisfy was rather more than could be expressed merely by looking at the average growth rate of the union. There should also be a reduction of the disparities in income and employment between the different members of the union.

Professor Triffin closed the discussion. He challenged the suggestion that his paper had shown him as in favour of closed regions. Much of his argument was really against such regions. After the formation of the Zollverein, the nation which emerged was still able to choose between free trade and protection. If the Common Market were successful, it should lead to a more liberal policy *vis-à-vis* the rest of the world. On page 9 of his paper he had not meant to imply that all various levels of integration could be complementary. He had been impressed by the academic nature of international trade discussion — for example, on the rates of exchange to be chosen after devaluation in 1949, or indeed in 1946 when the International Monetary Fund had started. He was struck by the fact that the conflicts which arose in practice were rarely on a world-wide scale, but in a much smaller context. World-wide agreement was difficult to arrange and negotiate, and it would add little to local agreements. For example, a fishing dispute in the Baltic could be solved in the Baltic ; we did not need to wait until Bolivia and Peru agreed to the solution.

Professor Triffin said it was true that it was sometimes hard to reconcile different levels of agreement. For example, in the early days of OEEC there had been controversy over whether its formation might lead to discrimination against the United States. In fact, it had led to liberalization being extended to other areas, including the dollar area, which was a great deal more than had come from Article 14 of the IMF agreement. The problems in organizing these concentric circles might be great, especially for countries whose interests were equally divided between two blocs.

The already-existing closed system of relationships between the United Kingdom and the rest of the sterling area was the main instance of this, but even so, it did not present an insuperable difficulty. The distinction between *de jure* commitments and *de facto* policies should be borne in mind. The former were more easily enforced locally than on a world scale. The 1914 gold standard had applied its rules only to Europe, the United States and their dependencies, but it had established a pattern for the whole of the world, even though Latin America, for example, had had flexible exchange rates. He thought we were moving back to some such system.

The reason why he had not been worried about the existence of several closed systems was that integration presupposed some surrender of economic sovereignty. This was always difficult to arrange and so unlikely to occur at all, unless there were powerful incentives for accepting such a surrender. In fact, in Table II of his paper, the proportion of 'other countries' exports to the European Payments Union area and to the dollar area was so large that what was left for trade between the rest of the world was insufficient to lead to the creation of a new group. The rest of the world could not establish markets big enough to equal the enormous proportion of the trade of the EPU area which was intra-regional — especially if there was some link between the Common Market and the sterling area.

Professor Triffin agreed with Dr. Fabricant and Dr. Marsan that no country would be prepared to surrender its own sovereignty merely in order to allow the average of other countries' rates of growth to go up. Finally, Professor Triffin offered his thanks to M. Duquesne who had put the philosophy behind his paper in an admirable way.

TENTH SESSION

Tuesday morning, September 17th, 1957

THE DISCUSSION OF THE PAPERS BY PROFESSORS SCITOVSKY, VERDOORN, AND MARCY

Chairman : PROFESSOR SVENNILSON

Professor Patinkin, who opened the session, conceived of it as a continuation of the previous afternoon's discussion. He was not going to spend much time dealing with Professor Verdoorn's statistics, but would consider Professor Verdoorn's paper as a study of the trade-creating or trade-diverting effects of a specific Customs Union experiment. This was not the proper place for a technical discussion of statistical methodology, and many of the points raised in the morning's papers went back to earlier discussions. There was wide agreement on the fact that small countries were more dependent on foreign trade than large ones. But, before drawing conclusions, we must specify a particular degree of development.

Report on the Proceedings

It was possible to find some small under-developed countries like Afghanistan, which were only very slightly dependent on foreign trade.

The correct formulation of our question was that, for a given level of *per capita* income, a small country must be more dependent on foreign trade than a larger one. Professor Kuznets' data supported this. On this basis, we could consider the advantages and disadvantages of such dependence. Professor Marcy's paper had referred to classical and neo-classical economists. There was a discussion of these advantages in Mill, and, later, in Edgeworth. The small country would obtain all the advantages from international trade, in the two-country model, as against a large country, since the large country would have only *partial* specialization. This presumed the usual classical assumption of constant costs. Once we abandoned this assumption, the conclusion was different.

A small country in terms of population need not be small from the point of view of trade in certain commodities. Israel, Switzerland, and Denmark, small, developed countries, were more specialized in given commodities than larger countries. This implied, *ceteris paribus*, that small countries were more likely to run into terms of trade difficulties than bigger ones.

Professors Scitovsky and Marcy had analysed the advantages to be derived from trade and Professor Scitovsky had drawn a distinction between technological and economic advantage. The former occurred when a small country was able, through foreign trade, to expand output to the level where plants were able to produce an optimum output. Another advantage was that there were sometimes not enough units in a small country to provide a reasonable degree of competition, but export markets provided the opportunity for competition, which kept firms on their toes and held down prices. He would add a third advantage, related but more classical ; namely, extreme competition which would eliminate industries in which the country had no comparative advantage at all.

Another point which had arisen earlier was that all the papers assumed that dependence on foreign trade was a *less* desirable state of affairs than having a market big enough to allow one to depend completely on domestic production. *Was* foreign trade more risky ? Professors Scitovsky and Verdoorn both seemed to think so.

Professor Verdoorn's paper returned to the subject of the previous afternoon — the economic implications of a Customs Union and its trade-diverting *versus* trade-increasing effects. His desire to analyse the Benelux data had made it necessary for Professor Verdoorn to take 1928 and 1938 as base years ; a before and after picture would be more interesting, perhaps one which compared 1949 or 1950 with 1956. But the special post-war situation made the use of a post-war base year impossible. As a result, it was difficult to isolate factors due to the establishment of the Customs Union from general growth and changing structure. Professor Verdoorn had analysed the Customs Union in terms of changes in the *share* of exports and the *share* of imports in order to get magnitudes which were less affected by changes in the European situation since 1938. But

Professor Patinkin wondered if we had any knowledge of specific industries in Belgium and Holland which had suffered an absolute decline in output and whose output had been replaced by imports from other Benelux countries. If there *were* any such industries, it would show that the Customs Union agreement was trade-creating.

Professor Patinkin's final point on Professors Scitovsky's and Marcy's papers was on the position of third countries with respect to the Common Market. He said he was thinking particularly of small third countries, not of the United States or the United Kingdom but of countries like Switzerland, Austria, Scandinavia, and Israel. What would be the impact of the Common Market on these countries ? What forces prevented them from joining today, and how would their future be affected ?

Professor Verdoorn said Professor Patinkin had asked whether there were specific industries in Benelux which had suffered an actual decrease in production as a result of the creation of Benelux. He could think of no specific industry. Besides, it rather depended on what was meant by 'industry'. If one looked only at very broad categories of output, one could find no absolute decrease of output in any of the eleven branches of industry which he had distinguished.

Professor Patinkin then asked if there were any data which would give this information for a later base year, say 1947.

Professor Verdoorn replied that 1947 was not a good year for comparison. Exports were low then, and there had been a steep rise in exports since. He suggested that perhaps M. Duquesne might have more information about Belgian industry. There had been complaints that some branches of the Belgian textile and shoe industries had suffered, but he did not know whether this had meant any *absolute* declines in production.

M. Duquesne pointed out that the answer to this depended entirely on the size of the aggregates which we studied. There were no decreases if one took large aggregates, but if one considered particular sectors there were declines in the furniture, shoe, and other small industries. The output of those industries might tentatively be estimated at 3 to 5 per cent of total Belgian manufacturing output. Difficulties first appeared in 1952–53, when there was a slight decline in world trade at a time when internal costs had increased because of the Korean boom. Since the recession ended, these Belgian complaints had entirely disappeared.

Professor Robinson thought we should remember that Professor Patinkin's problem would be equally solved if there were trade-creation in the sense of greater specialization in the plants *within* an industry : if, for example, particular boot and shoe firms concentrated more on producing goods in which they had special advantages.

Professor Patinkin, however, explained that he was not interested merely in finding cases of decreases in the output of specific products. What he was looking for was reductions in output *offset* by increased imports from other Benelux countries. He wanted to find a specific example of a Customs Union really working as it theoretically should.

M. Duquesne said this was just what he meant. The decreases in production he had mentioned were caused by increased imports from the partner country. There had been some specialization, if we took an industry as a broad category. He knew of one fertilizer firm which had produced both sulphates and nitrates in plants on both sides of the border. After the Customs Union had been set up, the sulphuric acid plant in Belgium had been closed, as had the nitric acid plant in the Netherlands, and output had doubled in each case. This was, of course, an extreme situation.

Professor Verdoorn wanted to ask a further question of M. Duquesne, who had told us of an absolute decline in output in some industries. There was a slight recession in Belgium at the time, and it coincided with an export drive in the Netherlands. Belgian tariffs being already modest before the union, would it have been possible for Belgium to avoid the consequences of this export drive if there had been no Customs Union ?

M. Duquesne thought this was the case, to a considerable extent. These industries would have been in difficulties even without Customs Union ; but because of the Customs Union the problem became more acute.

Professor Triffin wondered if the change in the chemical plants' specialization was prompted by a desire to reap economies of scale, or was there an element of comparative cost which determined the way the shift worked ?

M. Duquesne replied that economies of scale were strongly in favour of specialization, but he had no idea why the firm decided to concentrate on sulphuric acid in the Netherlands and nitric acid in Belgium.

Professor Jewkes wanted to know why the specialization had not occurred before the Customs Union, if the plants belonged to the same firm.

M. Duquesne answered that before the Customs Union the advantages of specialization had existed, but were offset by high tariffs.

Professor Verdoorn quoted another example of specialization. In the automobile industry there was a Ford assembly plant in Amsterdam and a General Motors one in Antwerp. Before the Customs Union, both made cars as well as trucks. Now one specialized on cars and the other on trucks. In other industries, too, for example, woollen yarns, cardboard and wallpaper, some degree of specialization had been effected.

Professor Scitovsky said he knew little about customs duties, but were not these chemical goods ones on which duties were very low indeed ? Again, was specialization purely haphazard or was there some reason for it ? If the plants had been owned by different firms, there might well have been no specialization at all unless there were very strong reasons leading towards it.

Professor Weiller suggested that in these particular industries agreements for specialization between manufacturers were now not common.

M. Duquesne said there was no formal answer to these questions. In his example, if there had been two different firms, the Benelux governments might have helped to promote an agreement between them. Most branches of Belgian industry were not sufficiently oligopolistic to make such agreements easy. Those agreements which now existed were entirely spontaneous. The woollen industry in Belgium had specialized on woollens to be exported to the Netherlands; the Netherlands had specialized on worsteds. Again, in the women's clothing industry there was Belgian specialization on semi-luxury articles, and Dutch specialization on more commonplace articles of ladies' clothing. This was quite spontaneous specialization.

M. Uri wondered how far we could draw lessons from Benelux. He had some doubts about Benelux, which had certainly had special difficulties, but had also enjoyed special good fortune to get over them. One difficulty was the different reactions of Belgium and the Netherlands to the devaluation of the pound. The Netherlands went all the way with the United Kingdom; Belgium, in a very difficult balance of payments position, only devalued by 12 per cent. Why, then, did the system not break down in the face of the sudden opening up of a tremendous difference in wage rates between the two? The difficulty was overcome by the fact that Belgian industry had a long-established industrial tradition while the Netherlands' industries were in an earlier stage of development. Differences in wage rates were compensated for by differences in productivity. The answer was probably that *ententes* not only encouraged specialization but probably also restraint in mutual relations — they limited the impact of industry in one country on the markets of another.

The second difference was that agriculture followed a very different pattern in the two countries. In theory, that was all to the good, but from a sociological point of view would the impact of the Customs Union be tolerable? And would it be politically acceptable? The introduction of the Customs Union in agriculture had been delayed, and now it would never have to be fully applied because Benelux would be merged in the larger Common Market, where the effects of the advent of the very efficient Dutch farming industry would be widely spread. Benelux raised very relevant questions, for example, on the optimum size of a customs union.

Professor Hague wondered whether the specialization M. Duquesne had mentioned between woollens and worsteds had been going on for a long time. Surely new machinery had not recently been purchased to allow the change.

Professor Jewkes pointed out that specialization between woollens and worsteds was a long-standing phenomenon all over the world and was indeed a classic illustration of specialization. If it had taken a customs union to induce this specialization in Benelux, the industries must have been very backward before.

Professor Prest suggested that specialization was, in any case, much greater in a large country than in a small one. People might know the advantages of specialization, but the market might be too small to make it possible to take advantage of them.

M. Duquesne said we would not now be considering the Customs Unions if we did not know the advantages of specialization. The table on page 20 of Professor Verdoorn's paper threw light on specialization between spinning and weaving. The table showed that the share of finished products in intra-bloc trade had increased very considerably. Did this mean that before the Customs Union, finished products were barred from international trade ? If so, perhaps we could expect an increase in the share of finished products in trade between the members of future customs unions.

Professor Scitovsky, on the other hand, wondered if customs unions would not have the result of increasing trade in intermediate products. Professor Jewkes had pointed out that even in production industries, like those making motor-cars, a large part of industry was operating on a smaller scale, producing parts for the assemblers, and had asked whether these smaller-scale plants could not be located in smaller countries. We were told that sub-contracting across national frontiers was difficult. But what about the Dutch bicycle industry, which used German parts, and the Dutch parts which went to the German bicycle industry ? We might be told that this was exceptional, but would not such things become easier and less exceptional in a future customs union ?

Professor Robinson recalled that until 1914 almost all the world's cars used German magnetos, and the world was none the worse for it. Even in 1915 British aircraft still used Bosch magnetos acquired through Switzerland.

Professor Edwards said there was a generalization underlying all this which was a half-truth, and had been set forth by Professor Scitovsky ; namely, that mass production called for large, stable, homogeneous markets. There was a stage in technology where this might be true, but recent American experience showed it to be only half true. There was now a trend in machine design away from the highly specialized machine towards more adaptable ones. In product design, too, the trend was to favour mass production, but also to favour adaptability. For example, in making small connecting links in radio sets, originally a score or so of small wires, the machine used was formerly highly specialized. But the job had been rethought for mass production, and was now done by spraying a small blank with conducting material on one side, and then grinding off all the superfluous conductor. Obviously one could grind to any desired pattern.

When industry first evolved from a handicraft process, and regarded mechanization merely as an application of power, specialization was all-important. But when firms became large enough they were able to think of mass production on a smaller scale and with more varied products. The American automobile industry, the symbol of mass production, was now moving in the direction of differentiating its product, and making more and more rapid model changes. Ford had recently announced that it would make substantial changes every year instead of every other year. In part, this reflected a desire to induce obsolescence deliberately ; a desire which had overridden the economies of mass production. But there was also a desire to attain greater flexibility in mass production.

Professor Jewkes thought that what we wanted to know was how far and in what ways a customs union would lead to specialization. One way of finding out was to use our before-and-after studies. Another would be to take, on the one hand, a big free trading area like the United States and, on the other, an area like Europe, where tariffs were supposed to be impeding specialization. By comparing the two we might find our answer. Was there really more specialization in United States industry?

Professor Edwards wanted to raise a related matter from Professor Scitovsky's paper. Professor Scitovsky had assumed that mass production implied a lowering of quality. This was only a quarter truth. In a few industries, like those making women's dresses, it was true, but where a precision fit of parts was required it was conspicuously untrue. Since mass-production techniques were aimed at large numbers of consumers, they had, by definition, to aim at a level of quality which would yield a product priced at the level which would attract most customers. One would clearly not undertake mass production where one intended to set such a high standard that very few people could afford to buy the article being produced.

Professor Scitovsky agreed with Professor Edwards about this, although he thought he had made this fact clear in his paper. European business-men realized all too rarely that high quality could be achieved with mass production. There was a feeling that quality must be sacrificed when switching to mass production and this was not necessarily true.

As to whether the trend was now away from single-purpose machine tools in the United States, Professor Scitovsky said he was aware of this, but he thought the generalization was true only by contrast with earlier American methods and not true by contrast with European handicraft methods.

Professor Weiller thought this meant that the big country still had the advantage, but *Professor Edwards* could not agree. He had no doubt that the United States had been forced to go through a period of inflexible mass production. But in all international borrowing of ideas the borrower could skip many steps the originating country had to go through. People now wanting to make mass production flexible were more likely to succeed than those who, themselves, had originally developed these techniques.

Professor Gudin wondered if the tendency of machinery in the United States to become less specific affected the problem of indivisibility.

Professor Edwards thought it did, in two respects. First, it permitted the production of components by small companies. Second, although a country of a given size had not sufficient demand for one specialized product, it might have a demand for a range of products which could be produced by one less-specialized machine.

Professor Baudin said he would answer the question on page 272 of Professor Marcy's paper, namely, how far could customs unions be created between heterogenous nations? There might be shorter- or longer-term difficulties. He would refer to the Greater Colombian Union

Report on the Proceedings

(Charter of Quito), which was open to countries with the same fundamental common characteristics, race, religion, and language, plus common economic characteristics. Differences in the degree of development ruled out the United States and even Argentina. The members were Ecuador, Peru, Panama, Colombia, and Venezuela. Venezuela later had political difficulties, but the Union had led to the creation of a common fleet. Because the Union was based on factors of homogeneity, it avoided the risk of domination, or lack of balance. This policy was called 'intra-national' in South America.

Dr. Rothschild thought that where the nations in a union were heterogeneous, especially as regards size, the experience of Benelux was, from this point of view, not much use as a model. His own doubts about the free trade area solution were as follows. He realized, of course, the advantage of more foreign trade, and the desirability on these grounds of bringing in small nations. But what would happen to small countries was not simply a question of the economic efficiency of firms, but also of the size and location of firms. A small country might have small but efficient firms. If the frontiers then opened, there would be an increased opportunity to expand the scale of production. The small firms now had to try to enter new markets and to establish themselves quickly, which was a matter of capital, advertising, and so on, and hence an expensive business. Professor Hoffmann's 'integration effect' might suit Germany, but in small countries efficient firms which had not sufficiently large capital resources to expand rapidly could not grasp the new opportunities quickly enough to become large-scale firms. With open frontiers, the firms in question might not be able to survive against aggressive competition from outside. Was this effect of severe competition the desired effect ? Toes would be trodden on, but if all toes were not of the same size, was this what one wanted ? It was the infant industry argument over again, but all the industries were not necessarily infants.

An international capital market itself was not the solution. There was no guarantee in Europe that capital would move from developed to less-developed countries. There was a much greater likelihood that capital would go to well-established centres. It was an already-established point that we had no guarantee that private capital would move according to the economic potentialities of the various nations. This answered one of Professor Triffin's questions. He asked whether we should not split small nations into still smaller regional units ; but unless we had a really homogeneous supranational community, there would be a real distinction between the different regions *within* a single nation, and the different nations in an international community. If there was unemployment *within* a country, the problem could be settled comparatively smoothly within that country ; but if one had an international community, would a small country have a loud enough voice to be sure that its own problems would be settled ? There was danger in easy optimism. The creation of a big area did not mean the immediate solution of small countries' problems.

Dr. Rothschild thought it was difficult to find out what had been the effects of the Coal and Steel Community, as distinct from the effects of the period of prosperity we were living in. Coal and steel industries in countries outside the Community had expanded as much as the industries inside — in Austria, Britain, and Sweden, for example. Austrian steel had done well because there was a lively demand for the quality of steel she was lucky enough to be producing.

Professor Marcy agreed with Dr. Rothschild that it was not enough to set up a customs union to solve all problems. Preliminary difficulties which had to be solved were, discrepancies in wage levels, and the fact that many people supported a union only in the hope that it would adopt a hostile attitude towards third countries which were more powerful and more developed. Professor Marcy thought that in the minds of many French supporters, the Customs Union was intended to have the fundamental purpose of solving the dollar shortage. Clearly, such members of a customs union would be strongly against a third union, and this would be catastrophic. Perhaps that was why the Scandinavian countries were so strongly against a customs union, because they were more dependent on outside trade than, for example, the French.

Professor Hoffmann said he was looking for examples of when it was profitable to join Unions — great or small. Why were the Scandinavian nations, with a high degree of cultural similarity, unwilling to join a customs union ? Intra-Scandinavian trade was very small, and, he thought, mainly centrifugal. Norwegian shipping capacity was such that the Scandinavian market could not employ more than a small proportion of it. Sweden's iron and steel output went far beyond the capacity of the Scandinavian market to absorb it. The propensity to join a customs union seemed to depend on the opportunity to develop new markets as a result of the union. The idea of customs unions was a very old one. If there were natural reasons for forming them, we should surely have more. The Commonwealth was a special case, so he wanted an answer in terms of Scandinavia.

Professor Svennilson said that agriculture was one obstacle to Scandinavian union. Danish agriculture was superior to large parts of Norwegian and Swedish. Norway and Sweden did not want to give up their own agriculture, and Denmark would not like to join unless this happened. In Norway, the infant industry argument was very important. The Norwegians feared that in a customs union Danish and Swedish industry would get a quicker start, and take the market before they had time to develop their own industry.

Professor Robinson wanted to go back to Dr. Rothschild's argument — whether a customs union of different sorts of nations at different stages of development was advantageous to its smaller members. This linked with an important point in Dr. Marsan's paper. Suppose we had a customs union between advanced and less-advanced nations. As an inexpert model builder, he would think it was not difficult to design a theoretical model in which the union acted to the disadvantage of the backward country. With perfect mobility of capital, labour, and entre-preneurs, and perfect adjustment of real wages, the union ought to act to the advantage of both partners, but if one removed any one of those assumptions, doubts began to arise. In the case of North and South Italy, for example, where there was not perfect mobility, if investment could not be attracted to the South, the model would have to include a depressed area. Increasing the openness of Southern Italy would merely result in even more expenditure on imports from the North. The balance of pay-ments between North and South Italy would only balance if real incomes were kept so low in the South that she could not buy more than she could afford to pay for from the North. This seemed to be a perfectly possible result of a union with great disparity between members.

Professor Robinson thought that what we needed was a period, not of *removing* discrepancies in wages, but of *achieving* such differences as reflected differences in efficiency. It was difficult to have discrepancies in *real* wages within an open economic system. It followed that we could work out a model of an integration which was to the disadvantage of the weaker nation.

This led to the problem of whom one wanted as a partner. This depended on the type of customs union. In a Benelux-type union, one had rather equal partners, both manufacturing nations. One objective of the union was then to make possible increased specialization and an increased scale of manufacture. But there were equal advantages in a union of a different character, which gave the sort of gain which one found in the United States economy. What one was trying to do in this second case was not so much to achieve greater economies in manu-facture as to give confidence to the different parts of the Union and so to allow them to expand and to find markets within the Union. This was the advantage derived from integration between France and the French overseas territories. Similarly, within the sterling area, the emphasis was not so much on the division of labour, as on the assurance that any expansion of specialist activities would meet with reasonable access to sufficient markets. The two were not incompatible in a large enough area.

Professor Gudin thought too much had been made of the so-called effect of domination in international trade theory. He thought that the first part of Professor Marcy's paper might have been clearer if the emphasis had been on reciprocal demand.

M. Uri said he had been provoked by Dr. Rothschild's comments on the Coal and Steel Community. He was aware that the high level of economic activity in recent years had confused the picture, as with Benelux. Adjustments had been less necessary, and the high level of economic activity had made the experiment less fruitful in yielding con-clusions about its effects.

To Professor Robinson, M. Uri said that the setting up of the invest-ment bank in the Common Market proposal had been advocated precisely because of the cumulative process Professor Robinson feared. But we must distinguish between small and large countries, and between advanced and backward areas, the backward areas belonging mostly to the larger countries in the union. Was not the problem much the same in the free trade area ?

On the type of customs union which ought to be built, M. Uri fully agreed that we must consider the kinds of country we were uniting ; the policy of the Union would depend on this. There was not one ready-made pattern for all types of union.

M. Duquesne said he was absolutely in agreement with M. Uri. It was impossibly unrealistic to discuss customs unions on the assumption of perfect competition and perfect mobility of factors. It was indeed necessary to devise a conscious and suitable policy if we wanted a customs union to yield all its potential advantages. When Benelux had been set up, the Netherlands was far less industrialized than Belgium, and there had been no guarantee at the outset that Dutch industry would exploit the possibilities of the Customs Union. Since 1950, however, the Dutch industries had developed, and one could now say that the Customs Union had greatly favoured the industrialization of the Netherlands. One could, of course, argue that if Germany and Belgium entered a customs union, that union would be dominated by German engineering. Yet, by joining, Belgium would exchange a small, not very well-protected market, for a large one. We must discover a method that would enable us to reap *all* the advantages of customs unions, and this depended on economic policy and on the efficiency of entrepreneurs.

M. Duquesne agreed with Professor Robinson that the advantages of the Customs Union would be mainly in giving opportunities for the region to adapt and develop its economy within an improved institutional framework.

Professor Leduc said he wanted to support Professor Robinson on the disadvantages of any tendency towards more equal wages within an economic union. In France the trade unions maintained the same level of wages in Paris as in the provinces, to the disadvantage of the provinces. This problem was even more real in overseas territories. Presumably, in any customs union, the policy would be to equalize wages in all territories inside the customs union with those in France. Such a uniformity would be to the disadvantage of the economies of overseas territories, and might well slow down their development.

Professor Verdoorn was glad that Professor Robinson had raised the problem of depressed areas. Just as in a generally prosperous country one or more 'black areas' might persist, it might well be that a certain country by joining a customs union would become a permanent loser instead of a winner, if at the outset it was less efficient than the rest. There was nothing in the theory of international trade to prevent this kind of development. The only way out was to a state of full employment and so to ensure sufficient demand for the produce of the less efficient countries. If the maintenance of full employment was not feasible, then it was vital to have a co-ordinated economic policy in order to spread employment more equally over the whole area.

Professor Verdoorn wanted to underline the importance which should be attached to ease of negotiation. It was rather depressing to see the long list of negotiations needed to set up even a modest union like Benelux, although the governments concerned had agreed relatively easily.

Professor Scitovsky said he agreed mainly with Dr. Rothschild. A customs union might be very hard on some of the smaller countries, and might harm all the under-developed areas of Europe, so that their future development might become an even greater problem under a customs union. The only solution would be an all-European investment plan.

Professor Scitovsky said he had not stressed increasing competition within customs unions, because it was not so very important or desirable. He himself was all against economic insecurity. Any European Customs Union would require much economic planning, and the co-ordination not only of investment policy but of nearly all economic policy.

Professor Triffin said that he would mention only his disagreements. To M. Uri, he would say that he disagreed on the question of the dislocation in Benelux trade caused by the differential devaluation of 1949. His own view was that this was one element which *smoothed* the adjustment. Before devaluation Belgium had been much nearer overall equilibrium in her economy than the Netherlands.

Professor Triffin was puzzled to hear that a small country, according to Professor Patinkin, was more likely to specialize, and so was at a disadvantage because it would have to give big price concessions to expand output in a customs union. This implied that a small country enjoyed a monopolistic position. Surely this was an advantage rather than a disadvantage. Again, if a country was very small, it was unlikely that the elasticity of demand for its product would be small.

To Professor Leduc, Professor Triffin said that no customs union would involve the equalization of wages. There were large differences in wages within the United States, and he thought that some diversity in wage levels was essential to the satisfactory operation of a customs union. Finally, on Dr. Rothschild's point, he thought that many of the arguments traditionally used about the advantages of scale within customs unions were only secondary. It was not so much a question of obstacles to trade, but of the *security* of the institutional framework rather than its nature. A customs union gave guarantees against sudden unilateral action, and also encouraged more positive measures of co-operation between countries. Customs unions could not operate successfully within a narrow framework. When we thought of integration, we must beware of the false dilemma of attaching too much importance to a rigid notion of what was a border and what constituted integration. Between complete nationalism and complete integration there were many intermediate solutions. This was the real challenge ; to reconcile some degree of political independence with a smaller degree of economic independence. We were not yet ready for world government, but did we have to wait for that before we could have any degree of economic interdependence ? Surely some regional solutions were possible.

Professor Verdoorn thought that so far as the smaller members of a customs union were concerned, so long as full employment could be maintained, the elasticity of supply would not be sufficient to allow excessive 'stepping on toes', as Dr. Rothschild would say. It would not be possible for the German cement industry, for example, to eliminate its competitors in all partner countries, because full employment would prevent a sufficiently rapid expansion. The greatest fortune of Benelux was to be launched at a time of full employment. Belgian wage costs were in 1954 still some 30 per cent above those of the Netherlands. If wages were 40 to 50 per cent of total costs, this gave a cost advantage of some 15 per cent to Dutch producers. Dutch exporters, however, were not foolish enough to give away this advantage in lower prices. Working at near-full capacity, the elasticity of supply was low, and exporters were only too ready to maximize their profits instead.

One aspect of his paper had not been discussed. Experience with Benelux made it plausible that the shifts in Dutch exports to Belgium which had taken place had been towards goods in which the Netherlands had a comparative advantage (page 17 of his paper). For, since the shares of total Dutch exports to Belgium held by different goods were now much more equal (the inequality had been reduced by 50 per cent), the pattern now conformed more to the general Dutch comparative advantage than in 1938. A customs union, even if the increase in the volume of trade to which it led to was only 25 per cent, appeared, therefore, to bring about a more efficient allocation of productive resources.

ELEVENTH SESSION
Tuesday afternoon, September 17th, 1957

A CONTINUATION OF THE DISCUSSION ON THE PAPERS BY PROFESSORS SCITOVSKY, VERDOORN, AND MARCY

Chairman : PROFESSOR PREST

M. Uri turned from the morning's discussion to the current proposals for the European Economic Community of Six, and its relation to the proposed Free Trade Area. He said it was constantly being asked how the EEC Treaty stood up to the tests we had discussed here, and which could be summed up under four headings : efficiency, vulnerability, stability, and development. Under efficiency, the crude argument was that large-scale production required a large market and that a large market was more efficient than a small one. This argument should be discounted. The Common Market's supporters had never relied on such simple theorizing and had never suggested that the individual European economies were too small to allow firms of optimum size to be set up — though this might indeed not be possible in some industries. For example, many European countries were too small to provide work for a steel strip mill. Professor Scitovsky's argument was that the intermediate stages of industry could provide markets for each other, and hence achieve optimum size. The strength of this argument could be illustrated from the relationship of the French steel industry to the French engineering industry. The weakness of the French steel industry was not an inherent one, but arose from the relative weakness of French engineering.

All these four tests had been very much in the minds of those who had worked on the plans for a European Economic Community — and this went much further than a Free Trade Area or Customs Union, simply because such problems had been recognized. It was all very well to decide to abandon protection, but we must establish such conditions as would ensure that a return to protection was not inevitable. In particular, governments would have to intervene to avoid either inflation or deflation. If they did not work in common, they would fall back on the old means of self-protection.

M. Uri said he would try to define, in terms of the concepts we had been using, the general characteristics of the EEC area. First, the countries were largely homogeneous in the sense that all were engaged in many lines of production. Second, nearly all were self-sufficient in food. Third, all were developed countries with a high level of culture. It was often said that in many fields the differences between these countries were not very much bigger than the differences between the regions of a single large country.

M. Uri proceeded to recall those provisions of the EEC Treaty which were relevant to our four criteria. First, efficiency could be treated from the point of view of the firm and of the best allocation of resources. For the efficiency of the firm, incentives were of paramount importance, and Professor Scitovsky's sociological analysis of the attitudes of European entrepreneurs showed how necessary it was to force them to become more competition-minded by exerting outside pressures. But since stability was essential, it might require a large country and many branches of industry to reconcile stability with competition. Participants had already said that when the pooling of markets started, the advantage would lie with the enterprises in larger countries which would have sufficient funds to be able immediately to develop markets in other countries. Was there not an answer to this in the fact that the establishment of the Common Market would be gradual, taking twelve to fifteen years? During that time many other things would change too and capital might well become more mobile once markets began to expand.

The second criterion of efficiency was the allocation of resources. Here we needed rules for competition. The problem was clearly posed by the differences between the EEC plan and that for a Free Trade Area, where a major problem arose over subsidies. We had to try to distinguish between those subsidies which prevented competition and those which compensated for the initial disadvantages of under-developed countries, or which formed part of social policy and affected consumption but not production. There was no distinction between export subsidies and other subsidies in the Treaty, it being assumed that subsidies on costs of production might frustrate economic efficiency. The British approach, for the Free Trade Area, was to distinguish sharply between export subsidies, which must disappear, and other subsidies, which were not regarded as inconsistent with the outright liberalization of trade. M. Uri wondered whether the value of the wider Free Trade Area did not depend on very big differences in price structures, affected in different ways by government policy. Was the system effective if the production of one industry depended not on its costs but on the policy of a government which gave it artificial aid to keep it competitive ?

In the Treaty the preoccupation with conditions of competition went further, the negotiations had considered the problem of distortions and how to eliminate them. This problem had played a major rôle in all the discussions which led to the Treaty, but he did not know whether it had been elaborated scientifically by the theorists. He would like to exemplify the problem by a model which considered social security and its financing in an industry like coal mining. The Continental system financed social security, in principle, from employers' contributions calculated as a pro-portion of the .wages they paid. The British system relied more heavily on payments from general tax resources — mostly direct taxes on income and profits, and indirect taxes on luxuries. The result was that the dis-tribution of the burden between different industries was not the same. The Continental system put a heavy burden on industries employing much labour, while the British system was less closely connected with the amount of labour employed in a particular industry. There was no distortion for the economy as a whole, but for some particular industries, especially coal, a large part of their different prices was a result of this difference in the way social security was financed. If the problem were not tackled, there would be big differences in coal prices, between Britain and Europe even though the miners' wages and output per man-shift were similar in Britain and in Europe. In theory, there should be an increase in the demand for coal in Britain and a decrease on the Continent. In practice, this would be impossible in a Common Market. To prevent the demand for British coal being impossibly large, there might be a steep increase in British prices, which might lead to an enormous rise in profits. Or there might be export restrictions, which were incompatible with the Treaty. Something had to be done about such problems. To say this was not to imply that one system was bad and the other good ; it was just that they were incompatible. This was the kind of distortion he had in mind.

How far any limitations on the scope of the free market arrangements would in themselves lead to big distortions was hard to say. If all products did not come within the Free Trade Area arrangements, and food and services were excluded, what were the consequences for competition ? Would these exclusions hamper the correct working of competition, and would competition be distorted if it were only partial ? It had been said that the Coal and Steel Community rested on a distortion. These were industries which had been asked overnight to compete, through the abolition of protection, though they were parts of national economies which pursued different tariff policies and had very different standards of living, wage levels, and so on. This problem might be very serious over a much wider field than its effects on food producers alone. It might well affect competition between industrial goods if they were produced by workers whose food supplies were obtained in very different conditions, with some countries self-sufficient and protected, and others buying at lower world prices. For would not differences in food prices lead to differences in money wages ?

This brought M. Uri to his second test of the Common Market, the test in terms of vulnerability. He said it was obvious that one basic factor of the Common Market was reciprocity. A nation could not be required to give up any kind of protection without some reward, but if the introduction of the Common Market led to the closing down of any branch of a nation's industry, that nation could rely on getting regular supplies on equal terms from outside. The elimination of export restrictions and dual pricing was a pre-condition for the elimination of protection, and in particular industries, like coal, engineering, and steel, it was an important pre-condition. There must be some guarantee against unpredictable and one-sided changes in national policies ; one could not expect any country to abandon one of its national industries if it were not assured of regular supplies of that product from abroad. Vulnerability also raised the question of the meaning of common tariffs in relation to the rest of the world. We could not conceal the fact that one reason for setting up the Common Market was to enhance the bargaining power in tariff negotiations of all member countries taken together. It was all to the good that the bargaining power of 'the six' would match the power of the United States in tariff negotiations and would make more likely the lowering of the United States tariff, which would be trade-creating. We should think, not in static terms, or of effects on paper, but of reality.

One argument encouraging agreement on a common tariff that was not excessive, was that if any industry could withstand competition from within the Common Market area, it had not much to fear from competition outside that area, and would not need very much protection from the rest of the world. Increased competition within the Common Market might be just the thing which was needed to make the industry competitive with the whole world. This was obviously trade-creating, making it possible to reduce protective tariffs against industries in third countries.

On stability, M. Uri felt that the Common Market proposals recognized that everything could not be left to automatic adjustment ; some governmental intervention was essential to both stability and development. We did not want a system where governments could not intervene at all, but one where they could intervene in a systematic way or at a higher level. This was true, for example, of the balance of payments problem. Here we must distinguish between different types of balance of payment disequilibrium ; otherwise any attempt to restore equilibrium would have to work through readjustment downwards to the level set by the most deflationary country. The achievement of expansion without recurrent balance of payments difficulties would be a greater contribution to raising standards of living than any reallocation of resources resulting from freer trade in a wider area.

Finally, on development, M. Uri drew attention to two preoccupations embodied in the Treaty. In Europe, we could not ignore the fact that an important prerequisite for any increase in productivity was to obtain the support of organized labour. A few years before, trade unions had been wholly opposed to increasing productivity, because they thought it must mean lower wages. We had to enlist trade union co-operation for the productive *redeployment* of labour if this were made necessary by the Common Market. With all the fears of European labour, it might be very important to set up a fund to finance such redeployment.

There had also been preoccupation with possible discrepancies between rates of development in different areas, and it was possible that some areas, despite their potentialities, would be net losers from the Common Market, simply because they were not yet advanced enough. The same might also apply to some firms and industries. It was for precisely this reason that there was provision in the Treaty for a special investment bank and for special facilities for pump-priming. Such provisions would make it possible for areas now at a disadvantage to catch up and take advantage of their potentialities. Many twentieth-century liberals had assumed that free connections between different areas would raise productivity and living standards, and this idea had been accepted from the start. But it was not enough. We needed a common infra-structure to allow new enterprises to be set up in under-developed areas. The liberal assumptions might well hold true only after the first phase of conscious pump-priming.

M. Uri's general impression was that, with the progressive character of the provisions of the Treaty, and the nature of the area as it now stood, one need not expect any large shift of industry when the Common Market came into being. In every country, each individual industry would probably need to reorganize and try to become more efficient, but he did not see why there should be any need to close down large sections of industry, unless some nations had very large competitive advantages. Perhaps the biggest need would be to do away with foolish economic policies. It was an open question whether common European policies would be better or worse than the policies of individual governments. That depended entirely on the efficiency of the institutional framework. Partnership would surely prevent the most foolish of the economic policies of any individual country being continued, and would therefore eliminate those policies which had most seriously held back progress in member countries.

What had been attempted from a policy point of view was to turn the six countries into a single large country in their policies towards the rest of the world. There were qualifications, of course, but the provisions of the Treaty pointed in that direction, and that was the way in which economic union had been construed in the parliaments which had ratified it.

Professor Jewkes said he wanted to speak not as an economist but just as one European who believed in a general way in the creation of large markets, and was passionately concerned for the re-creation of European unity. He was longing for bonfires of passports ; he hated customs officials ; and he was convinced that their abolition would be a good thing. But as he listened to the arguments of economists who supported the Common Market, he felt they were promising too much. Many of their arguments were mutually incompatible, and some of them highly dubious. In spite of the soothing phrases of M. Uri, and the assurance that all difficulties had been thought of and eliminated, he still felt that in some way the economists were taking him for a ride.

One reason for his doubts was to be found in the way in which the word 'competition' was used to mean many different things. If we asked, 'Why will a large Common Market be good ?', the simple answer was, 'Because it will bring more competition'. But why should more competition be good ? There were several reasons. The traditional explanation was that if tariffs were abolished there would be a redistribution of resources, a beneficial change in the location of industries, the elimination of marginal firms, and so on. Production would be in the hands of more efficient agents. But it followed that the advantages of competition were derived only through a considerable amount of upset, and the advantages were the greater in proportion as the upset created was the greater. In other words, we had to pay the price of efficiency in terms of disturbance.

At that stage, the economist made a *volte-face*. He suggested that perhaps these disturbances need not occur ; he described the process of competition in another way. When two firms were separated by a tariff, the explanation now ran, and this tariff was abolished, the high-cost producer would intensify his efforts, improve his efficiency, become a low-cost producer, and thus minimize the need for economic readjustment. Professor Jewkes felt that this second explanation of what would happen was not consistent with the first. It might or might not be true that a firm could be made more efficient by threats.

The third concept of increased competition was that of Professor Scitovsky, who took the view that competition between small firms was not competition at all. According to Professor Scitovsky, present European-style competition was not what we needed. When the Common Market was founded bigger units would come into existence — mergers and amalgamations would be formed — and there would be more valuable competition between these units. Professor Jewkes did not see that this would do much good. We had had plenty of mergers in Europe in the last few years, but had they really increased efficiency ? Indeed, he hoped that the Common Market would include an institution charged with the duty of preventing and controlling mergers, as in the United States.

In so far as the Common Market eliminated distortions, Professor Jewkes felt it was bound to mean changes, and therefore to be painful ;

to deny that was to be quite unrealistic, and would mean great disillusionment later on. Any devices introduced for easing the transition should be scrutinized carefully to make certain that they did not do more harm than good. If, for example, compensation was going to be paid to business-men, and plans made to help firms to remain in uneconomical industries, this was merely storing up problems for the future.

M. Uri had asked what was the optimum size of a customs union. His own answer was 'one which included the United States'. He could not understand the American attitude on this matter. Americans were conscious of the advantages of a large free trading area in their own country. Why should European countries not be given an open invitation to join an American Customs Union ? This would save the United States a good deal in economic aid, and encourage European countries to help themselves. It would also have the advantage of initiating a common market on the optimum scale.

M. Uri replied that there was no provision for compensation or help to maintain firms indefinitely in bad locations. All that had been envisaged was some attempt to help the reconversion of enterprises through loans. He was not sure whether the notion that one could only gain if someone else suffered was really in contradiction to the notion that enterprises should adjust to the changing conditions rather than disappear. It was true that activity would need to be redistributed, but this might not necessarily occur only at one point in time ; and we might also argue about the identity of an enterprise. If it reorganized itself very profoundly in the six months before the Common Market was set up, or if it changed its activity, was it the same enterprise or was it another one ? From a human point of view, it might employ the same workers and the same entrepreneurs. In that sense, there was no contradiction between avoiding painful shifts in employment and the possibility of a necessary reorganization within the firms themselves. This was what the transition period meant ; change without suffering. But the transition could not last for ever, and there must be limited, and not unlimited, help to firms.

Professor Prest said Professor Jewkes had told us we could not have it both ways ; but M. Uri took the view that we could have advantages without disadvantages if we brought in the Common Market slowly. One relevant point might be that in the United States the development of a large common market had been accompanied by a rise in national income, and a rise in population faster than would ever be possible in Europe.

Professor Scitovsky did not see any incompatibility between Professor Jewkes' first two definitions of competition. His own guess was that there would be as much, or more, reallocation of resources *within* individual countries as there was between countries. In some European countries, for example France, efficient and inefficient firms were standing side by side, with the government subsidizing the inefficient. The creation of a customs union would force governments to reconsider the social policies allowing such subsidization, and this would lead to the reallocation of resources within countries. Nor was it incompatible with the second meaning of competition — added pressure on individual firms to mend their ways. No one expected great changes in human nature, but some pressures would be brought to bear on backward firms. He believed that this would involve some dislocation and some suffering, and to that extent he was not even sure that this second type of competition was very desirable. We should certainly not take it for granted that the costs of change could never be too high.

The meaning of Professor Jewkes' third type of competition was not clear. His own argument had been that one advantage of competition might be to encourage investment in large modern plants. A long-established industry of small firms might lack the capital resources of a single large firm.

M. Duquesne wondered whether we were not bogged down by a static outlook. We were asking what would happen to the present structure of European production after the EEC had come into existence. But the important question in the long run was what would be the influence of the Common Market on the future development of European industry. This was far more relevant. If we could increase the rate of development of our industries by 15 per cent, the long-term results would be much more beneficial than anything we could expect from a reallocation of our present resources.

Professor Weiller said that when talking of the economics of the Common Market, one of the most interesting features was that the discussion took a poetic turn towards more or less wild dreams. One might claim that the United States would give up its present economic policies, but this was only a dream. It was also only a dream to hope to answer all possible objections beforehand. M. Uri had answered all our questions, but experts could only propose, not dispose, and the job of economists was to try to see what the response to particular policies would be. Was there incompatibility ?

Professor Weiller said that governments were apt to make mistakes, and he was concerned about the Common Market's vulnerability to nationalism. Where economic vulnerability was greatest, vulnerability to nationalism was greatest too. He did not see why France was regarded so often in the recent discussions as the most vulnerable country. It might be that if monetary policy was regarded as the only method of solving transitional problems — at least, if it was the only permissible way of solving them according to the rules of the game — any Common Market country might then be committed to a long period of deflation which the population would not stand for.

Professor Weiller felt we were bound to think in terms of world relations for each of the participating countries. Whether we had a Common Market and a Free Trade Area or not, we must keep in mind attempts to increase exports to other markets too ; for the French, there was still such a thing as the franc area. But it was necessary to think more generally of expanding trade relations in the near future, especially with the under-developed countries, and all this without forgetting the efforts that must still be made to fill the dollar gap.

On the first part of M. Uri's argument, Professor Weiller said this was an interesting and attractive attempt at comparative statics. Reverting to the previous arguments on tariffs, he recalled that one could have an average of 25, 15, or 0 per cent, but that a certain flexibility in policy was needed, especially to avoid depression (and that was true whether the tariff was at an average level of 50 or 0 per cent in the long run). A zero tariff might be attractive, but where the tariff was 0 per cent flexibility was difficult. If all the world would enter into a customs union, that would be well enough, but it would be dangerous if there were no possibility of any escape clause. It would be a pity if we could not apply any emergency measures under the Common Market and governments could not make adjustments to cope with such things as short-period balance of payments deficits.

Professor Hoffmann was anxious to point out that there had now been ten years of discussion in Europe on the problem of integration and that the Treaty was actually signed. Surely what we now had to do was to see what we could make of the existing situation, even the Treaty itself contained a lot of economic contradictions, which were the price of political compromise. For it *was* signed. Professor Scitovsky was anxious not to pay a high human price for the Common Market, but one could argue from the German example in the post-war world. The United States had given a great deal in order to offer the German economy an opportunity for rapid development. This had been an enormous success, and a high rate of growth, perhaps temporarily an abnormally high rate, had been achieved. As a result, there was relatively great political stability in Germany. One could well imagine that if there were an increase in the growth rate with the Common Market, the political stability of Europe would become greater ; this in turn was a necessary condition for a high rate of investment.

Professor Hoffmann wondered if it really was necessary to assume that the aim of the European Customs Union was to build up a Chinese Wall round it ? Economists had certainly not been thinking in those terms. The internal situation in Continental Europe would not allow a high tariff wall round the six countries, and, in fact, the Customs Union meant a contribution to the further liberalization of international trade.

Professor Hoffmann said that many people stressed the demonstration effect in less-developed areas. Would not the demonstration effect work even more successfully within the Common Market, and give incentives for new investment ? The old vicious circle of poverty in under-developed areas could possibly be broken by the Investment Bank of the Common Market. The Common Market would also be a guarantee of the continuity of investment. Why did capital not move enough between different parts of Europe ? Because there were no guarantees that monetary and fiscal policy would not change. Yet within the Common Market such a guarantee would be given. The Common Market might also overcome the Italian social problem of how to encourage development in the South and allow investment to take place. Differences in the quality of labour within Europe were vast, and this was an advantage. It allowed us to build up new industries to use these different qualities of labour, and this meant new chances for investment.

Professor Triffin was puzzled by the tone of the discussion. Many of the economists who used to be strongly anti-protectionist were now terrified of the dislocation which would be caused by abandoning tariffs. He suggested two counter-arguments. First, we argued too much as though we had a really rational tariff system, exactly designed to reduce the distortions in the world economy to a minimum. A study of French tariffs showed their complete irrationality — the result of past history. One would expect low tariffs on goods that were important French exports. In fact, the opposite was the case. Second, we forgot that without a Common Market nations could meet big rises in each other's tariffs. Surely we needed institutions to prevent the dislocations which had been the cause of so much trouble in the past.

Professor Edwards held a position half-way between Professor Jewkes and M. Uri, he agreed that we should not accomplish much if the Common Market merely substituted private for public restrictions. That said, however, there was surely a basis for optimism, though we must reconcile ourselves to facing some dislocations. The discussion had proceeded in terms of readjustments in the costs and efficiencies of business enterprises, in so far as these were capable of control. In other words, we had been concerned with internal economies. In creating a wider economic area, however, we should, irrespective of what happened to internal economies, create the possibility of achieving substantial *external* economies. Efficient service industries would become available in a way that would not happen in smaller economies. So, while particular enterprises might suffer hardship and readjustment, there would be increases in efficiency arising from the external advantages offered by the Common Market.

M. Duquesne said he would quote one example to illustrate what Professor Edwards had just said. A study published by the cotton industry of one European country complained about the insufficiency of the tariff protection afforded to cotton, but at the same time regarded the protection given to machinery and dye-stuffs producers as excessive. This proved that national protectionist policies might well be self-defeating and involve contradictions.

Professor Weiller said we were dealing here with comparative statics and must remember that the problems of an economic union must be studied from a number of points of view. For instance, we might like the customs tariff to be zero, but that could not happen immediately for at least two reasons. First, it could not happen because of the existing pattern of trade, which reminded him of one of Professor Lionel Robbins' sayings that though free trade was desirable in principle, in existing conditions we still needed the sterling area, imperial preference, and so on. Second, it could not happen because of economic fluctuations ; in order to have the utmost flexibility in policy, we needed some kind of tariff —

perhaps close to zero, but obviously not quite zero.

Professor Triffin thought there was a large degree of truth in what Professor Weiller had said, but it was only half the truth. He had heard the same argument from a Swiss colleague in the European Payments Union, who stressed the need to be able to use policy in a flexible manner. The answer, of course, was that if similar flexibility were enjoyed by sixteen other nations, the Swiss colleague would be in a worse position than where all had to accept the same restrictions. When we discussed flexibility from a national point of view, we forgot that it would multiply our problems.

Dr. Rothschild said he shared Professor Jewkes' doubts and could not follow all the counter-arguments. It was too simple to say that Communism was weak in Germany because of the high rate of post-war growth. To say that was surely to ignore the whole of Germany's history since 1914, and particularly since 1933. It might help to sell the idea of the Common Market, but it did not help us to see whether a Free Trade Area would assist under-developed countries.

Dr. Rothschild agreed with Professor Triffin that every country would like complete freedom of action in trade policy, but this dilemma could not be solved by the creation of the Common Market, because we could not guarantee that the Common Market would itself pursue a correct policy. How could we ensure that the right policy was followed ? Through OEEC or through supranational authorities ? So long as there was full employment, the Common Market would work, but so would OEEC, and so would GATT. Moreover, the OEEC system was not an irreversible one ; retreat was possible. It would also be possible in the transition period of the Common Market, but not later on. M. Uri had assumed that common policy would always be wiser and better than that of a single nation, but Dr. Rothschild was not so sure. Some individual countries might act more wisely than a common authority, and might arrange their regional interests more effectively. He did not think the demand for disintegration at certain stages in history was pure chance or mere emotionalism. At the break-up of the Austro-Hungarian Empire, certain areas, Czechoslovakia for example, were extremely anxious to leave the empire, and they had developed more rapidly after 1918. There were economic arguments in favour of forming a bigger trading area, but unless we had a clear idea of its policies and its institutional set-up, the consequences might be disastrous. It was true that the process of integration in Europe would be gradual, but none of us knew which was the decisive stage in tariff reduction. Where did one start to feel the full blast of foreign competition ; after the first 5 per cent reduction of the tariff — or after the last ? We must realize that this problem was not so simple as it looked.

M. Uri summed up the discussion. He said he had been struck by the view of Dr. Rothschild that the OEEC system was reversible. He thought it was the opposite. If one wanted to improve an organization, it was essential *not* to admit that a retreat was possible, or interested parties might go to their governments and press for this reverse process. Proof was impossible, but, on the face of it, the possibility of gradually engaging in an irreversible process was very important in forcing on adjustment.

On external economies, it was important to remember that most business-men did not think of all the other things which could change while tariff barriers were being reduced. Over fifteen years a 60 per cent increase of production in Europe was quite possible, so that competitors would not have to share only the present European output, but a future increment of output as well. Changes were not a hardship if firms did not have to reduce output absolutely, but only to accept a smaller share of an increased output. Over fifteen years, too, the whole structure of costs would change. Similarly, changes in basic economic conditions could well do away with the handicaps under which some parts of industry were working. Nor should one draw inferences from competition with the dumped exports of protected economies. In the Common Market, one would have to sell on other markets under exactly the same conditions as in one's own. One snag about trade liberalization under OEEC was that it implied no integration of cost structures, and it followed that a more far-reaching system might be better balanced, and mean far more than just doing away with quantitative barriers to trade.

M. Uri closed by saying that Professor Hoffmann was quite right when he said that the Treaty bore the marks of a great deal of negotiation, much of it window dressing. But that left us with the practical problem of extending free trade beyond 'the six' to a Free Trade Area. A lot more thinking was necessary on the kind of conditions which would make the Free Trade Area acceptable and workable. Fortunately, the reasoning behind the Common Market Treaty could teach us much about the problems of the Free Trade Area.

INDEX

Entries in the Index in Black Type under the Names of Participants in the Conference indicate their Papers or the Discussion on their Papers. Entries in Italics indicate Contributions by Participants to the Discussions

Index

Capital accumulation, differing rates of, 7-; in small nations, 26 ; in Switzerland, 66

Capital investment, international flows of, 23

Capital markets, domestic, 7, 335

Capital stocks, of Switzerland, 66 ; of United States, 36

Cartels, international, 8, 123-6 ; national, 8, 58, — objects of, 372

Chemical industry, Italian, 154 ; Swiss, 64-5

Clark, C., 36, 51 n., 61, 172 n.

Classical theory of foreign trade, inapplicability of, to developing economies, 182

Cobb, C. W., and Douglas, P. H., 38

Cobb-Douglas production function, 38

Commodity agreements, difficulties of, 284

Common market, European, *see* European Economic Community

Comparative advantages, exploitation of, by small nations, 17

Competition, attitudes to, 374 ; character of, xvii, 120, 343, 368, 372 ; effects of size on character of, 122-3, 127-30, 160-62 ; effects of, in United States, 346 ; increases of, in customs unions, 273, 286, 432 ; intensity of, with free trade, 285-6 ; public policy towards, 128-9

Concentration of foreign trade, indices of, 21-2, 72, 74

Concentration of industry, and competition, 159-62

Convertibility, key rôle of policies of major trading nations in, 262

Costs, relation of, to size of firm, 105-8

Creamer, D., 39 n.

Credit markets, international, 2, 10-12

Cultural discontinuities at national frontiers, 2, 335 ; as barrier to international division of labour, 25

Cultural factors in dynamic adjustment, 130, 383

Customs unions : advantages to small members, 428 ; aims, 291 ; competition, 273, 286-90, 410 ; cultural homogeneity, 375 ; credit facilities, 412 ; effects on non-member small nations, 275-6 ; effects in reducing vulnerability of member countries to foreign shocks, 259 ; effects in giving large nation advantages to small nations, 265-81 ; limitations on efficient producers, 258 ; market expansion, 272-4 ; monetary integration, 258, 410 ; optimum size, 419, 433 ; primary effects, 295-310 ; rates of growth, 414 ; risks of inflation, 257-259, 409 ; trade creating and trade diverting effects, 252-7, 275, 406-15, 416 ; traditional arguments against, 253-5 ; Scandinavian attitude to, 423 ; structural changes in member countries, 411

Cyclical stability, international comparisons of, 71

Defence, government expenditure on research for, 111 ; economies of scale in research costs of, 236 ; wastefulness of research expenditure for, 376

Defence expenditure, determinants of, 234-6, economies of scale in, xxi, 26, 236-8, 396 ; international comparisons of, 336-7 ; in small countries, 26-7 ; in under-developed countries, 149 ; minimum, 136

Demand, homogeneity of, in large countries, 41, 370

Democratic institutions, relation of, to competition, 375

Demonstration effect, 361

Denmark, 30 ; resources of, 17

Depressed areas, effects of inclusion in customs unions, 424-5

De-stabilizing forces, propagation of, 194

Developing countries, problems of, 133-50

Development, degree of, as element in stability, 207

Development expenditure, *see* Research and development

Development plan, Italian, 164

Diplomatic services, costs of, 149

Discontinuities at national frontiers, 1-2 ; elimination of, 9, 339

Disintegration, economic effects of, 378, 385

Diversification of firms, in United States, 119-20, 367

Diversification of industries, degree of, xvii, 16, 72

Domestic capital markets, growth of, 7 ; lack of, in Portugal, 187

Domestic market, minimum efficient size of, 152 ; size of, as limiting factor

Index

in development of small nations, xvi, xxi, 6, 40, 152, — in relation to efficiency, 35-53

Domination effect, 22, 81-2, 86, 183, 188

Douglas, P. H., and Cobb, C. W., 38

Duncan, G. A., 267

Dupriez, L. H., 207

Duquesne de la Vinelle, L., xvi, **78-92**, *335, 343, 344, 345, 346*, **348-58**, *355, 357, 364, 377, 378, 381, 383, 402, 403, 409, 413, 417, 418, 419, 425, 434, 436,*

Durand, D., 39 n.

Dynamic adjustment and size of nation, 131-200

Economic growth, specific aspects of, in small nations, 14-32

Economic homogeneity, concept of, 134

Economic integration, degrees of, 271, 426 ; reconcilability of varying levels of, 252, 412, 414

Economic nationalism, consequences of, 149-50 ; vulnerability to, and size of nation, 247-64, 406-15

Economic policies and rate of growth, 217-18, 382

Economic services, economies of scale in, 232-4 ; international comparisons of expenditure on, 233

Economic sovereignty, need for limitations on, 251-2, 262-4, 414-15

Economic structure, concentration of, in small nations, 15-18 ; diversification of, as function of level of development, 16

Economic take-off, concept of, 215

Economies of scale, availability of, to small nations, 276-81 ; extent of, xvii, 95-116, 278-81, 358-66 ; in administration, xxi, 227, 238-9, 394-395 ; in defence, xxi, 26, 236-8, 396 ; in industry, xvi, 25, 102-8, 136, 340 ; in professional activities, 25 ; in research and development, 103-13, 154, 157-9, 236 ; in retailing, 25

Education and training, investment in, in Italy, — in Switzerland, 69-70, — in United States, 25, 37 ; international comparisons of expenditure on, 230-32

Edwards, C. D., xvii, **117-30**, *334, 346, 347, 354, 360,* **366-77**, *369, 373-5, 377, 382, 383, 392, 394-7, 398, 403, 405, 413, 414, 420, 421, 436*

Efficiency, definitions of, 37, 78-9 ; international comparisons of, 47-50 ; measurement of, 36-40, 340 ; and size of the economy, 43-4, 35-53, 85-88, 136, 341, 343 ; of small nations, 54-77, 78-92

Eliasberg, V. F., and Abramovitz, M., 399 n.

Ellis, H. S., *344*

Employment, problems of, in small nations as result of policies of other countries, 249

Engineering industry, dependence of, on government expenditures, 85-6 ; development of, in relation to speed of expansion, 87 ; international collaboration in, 114 ; inventions in, 109 ; in Italy, 155

Euratom, 9, 163

European Coal and Steel Community, 9, 164, 165, 213, 252, 412, 423-4, 430

European Economic Community, conditions of competition in, 429 ; establishment of, 151, 252, 427-38 ; investment bank in, 431 ; opportunities afforded to Italy by, 163 ; vulnerability of, 430

European integration, impacts of, on trade of rest of world, 261-2

European Payments Union, 10, 81, 252, 254, 258, 259, 260, 261, 412

Export industries, specialization of, in small nations, 12, 63-5, 72, 89

Export market, size of, in relation to domestic market, 152 ; risks of, xix, 9, 17, 144, 153, 197, 284, 338, 378, 416

Exports, international comparisons of volume of, 180 ; ratio of, to total output in small nations, 19, 63-5 ; sensitivity of, to monetary policies of other nations, 198

External relations, influence of, in stability, 209-19

Fabricant, S., xvi, **35-53**, **339-48**, *341, 343, 344, 348, 350, 351, 359, 369, 381, 390, 399, 400, 401*

Factor mobility, within large countries, 2, 6, 341, 392

Federal nations, discontinuities within, 3

Firm, definition of, 118-19 ; minimum efficient size of, xvii, 85 ; size and efficiency of, 45, 105-8, 117-30 ; specialization of, xviii, 100-2

Index

Florence, P. Sargant, 98 n.
Foreign investment in small countries, 23
Foreign subsidiaries of national firms, 65-6
Foreign trade, as escape from penalties of smallness, 113-14, 211, 265-90, 415-38 ; classical theory of, and inapplicability to developing economy, 182 ; difficulties and risks of, 9, 17, 144, 153, 197, 270, 283-5, 338, 378-9, 416 ; in economies of small nations, 18-24, 63-5 ; indices of concentration of, 21-2 ; *per capita* in relation to *per capita* incomes, 19-20 ; political factors limiting dependence on, 26 ; ratio to national incomes, 20
Fourastié, J., 61
France : Defence expenditure, 237 ; general level of productivity, 347 ; real expenditure on public services, 228-9 ; size of industrial units, 365
Frankel, M., 48, 50 n., 341
Free trade, classical principles of, 247-8
Free trade policies, need for long-term commitments to, 271
Friedman, M., 45

Galbraith, J. K., 104 n.
Gehrels, F. G., and Johnston, B. F., 270 n., 271, 272, 275, 276 n., 278 n.
General Agreement on Tariffs and Trade, xx, 247, 250, 271, 437
Germany (Western), occupational structure of, 73
Gilbert, M., and Kravis, I. B., xxi, 36, 48, 224, 228, 229, 237, 401
Goldsmith, R. W., 37 n., 341
Government action, greater ease of, in small countries, 209 ; in stabilization 192
Government activity, differences in extent of, 396
Government authority, as factor in national integration, 1, 3
Government expenditure, in engineering industries, 85 ; in fundamental research, 157-9 ; in research for defence, 111-12, 236, 376 ; variations in, 395-7
Government planning, rôle of, in Portugal, 186
Government policy, results or errors in, for small nations, 80-82

Government services, variations in costs with size of state in Australia, 241-3
Growth, policies most likely to ensure, 217-18
Growth rates, comparisons of, 389, 390 ; inequalities in, 202 ; trends of, 205
Gudin, E., *344, 376, 388, 408, 421, 424*

Haberler, G., 253, 254
Habsburg monarchy, consequences of dissolution of, 168-72
Hague, D. C., *359, 362, 372, 419*
Harrod-Domar model, 185
Health services, *see* Social services
Hertz, F., 170 n.
Hirschman, A. O., 21, 348
Hoffmann, W., 61, *337, 344, 352, 359, 362, 381, 389, 404, 410, 413, 425, 435*
Home markets, uniformity of, 6
Housing expenditure, *see* Social services
Hultgren, T., 49 n.

Imports, ratio of, to total output in small nations, 19
Incomes, discontinuities in, at national frontiers, 6 ; distribution of, in small countries, 30
Increasing returns, mechanism of, 45-6
Industrialization, effects of size of economy of pattern of, 82-6 ; international comparisons of, 62-3
Industrial concentration, degree of, 103 ; rôle of mergers in, 104 ; effects on character of competition, 120-2 ; and specialization, 159-62
Industrial production after world wars, international comparisons of, 178-9
Industrial research, conditions and costs of, 108-13
Industry, diversification of, xvii measurement of size of, 40-2 ; relation of size to efficiency of, 42-3, 102-8 ; size distribution of firms in, 100-2
Inflation, effects of differing rates of, xx
Innovation, as element in rapid progress, 209 ; attitudes towards, 188, 370, 374 ; characteristics of, 108 ; in United States economy, 52
Innovations, expenditure on development of, 110-12
Instability, causes of, 191-5, 207-18 ; coefficients of, 190 ; dangers of, for

442

Index

Index

Managerial capacity, as factor limiting growth of firms, 362, 364
Marcy, G., xx, **265-81**, *265*, *388*, *415-438*, *423*
Markets, size of, xvi, xxi, 17, 117-30, 134,—as determinant of rate of growth, 390, — measurement of, 40-42, — in Italy, 151, — in Belgium, 85, — in United States, 35-53 ; uniformity of, 6
Market expansion, opportunities for, in customs unions, 272-4
Market expansion schemes, implications of, for under-developed countries, 146-9
Markham, J. W., 104 n.
Marsan, V. A., xix, **151-67**, *356*, **377-86**, *381*, *386*, *402*, *414*
Marshall, A., 41, 52, 53, 102, 359, 362
Martin, A., and Lewis, W. A., xxi, 223, 224, 231, 233, 240, 401
Mass production, inadequacy of international trade as basis for, 286 ; necessity of, in customs unions with increased competition, 289
Mass production techniques, adaptability of, 420-21
Meade, J. E., 275, 297 n., 299 n.
Mergers, rôle of, in industrial concentration, 104
Migration of labour, national attitudes towards, 6
Mill, John Stuart, 182, 186
Minimum efficient size of plant, xvii, 17, 360, 373 ; and technique of production, 364
Monetary integration, extent of, in customs unions, 410
Monetary policy, effects of, on expansion, 79-82 ; of great powers, and small nations, 81-2, 197
Monopolies and Restrictive Practices Commission, 106-8
Monopoly, necessity of, to achieve economic scale of production, 160-1, 187
Moos, S., 177 n.
Moret, M., 265 n.
Morton, G., and Makower, H., 275
Moura, F., 184 n.
Multi-product firms, varieties of, 370-71

Nation, concept of, xiv, 1-13, 133, 201, 333, 336, 339, — in classical economics, 265-6 ; optimum size of, 137

National development programmes, as factor in national integration, 8
National economy, concept and measurement of, 112-20
National frontiers, discontinuities at, 1-13, 333-9 ; economic significance of, 118, 263
National integration, degrees of, 3-8
National political organizations, inadequacy of, for major policy decisions, 264
Nationalism, economic consequences of, 149-50
Nationalization, United Kingdom experience of, 105, 363
Nations, economic interdependence of, 202
Natural resources, and geographical area, 16 ; variations in endowment of, 28, 142, 353
Netherlands Central Planning Bureau, 291 n.
New entry into industry, limitations on, in Portugal, 187
Nunez, J., 184 n.
Nutter, G. W., 103

Olson, E. C., 47 n.
Optimum population, concept of, 138
Optimum size of nation, concept of, 137, 211
Organization for European Economic Co-operation, growth of output of member nations of, 79, 90 ; percentage distribution of exports of member nations, 255 ; trade liberalization under, 252, 257, 259, 271
Output, comparisons of growth of, 79, 343
Overseas empires, as development blocs, 213

Paley Report, 44
Paretti, V., and Bloch, G., 79, 87, 89, 343
Participants, list of, ix
Patent laws and technological competition, 128
Patent licences, manufacturing under, 13, 65-6, 159
Patinkin, D., **208**, *338*, *347*, *349*, *352*, *356*, *377*, *378*, *379*, *383*, *392*, *401*, *403*, *415-7*
Peeters, M., 89 n.
Per capita income, international comparisons of increase of, 204

444

Index

Pereira, G., *384*
Perroux, F., 82, 182 n., 183 n., 201, 203, 205, 206, 216, 390, 393
Pinto, L. T., **182-9, 377-86**
Plants, minimum scale of, 17 ; size distribution of, within industries, 100-102 ; trends in size of, 97-100
Polak, J. J., 300
Polanyi, M., 95 n.
Political factors, limiting dependence on foreign trade, 26, 380
Political nationalism, as factor in national integration, 4, 8, 334, 338
Political régime, as factor in national adaptability, 383
Population, effects of increase in size of, 140 ; percentage of, in large cities, 178
Population movements, restrictions on, 144
Portugal : bargaining position, 184 ; capital markets, 187 ; development problems, 182-9, 384-5 ; distribution of working population, 184 ; government planning, 186 ; innovation, 188 ; poverty, 183-5 ; effects of, on market structure, 187-9 ; prevalence of monopoly, 187, 384 ; size, 183
Preferential tariff reduction, effects of, 253
Prest, W., **241-3**, 347, 377-8, 391, 400, 401, 419, 433
Price cutting, reasons for, 347
Product design, American skill in, 347
Production runs, length of, 346, 360, 363
Productivity, international comparisons of, 47-50, 54-57, 59-62, 342, 344, 345
Profit margins, excessive size of, in small nations, 286-90
Progress, relation of, to size and stability, 190-219 ; standards of measurement of, 201-3
Propagation of de-stabilizing factors, extent of control over, 194
Public expenditure, international comparisons of, 225

Regional integration, *see* Integration
Research, as an economy of scale, 103-113
Research and development, economies of scale in, 154, 157-9, 236, 374 ; government financing of, 157-9, 376

Research and development expenditures, 12-13, 37, 103-4, 108-13, 129, 376-7 ; burden of, for small nations, 136
Resources, mobility of, within national frontiers, 2, 392 ; availability of, as function of area, 16-17
Ricardo, D., 186
Roads and transport, international comparisons of expenditure on, 233
Robinson, E. A. G., xiii-xxii, **223-39**, *333, 336, 343, 345, 347, 349, 351, 353, 359, 360, 362, 365, 370, 371, 376, 377, 379, 381, 382, 388, 391,* **394-406,** *397-398, 399, 400, 401, 402, 403, 405, 408, 412, 417, 420, 423-4*
Rosenbluth, G., 46 n.
Rostas, L., 47, 48, 50 n., 341, 345
Rostow, W. W., 215
Rothbarth, E., 41 n., 343
Rothschild, K. W., **168-81,** *338, 347, 353, 361, 366-8, 371, 375,* **377-86,** 387, 390, 399, 408, 422, 436
Rustow, A., 56

Samuelson, P. A., 104 n.
Sauvy, A., 174
Say, J. B., 192
Scale of plant, minimum and optimum, 17
Scandinavian attitude to customs unions, 423
Schilder, S., 1170 n.
Schumpeter, J. A., 368
Scitovsky, T., xx, 208, 271 n., 273, 276 n., 277, 278, **282-90,** *335, 338, 339, 342, 344, 345, 347, 360, 361, 362, 368, 369, 379, 390, 392, 401, 405, 407, 408, 409, 410, 413,* **415-38,** *418, 420, 421, 426, 433*
Second World War, effects of, on Austria, 172
Size, definitions of, xv, 134, 200-1, 377, 387, 406
Size of factories, international comparisons of, 114-15
Size of firm, minimum efficient, xvii, 85 ; relation of, to efficiency, 45, 117-30 ; relation of, to size of economy, 120-23
Size of markets, *see* Markets
Size of nation, and cost of administration, 223-39 ; difficulties of definition of, 212, 335-8, 387 ; and dynamic adjustment, 131-200, 377-86 ; effects of, where foreign trade is

Index

impossible, 24-7 ; effects of, on pattern of expansion, 79-83 ; effects of, on rates of institutional and technological change, 127-30 ; effects of, on stability, 190-219, 387-94 ; effects of, in viability, 168-81, 377-86 ; as factor determining growth, 14-25, 139-44, 388-94 ; irrelevance of, in free trade system, 248 ; and vulnerability to economic nationalism, 247-264

Small nations, concentration of foreign trade of, 21, 349 ; contributions to flow of international trade of, 268 ; cultural homogeneity in, 29, 128, 369 ; dependence on foreign trade of, 18-24, 266-8 ; domination by policies of larger nations, 81, 218, 249, 388-9 ; economic structure of, 15-18, 29-30 ; effects of international cartels on, 126 ; entrepreneurial policy in, 286-90 ; general characteristics of, xix, 11, 15-18, 353, 120-2 ; government action in, 80-2, 209 ; growth in, 14-32, 282-3 ; limits to industrial expansion in, 274 ; social adjustments in, 28, 352 ; sources of capital for growth in, 23, 280 ; specialized enterprises in, 124-126 ; vulnerability of, 197, 248-9, 381

Small primary producing countries, rigidities in, 392-3

Smith, Adam, xiii, 139

Smith, Caleb, 45

Social adjustments, in process of economic growth, 28, 29, 352

Social insurance, *see* Social services

Social invention, as prerequisite for economic growth, 32

Social services, economies of scale in, 231 ; public expenditure on, 231-2

Specialization, advantages of, 334-5 ; and instability, 193

Spontaneous innovation, rôle of, 52

Stability, and size of nation, 190-219

Standardization of industrial products, 340, 361

Steel industry, Italian, competitiveness of, 156 ; oligopolistic structure of, 161

Stigler, G., 42, 52, 103, *337, 342, 345, 358, 361*

Stolper, G., 170 n.

Structural changes with economic growth, patterns of, 206

Summary record of the debate, 333-438

Svennilson, I., xiv, **1-13,** 87 n., **333-39,** *334, 339, 348, 351, 352, 356, 369,* 370, 391, 392, 423

Switzerland : capital stock, 66 ; cyclical stability, 70-1 ; export orientation, 63-5, 379 ; freight costs, 57 ; general characteristics of economy, xv-xvi, 27, 30, 54-77, 354-5 ; gross investment, 67 ; industrialization, 61-2 ; labour force, 60-1, 68-70 ; neutrality, 59 ; occupational structure, 73 ; research, 70 ; size of economic units, 57-8 ; terms of trade, 64-5 ; tourism, 354 ; watch industry, 64, 373-5

Tariff policies, and economic nationalism, 149 ; effects of, on small nations, 248 ; and suboptimal firms, 161 ; in Belgium, 83-4 ; in Italy, 162

Tariff reductions, impact of, on intrabloc trade, 293

Tarshis, L., **190-9,** **386-94**

Taussig, F. W., 344

Technical knowledge, international mobility of, 12-13, 24, 129, 348

Technological factors limiting dependence of small countries on foreign trade, 24

Technological optimum size of economy, concept of, 283

Textile industry, in Belgium, 82-4 ; inventions in, 109 ; in Switzerland, 64

Timing of economic development, importance of, 356-7

Trade, *see* Foreign trade

Trade diversion, as result of customs union, 252-7, 407-9 ; effects on balance of payments of, 256 ; effects on employment of, 256 ; effects on prices of, 257

Transport costs within national frontiers, 21, 337

Transport policy, in Belgium, 84-5

Triffin, R., **247-64,** *386, 394, 403, 404,* **406-15,** *409, 410, 411, 414-5,* 418, 426, 436, 437

Tyszynski, H., 87 n.

Under-developed countries, applicability of normal concept of nation to, 338 ; characteristics of, 144-9, 185-186 ; dangers of instability for, 216 ; position of, in economic unions with

Index

THE END

PRINTED IN GREAT BRITAIN BY
LOWE AND BRYDONE (PRINTERS) LIMITED, LONDON, N.W.10